DEAL

DEAL

My Three Decades
of Drumming, Dreams, and
Drugs with the
GRATEFUL DEAD

Bill Kreutzmann
with Benjy Eisen

ST. MARTIN'S PRESS
New York

Endpaper artwork: *1000 Mics*, © Bill Kreutzmann.

Designed by Kathryn Parise

The Library of Congress Cataloging-in-Publication Data is available upon request.

ISBN 978-1-250-03379-6 (hardcover)
ISBN 978-1-250-03380-2 (e-book)

First Edition: May 2015

10 9 8 7 6 5 4 3 2 1

If I told you all that went down/
It would burn off both your ears.

—"Deal" (Lyrics by Robert Hunter)

DEAL

INTRODUCTION

A Dance with the Divine

Rock 'n' roll was never meant to be institutionalized. When it first came out, it couldn't be contained. It broke every rule and regulation, amendment and guideline. It played by its own set of rules and then it broke those, too. It was supposed to inspire an uprising and fuel the revolution. It was meant to be something your parents feared and your teachers scorned. The very moment that Bill Kreutzmann dedicated his life to rock 'n' roll, his father warned him, "You'll never make any money at it." Parents aren't always right, you know. That might be the first lesson of rock 'n' roll.

Look: Rock 'n' roll was meant for rebels and revolutionaries. It was meant for outcasts and outlaws, misfits and desperadoes. That's why it was meant for every kid in America. That's also why it was the perfect outlet for the Grateful Dead. They may have been seen as subversive in the context of their mid-1960s birth, but even that helped cement their status as the quintessential, All-American Band. They waved that flag. If you bought the ticket, they'd take you on that ride.

Even though they played shows in front of some of the largest audiences of all time, they were still considered an underground phenomenon. Eventually, their secret handshake became so well known that the exclusive became inclusive; by the time Deadheads started proclaiming—validly—that "we are everywhere," the band's insignia had become an international symbol of American counterculture; the David had turned into a Goliath.

But on a small island of the Hawaiian archipelago, two decades after the Grateful Dead disbanded, drummer Bill Kreutzmann lives a pretty normal life. Well . . . "normal" as far as the hippie lifestyle goes. He lives on an unassuming island property, with cockroaches in the basement and two black Labs—"Iko" and "Lucy"—running around the yard. It's the kind of house you might go to for a Friday night game of poker with the boys, but it has a few aces up its sleeve, of course—like a gold record stashed behind a pile of stuff in the living room and a Grammy Award on the bookshelf.

It took more than a month of me coming over to Billy's house, every day, before I even noticed the Grammy Award. And, sure enough, sharing shelf space with the Grammy—and an array of interesting books—is a Rock and Roll Hall of Fame statue. Billy could give a fuck about the statue itself; after all, it's just a fabricated object. It's not a totem and it doesn't have magical powers. (If it did, surely he would've already tried to eat it—or smoke it—by now.)

"Oh, that? It's a good bookend," he said, almost absentmindedly, when I finally asked him about it one day. We had been up late, drinking, getting high and talking about the days of the Grateful Dead. I understood his point, so I wrote down his response and nodded in agreement; but I didn't forget that, as a teenager, I would sing "Scarlet Begonias" in the shower before school every morning and daydream about my next Grateful Dead concert. Bill Kreutzmann is in the Rock and Roll Hall of Fame. As well he should be.

When you're with him, it's easy to forget the superfluous. He doesn't measure himself by awards or accolades. When we started converting his life story into words on the page, he was never afraid to say things like,

"We really blew that one!" (Woodstock . . . no big deal), or "What were we thinking?" (the album cover for *Go to Heaven*).

Rock 'n' roll might be part smoke and mirrors, but the Grateful Dead bored easily of such trivialities. They didn't have synchronized dance moves and they didn't set their instruments on fire. Who they were on-stage is exactly who they were when they walked off it.

Rock stars are supposed to be immortal, even after death. The Grateful Dead's very existence, however, was fragile from the start. They were infinitely human; it was their music that seemed to come from another dimension entirely. It transcended the earth while grounding you to it, connecting you to everything on the planet all at once. The band's immortality was a result of their rhythms and melodies, not their show outfits and stage banter. They went for what mattered most. It didn't always work and it wasn't always good . . . but when it was, it was better than great. It was a dance with the divine.

Billy was there from the very beginning, before the ragtag group of music-heads that would become the Grateful Dead were even called that. Back then, they were just wild-eyed kids, standing around the back room of a music store in Palo Alto, rubbing two sticks together. But those sticks quickly heated up and caused a spark that caught just enough wind and air to ignite, eventually exploding across the sky like Kerouac's "fabulous yellow roman candles." And, when it did, it set the rickety ole house of rock 'n' roll ablaze. It burned down the walls. It turned the ceiling into ashes. It refused to be stuck inside any confined space . . . or time.

Rock 'n' roll, by its very nature, likes to shed its skin every generation or so. But when the Grateful Dead formed, there was nothing there yet to shed. Rock music was still too new. It was always about breaking the rules, but the rules had yet to be written down. So the Dead broke them all.

They didn't play their hits. They barely even had any hits, at least in a traditional sense. They would practice endlessly, but it was impossible to "rehearse" music that's meant to be in the moment. And although that moment ended, in some ways, in the Summer of 1995, it is still a thirty-year moment that will live on forever. And not just in the minds and in the memories of aging hippies, prep school dropouts, and those lucky enough to have seen the band play live. Already, Grateful Dead music has been passed down to the next generation and it will be passed down to the generation after that. Nobody knows why it endures so persistently, although plenty of other books have attempted to answer that question. This book doesn't even attempt to ask it.

That's because this is not the story of the Grateful Dead. It does include that band's entire history, in a comprehensive manner that may be more complete than any other book out there. So let me rephrase that: this is not *just* the story of the Grateful Dead. This is the story of the man who drove the Grateful Dead's music forward each night with his beats and with his rhythms. His beats have become all of our rhythms but his stories are uniquely his.

And it's a story that took him from poaching deer on the side of Highway 1 in California to living out of a tepee in the Nevada desert under the guidance of a shaman. It's a story of sex, drugs, and rock 'n' roll, sure. But it's also a story of cowboys and Indians, a story of cops and robbers, a story of heroes and crooks. It's a story of Northern California in the last half of the twentieth century. It's a story of friends lighting things on fire and racing cars and causing all kinds of trouble in hotels across the world. It's a story of endless renewal. Like any good story, it calls upon the angels of love to sing its chorus. But like any story worth telling, it also wrestles with the demons of loss, who huff and puff the verses like sheets of rain against the walls. It's the story of staying high, if not dry, and of weathering the storm. Of staying the course. It's the story of an extraordinary life well lived, and it is a story that is still far from having an end.

Lots of people can tell you about the Grateful Dead, and all of them will allow that there are many sides to that tale. This is Bill Kreutzmann's side. This is Bill Kreutzmann's story. This is his . . . DEAL.

—*Benjy Eisen*
San Francisco, December 7, 2014

1

Hawaii

Sometime in the late 1980s, Jerry Garcia and I took a trip that didn't involve dropping acid, but it was still long, strange, and psychedelic. Our band, the Grateful Dead, had recently hit the high-water mark, both creatively and commercially. After twenty-some years of taking stabs in the dark, our latest album, *In the Dark,* was a hit. We had a Top Ten single ("Touch of Grey") and its accompanying video was in heavy rotation on MTV. We sold out a five-night stand at the world's most prestigious arena—New York's Madison Square Garden—and we had recently come off an incredibly successful stadium tour with Bob Dylan.

We decided to celebrate by getting as far away from it all as possible.

The Grateful Dead had toured all over the world—including Alaska, Luxembourg, and even a few shows at the base of the Great Pyramid in Egypt. There were few places we could go where someone didn't come up to us, telling us that they met their future husband or wife at one of our concerts, or that in the middle of one of our jams they realized they wanted to change careers, or—even—that they came out of a coma when their family played them a tape of one of their favorite Dead concerts. Every experience was different; personal, intimate. But they all had one thing in common: the Grateful Dead changed their lives. It's hard to explain how that makes you feel, being a part of it. In some ways, I was no more a part of it than anyone in the audience. But as a band member, I also knew that with that privilege came a duty to the fans and to the music. Everyone felt like they owned a little piece of the Grateful Dead, and I think, philosophically speaking, that's probably true. For those of us on stage, however, all of that came with a great and heavy responsibility to always be the band that everyone wanted us to be. That was a weight that we were glad to bear. But that was a weight.

Gravity has different rules, underwater, though. Weight is balanced by buoyancy. So we decided to give it a try and see if we could become weightless in the deep.

There was a dive shop across the highway from where we recorded *In the Dark*—in San Rafael, California—and we signed up for lessons. It was me, Jerry, and our roadie, Steve Parish. I was the only one who had gone scuba diving before, but it was reckless: I had no experience and little instruction. It was in Laredo, Mexico and I didn't know what the fuck I was doing. I wasn't certified. I never minded getting in over my head, but I knew it wasn't safe.

I decided to get certified and I convinced Jerry and Parish to do it with me. We flew to Hawaii for our open water certification dive. Jerry was in a wetsuit, with an oxygen tank strapped to his back. In that moment, he didn't look like a famous guitarist. He looked like an explorer. Which, I suppose, he was. He also looked like something straight out of a comic book or, perhaps, a character from one of the sci-fi novels that he loved so much. The underwater world that we were about to explore was easily as strange and unusual and captivating as anything we had read about in Kurt Vonnegut books. That was fiction; this was not.

Also: It was as psychedelic and far-out as anything we had seen during the Acid Tests, or at Woodstock, or during our strange days wandering around San Francisco during the Summer of Love. And yet, we were sober for this one. After years of persistent pot smoking, psychedelic excesses, alcohol benders, cocaine binges, and heroin abuse, scuba diving was going to be our new drug.

The first time out together, we just got our feet wet. We were in, maybe, twenty feet of water, just off a pier. We didn't really know much about diving yet. We were there to learn. But one thing we did know was that we were on the other side of the forest from the multi-beast known as the Grateful Dead.

Jerry and I were submerged under the water, digging this weird, new landscape and trying to get lost in its vastness and implications. Just then, a woman instructor swam up to us, with a waterproof notepad that you can write on under water. It looked like she was about to write an instruction but, instead, she asked Jerry for his autograph. Twenty feet below the surface! I nearly spat out my regulator from laughing so hard.

Afterward, back on solid ground, Jerry looked at me and said, "I can't get away from it, Bill." I nodded: "We'll get deeper next time."

Which we did. Many times, in fact.

We started doing exotic dives with a shop called Jack's Diving Locker in Kona. The Big Island. We went diving with dolphins and pilot whales and white-tipped sharks and conger eels and all sorts of strange, far-out creatures that we never even imagined existed. That far out on the water, and that deep under the surface, we found that we could, actually, get away from the world above. It was the one place we could go where we weren't rock stars; we were just friends, exploring an underwater landscape. It was our great escape.

Palo Alto, California

The first time I met Jerry Garcia, he was standing in the doorway at my parents' house, asking for my dad and clutching a fistful of dollars. My father always wanted to play a stringed instrument, so he bought a five-string banjo. But he wasn't very good at it, so he listed it for sale in the classifieds of the *Palo Alto Times*. He ended up selling it to Jerry for fifteen bucks. Years later, when Jerry and I reminisced about it, he said, "You know Billy, it's actually a really great banjo." He enjoyed playing it.

Jerry's banjo playing would become world-famous, but it was his skills as a guitarist, singer, songwriter, and improviser in the Grateful Dead that made him a legend. I played drums in the Grateful Dead from our very first rehearsal down to our very last gig, thirty years later. During those three decades, we sold millions of albums and moved even more concert tickets. We toured the world and played thousands of shows. We traveled Canada by train, Alaska by plane, Europe by bus, and Egypt by camelback. A nation of Deadheads followed us wherever we went, bearing torches lit from the flames of the 1960s even when the rest of the country got swallowed up in 1980s bullshit. We weren't just a band; we were a community, a culture. We became a brand and a lifestyle. And Jerry Garcia was our leader, our nucleus, our heart.

But that day, I had no idea who Jerry Garcia was, what he did, or why he wanted that banjo. It didn't compute. I must've been around twelve years old and I wasn't listening to bluegrass or any kind of banjo music at all.

∽ Jerry Garcia: I was his fan before I was his bandmate. *(Herb Greene)*

And, even though he was four years older than me, which at that age feels like lifetimes, in truth, Garcia was also just a kid. He was just someone in the doorway, buying something from my dad.

Hawaii

During one of our Hawaiian scuba diving trips—either in the late '80s or early '90s—we were hanging out and talking in the back of the dive boat. We were both high from being in the water. On it and under it. We really loved diving. We loved being in the Grateful Dead, too, but it wasn't exactly calming. Not like being in the ocean. Back on the mainland, everything around us was whirling and buzzing, a constant three-ring circus, going full-throttle all the time. Tours, records, fans, press, parties, nonstop noise. But out there on the water, we could really relax. It was also good for our health. When you're diving, you can't drink your weight in booze the night before or stay up all night plowing your nose through a pile of cocaine. Your eyes, your nose, and your mind all have to be clear.

I can still picture us in the back of that boat, watching the water go by, with no sign of land in any direction. Jerry and I looked at each other and made a promise that if the Grateful Dead ever ended, we would both move to Hawaii, go on dives, get healthy, and live a much different lifestyle. He never had a chance to fulfill his end of the bargain. But after he died, on August 9, 1995, I fulfilled mine.

I chose the island of Kauai because it was the most remote, the least touristy, and it reminded me, in a way, of California's "Lost Coast," up in Mendocino where I lived on a ranch for many, many years. At first I moved to Kapa'a, then up the shore some to Anahola, which is basically a small residential community that's mostly made up of island natives. Pacific Islanders. They're suspicious of Americans, no matter how long you've lived there. There remain various tensions, unspoken resentments, injustices, racial undercurrents, and all that horrible crap, between Pacific Islanders and mainland transplants. The natives call the white intruders haoles ("howl-ies"). All Caucasians are haoles. It means "without breath" because, when Captain Cook "discovered" the archipelago in 1778, he refused to greet people the traditional Hawaiian way, by inhaling their breath. He opted for shaking hands instead.

Well now, I found a house right on the beach in Anahola, and I decided to take it. I dug right in. I bought a twenty-two-foot Sea Cat, a power boat that I named the Far Eagle, and kept her right out front, in my yard. This really, really large Hawaiian nicknamed Big Joe used to walk past my house and harass me all the time: "Billy, when are you going fishing in that thing? Get the boat out! C'mon, the fish are running today!"

Big Joe wasn't the friendliest to haolies like me; in fact he had a reputation for altercations. That's putting it kindly. But for whatever reason, I was the exception. He was an experienced fisherman, so I agreed to take him out fishing if he'd help me get the boat in good shape. It was a deal and we went out fishing for our first time together.

As soon as we got out there, a big squall came in and started dumping rain on us. Suddenly, we had a bite. We hooked up what we guessed was a marlin, because it just started running line like crazy. Joe and another guy on the boat with us start yelling at me, in Hawaiian. "Hana pa'a! Hana pa'a!" I was new to fishing, new to the island, new to Hawaiian culture; I didn't have any clue what they were saying. Why would I? They were trying to tell me that we were hooked up to a fish. They thought I understood that it was my cue to gun the boat for a few seconds, push her forward, because it would sink the hook in the mouth and get us one step closer to bringing in the fish. So what did I do? I backed off the gas, instead.

"Okay," I thought, "Let's stop and reel it in!" The fish instantly spit the hook and got away. I got yelled at a few times during all of this. That's how I learned what "hana pa'a" means and also what to do when I heard it. I wouldn't make that same mistake again. But I still had to prove myself to Big Joe and his friends. And I had to prove myself to the island. I had to prove that I was worthy.

The next time out, it was just me and Big Joe. We managed to catch two really large ahi tunas. They might've been 100-pounders. It was serious. I didn't fuck up this time. I started driving the boat home while Big

Joe got to work cleaning the fish. He gutted them efficiently, then threw them on ice in the fish boxes. When he was done, he sat down next to me—it was a good day at sea. We were happy fishermen. But something caught my eye: in the back corner of the boat, there was this triangular fleshy thing, with a white valve on it. "What the fuck is this?" I picked it up with my hand and, lo and behold, it was beating. It was one of the fish's hearts and it was still beating! I was totally shocked. I grabbed Joe's arm and shook his hand with it. He tried to play cool but his eyes betrayed him. I caught him off guard.

I knew what I had to do. I took the heart back in my hand, looked Big Joe in the eye . . . and then ripped into it with my teeth, taking a bite out of it. It was easily the worst thing I've ever put in my mouth. Fucking horrendous. Worse than anything on the menu at Applebees. I could feel the heart beating between my teeth. I spat it out, guzzled a Budweiser and fought to get my composure back. Then I looked at Big Joe. I stretched out my hand and offered him the rest of the heart. Here was this 300-pound Hawaiian whose acceptance and respect I had been trying to earn. But suddenly, there I was, daring him—challenging him—to take a bite out of a beating, disembodied fish heart. He looked back at me with big, alarmed eyes; he knew damn well that it was a test. The tide had turned. He took a little bite, spat it out, chased it with beer, and then said, "Holy shit! That was disgusting!" We laughed about it, all the while knowing that we had just cemented our friendship. I passed his test; he passed mine.

Big Joe's face softened up and he, very gently, said, "Don't tell any of my brothers about this. I don't want them to know." He made me promise I wouldn't tell, and I promised, and for years I kept that promise. The only reason I can tell you now is because, eventually, he took to bragging about the whole thing.

Later on, when we became regular fishing buddies, Big Joe would shout orders at me, like, "Hold that pole like a man, Bill!" He didn't give a shit that I was in the Grateful Dead. We caught fish together and that was all that mattered.

Palo Alto, California

People have always called the Grateful Dead a San Francisco band, but the truth is that we were a San Rafael band that started out as a Palo Alto band.

I was born in Palo Alto, a small town about thirty-three miles south of San Francisco. It's less than an hour's drive to the city—usually—but it can feel like continents apart, and not just because of all the standstill traffic. It's a whole different culture.

I spent most of my time in Palo Alto just trying to figure a way out. I needed something bigger, something more. I wanted to break out.

My parents met at Stanford University. My dad was from San Francisco and my mom was from New Orleans. The hospital where I was born, Stanford Hospital, is now a rehab center. Kind of apropos, huh? That was May 7, 1946.

I have one sister, Marcia L. Kreutzmann, thirteen years younger than me. I was an only child for thirteen years. Our house was at 1512 Byron in Palo Alto. It's still there.

The first music concert that I went to was in Palo Alto. It must have been some time in the summer and it was on the back of a flatbed truck. I think it was a country-and-western/rock band, and I watched the drummer play and it looked really cool to be able to play music and still get physical with stuff. It was the music and movement, working together to create rhythm that I really liked. I wanted to play piano and I wanted to play trumpet, but I never picked up either one. My parents didn't have a piano so that wasn't going to happen, and drums just became the thing.

And yet, I hated the snare drum, growing up. Our house was in earshot of a military academy; every afternoon, we'd be forced to hear marching band practice. I was always aware of the time, because they would start at 2:30 and for the next hour, the marching band would be louder than my thoughts. And my thoughts were, "I hate those drums." There was no escape. You could hear it all throughout the neighborhood. I was sick of stupid march music. I wanted nothing to do with it and never wanted to hear another snare drum in my life. But then I saw my first live band and the drummer had a full kit and it was a whole different ball game. He used all four limbs and the snare was just one thing in his arsenal of sound. Also, I think this might explain why I had an aversion to Mickey Hart's marches, decades later. But we'll get to that.

By the time I was in sixth grade, my last year at Middlefield Elementary School, all I wanted to do was to play music. I was so determined, that I joined the school's god-awful band class, even though it didn't sound like music to me. Whenever I walked by that classroom, all I heard was noise. And the poor teacher taught all the different instruments, including the drums. Every instrument. A lot of the kids from wealthier families had their own equipment, but since I didn't, I was assigned one of the school's drums. I was handed a big old marching bass drum, covered with dust as if nobody had ever played it. And then the teacher handed me sheet music and I was supposed to read it and play along on the drum. I had been told that much, but I hadn't been told how to do it. I could tell during that very first class that this wasn't going to work. About a minute into the second class, the teacher came over and kicked me out. She said, "You can't keep a beat."

My response was, "Okay, good." The music sucked. I didn't really care. I just hit the bass drum any time I felt like it—kind of like I do today. There was nothing for me to keep a beat to; the notes on the page looked like someone spilled an ashtray across the sheets after a full night of partying. The splotches of ink made no sense to me. And I didn't hear anything that I wanted to play along with, anyway. It wasn't music to my ears. I'd been listening to Ray Charles and Fats Domino and all this wonderful stuff as a kid. My musical tastes were already hip. Remember, my mom was from New Orleans. So whatever the teacher was trying to get these kids to play, it was like, "What the fuck?"

Lucky for me, both of my parents loved black music, and they would listen to the black radio station, KDIA in the East Bay. "Lucky 13." It's still there today, I believe. For many years it was the heartbeat of soul music in the Bay Area. Our whole family tuned in to it. We wouldn't be caught dead listening to KDIA now, though, because it devolved into a Christian rock station.

My dad worked up at the Emporium—one of the first real department stores—and I'd go to work with him some days, just to hang out or go to a movie, and he would always have the dial tuned to KDIA. I don't remember all the music—a lot of it embarrassed me, because it was so frank compared to the white stuff—but my parents loved it. It was cool.

After I got kicked out of band class, I got on my bike and rode up to old town Palo Alto to a music store, and there was a sign in the front window that said, "Drum lessons, three dollars per half hour. Call Lee Andersen at this number." I called him and that very Saturday he met me at the music store. That's when I bought my very first pair of drumsticks. At $1.95, they were too expensive for me, but Lee loaned me the money, and I remember those sticks to this day. They were the most precious thing I'd ever owned. It was like, "Ah, this is *me*! I'm holding *me* for once." I finally had something that really meant "Bill." Something that I could identify with.

Lee Andersen became my drum teacher. Immediately after my first lesson, I went home and took out all my mother's pots and pans, and started playing on the kitchen floor. I didn't have a drum set yet, but my parents weren't home. So I did that for hours.

Lee lived up behind Stanford University on a street called Perry Lane, which is where Ken Kesey was writing his novel, *One Flew Over the Cuckoo's Nest*. They were almost next-door neighbors. Kesey was working on his book at the same time that I was taking drum lessons, just a few houses over.

Walking inside Lee's house was like taking a trip to the Hawaiian Islands—it was decorated top to bottom in Hawaiian style, with fake palm trees and hula skirts lining the bar. It was my first trip to Hawaii. Little did I know I'd end up living on Kauai.

Lee had a silver Slingerland drum set sprawled out like furniture across the living room, with a bass drum that doubled as a floor tom if needed.

During my lessons, he also taught me some more advanced stuff, such as the finer points of making multicolored mixed drinks. You have to layer them so the colors don't run together. That was very important. So was drinking them. At the beginning of the lesson, he'd tell me about the woman he had been with the night before, what she looked like naked, and all these other things. It was all part of the drum lesson. It was learning the rhythms of life.

After one of the lessons, Lee started high jumping with some friends of his, over a high bar that they had set up outside. Kesey was there, too, and came crashing over the bar. At age thirteen, it was too high for me, so I went back inside the house and banged on Lee's kit until dark. He never stopped me or told me to quit.

Lee got a physics degree at Stanford, then regretted it. When you're a physicist, who wants to hire you the most? The government. And what do they want you to do? Make nuclear weapons. Lee said fuck that. He wanted to invent. He had the idea that he was going to invent a machine that detected gold.

My whole focus was on getting to that drum lesson every Saturday afternoon. I had to ride my bike up the hill behind Stanford University and I can still remember the smell of the eucalyptus trees along the way. It was the beginning of fall and the trees still held the smell of summer. The scent of the trees, with the feeling of the drum sticks in my pocket, gave me the motivation to ride uphill, as fast as I could go. I never missed a lesson.

I barely noticed any of the other houses around Lee's, but Phil Lesh told me a funny little story once about one of them. At some point, Phil actually snuck into Kesey's house and read part of the manuscript Kesey had been working on, *One Flew Over the Cuckoos Nest,* before it was published. He came back and said, "Kesey's a really good writer." Everybody knew he was writing a book, so the buzz was already out among a certain crowd. But Phil had the courage, the audacity, to go in and read his stuff. "Yeah, he's a good writer." I didn't know Phil yet, but that would change.

Not far from Perry Lane was a boarding house nicknamed the Chateau, where Phil, Jerry Garcia, Robert Hunter—who became the Grateful Dead's lyricist—and many other creative types lived at various points. Some of them would in some way intersect with my life in the years that followed, some were just transients. Jerry and Robert actually lived in their cars, out back, at first, before they could afford rent. I didn't know anything about Jerry, or the others, when I visited there, though. I was the high school kid; they were the beatniks.

I knew some of the other musicians staying at the Chateau but I only remember Danny Barnett, a good jazz drummer who's no longer with us, darn it. Somebody must've invited me to go over there once and I stumbled into a really hip scene. Almost too hip for me, at the time. I don't remember smoking dope or anything, I just remember being there. There was a great jam session in the living room and that's what I was really after. I sat in on the last song of the night, where I got to show off my newest trick: a shuffle. I was nervous. I was also elated.

I always gravitated to places where I could hear music that was far-out. In downtown Palo Alto there was a coffeehouse called St. Michael's Alley, next to the movie theater on University Avenue, where I would go to check out live music. Jazz. And there was another place I used to frequent called the Tangent, which was where Garcia played banjo with Mother McCree's Uptown Jug Champions.

The first time I played music in front of people wasn't at a gig. It was just playing around, in front of friends, for fun. My dad drove me there. I was probably thirteen or fourteen years old. I didn't have much of a drum kit, though. My dad rented me a snare drum and a hi-hat, and that was it. The bassist's dad rented him a bass and a bass amp, and he knew about as much on bass as I did on the drums. The guitarist was this hot local player who knew some rock 'n' roll songs, and we sat there and played for a while. The last song we did at the end of the session was "Johnny B. Goode." The guitar player really got it right and, to my surprise, my friends on the couch all got up and started dancing, and I said, "Yeah!"

That moment was the catalyst for everything. It was the first truly joyful moment of my life. I was given the gift of finding something that was so clearly my passion, it was undeniable. That was my direction from then on.

Afterward, my dad came to pick me up and on the way down the front stairs, he saw something sparkling in my eye, lighting up my entire face like a kid at his first Macy's Thanksgiving Day Parade, watching his favorite cartoon character waltz across the sky. I was lit from doing something that I really loved. And from out of nowhere he said, "You know, Billy, you won't earn any money playing music." I said, "Dad, I didn't even think of that." My head was still somewhere else, still high from the experience of playing music and the unexpected joy it brought me when I saw those kids dancing to my beat. It was my own little acid trip, years before I first tried acid. I learned a lot about my dad in that moment and I knew that he had seen something new in me that wasn't there before. I now had desire in my life. Passion.

My dad was so concerned with money and that was very strange to me. The war had ended something like twelve or maybe fifteen years earlier, but it had taken him out of Stanford, where he was studying to become a lawyer. He had to become a soldier instead.

My dad wanted me to go to college and become a businessman and

∽ Legends in our minds—my first band, the Legends, and that's my first drum set. This must've been taken in Palo Alto High School, sometime in the early 1960s. *(Photo credit unknown; image courtesy of the Kreutzmann family archives)*

make a respectable income. Musicians were still second-class citizens—the "help," back then. My dad loved me and he supported me, but he never thought I'd have much of a career being a drummer. I think he wanted his own second chance, through me, and didn't think that it would happen if I ran off chasing fantasies with a rock 'n' roll band.

Years later, he returned to Stanford, but this time to watch the Grateful Dead play a sold-out concert at the Frost Amphitheater. He wore a shirt that said, "Grateful Dad."

I got a paper route so that I could buy my first drum set. I'd throw my papers the same way that most paperboys do. You know how kids ride without holding onto the handlebars? That's what I did. It was a flat and easy paper route, so I'd just practice playing drums on the handlebars as I rode along. It was fun to do that; I didn't think anything of it.

Around this time, I got totally hooked on rock 'n' roll. I couldn't have been more into it. There was so much to learn but I was an eager student. I started playing Ray Charles songs, like "What'd I Say." I found out that a lot of the stuff that I liked in my playing came from Fats Domino—more of a 12/8, more of a shuffle feeling, a New Orleans feeling. That's really my style more than straight sixteenth notes. It bounces a little bit and it feels good. Anyway, that came from listening to that earlier music—Fats Domino and the music from New Orleans. I don't remember many of the other artists by name. My mom had lots of albums by black groups that were really good. She had an album by a band called the Olympics that had one or two really great songs. And she had Duke Ellington.

The first time I listened to James Brown was when I was a senior in high school. I had my own apartment where I could play drums and nobody would complain, so I would put on albums and try to play along and learn the parts. But when I tried to do that with James Brown, I went, "What the fuck is that guy doing, and how the fuck is he doing it?" Of course, years later, I learned that he had two drummers on those albums. That's interesting to think about now. Two drummers, eh?

I liked jazz a lot, too, but my heavy jazz stuff didn't really start until I was nineteen and living with Phil Lesh. So that came later. Mostly, I listened to early Ray Charles, just to get off on the way the drummer played so musically. I was fascinated by the different rhythms he used throughout the album and the way the different parts and instruments all fit together. I loved that music. I loved hearing Ray Charles's *Live at Newport*—that was a really big one for me, because it had "The Night Time is the Right Time" on there, with a killer intro sax solo. I used to listen to that all the time. I also listened to some funk.

I joined my first band before that—the Legends. They were all guys from Palo Alto. One of the members played football on the high school team—I was still in junior high. The others were all perfectly fine muggles. I haven't kept in touch with them but one of the guys got into politics and became some kind of town representative in Palo Alto.

We had matching band costumes—we wore red sport coats and black pants and black ties. It was all corny, straight stuff. Nobody had taken psychedelics or smoked pot yet. The Legends were still a straight band. We were just copying other songs; we didn't have any original material. It was just a platform to learn and play music, while having fun.

We had a sax player and we played whatever was popular then. We'd do "What'd I Say," which I already said I loved and knew how to play. And we did stuff like Buddy Holly's "Not Fade Away." We also did some Ventures' songs—"Walk Don't Run" was one of them.

Our first gigs were at the YMCA. They were always big events for us. I wasn't sixteen yet. My dad would drive us all over there. We would load everything into his Ford station wagon and then he'd help me set up. It was always a horrible scene: the Mexicans would beat up the white guys. I was glad to be on a drum set, playing, so I didn't get in a fight. It was terrible. They were such fighters, but we were just white, middle-class kids. For a while I grew up frightened of Mexicans.

My parents got divorced when I was in eighth or ninth grade. My mom couldn't handle me at home. I was too wild or something. At least, in her eyes. So she sent me away to a prep school that was run by a headmaster who was once on a football team that my grandfather coached.

My grandfather, Clark Shaughnessy, coached the Stanford University football team that won the 1941 Rose Bowl. He modified the T Formation and tweaked it until it was wild enough to win championships. It was innovative and crazy at the same time. It made him famous. He eventually accepted the position of head coach in the NFL with the Los Angeles Rams and then, later, coached the Chicago Bears. He was a really good man. I loved him. Still do.

Until Stanford won that championship, though—at the end of his first year as head coach—they were really uneasy with his nontraditional approach. They were worried about his twenty-fifth-century way of thinking. They had never seen plays like his before, and that concerned them. When someone comes along and changes the way something is done, if it doesn't work, they call it foolish. But when it works, they call it revolutionary.

Whether you loved the Grateful Dead or felt differently, there's no disputing that we changed the way things were done. Even when we tackled traditional songs, we always approached everything with an eye toward innovation. Some of it worked and some of it didn't, but we put more money on risky chances than on sure bets, every time. People told us we were crazy, pretty much every day of our career. Yet, we ended up in the Rock and Roll Hall of Fame. My grandfather ended up in the College Football Hall of Fame (and accumulated other, similar accolades as well). So, as the drummer, you can see where I got it from.

After playing for my grandfather, Charlie Orme became headmaster of the prep school that his father founded in Prescott, Arizona: the Orme School. My mom sent me there. I ended up only going for a year—ninth grade—but it was an interesting year. Not my favorite.

I didn't get in there on my grades or accolades; I got in because my granddad was a well-known football coach. They made me repeat the ninth grade, but it was either that or military school. That was the ultimatum my mother gave me. I really had no choice at all. It was either horses or guns. But with horses came the promise to play football. Guns we'll get to later.

I had been playing music for a few years at that point and really getting into it. Being sent to prep school meant that I had to be away from my drums, but not my drum sticks—I brought those sticks that Lee Anderson bought me. In bed at night, after lights-out, I would count the days until I could be reunited with my drum set. It was like suffering a punishment for a crime I didn't commit.

For sport, at this prep school, I played six-man football. We had a really good team. We won every game. But I couldn't keep a grade point, so they kicked me off. It's embarrassing telling you all this now, actually. But I was big for my age, so I was a redshirted freshman. I was on the varsity and played with all the seniors and did really well—just because I was big, not because I was any good at football. When they booted me from the team, they said, "Now you have to ride horses."

That didn't sit very well with me. The other people that rode horses were mostly girls, and they weren't exactly pretty, so it was kind of like, "Ehh." And I wasn't able to play any music. Whenever I could, I would practice by hitting my drumsticks against my pillow. Every night, I'd listen to Ray Charles and the cool stuff from when he was in his R&B period, when he first started playing, and I'd fall asleep happy.

Every day, I begged my mother to take me out of prep school. I wrote her letters from study hall, insisting she let me withdraw. But she didn't. Then my dad did the coolest thing. He crated up my drums and shipped them off to Arizona. I didn't know they were coming. When they arrived, I pried open the crates, not knowing what to expect. At the very first glimpse, the very first second I saw that my drums were in there, love and meaning and passion all came flooding back into my life. I had my drums back.

The school allowed me to play those drums after class instead of riding horses, which was really cool of them. They let me set up my drums in the multipurpose room, which actually was a reconditioned barn, with a stage.

I could go in there and practice every day after school, just about whenever I wanted, unless they were holding meetings. One day, I was playing away and in walked the headmaster with this guy that had these really thick coke-bottle eyeglasses, and the headmaster signaled me to be quiet.

You know, "Come on, shut up, enough already." But his guest didn't mind. He prodded the headmaster in the side with his elbow. "No, tell him to keep playing. I've never heard anything like that." I liked that guy. It turns out, that guy was Aldous Huxley, the author.

I had no idea who Aldous Huxley was at that time. He was there to give a lecture later in that very same room to the student body. We heard the lecture that night. I remember being there really well, I just couldn't figure out what the hell he was talking about. I recognized that his words had a really good energy to them, but I didn't understand what they meant. Years later, it began to make sense.

Huxley's most famous book, *Brave New World,* was about his fear of a government that could manufacture people, creating a nation of exact duplicates. The cloning of the masses. Huxley's trip was that we're approaching a point where we'll have the technology to do that. Give a government enough power and control, and they could start mass-producing obedient citizens. And it would be a total nightmare. A living hell.

Huxley was English, and he experienced the horror of Germany during its darkest period. Hitler wanted a world of clones. Huxley did not. He had a fear of a country—not just Germany but maybe even America—trying to artificially make their own flawed idea of the perfect race of people. That was the theme of his lecture.

I have that same fear and it's even more relevant today. In more ways than most of us care to admit, America isn't that far away from doing something like that right now. It's just more insidious than in *Brave New World.*

But the coolest thing about my serendipitous encounter with Huxley is that Huxley was also an acid head. A few years later, so was I. In fact, in different ways, we're both now famous for our love of acid. And because of it.

Anyway, that's one of my clearest memories of being a kid. My other memories include my parents doing some pretty wild stuff. My dad taught me rocketry class. It should've been called missile class. This was earlier; I think I was around eleven or twelve at the time. He said, "We're going to learn to make rockets, Billy," and I said, "Okay, let's do that." We packed black powder into copper tubes, put firecracker fuses on them, and fired those fuckers off. I got the hang of it pretty fast. We'd shoot them out across the road, carelessly. Luckily, we didn't hit anything. At least, nothing that mattered or complained.

Then one day, my dad said, "Okay, I'm going to teach you about thrust." We had a wood swing in the backyard, hung by metal chains. He took clamps and bolted an eight-inch metal pipe to the swing, packing it with black powder. Passersby would have not-so-causally thought, "Hey, why is there a pipe bomb stuck to this kid's swing?"

I had a sneaking suspicion that this might not be set up correctly, so I went over and got a piece of plywood and hid behind it. I'd seen what the smaller copper tubes could do and this one looked like it could've belonged to NASA. As soon as he lit the thing, it made a loud whooshing sound and the whole area instantly filled up with smoke. It was a complete white-out. I couldn't see a thing but the swing hadn't moved—not an inch. The rocket itself was gone. My dad told me to go inside. "If anybody asks," he said, "tell them the car backfired." When I felt it was safe to come out, I found my dad looking through our orange tree at a brand-new six-inch hole in the back of the house. At least we knew where the rocket had gone. That was my dad, for you. He was pretty carefree like that. We did lots of wild stuff together. But that was the end of rocket class.

After that, my dad said, "That's enough, no more black powder." But he'd leave to go to work and I knew where he kept the black powder, so I went in and continued the experiments. There was this really wealthy kid down at the end of the block, Jeffrey Smedburg, and we wanted to prank him. We had a Prince Albert can—way before we used them for marijuana—and we took it and I filled it about half full of this black powder. I said to him, "When you light it, whatever you do, don't look in it. Hold a match out in front of you; don't let go," and I heard this big whoosh and saw a giant cloud of white smoke. When the smoke cleared, the hair on Jeffrey's face was completely burnt off. We were just kids, so there was no mustache or facial hair, but his eyebrows and eyelashes were gone, his hair was burnt way back, and his face was black. I took him inside and scrubbed him up. I washed him off as hard as I could, hoping to make him look good so his parents would believe the story I was going to make up for him. It finally came to me: "Tell them you've been to a séance." I didn't even know what a fucking séance was. "Tell them you've been to a séance." And that was the last that Jeffrey Smedburg was ever allowed to play with me. With other kids, we just did stuff. We grew up. We did whatever kids do.

I started smoking pot when I was sixteen and I loved it. The first time I got high was right next to my junior high school, at some guy's house in downtown Palo Alto. He had a matchbox full of marijuana—it looked like oregano to me, but when we smoked it, all of a sudden we got this funny buzz and went outside and said, "Oh, this is fucking great!" and we walked all around Palo Alto, stoned. It felt like I was walking on mashed potatoes. Everything was gravy. The next time we bought weed from him, he sold us actual oregano. Bait and switch. So I learned right away what the difference was. You learn about these things as you go; it's a wonderful part of growing up. You learn, you grow. I'm growing now.

Both of my parents went to Stanford and they had a great library. There was never anything good on television, even back then, so whenever I got bored, I would go through my parents' books. When they weren't home, I'd investigate and start reading whatever interested me. I read a bunch of Faulkner and it was kind of intriguing—he wrote in such a weird way. I loved Steinbeck, too, of course.

I don't think I got Jack Kerouac's *On the Road* from my parents' library, but it came to me somehow. I read it before I really knew the other guys in the Grateful Dead—I know that—but it was an important book to all of us. It became influential to me in the same way that certain music was influential. It was jazz, on the page.

I never met Jack Kerouac but I eventually became friends with Neal Cassady, the real-life hero of *On the Road*. His character, Dean Moriarty, was larger than life. Even in real life. He was Kerouac's inspiration behind that novel, but he also was an inspiration to anybody who ever crossed paths with him. Myself included. And Ken Kesey. And his Merry Pranksters. And Jerry Garcia. And the Grateful Dead. That was all to come; sooner than you might think.

But when I first picked up *On the Road*, it was my boarding pass out of Palo Alto and into destinations unknown—my life's great adventure. It seemed to say that there was something greater out there, and even if it didn't appear within my reach, I could grab ahold of it anyway, just by believing that it was possible. That's really important. Because after that, I started reaching for it. And sure enough, I was able to grab ahold.

This was right at the age when everyone started getting their driver's licenses and we got to experience some of the freedom that Kerouac talked about in *On the Road*, but for real. This was the teenage version because we still went home at night. The first car I had was a '58 Dodge station wagon, not unlike my dad's. We wore grooves in the asphalt on Highway 101 going up to San Francisco. Sometimes we'd hit Skyline and take the back roads up. That's how I learned that the best stuff is often found on the alternate routes.

In San Francisco, there was a club called the Jazz Workshop and they used to have an eighteen-and-over section. You could sit behind a screen of chicken wire and watch artists like Cal Tjader play. They had to keep us separated from the bar because we weren't old enough to drink, but I'd go there because I could hear live music—live, far-out music—and that was always my calling. I'd find myself in Santa Cruz . . . I remember Big Mama Thornton singing at a club across the street from the boardwalk. Since I wasn't twenty-one yet, I had to look through a hole in the wall, but I could hear the music. I'd always do that kind of thing—anything to get within earshot.

When my parents finally got divorced, it had a much bigger effect on me than I first admitted. It hurt because you can't really side with one or the other. You love them both. You don't want to see them fighting. I came home from prep school after only one year. At first, I stayed at my mother's house. Then my dad helped me get my own apartment. I left home, basically, at sixteen. Still in high school.

In order to pay for my first apartment, I worked any kind of job I could get. I gave drum lessons, just trying to get by any way I could. I worked at the weirdest job ever—I sold human hair wigs. "That wig is so you; you look ten years younger!" That was when I was a junior in high school.

I wanted to be in a band again, so I tried to get my gig back with the Legends. I lucked out when they didn't let me rejoin. They said, "Oh, you left." "Well . . . okay." "You were sent away to school. . . ." "Yeah, I know." Thank God they didn't take me back, because soon after that, I went and saw Jerry Garcia play at the Tangent and that led to being in a band with him and that led to everything that followed. The rest of my life.

I played a gig with Jerry before that, but with him on bass. He didn't even sing. He did it just to do it. That group was called the Zodiacs. A guy named Ron McKernan played harmonica. You know who that is? That's Pigpen. He didn't have that nickname quite yet. The guitarist's name was Troy Weidenheimer; he was a hotshot player from Palo Alto and it was his band. Jerry was the hired bass player and I was the hired drummer. I only remember playing that one gig with them, but I was in way over my head. I always did that. I always played things that were really hard and it didn't matter. I just went for it.

The night that I saw Garcia at the Tangent, he played banjo with a jug band called Mother McCree's Uptown Jug Champions. I had forgotten that he bought my dad's banjo. He might've even been playing it that night.

It was an amazing night. He had the whole place totally under his spell. I sat right in front of him, spellbound. Right then, I became the first Deadhead because I said, "I'm going to follow this guy forever." I really did say that to myself, and I'd never said that about anything or anybody before. About two weeks later, he called me and said, "Hey, you want to play in a band?" "Yeah, sure." Suddenly I had a band again. We called ourselves the Warlocks, then we changed our name to the Grateful Dead.

Everything was about to happen. I was about to start eating a lot of acid. So were my bandmates. We were about to transform from a garage band—or, technically, a music store blues band—to the sound-track band of the psychedelic revolution. The long strange trip was about to kick in.

The summer before my senior year in high school, I started dating a girl named Brenda and we had the kind of romance that really blossoms in the schoolyard; we loved making out at the train station and fogging the windows up in the car. The very first time we made love, I got her pregnant. I remember it. It was in a blue-light cheap motel. I even remember the street it was on: El Camino Real. We'd been wanting to do it for days and days. You know how teenagers are always swinging for the big home run. When you're seventeen or eighteen, you're at the top of your game. You can't be held back. And contraceptives were about as foreign to us as social security, so that was that.

Brenda had red hair and freckles. She was cool, she was beautiful, and she was my first real girlfriend. I tested the waters with various girls before

Brenda, but even at that age, I was a relationship guy. I liked to stick to one at a time. And it worked. For a while, anyway.

When I got Brenda pregnant, there was never any talk of an abortion. That wasn't really common back then, so it never even crossed my mind. And, besides, she was going to have the baby anyway. So she gave birth to Stacy, my daughter. Our daughter. Stacy was born on July 3, 1964. I wanted to be an upstanding guy because my dad raised me that way. So, even at that young age, I thought I should get married and have the kid and have a job and have an apartment and play drums in a band, and still go to high school. Forget it. It doesn't work. Something had to give. And it wasn't going to be my band.

I was too young to have a daughter, I was still just a son myself. But once the baby arrived, I had to be a man. Or at least try. It wasn't a shot-gun wedding, but I didn't exactly propose to Brenda. I simply took her to Reno and married her there. I was eighteen, but you had to be twenty-one to get married, so I faked that I was of age. That's also how I got out of the marriage. A few years later, I had it annulled. My dad was an attorney by then and said, "You weren't twenty-one." It was never a divorce because it was never a real marriage.

It was hard on Brenda and Stacy, but what can I tell you? I didn't make the best decisions when I was eighteen, as far as those kinds of things went. There was so much going on in my life. Haight-Ashbury had just come alive. I was plugged into that whole scene. I was making electrifying, new music with the band that was soon to become the Grateful Dead. That was a big transition time. It was the Summer of '65. It was hard to be a husband and a father. In the end, I wasn't able to do it.

Our apartment wasn't free, neither was starting a family, so I would give drum lessons at students' homes while Brenda and Stacy would wait in the station wagon. And I also taught drums at a music store in Palo Alto called Dana Morgan's, named after the owner. The same place where Jerry Garcia was teaching guitar. At night, after the store closed, Garcia and some of the other employees would take the instruments off the wall and play music right in the shop. This may have been Pigpen's doing. He swept floors or something there, and he really wanted to form an electric blues band. That's what he listened to. That's what he loved. His dad was a DJ at a local radio station and had a tremendous record collection. It was all blues music. So that's where Pigpen was coming from and where he wanted to go. He was able to get Jerry and a young kid about my age named Bob Weir on board for this thing. They were all in Mother McCree's Uptown Jug Champions together, covering jug band material and playing out. Back at the shop, they started playing rock music on electric instruments.

That's when Jerry called, asking me to join this new group. He was now on electric guitar. Weir too. Pigpen on harp. They recruited Dana Morgan's son, Dana Jr., to play bass, mostly because his dad owned the music store, which meant his dad owned the instruments, which meant the band had instruments.

Dana Jr. gave me a sparkling gold drum set, a Ludwig, and he also supplied Jerry with some of his guitars and amps and stuff. The flip side of that deal was that Dana just bought himself a position in the band, on bass. But he wasn't much of a bass player. It wasn't going to work. No offense, Dana.

We tried to do some gigs and they were as disastrous as open mic night at the School for the Tone Deaf. The guy just couldn't play the bass. I don't know what to tell you. Technically, we played our first show at Menlo College in Menlo Park, one town over from Palo Alto. That was on April Fool's Day, '65. No joke. The same date listed as my birthday on my fake driver's license. Also no joke.

Our first public show was about a month later, on May 5, at a pizza joint in Menlo Park called Magoo's Pizza Parlor. That's when we started calling ourselves the Warlocks. We played a couple more shows there. At one of them, Phil Lesh was in the audience and even though I still hadn't met him, I remember watching him that night because he was trying to dance, and you weren't allowed to dance there. The pizza parlor didn't have a dance permit which, in those days, believe it or not, you needed. Otherwise you'd get in trouble.

You know, I don't really remember ever formally meeting Pigpen or Bobby. I just remember that we all met at Dana Morgan's and that our first practices were at that shop. After closing time, we'd practice while our friends Sue Swanson and Connie Bonner just kind of hung out. They encouraged us. They were our first fan club. They later worked for the Grateful Dead—for years and years. Those two gals really liked us, and I think one of their parents was wealthy, so we went to their house in Atherton and would practice there sometimes. Atherton is a rich community in the Bay Area. Weir was also from Atherton and we practiced at his house once too. His mom took Jerry and Phil aside and made them promise that, if she let Bobby stay in the band, they'd make sure he finished high school. They broke their promise.

I don't remember much about about those first band practices. They were with Dana Morgan Jr. on bass, and there wasn't much that was memorable there. Then one day Jerry came to me and said, "Billy, we have to get a new bass player." No shit. I agreed and he said, "I have this friend who could do it. He's up in Berkeley, but he'd move down here if we let him in the band."

So I asked, "Is he a bass player?" "No." "That's interesting." But, sure enough, his friend—Phil Lesh—came down to Palo Alto and got a house near University Avenue and it became the spot where a lot of future shenanigans went down. It was on High Street. Aptly named. We'll get to all that. But first, one cool thing I have to say about Dana—he never asked for the gear back.

When Phil first joined, he got himself a little red Gibson four-string bass and he learned how to play that thing in about an hour, I think. He knew music, so he just had to apply it to that instrument. To this day, Phil has a very unique style of playing bass. The Grateful Dead had a very unique way of playing rock 'n' roll. You have to remember that it wasn't that we were trying to be different—that, too—but we had no blueprint. The Rolling Stones had only been around for three years. The Who had just formed. Pink Floyd were just forming. Led Zeppelin didn't exist yet. We were making it up as we went along. All of us.

So Phil joined the band and the first time I took acid was at his house on High Street. Robert Hunter was my partner for that trip, and I've loved him dearly ever since. I was eighteen and it was the earth-shattering, life-changing experience that I had hoped it would be, but that I never fully expected. I ate the acid and those however many micrograms of LSD-25 hit me like a teardrop falling into a huge body of still water—one minuscule drop was all it took to send ripples out in every direction, progressing into waves by the time they came crashing down on the shores of consciousness. First the drug itself was that drop, then I became that drop, splashing into the same vast ocean whose shores I had been standing on for eighteen years, always scanning the horizon, always looking out beyond the reflection of the lighthouse, always balancing on the edge of some bluff, catching the spindrift, wondering what would happen if I dove on in.

Taking the LSD was me diving on in. And, just as I had suspected, there was a never-ending parade of incredible things—sea creatures of the wildest imagination, ranging from fish that can camouflage themselves as your best friend from high school to mermaids who will love you then leave you to drown just to get back at their landlocked underlings—all brimming and buzzing underneath the unfathomable deep blue. And all it took was a tiny drop to penetrate the surface, to break on through. And even in the dark, down deep, there was little fear but no shortage of curiosity. "What's this?" "What's over here?" I had goggles on that gave me perfect vision. Not only could I see all these strange and fabulous creatures around me, but I could also see their intention. I could see more than just their shells.

Ever since I picked up *On the Road*, I knew that there was more out there, that there was something more than just life in the suburbs where people worked all day and then sat around watching television after dinner until they were ready for bed. I always believed that the America that Kerouac wrote about so convincingly was not just a place to visit in books, but a place to visit in the flesh. It was where I wanted to be, and I always knew I would arrive there, just by knowing that I would. If *On the Road* was my boarding pass, then acid was my vehicle of choice. Before the drug even fully came on that night, I could feel that it would forever change my life. I was right.

Hunter and I watched the garbagemen picking up trash in the morning, while still tripping, going, "Far out!" And it really was far-out, too. They were as strange as any other psychedelic crustacean. They would stop in front of all the houses, one at a time, and do a little preprogrammed, emotionless dance that involved dumping strangers' trash cans into the back of their truck, tossing the cans like yesterday's news, and then moving on without ever looking back. No mercy. The truck was the biggest trash compactor I had ever seen—and it was on wheels! It made an incredible noise every time it started up and it would screech a few feet later at the next stop. Just really crazy jazz. Horns and a snare. The garbage men, meanwhile, were like automatons with hair and grease and dirt. I could see their auras. They were neither happy nor unhappy. Just containers of electricity, plugged into the current.

I looked at Robert Hunter like I had just seen a brave new world, and repeated myself—"Far out." Then I jumped into Sue Swanson's car and drove for hours, driving all around Portola Valley. We stopped by some redwoods and I ran up to the biggest one I saw, with a trunk as wide as the number one wide receiver in earth's biggest football league—a game of giants—but its countenance was still and solemn, revealing a lifetime of staunch service to the forest. It had a consciousness. I could see it sure as I could see the auras of the garbagemen earlier.

Redwoods are hard on tree huggers because you can't even begin to wrap your arms around them. Much less your mind. "You're alive!" I shouted, with my neck craned, looking up at its 250-foot declaration of a life well lived. "You're alive!" And it was, too. And so was I. And all of that was far-out. And then it occurred to me that the tree was maybe even more alive than most of the people we drove past that morning, on their way to work. That's one of those perceptions that you have on acid, but is it also not true?

Almost everybody in the band took acid that day. One of Phil's friends, Hank Harrison, insisted on it. Hank wanted to manage us, so we gave him a shot and that lasted all but a few days. He was a terrible manager. Granted, I'll probably say that about all of our managers; I have issues with management. Hank didn't work out for us, but he did go on to father a famous singer—Courtney Love.

Under Hank's temporary stewardship, he suggested to us—very strongly—that we all take LSD together and play music. What a great idea. And everybody but Pigpen, to the man, went "Yeah!" So we took acid and jammed. This led into the Acid Tests and a whole series of gigs with Ken Kesey and the Merry Pranksters, once a week, for a while.

But we had a string of strange gigs before then, straight gigs that didn't really work for us. Our first gig with Phil was June 18, 1965, at a place called Frenchy's Bikini-A-Go-Go in Hayward, which is a city in the East Bay, about twenty miles from Palo Alto. Our first road gig. Phil's first show. I don't think we played that well. It was awkward. We weren't the right band for the place. We weren't a Top 40 band. When we went back the second night, we found out they hired another band instead. Someone told me they were a clarinet, accordion, and upright bass combo, which is pretty strange. Guess that's where the money was.

The clubs around there in those days often had topless dancers. That November, we played a topless club up in San Francisco—Pierre's in North Beach—and while we were playing, one of the dancers had sweat pouring off her boobs like crazy. She turned around and asked us, "Hey, can't you play any shorter songs?" We were having a great time playing and looking at her boobs, so we didn't care. I think Bobby took her home that night. At least he wanted to.

In the fall, before that gig, we landed a residency at this club called the In Room, which was located in Belmont, directly between Palo Alto and San Francisco. Six weeks straight, five shows a week, five sets a night, forty-five-minute sets, fifty-minute sets, something like that, stop, start, all that. They wanted us to play loud and stop between songs so people would order more drinks. The In Room was hardcore. There was no shortage of meth, alcohol, or loose women. That was the vibe. Real angular. Cigarette smoke filled the air.

From the very beginning, we would cover Rolling Stones songs. We'd play stuff like "Get Off of My Cloud" and "Satisfaction." They were just fun, easy tunes to do in the nightclubs we were playing back then and that's what the people in those places wanted to hear. Toward the end of our career, we would cover "The Last Time" a lot. People thought we were trying to convey a secret message because the chorus goes, "This may be the last time," and there were all those rumors about Garcia's health and the health of the band—Deadheads would read stuff into it. But that wasn't the case at all; we just liked playing it. In fact, Phil has said it was one of the songs that first got him into rock 'n' roll.

At the beginning of the In Room residency, we backed up Cornell Gunther and the Coasters. The Coasters were already a popular band with hit songs like "Little Egypt," "Love Potion No. 9," "Yakety Yak," and "Poison Ivy." Gunther brought a musical director with him who doubled as a rhythm guitarist. He tried to teach us the songs in mid-performance—even though we already knew them. He insisted on playing in the band and it was just miserable. We didn't respond well to somebody sitting there telling us how to do it. The next night, we said, "Don't bring him," and we played the songs perfectly because they were so easy. Gunther loved it. He was just gay as could be; a wonderful cat. We hung out afterward and it was cool.

The In Room was really where we got our first chops as a band, in front of an audience. It's also where we really first started improvising. We didn't learn how to get that far-out with our music until the Acid Tests a few months later, but we started jamming—improvising in the jazz sense—at the In Room. When you have to play all night, every night, and you don't have a lot of material, you almost have no choice. We learned that we could make one song last an entire set. And nobody really noticed. That was nice.

When we would stretch out and go long, when we got really loud and into it, the dancers would look at us uncomfortably and start glancing at the bartenders for help. But rather than putting an end to it, this one particular bartender, who had a glass eye, would add to the freakiness. He would pour lighter fluid all along the drainage ditch of the bar, pop his glass eye out of its socket, spin it on the bar top, and then set the whole damn thing on fire. From my perch on the drum riser, it looked like a curtain of flame with a madman's eye spinning right through it. Everyone was like, "What the fuck is going on here?" We seem be a magnet for that kind of thing; maybe there's some kind of chemistry that attracts that kind of weirdness. But the In Room nurtured us as a live act and allowed us to discover who we really were as a band.

It seems like so many bands that have really made an impact with their own unique sound all have one thing in common—they all did some kind of residency during their infancy. A place to learn and grow, to play and play and then play some more, to let loose and then get tight, to see what works and, also, what's what. That was the In Room, for us. Although the manager did once tell us that we were never going to make it. I'm not so sure that he was right about that. (I think most successful bands have a story like that in common, too).

We get credited for starting the jam band scene and maybe that is true, but jazz musicians jammed way before rock musicians. John Coltrane jammed way before the Grateful Dead. Some of us loved jazz and loved John Coltrane but, oddly enough, Garcia wasn't so into it at first. He once told me that he didn't get Coltrane. That blew my mind, but who knows? He sometimes made comments like that to me about other music and I would discover later that he only meant it in the momentary space of a particular mood.

Years—decades—later, there were moments on stage where occasionally it would just be Jerry and me playing for a few minutes. An unintentional duet. I don't remember what shows they happened at, and we didn't get to do them nearly as often as we should've, but Lesh came up to me once, after one of those shows, and said, "Man, you guys sounded like John Coltrane and Elvin Jones up there." I knew better—we hardly sounded like that. But what he meant was that we were able to be completely open and free, without being restricted, without having to play in fours or in twos or any disco crap. We played so loose, it was like water going over a waterfall. The water flows over different rocks and splashes off here and there at unpredictable moments where it's just pure nature and beauty and art and it can't be practiced and it can't be planned, it just is. It was a blending of a certain amount of strangeness with something that was still understandable. It was really satisfying to play that way, too. Nothing about it was obvious and none of it was literal. That's the music that I like the most. Jerry and I used to really get off on those duets.

Phil was the one who first turned me on to John Coltrane—and to Elvin Jones, his drummer—a year or so after the In Room, when we were living together on Belvedere Street in San Francisco. I was high on some kind of relaxant; there was something going around for a while that they were lacing weed with—way before rat or any of those horrible things. I think it was the same as smoking heroin. Whatever it was, Phil rolled it in this joint and I loved it. Then he played me Coltrane and I got drenched by the sound. I let it wash all over me: "Yes!" I wasn't listening for structure and I wasn't looking for theory. I didn't try to understand that music from any academic standpoint. That would've been totally misguided and would've missed the point, anyway. When you listen to music that moves you, you don't sit and count the beats. That music is about being free. And being in the moment.

That's exactly what we were trying to create ourselves, beginning at the In Room. Once we started playing high on acid at the Acid Tests, it all went into high gear. Meanwhile, during this initial phase, we played in all these rough nightclubs. It was the fall of 1965, so none of us except for Jerry and Phil were even twenty-one. Unless, of course, you looked at our fake IDs.

Phil's girlfriend somehow got her hands on a stash of blank draft cards around the same time that I took a day job at the Behavioral Research Center at Stanford. I was essentially a gopher for all the professors.

With fancy typewriters at my disposal and everybody minding their own business, I did what any acid-eating, pot-smoking hippie would do: I took the blank draft cards and filled in all the numbers, using the exact same dot matrixes that are on the official cards. I made sure they were a perfect match. We may have been technically underage at the time, but we had documentation that "proved" otherwise.

In fact, the cards were so good, that the authorities couldn't bust us. A couple ABC guys strolled into a bar where we were playing once, and when we handed them our forgeries, they tried not to laugh: "Unbelievable! These check out. Somehow."

The gig where that happened was actually at a place called the Fireside, right before the In Room residency—August 1965. The Fireside was the same kind of gig as the In Room except we didn't last there but maybe a week. And it was, again, one of these raunchy bar scenes—they wanted rock bands in there. We got away with the underage thing, but then we were asked to leave anyway. So that gig didn't work out.

Here's another thing I got away with that same year, talking of draft cards: I'm pretty sure it's safe for me to talk about this now. From the moment the Warlocks started, the band was my life. That's what I was doing. I wasn't going to let the war in Vietnam interrupt band practice. Some of my friends were getting drafted—one of them shot himself in the foot with a 30/30 to get out of it. When I got my notice, my dad said, "You've got to go report. They'll come after you and put you in jail if you don't report." That got through to me. So I went down to my draft board in San Jose, and I looked at the address of the induction center where I was supposed to go, and when I got there, all I found was a burnt-out shell. There was nothing else there. Somebody must have torched the building. Some of the Jesuits were allegedly burning down induction centers, and I'm not sure if they burned mine down, but I'm positive that it was gone. There was no more "Bill Kreutzmann" in the system. That was the age of two-inch computer tape—not like today's digital age where information is more permanent and stored in the cloud. My file was gone. It was remarkable. Whoever is responsible for that, here's to you.

When I got there and realized that the whole damn building was gone, I said, "Fuck that. I'm out of here!" A thousand other guys lucked out too, I bet.

So I didn't go to war and instead I got to stay in the Warlocks, even though that was a horrible name for a band. I'm glad we decided to look for a new one. We had to. The Warlocks name was already taken. At least, that's what someone in our group told us. Now, maybe they made that up, just because in later years nobody was really able to track that other band down. Either way, a name change was for the best. There were a lot of fortuitous things that happened to us. This was one of them.

I remember we were at Phil's house one day trying to come up with a new name. Garcia sat on the couch with a giant dictionary and he came across the words, "Grateful Dead." The words jumped off the page. We were all there, the whole band together, all clustered around the couch. When the phrase "Grateful Dead" came up, everybody went, "What?" We'd just been smoking DMT and those words stuck out. They were so incongruous. "How could you be grateful and dead? How could you possibly be both of those things?"

And then we learned the beautiful story behind those two words. There are a few different variations of the "grateful dead" folk tale throughout history, and from different parts of the world, but the essential motif, or common thread, behind them is that there is a traveler who comes across a burial scene. The villagers refused to bury some body because they hadn't paid off their debt. In a tremendous act of good will, the traveler pays the debt for them and continues on their way. Then along comes this spirit, this ghost, and says, "I'm the grateful dead and I'd like to reward you for your good deed."

A whole bunch of ballads are written about that. I thought that was a beautiful story, although I wasn't convinced that it would make a good band name. At first, I voted against it, but then I finally consented. "Fine. We'll be the Grateful Dead." I'm glad I lost that argument.

Another one of those fortuitous things that happened was that we were all invited up to one of Ken Kesey's wild parties at La Honda. By this point,

Kesey had published his second novel, *Sometimes a Great Notion,* and a bunch of his freaky friends started calling themselves the Merry Pranksters. In 1964 they went all the way to New York and back on a school bus that Kesey bought with some of his book money. They painted the bus in Day-Glo colors and called it Furthur. There was a lot of LSD involved.

Most of the Pranksters had nicknames, like Mal Function, dis-MOUNT, Gretchen Fetchin and, of course, Wavy Gravy. Jerry Garcia's future wife, Carolyn, was nicknamed Mountain Girl. The Grateful Dead didn't actually go on that cross-country Furthur tour. We weren't Pranksters—we were the Grateful Dead. But some of us got Prankster names, anyway. We were initiated into Pranksterdom. Garcia got Captain Trips. I got Bill the Drummer.

With his success, Kesey was able to move out of Perry Lane to a bigger property in La Honda, about forty minutes west of Palo Alto. La Honda was up in the redwood forest in the coastal mountain range of California. It's a gorgeous country place, real quiet. It's foggy in the summertime, like most coastal areas in California. La Honda was more like a psychedelic ranch, a commune for the Pranksters and their friends, than a writer's retreat, which is what Kesey may have originally wanted it for. That didn't happen. Oh well.

When we made it over there for that party, we didn't even bring our instruments. We were just up there, hanging out and partying. That's where I first met some of the Hells Angels. I know they can smell fear so I just put on my game face and wished for the best. But that's also the night that I first met Neal Cassady. He was always really wired, juggling conversations, sledgehammers, girls, and drugs—all at once, although nobody could keep count. He was jazz personified. All horns and a snare. He hit me up for dexamyl and shook me down for speed. By this point though I think he was getting more into acid. We all were.

The first Acid Test was more like a pop quiz than a test. We all aced it. It wasn't a gig. We just went to get weird, and that's exactly what we did. It was a house party at Ken Babbs'—one of the Pranksters—place in Santa Cruz.

We played our first show as the Grateful Dead about a week later—December 4, 1965—at what was really the first public Acid Test. How's that for a perfect pairing? Two one-of-a-kind firsts. Or was it two of a kind? It was held in San Jose at the house of a friend of Kesey's that he nicknamed Big Nig. That was Kesey's way of poking fun at racism, since Big Nig was a big black man. The Rolling Stones were playing a concert down the street from his house and some effort was made to get Mick Jagger or Keith Richards to the party. But, inside the Acid Test, something more important happened. We had already played all those shows as the Warlocks, but this was the start of something new, something different. It was bigger than itself for the first time.

The Rolling Stones never showed up, but Jann Wenner was there, in the audience. Two years later, he founded *Rolling Stone Magazine*—with a feature on the Grateful Dead in the very first issue.

The Acid Tests were the physical manifestation of what goes on in your mind during an acid trip. Things don't always make sense. Some sounds are noises, some noises are music, music is being played, but not everything being played is music. Some things you hear over the loudspeaker are snippets from a conversation you had earlier on in the night with a friend of yours. Did you really say that aloud? You must've because now it was being looped over the PA system, along with weird announcements and proclamations. And you can't trust anything you see because you're seeing things that just can't be. Or can they? It was a psychedelic circus and everyone was the sideshow and everyone was the main event, but was there even any main event at all? Nobody could say for sure.

After Big Nig's Acid Test in San Jose, we started playing Acid Tests about once a week. Some are more memorable than others and, then too, some are more famous than others. But they were all historic. The Muir Beach Acid Test, on December 11, 1965, was held in a lodge about 100 yards from the ocean, and it's where a guy named Owsley Stanley first came into the Grateful Dead story. I don't actually remember meeting him that night, so he doesn't come into my own story quite yet. At least, not for another paragraph. But at the Muir Beach Acid Test, I do remember the Pranksters showing movies of their bus adventures, projected onto a screen. As the acid was coming on strong, Babbs would ask over the sound system, "Are you watching the movie? Are you in the movie? Now, are you in the movie, watching the movie?" Overlaid, it was like the mirrors in barbershops that ricochet to infinity. You're watching the movie and, pretty soon, you are the movie.

The same could be said for Owsley—first he was watching the movie, then he was in the movie. There is an account of him at the Muir Woods Acid Test pushing around a heavy, metal chair that made a horrible scraping noise on the floor, then getting so wrecked he wrecked his car going home that night. Yep, sounds like him.

Pretty soon, I learned that he made the stuff that made the Kool Aid so electric. At first we were eating acid by taking capsules that came straight from Sandoz Laboratory in Switzerland. Official stuff. Sandoz didn't actually cap those things; the Pranksters did. But Sandoz manufactured the stuff inside. You'd hold it up and look in the light and see this little teeny speck of dust. You were almost sure there was nothing there, but it sure got you high.

When that supply disappeared, we started taking Owsley's. He very quickly came onto the scene with a reputation as the guy who made the best acid. And it was true—he did. He'd get really, really high when he concocted it. If you don't get high while you're making it, you're not making it right. He told me that.

Owsley had a lot of beliefs that were questionable, but in his mind, they were unquestionable truths. When we first went to his place in Berkeley—a couple blocks down from Telegraph Avenue—he told us he could talk to electronics, mentally talk to them, like people talk to plants. He talked to electronics and chemical compounds. And for all I could ever tell, they actually listened. Sometimes they just listened slowly, that's all. And they didn't always talk back.

Owsley studied chemistry at Berkeley. I'd go to his place with Brenda and the band on the weekends and take acid and mess around. Sometimes we'd paint the floor Day-Glo colors and stuff. We didn't play music there, because of his neighbors, but he showed us all his tricks—his electronic wizardry and stuff. So, immediately we got enthused about getting involved with him somehow and bringing him into the Grateful Dead fold. He became our first soundman but, more than that, he also started financing the band, once his acid sales took off. Once he earned the nickname: "Alice D. Millionaire." Get it?

While studying chemistry at Berkeley, Owsley met Melissa, one of the great loves of his life. Great lady. She was a chemistry student and she and Owsley took classes together. He didn't give a shit about most of it, because he already knew what he wanted. He just needed a lab. So he went in there and at first he made speed, and then he made acid. Nobody knew what he was doing, of course. But he did.

Meanwhile, Ken Kesey got turned on to acid by volunteering for CIA-financed psychedelic experiments at the Veteran's Administration Hospital in Palo Alto. He volunteered to be one of the guinea pigs, and after so many trips, the doctor asked, "How are you feeling, Ken?" He replied, "I don't feel anything this time, Doc," as he watched the doctor's face turn into something from a science-fiction film yet to be made. "Nothin'." He went outside, high as a motherfucker, and said, "This is so much better." That was the last time he ever took acid at the hospital.

So, the Acid Tests started out fueled by Sandoz product and then Owsley's acid came in and took over. Owsley had a way of doing that with everything. He even took over the band for a while. He was our medicine man, our soundman, and our patron saint . . . but at a cost.

The first time I remember meeting Owsley was at an Acid Test at Longshoreman's Hall, which is this weird, far-out building down in San Francisco's Fisherman's Wharf neighborhood. Down by the docks of the city. This wasn't just an Acid Test though—this was a weekend-long psychedelic convention billed as the Trips Festival. A newly formed Big Brother and the Holding Company also performed at this one. Before we played, we went across the street to a friend's apartment—I don't remember who—and they had white caps that they said had acid in them. It didn't look like anything from Sandoz. They said, "No, this is new Owsley. This is what you want." The whole band, except Pigpen, dropped a white capsule of acid that night and got really high and had a great Acid Test.

That's the same night that Kesey came up to us and said, "You guys are going to be more famous than you realize, not just here in San Francisco." He saw that there was something going on here, even if Mr. Jones didn't know what it was, just yet. Kesey was wearing a spacesuit with a mirrored helmet. It was a disguise because he was running from the law. Back on his property in La Honda, he had been set up and busted with less than an ounce of weed. It was supposed to be some kind of slap on the wrist, so that they could make an example out of him, but Kesey called bullshit and went on the run. At the Trips Festival, there were a lot of people in costumes, so he wasn't the only person incognito. Still, it was pretty outrageous. He was a fake spaceman but a real American hero.

Another Acid Test story, this one from Portland: Neal Cassady drove most of the gang up to Oregon in a rented U-Haul, in treacherous road conditions, after Furthur had broken down en route. Cowboy Neal was at the wheel but Sue Swanson and I had decided to fly up to Portland from San Francisco instead. We took acid before the flight and got really high while we were in the air. We were supposed to be picked up by somebody who we didn't know and we sat in the Portland airport, PDX, for what seemed like hours, so high on acid that we couldn't recognize faces or see straight or do anything useful. The person who was supposed to come get us was there the whole time. Finally he came up to us and asked, "Are you Bill and Sue?" He'd been waiting for us since we landed. We were just so completely high. The next night was the Acid Test.

The thing about acid is that it's tricky to take two nights in a row. You have to double up on the dosage the second night if you want to get to the same level. And even then, you don't always get there. That's one of the many interesting things about that drug; there are a lot of interesting things about it. Anyway, I more than doubled up. I wanted to make sure we had a really great Acid Test. We played in a small, open-seated theater. It was more of an "Acid Test Show" than a fully realized Acid Test. Needless to say, we passed it. With flying colors.

"Music from the Pink House"

Throughout the thirty-year history of our band, people have always accused the Grateful Dead of trying to sabotage our own career. It seemed to outsiders, many times, like we just didn't care about success. At least, not in the big Hollywood-superstar kind of way. But in February of '66, we moved to Los Angeles because we wanted to make the big time and we thought that meant we had to be in L.A. for some reason. We learned a lot of lessons about all of that, but those three months also gave us an entire lifetime's worth of adventure. Or, at least, a chapter's worth.

I always found it funny that The Band had an album called *Music from the Big Pink,* named after a house they all shared in the mid-Hudson region of New York. Around the same time The Band lived at Big Pink, the Grateful Dead also lived in a big pink house, but in L.A. (The Band recorded some of the *Pink Album* in L.A., making a further connection.) We could've made a record called *Music from the Pink House.* Instead we just made memories.

Our version of the Big Pink was in the Watts district of Los Angeles, a black neighborhood that made headlines the previous summer when the Watts Riots broke out. Ignited by racial injustice on behalf of—who else—the local police, the weeklong riots killed a few dozen people, injured around 1,000, and resulted in more than 3,000 arrests. Later I would learn that Robert Hunter was one of the National Guardsmen who was called up for duty, to report to the scene. I wonder how effective he was in maintaining order.

All sense of order was lost, anyway, once we moved into the hood. But in a totally different sense. The Pranksters accompanied us on our journey south, with the ultimate goal of reuniting with Kesey, who was at-large in Mexico. A fugitive. But before meeting up with him, the Pranksters took advantage of our southern migration by throwing a few Acid Tests in and around Los Angeles. In my mind, those Tests really exposed all the elements of why L.A. just wasn't going to work for us.

The Doors were a good example of the Southern California scene. They wore that outfit well, what with the leather pants and the affected swagger and all. But the Grateful Dead were ambassadors from the north. We realized this soon enough. Learning what we weren't helped us define what we were.

In the meantime, the most outrageous things happened at the Pink House. Owsley lived with us, which meant we took a lot of acid. We'd dose once a week, on Wednesdays. Always on Wednesdays. I don't know why we chose that day in particular, and sometimes we'd do it more often—but getting high on acid every Wednesday was part of the ritual of the house.

That was one of the things I really liked about being in that Pink House, and about being in the Grateful Dead, period, during the early years: everybody had a sense of adventure. We were never satisfied with everyday occurrences. It took something weird to grab our attention, to deserve our attention—and once it got our attention, that was it. Then suddenly we could frame it in the living comic book that was our lives at the time, and put a punch line on it.

Watching stuff on TV just didn't cut it. That was somebody else's storyline. We were too busy living in ours. Playing music did the trick and we did that all the time. It was our number one occupation. But we needed extracurricular activities too, in order to feed the beast of inspiration. Whatever we did, part of the unspoken criteria was that it had to be far-out. It had to be an adventure. A good catalyst for that, a good motion-maker for this attitude of creativity, was to take LSD.

Lucky for us, Owsley was there with an endless supply of it. Some of his acid is still probably around today, hidden in people's freezers or basements like fine wine that they're holding onto for a special occasion. That's how much he made. But Owsley was more than just our supplier—as I mentioned earlier, he was also our financier and our patron. He invested in the Grateful Dead. We didn't have any money in our pockets when we were in L.A. We weren't playing many gigs and the ones we did play, didn't really pay. But we had the backing of the "L.S.D. Millionaire." Owsley paid the rent, bankrolled our wardrobes, and bought our food.

To feed us, Owsley would buy huge sections of cow, like the entire rump and topside. Literally. Raw and uncut. He'd plop the fucker right in the refrigerator. We had to cut off our own versions of steaks when we wanted to eat, using knives that were duller than a PTA meeting. But Owsley believed—religiously, scientifically, whatever—in a strict meat-eater diet. Carnivorous to the core. He never ate vegetables or cereal or pasta or yogurt or fruit or cheese. He never ate salads. No greens. No carbohydrates. He only ate meat. And since he had all the money, he controlled our diets. He felt very strongly about his dietary beliefs, which is fine, but he also forced them on us. So there was half of a dead cow in the fridge and a knife that got duller every time and our patience wore thinner with every meal. Brenda had to fight with him just to get oatmeal for Stacy.

But food wasn't the primary reason for living there; playing music was. Owsley supplied all the equipment and somehow we were placed inside his dream of building the perfect sound system for a live band. Unfortunately, his idea of perfect turned out to be pretty far from Eden. Eight years later—in 1974—it led us to the now-legendary Wall of Sound setup. That was the pinnacle of the great Owsley sound experiment. Of course, it turns out that having a wall of speakers—including 4,000 pounds of speakers above the drummer—was not the best idea.

But, at the Pink House, the wall of speakers and amplifiers that Owsley set up in the living room was awesome. We could rehearse whenever we wanted. And when we did, we were loud. Really loud. Predictably, the neighbors weren't too happy.

Well, one day, the old lady who lived in a two-story house to the right of us opened all of her windows and put a different sound device in each of them—a radio in one, a telephone in one, a television in one, a hair dryer in another, a blender in this one, whatever she could figure would make a sound. She turned them all on, facing our house, full blast, to bug us. She was trying to get back at us for playing music so loud all the time and probably just being loud in general. But, unfortunately for her, it didn't work. We loved it. We were all high on acid going, "Fuck, that's bitchin'!"

We probably should've been more concerned about the house on the other side of us. It wasn't until the end of our stay that we learned it was an outlaw gambling operation. That's all right. We kept to ourselves and laid low anyway. Especially in that neighborhood—fucking Watts.

While we were there, the Pink House was the center of the Dead's universe. My whole family was there, living in one room—Brenda and I had Stacy's crib in our bedroom. Phil brought along his girlfriend, Florence Louise (who later changed her name to Rosie McGee and wrote her own book about all of this). Owsley had Melissa. Jerry's family came down with him initially, but the relationship fell apart before we even moved into the house. So his wife and daughter, Sara and Heather, split back north. It was a three-ring circus with constant motion and people coming in and out.

It wasn't boring living there. I remember that Weir dated a Playboy Bunny once and took her home and that was exciting. She was in the house for a few days. And Danny Rifkin—who would soon start co-managing us with a guy named Rock Scully for many, many years—first stumbled into our world as a visitor at the Pink House. Danny came there with Harry Shearer, who became a famous actor. Harry was in that funny rock 'n' roll satire, *Spinal Tap,* as the bassist Derek Smalls, with the aluminum foil cock or whatever. He co-wrote that script and then, as you probably know, he went on to do many of the voices on *The Simpsons*. So, in a way, you could say Ned Flanders swung by the Pink House.

It's pretty cool to note that Harry's career first really took off with *Saturday Night Live*—there's a certain synchronicity to that and you'll soon see why. What's more, Harry came to SNL via a recommendation from Al Franken (a future Deadhead). He replaced John Belushi (a future friend). There were all sorts of crazy connections like this, everywhere, throughout our career.

Owsley was kind of the lone wolf at the Pink House, because he was always in the attic, making the sacrament or whatever he was doing up there. He had all the raw stuff and the pill press or the capping machine or whatever he used—I never paid much attention to that shit and I never saw it. But this was in the first half of 1966. LSD was still legal. We weren't worried about it.

I'm going to start referring to Owsley as Bear sometimes, because that's what we started calling him, at his insistence. It was a nickname he brought with him from childhood. Well, anyway, Bear was one of those guys who was sure he had all the answers. He was sure he knew what was best for everybody, all the time. We're still not so sure of that. We eventually had to part ways because it all just got to be too much.

Bear was as stubborn as red wine on white carpet. It became a burden at shows because, as our soundman, everything had to be perfect before we could start. Not our idea of perfect, but his. And he was constantly experimenting with new ideas for better sound, which were all fine experiments, but all too often they delayed our start time. Significantly.

It was mathematically correct that if you yelled at Bear once, he slowed down twice. If something was wrong with the sound, he'd sit there and really talk to these machines. It didn't matter to him if he was responsible for the gig starting two hours late. All that mattered was that, when it did start, he got the sound he wanted.

As pigheaded and difficult as he could be, he did have a number of visionary ideas that at least demanded consideration. He had an incredible theory about the weather that involved the polar ice caps melting. At the time, we all went, "That's nonsense. It'll never happen." But it's happening, all right. In 1966, Bear was talking about stuff that is actually going on today.

Another one of his "crazy" theories was about an incredible storm. The eye of it, he said, will start over Greenland and spread over both northern continents because of global warming. I don't think it's entirely correct science, but his speculation about the polar caps is coming true, so there's that. Bear postulated that eventually there will just be one giant cyclone that will never stop. It will be so large that it will regenerate itself and regenerate itself, like a comic book villain. He laid out his theory to Kesey once, in this long-winded rap, and you can watch some of it on YouTube if you want to look it up and get a feel for him. He was real serious about a lot of stuff. He always had the mad scientist's mind. He analyzed stuff.

Bear also manufactured some of the first designer drugs. He made at least one batch of STP, which was basically a speed-based psychedelic. I got to try it once—or, rather, he got to try it on me. As an experiment. He gave me a tremendous dose. I was up for seventy-two hours and laughed for most of it. I saw giant bubbles wherever I looked. It was far-out, but it was too harsh a ride for most people. People didn't like it, so Bear stopped making it. LSD was the hit. That was the one.

And, like everything, we took it as far as we could go. One time, up in the attic, some of the guys went so far as to shoot up with LSD. Inject it. You can't do it to yourself because you can't look at your arm with the needle in it; that's a heavy thing to see while hallucinating on acid. It comes on that fast. You're high. There's no come-on. You're just there. It's instantaneous.

As for throwing Acid Tests while we were in L.A., the one that stands out the most is the Watts Acid Test. It actually took place a few miles south of Watts, in a warehouse in Compton. It was on February 12, so the band had been in L.A. for less than a week and we hadn't moved into the Pink House quite yet. The police were likely still edgy from the race riots. Hippies, to them, fell in the same category as minorities. They didn't seem to like us. So, there was a big police presence outside the Watts Acid Test and that didn't go over well with anyone.

After the Test, we made plans to meet up at some woman's house. It was already morning by this time—Sunday morning. I had my station wagon with me but was too high to drive. I piled in the back and lay down on top of equipment while Phil drove. We got there before the Pranksters, and when their bus pulled up, Neal Cassady got outside and directed the bus right over a stop sign. He must have drunk as much Kool Aid as I did.

We watched him because just watching him, in his everyday life, was like watching an action film—comic, adventurous, frantic, with many frames per second. Embarrassed by his uncharacteristic mishap, Neal went over and held up the stop sign, trying to get it to stay upright again, as if to erase his mistake. When he walked away, it started to fall. So he immediately put his hand out and stopped it from falling all the way. He started leaning on it to hold it up, and in the meantime these two old ladies, dressed in their Sunday best, came walking down the sidewalk. Neal didn't want them to see that the stop sign had been run over, so he made it look like he was just leaning on it casually. No problem. Just being casual. As the ladies walked by, they looked at the bus, Furthur, and you could hear them cackling about it. Neal tipped his hat to them, "Morning, ladies," as they walked to church. As soon as they had their backs to him—plop! Down went the stop sign. It was perfect Buster Keaton timing. Neal was a true showman and we were his audience. He was always good for a laugh. Many of them, in fact.

One final L.A. story and then we can get back to San Francisco—there was another acid test in L.A. that nobody knows about because it wasn't advertised, the band didn't play, and there were only a few people involved. One of whom completely failed the test.

At the Pink House one day, out of the clear fucking blue, a friend of mine from high school, Rollie Grogan, shows up. He had just completed basic training for the marines at Camp Pendleton and he was on his break or whatever, right before he was going to be shipped off to Vietnam. He brought a buddy from basic training with him, a fellow marine. They were looking for something to do. A contingent from the Pink House had already made plans to go down to Venice Beach for the day and take acid. Have some fun on the boardwalk, whatever. I invited them to come along but I asked Rollie if he thought his friend could handle it. After all, they were getting ready to go fight a war. That's heavy stuff, even on a clean head.

But they signed on and sure enough, Rollie's friend had an intense trip. He went overboard and the next thing I knew, he ran up and down the boardwalk yelling a weird mix of orders and nonsense to people. "Mother! Fire! Brimstone! Hell!" He'd do an about-face and then go up to another civilian and do the same thing, snapping to attention and spewing a whole set of military commands that he had just been brainwashed with during basic training. They must have shown him some really scary movies. Dystopian, apocalyptic shit. I started to get nervous. Paranoid. The police were bound to show up. Rollie and I decided, "Well, fuck. We're outta here." We needed a place to hide.

There were really small waves coming in off the Pacific that day, so we lay down in the ocean with our feet out to the water and with our heads on the sand so that nobody could see us when the cops showed up. We were sure they were coming and, sure enough, they did.

We met a friend of Bear's earlier that day named Jean Millay, who was very hip and just the coolest gal. Her house became one of the focal points for all of us during that trip because she lived right there in Venice Beach and welcomed us over. Rifkin brought Rollie's friend there to talk the guy down.

Inevitably, the police came knocking on her front door. Keep in mind that this was half a year before acid was made illegal. The cops just thought they were responding to complaints about a drunk. Jean held them off. "Oh, we've got him calmed down. He just needs to sleep it off." Just as she said that, he let out this horrible rave: "The world's going to end today! Fire and brimstone! Get your guns!" All this insane stuff.

Somehow Jean was able to get the cops to leave and we handled the guy from there. As acid wears off, you come down and can change gears or switch scenes if you need to. I don't know what happened to Rollie's friend after that because we all went and did different things. I ended up at some guy's apartment, playing music for a while—hand drums and stuff—and then went off into the night.

This was pretty much the same time period when Jim Morrison would hang out at Venice Beach, cruising the boardwalk while high on acid or mescaline or whatever. It was the perfect place for the Doors. But it wasn't our scene. So, three months after arriving in L.A., we loaded our gear and headed back north, San Francisco bound.

We had sent the girls—Brenda, Florence, and Melissa—up to the Bay Area before our own departure, with the mission of finding a new band house. They got an A+ on that assignment, all right. Bonus points, gold stars, all of it. They found a hidden mansion in Marin County and signed the rental agreement. This would be the first time the Dead landed in Marin. We ended up headquartered in that county for most of our career. Marin borders San Francisco on the north and the place they found, Rancho Olompali, was at the northern tip, halfway between Novato and Petaluma, about half an hour's drive from the big city. Right off Highway 101. We moved in, beginning on May 1, 1966.

Olompali is now a state park and the place is historic, not just because of the legendary six weeks the Grateful Dead lived there. Although, that too. The property is big enough to hold an entire village. In fact, at one point, it did. Olompali was originally an Indian village—the Coast Miwoks inhabited the site long before we did. Long before any of us were born. Like, before Jesus Christ was born. By the 1200s or 1300s it became the biggest village in the entire region. The Indians controlled the land until sometime well into the twentieth century. None of this was lost on us when we moved into the twenty-six-room mansion. We could feel the presence of Indian spirits. Really. Not all of them were so friendly.

Brenda wasn't so happy at Olompali; the rest of us had nothing but high times, day and night. Maybe that's why she wasn't so happy. She was trying to raise Stacy while the rest of us were drinking Bear's punch and having wild, naked times around the pool. Really outrageous stuff.

I played the family card, so Brenda, Stacy, and I ended up with the nicest bedroom at Olompali. It was all wood paneling and overlooked the pool, which was out about fifty yards from the house. In between, there was this big grass area and a stone court below that. There was lots of land. I used to go out and mow the lawn. I loved that, for some weird reason. I'd do patterns and designs—crop circles.

The grounds were like a kingdom and the house, a castle. There were secret passages—you could go from my room, through Pigpen's room, down into the living room and come out below, where there was an Indian relic. There were Indian burial grounds all around Olompali. The mounds are still there to this day; people know better than to mess with them.

The house took the foundation from the original adobe compound, but it was renovated into a big, beautiful, Victorian-style estate. In the hallway, there was a large piece of glass with wood paneling around it that you could look into and see the old adobe bricks—a window into the ancient part of the house. Through the looking glass.

We'd get high on acid and see spirits and things come out of there; they just flooded the whole house with all this weird energy. Jerry, Bear, and Phil all saw horrible stuff coming out from the old bricks. They saw fire and saw that the house was eventually going to burn down, which I think ended up happening. The bricks from the original Indian house may have actually survived.

Olompali was a far-out time. We had all this land, a swimming pool, temperate weather—and no neighbors. We threw a couple wild get-togethers that people still talk about today, although, for us, it was like one continuous six-week party. Bear was with us so we had acid and a PA system. We played, other people played, we all got naked and went swimming or else tripped out on the Indian vibe.

Of all the places the Grateful Dead stayed as a group—and there are a few notable ones to come—Olompali was my favorite. None of our band houses lasted forever and that's just the temporal nature of things. The world turns. We spin. We were young adults, which meant that scenes changed with every season; anything that wasn't fresh was already stale. But Olompali was the one place that I wish we had been able to stay at forever. When I conjure up some of those memories, and I get the images to flash behind my eyes, I begin to understand that those six weeks have become frozen in time. Permanent. But they sure were fleeting at the time.

At one of our parties there, almost all the San Francisco rock bands showed up, just to hang. We were all friends and we were all just starting out. This was right before Janis Joplin joined Big Brother and just months before Grace Slick joined Jefferson Airplane. But both of those ladies—and both of those bands—hung out with us that day.

The end of the driveway intersected directly with Highway 101 South, and people passing by could see there was something going on because cars were parked alongside the road. Everyone was welcome and there was a certain natural attraction for certain types of people. It was almost like a big, impromptu afternoon Acid Test.

The band the Charlatans were there in force. They were really memorable, visually, because they wore their stage outfits all the time, even when they weren't playing. So they weren't really stage outfits, then. That's just how they dressed. Victorian garb refashioned into a Nevada City gambler vibe. One of the guys in the band, George Hunter, chased Jerry around with a loaded 30/30. It was a misunderstanding over some girl. It's always about a girl or money, isn't it? Or drugs. Garcia ran and, eventually, the situation was diffused.

There was another incident involving guns and Bobby at Olompali. Pigpen and I got our hands on a .22 and we were hungry for dinner, so we decided to shoot a deer that we saw in the driveway. I took the shot and thought I missed. The deer ran off. It turns out, the bullet went right through the deer's head and landed about three feet from Weir, who was sitting up on a hill on the other side. Later on, when he told us how close he was to the bullet, he said, "Also, there's a dead deer up there somewhere with a hole in its head." By the time we found this out, a few days had gone by and it was too late to eat the meat. We messed up everything with that one.

Neal Cassady came to those parties at Olompali and stayed overnight sometimes. He was in the bedroom that was over the garage. The band was in the main house. I walked in on him fucking this chick, a Prankster I think, named Anne Murphy. Cassady was famous for his ability to hold seven conversations at once while doing a dozen other things and, like a master juggler, never drop a ball. He also was known for fucking a lot of women. But when I walked in on him and Anne, he said, "Bill, you've got to get out of here. Now is not the time." Just like that. Ended the conversation. He didn't get mad that I interrupted him and his girl and he didn't miss a beat fucking her, either. It was simply, like, "Hi, Bill. Not now. Get out of here."

That Cassady story reminds me of a contrasting one involving Bear, which I'm going to tell you now, even though it took place some time later.

We were playing with the Allman Brothers and the Hampton Grease Band (led by my friend Col. Bruce Hampton) in Atlanta on May 10, 1970. In those days, and probably still in many cities across America, the local populaces were just straight as hell. If you weren't married, you couldn't be with a girl in your room. All these fucking rules. And the authorities always knew what hotel the bands were staying in. Especially back then. So Phil and I were hanging out with Bear and his girlfriend in their room. Phil and I were smoking a joint while sitting on one of the beds, while Bear was over there fucking his girlfriend on the other one, making all these weird sounds. When he fucked, he always made these really weird, strange sounds. Phil and I were yukking it up, "Oh, Bear, ha ha!" And the poor chick, you can imagine, "Oh God, what did I get myself into? What's this guy doing?" Bear wasn't a really big, muscle-bound guy, but he was completely addicted to sex. He wasn't afraid to admit it, either. He was balling the hell out of his lady, and there was a knock at the door— bam, bam, bam. It was the cops. The local cops. They were going to come in, one way or the other, so Bear got up like a flash of fucking lightning, opened the window, and tossed his pot stash, so he wouldn't get busted.

We tossed our joint, too, and tried to air out the room. To buy us time, I told the cops, "You're going to get in over my dead body," or something. They proceeded to knock the door in. This was at a hotel, so maybe they had a key. I was still sitting with Phil on the one bed, and Bear was still fucking the chick in the other. He didn't stop. He didn't miss a beat. He got right back on her after he threw the weed out the window. He was fucking her like crazy and the cops came with their guns drawn right at our heads, right at me and Phil. But they slowly lowered them as they became aware of what was going on in the other bed.

Bear and this chick were into this weird thing, and pretty soon the guns were held at rest, pointing at the ground, and the cops asked us, "Hey, can you guys get them to stop?" It was too uncomfortable for them.

I said, "I can't do that! He's our soundman. If I get him to stop, we'll have terrible sound tomorrow night." Finally, Bear succumbed to the cops and stopped doing it, and the cops just made us go to our own rooms. They were weirded out. We were just glad to be out of there. And that was Owsley "Bear" Stanley for you.

Well, anyway, moving on: We had to move out of Olompali after just six weeks. Not by choice. But we lucked out and relocated to a space not too far away that was equally unique—an abandoned Girl Scout camp in Lagunitas, a small town on the west side of the county. As you approached the town, you'd take a right at a road just before the main intersection, where the bar is, and it was right up there. Quicksilver Messenger Service and Big Brother also lived in West Marin, and we'd all hang out.

Our encampment in Lagunitas was like this: There was a garage out in the front and little cabins scattered throughout the property. A creek bed ran off to the left, throughout, and it was nestled under redwoods. There was a cafeteria with a commercial kitchen, like a mess hall, and we set up all our gear in the front of that room. That became our practice space. We also had all of our communal dinners there. We were all living together then.

Camp Lagunitas was really cool; we loved living there. We could rehearse as much as we wanted and we never got hassled by the police. At first. Eventually there were noise complaints or something, but it was a great run. We took acid there as regularly as we could. And we played in the river a lot. It was a cold river, so we only really got in during the afternoons.

This was also neat, and something I always remember: We didn't drink at Camp Lagunitas. Pigpen was the only one that drank. Nobody else drank at all. Nothing. No beer—nothing. We just smoked pot and ate acid.

I think Pigpen got dosed once or twice—either against his will or accidentally—although I don't remember the details. He was probably unhappy about it. I felt lonesome for him, because the band had found something that had become nearly as important to us as music. It changed us as people and as musicians and as a band—and Pigpen, by his own choice, was left out of all of that. I never judged him for it, and Pig never judged us in return. But it did make me sad that it was like that.

Pigpen was a very soulful guy. He loved to romance chicks and he loved to drink Southern Comfort. He and Janis were great friends, then lovers, and they'd sit up late at night, playing guitar, wooing each other. He was just a real salt-of-the-earth guy. He dressed sort of like a biker, but he wasn't one. He liked bikes, but he didn't really have a Harley or anything like that. Pigpen was pseudo-tough. He dressed tough and he acted tough—but on the inside, he was the sweetest guy anybody had ever met. We used to laugh about it, because people thought he was kind of this badass, but he wasn't. He was like a puppy, with an outer shell of motorcycle insignia, which didn't really say anything on it.

We met a guy named Gene Estribou, who had a studio on Buena Vista West in San Francisco, just a couple blocks up from the famous intersection of Haight and Ashbury. Phil once lived right around there, too. For a while, we'd drive down to the city from Lagunitas every day to record at Gene's studio. We recorded songs that a lot of people have probably never even heard of. A Pigpen tune called "Tastebud" and a Lesh number, "Cardboard Cowboy." I don't even remember how they go. We also recorded "Don't Ease Me In" and "Stealin' " at those sessions and ended up releasing those two tracks as a forty-five single that summer. We only pressed maybe 100 copies, give or take, and sold them exclusively at shops on Haight Street. Talk about a rare artifact; one of those would be quite a find.

I would drive the band down to Estribou's every day in my station wagon. With the roads in West Marin—and city traffic—it took us nearly an hour, each way. Man, we put a lot of miles on that thing and it showed. There was a leak in the radiator and we didn't have the money to fix it. Every morning, I fed the baby oatmeal, and then I'd go and pour raw oatmeal directly in the radiator and added water. When oatmeal heats up, it expands and that fixed the leak. It worked. It got us to where we needed to go—and back. Just in time for another oatmeal fix. That station wagon ended up dying in Haight-Ashbury a few months later, when we all moved into the city. It got up to where Phil and I lived, on Belvedere Street, and that was it. Rust in peace. To this day, I can see it sitting there, just watching it rust away. The city finally came and towed it.

We started getting regular gigs, mostly in San Francisco on the weekends, thanks in large part to our new management team of Danny Rifkin and Rock Scully. Rifkin lived with us at Camp Lagunitas, in the unenclosed arts and crafts space, but the Grateful Dead now had an official management office at a boarding house, a couple blocks up from Haight Street, on Ashbury. The band managers also managed the boarding house. The house would become famous. So would the band.

That summer, 1966, we were able to get our own practice space—away from where we lived—for the first time. It was at a heliport just north of the Golden Gate Bridge, in Sausalito. There was an open space that wasn't being used, an open room, and we just took it and used it. It had a bathroom and that's all we needed. So it became our practice hall. Being in Sausalito, it overlooked San Francisco and, of course, the bay between. Otis Redding wrote "(Sittin' on) the Dock of the Bay" on a houseboat just a couple of miles from there, during the same period. Otis once hit on Phil's girl, Florence—outright at a gig—but she said she just couldn't do it. Funny enough, she did it with me, and I didn't even hit on her.

Florence was a real free spirit and a photographer. As we'll get to in just a few more pages, Phil, Florence, and I all lived in a house in San Francisco's Diamond Heights district for a while. It was a split-level house on the hillside and I lived on the bottom. One afternoon or something, Florence came downstairs and asked if we could fuck. "It's okay," she said. She fucked my eyes out and Phil wasn't mad or anything. It was all okay. In fact, we all hung out afterward. That sort of thing didn't happen as much as you might think, really, but that one happened and it was kind of surprising. It's not the standards by which most of us live these days, and I think it had more to do with stuff between them—that they were going through—than anything to actually do with me. But I worked my way through it.

Anyway, our stay at Lagunitas felt like a summer camp, especially since that's what the property was literally built for. And, of course, it was summertime. We each had our own spaces. I was in a cabin with Brenda and Stacy. Other people lived in other cabins, or in the main house, or in the bunkhouse, or in other buildings originally built for a kid's camp. When we moved from Lagunitas, we left Marin County and went to San Francisco. I think one reason for that was that we couldn't find a house big enough to fit everybody, with me having a wife and daughter and all that. But that was about to end real soon.

One of the most difficult acid trips I ever had was at Lagunitas. It was nighttime and Brenda was having the hardest time. "This isn't working. I'm not happy." All that kind of crap. And here I was, high on acid, having the best time, playing music with the band in the cafeteria. I knew then that Brenda was right. It wasn't working. It had been a long time since she had been happy and, besides, living with the Grateful Dead was no way to raise a baby. Especially during that period. Our days together were coming to an end.

In late September 1966, when the band moved down to San Francisco, I made it official. Around the time that I broke up with Brenda, the band broke up with Bear. It was a mutual split. We were tired of his power plays and long delays, and he was tired of being broke, since he gave up making acid to work for the Dead. So he went back to just making acid. That worked for us. And it wouldn't be the last we saw of our brother.

Like the Pink House and Olompali, Lagunitas was really far-out. But in 1995, Jerry died at a facility that's a stone's throw from our old camp, and when I think of Lagunitas, I can't help but think of that.

Much has been made about the Grateful Dead house at 710 Ashbury Street in San Francisco but we're not really going to make much of it here. For one thing, I only really lived there for but a moment. A couple of weeks, at most. We can talk about it, but it didn't have the same magnitude, in my mind, as Olompali or Lagunitas or even the Pink House.

Our place on Ashbury Street was the same boarding house where Scully and Rifkin first set up the band's office, while managing both the band and the house. It was no coincidence that when we needed to leave Camp Lagunitas for the real world, rooms there mysteriously began to open up until we took over the entire building. "We knew the management." And that's how 710 Ashbury became the Grateful Dead house.

There was another Victorian across the street, at 715 Ashbury that, while not nearly as famous, is still a part of the story. Sue Swanson and Ron Rakow, both eventual Grateful Dead employees, lived there. So did Alton Kelley and Stanley Mouse, the famous psychedelic poster artists who did several of our album covers and whose art remains a big part of our identity today—most notably the "Skull and Roses" image. Also of note: 715

became somewhat of a nest for Hells Angels. So you had the Grateful Dead on the one side of that street, and the Hells Angels on the other. Kinda a nice juxtaposition—and the names play off each other, too.

Like many San Franciscan streets, Ashbury is on a hill. I heard that Ken Kesey was driving down it one day and his brakes gave out and he had to make a quick decision: he could crash into the Grateful Dead house, or he could crash into the Hells Angels house. He chose the Hells Angels. Wise choice from our perspective but perhaps questionable from any other.

The Grateful Dead posed for band pictures on the front stoop of the 710 house and one of those images is now rather iconic. A thin, beardless Jerry is grinning from the doorway, Pigpen's holding a rifle with a real outlaw aura to him, Bobby—by contrast—is playing the innocent; Scully and Rifkin are on the stoop, smiling; Phil is looking at me; and I've got my arm raised, finger pointed upward, as if in some kind of peaceful warrior battle cry. Photographed by Baron Wolman for *Rolling Stone*, over the decades it has become one of the band's most enduring images. Maybe that's why so many people, both Deadheads and otherwise, get their picture taken in front of that front gate whenever they visit San Francisco.

It helps that the house was just a few short blocks up from the intersection of Haight-Ashbury. When we weren't hanging out at the house, we'd walk down Ashbury, hang a left on Haight, and hang right there with the throngs of like-minded people gathered outside, on the street. That stretch became hippie central, a phenomenon, a time and place that has since made it into the history books. We really became entrenched in that scene, if not synonymous with it. Wandering around Haight, you'd end up bumping into everyone you wanted to find and—as the song goes—strangers would stop strangers, just to shake their hand. It was also a brisk walk to Golden Gate Park and its eastward extension, the Panhandle. Both of these public spaces would be "instrumental," so to speak, during our time there.

For the most part, during the band's tenure at 710 Ashbury, it wasn't where I spent the night, but it is where I spent most of my time. There's that story of Weir getting in trouble with the police for throwing water balloons off of the roof—that's been written about in every book (including this one, now). Stuff like that is probably the real reason that house became so famous. As at all of our group residences, outrageous shit happened at least once every time the hour hand circled back around. Sometimes, the minute hand, too. To this day, tourist buses still go down Ashbury Street to view the famous "Grateful Dead house"—minus the water balloons—and it's a permanent part of San Francisco's "map of the stars." It's become that kind of thing.

But living there wasn't exactly glamorous. There were too many people for too small a space, no privacy, and the whole building just became this electric zoo with an open-door policy for just about anyone. Phil and Florence wanted out of there. I wanted the same thing. And, back then, I also just wanted to follow Phil, as a person, in the same way that I wanted to follow Jerry, as a musician. Phil was like an older brother to me in those days. That's an important point to remember.

The two of us relocated to a house in a neighborhood called Diamond Heights, about two miles uphill from Haight-Ashbury. Phil brought Florence with him, and I still had Brenda and our daughter with me, at that time. So Diamond Heights had something of a family vibe going for it. When we wanted to run away and join the circus, which was on a daily basis, we'd head on down to 710 and take it from there.

I wasn't at Diamond Heights but for a minute before I broke up with Brenda and had our unlawful marriage lawfully annulled. I basically just woke up one day and told her that she got her wish. It was over. Time for her to leave.

The earth was spinning on its axis at a dizzying pace, and it's not that the world revolved around me, it's just that I was in orbit too, moving from place to place, keeping up with changes within me, changes within my country . . . and changes with my love life. It seemed like no time really passed between saying good-bye to Brenda and saying hello to a girl named Susila Ziegler.

I met Susila at 710 Ashbury although she lived at her parents' house in Mill Valley, which is an affluent town directly across the Golden Gate

Bridge, just minutes north of the city. We started hanging out, then we started going out, then we became a couple.

Susila was a very beautiful young woman, an artist, and in fact, she designed one of the first Grateful Dead T-shirts and began selling them at shows. That might not seem like a big deal now, but Susila was actually one of the first people to ever do this for any rock band. Remember: the concert business was just starting back then, just figuring itself out, and San Francisco led the way. Silk-screened T-shirts were fairly new, in and of themselves. Susila made and sold Grateful Dead shirts and then she made shirts for the Allman Brothers and suddenly T-shirt sales—and, later, other merchandise items—at live concerts became a key component of every band's income. Eventually, the Grateful Dead's merchandise arm would grow into a business unto itself, with everything from pint glasses to dog collars sporting the band's name, logo, or artwork. Anyway, Susila did well with that and sometimes I would even carry boxes of her T-shirts to the shows to make sure they got there. We were partners; we had a good time together.

I remember my first date with Susila. We drove from San Francisco up to Healdsburg, a charming little wine town in Sonoma, one county north of Marin. Northern California. She had a friend who had a farm up there. We got into a one-man sleeping bag and made love that first night and I knew that we were probably going to see each other a lot after that. It was freezing, so we had to stay really close to stay warm, and that was kind of romantic. Very romantic, in fact. Driving up to Northern California seemed like a big deal to me at the time. It was a great adventure and the start of a great romance and I ended up marrying Susila and having my son, Justin, with her. Justin was born on June 10, 1969, just in time to attend Woodstock. But we're still in 1966, having high times on Haight Street.

We were finally playing a lot of shows and attracting an audience. Not Acid Tests—actual shows. We'd practice at the Heliport in Sausalito during the day, and play out in San Francisco at night. We still played some tiny rooms, like the Matrix, which is down in the Marina District and is now some kind of ultra-lounge. But we were moving up in the scene. And fast. We were doing multiple-night runs at the Fillmore, which were promoted by a guy named Bill Graham. And we even played at his bigger room, Winterland, which was a repurposed ice skating rink that could hold more than 5,400 people. It's the same place where the Band filmed *The Last Waltz,* ten years after this. We also played a number of two-night stands at the Avalon Ballroom, a psychedelic dancehall run by Graham's competitor, Chet Helms, and his company, the Family Dog. Of course, all of these venues are now legendary (even though only the Fillmore survives). San Francisco became the cradle for the live music concert industry and these venues were its playpen.

When we didn't have a gig, we'd create one. We played for free, just for the fuck of it. At the time, it was making a virtue out of necessity: we just loved playing together as much as we could. It wasn't a business; it was an adventure. With Scully and Rifkin as our managers, we were able to make money without having to hold outside jobs. We could just play music—which is all we ever wanted to do. And we wanted to do it all the time. We were a working band. We played a lot of gigs around the Bay Area and those shows covered the cost of living for all of us. They also gave us the resources to put on free concerts whenever we weren't playing a ticketed show.

When we played for free, everything came together with a certain grace that seemed almost like divine intention. But it can take a lot of people to line the pieces up in order for them to fall into place. It takes a community to make a community. The Panhandle concerts were an example of this poetry in motion. In order to use electric instruments and a PA system, we needed power; there were no plugs in the park, obviously. So we ran extension cords from a friend's apartment, stringing them on streetlights over Oak Street and snaking them into the Panhandle.

On New Year's Day, 1967, we played a free show that the Hells Angels threw together for the Diggers, a radical group of hippies who thought that everything should be free, not just music. An appealing concept, but not really a sustainable one, with a message that resonates less and less as you get older. I wonder, do the Diggers still believe in the Diggers? Can they still dig it? That said, we played for free for them that day, along with Big Brother and the Holding Company, right there in the Panhandle. We were all so happy; it was just a beautiful happening.

A few months before that, on October 6, 1966, we performed in the Panhandle as part of the Love Pageant Rally, for rather unfortunate circumstances—it was to mourn the end of legal LSD in California. The rest of the country would soon follow suit. When acid became illegal, the hippies became criminals. Nonviolent, otherwise law-abiding, criminals. All because we liked to expand our consciousness. Much like a jazz funeral or a celebration of life, we decided to be festive about it and, after parading down Haight Street, we played for free in the park—again, with Big Brother and the Holding Company.

We also played a number of free shows in Golden Gate Park during this era, and one of them in particular stands out, because some have said it represented the peak of the whole Haight-Ashbury scene and the San Francisco hippie movement—the Human Be-In on January 14, 1967. More than 20,000 people filled the Polo Fields in the park that day. Most people walked—band included—right from Haight Street, through the park and to the field, without any agenda. It wasn't a rally and it wasn't a festival. It was simply a BE-IN. Be here or be square. Be a human be-ing. Bear handed out doses. Allen Ginsberg and Timothy Leary spoke. In addition to the Grateful Dead, all the other usual suspects were there, too, including Quicksilver Messenger Service and Jefferson Airplane. I remember playing it, but I don't remember much more about that day.

A year later, on March 3, 1968, we staged a coup on Haight Street and played on the back of two back-to-back flatbed trucks. Instead of concrete and cars, Haight Street became a sea of people. You couldn't see the street for the crowd. The previous month, there was some kind of incident involving police and hippies, and a near riot ensued. The city offered to close the street to traffic on March 3, for festivities, as some kind of peace offering. The Grateful Dead decided to take advantage of the situation

~ Dancing in the streets: Haight Street. March 3, 1968. *(Jim Marshall)*

and we suddenly stormed the street with a surprise show. There's a famous photograph from that one that remains one of my favorites. Of course, there were lots of other free concerts as well, each one special for one reason or another.

The concept of a free rock show has changed over the years, so let me make this clear: when we played for free, there were no sponsorships. No hidden deals. No kickbacks—just kicks. We played because we wanted to play. Sometimes those gigs were conceived of mere hours before we started playing, because one of us said that they felt like it. In hindsight, it was probably genius marketing, because massive crowds gathered once word spread, and every one of those shows expanded our audience. I guarantee it.

The more traditional way to gain an audience and become successful is to record records, release them, promote them, and go through the machinery of the music industry. Nowadays that's not quite as important and you can circumvent the system entirely and still have a respectable career. But back then, if you wanted to make it as a band, you had to first get a record deal. So, around the time we relocated to San Francisco from Lagunitas, we signed to a major label. Warner Bros. Records. We got a significant advance, given the standards for the time. Something like $10,000. We were on our way. We were only a little over a year old, as a band. We had a contract worked up by September and completed the deal later that fall.

In January 1967, we went back down to L.A., this time with the backing of a record label, and set to work recording our first album—*San Francisco's The Grateful Dead*. We were in Studio A at RCA Studios. We also were on a lot of Ritalin. The album sounds like it. We played everything too fast. We were nervous.

Phil was into speed—many years ago, not now of course—and he had a stash of Ritalin. He used to drive a mail truck on Market Street in San Francisco during rush hour and he became The Crazy Postman. He'd go out there and just beat everybody to the line and race like crazy. I can see speed working for something like that. But it didn't work for recording music. At least, not for our music.

Playing music on speed sounds like you're playing music on speed. It was our first experience with recording for the big league, and we all wanted the album to be popular. We wanted it to work. We even had a big-shot producer—Dave Hassinger, who came to us straight from mixing the Rolling Stones. Hassinger told us the record was great. It wasn't.

Some of the songs, like, "Morning Dew" and "Cold, Rain and Snow," became concert staples, for years and decades to follow. They were covers that we enjoyed playing, but their recorded versions failed to capture the energy that we had when we performed them live.

I felt like, "Okay, we've paid our dues. It's our time. The record is going to be a hit." But our time wasn't going to come for a while and neither would our first hit record. It wasn't going to be that easy. We weren't that good yet. We were still learning how to be a band. We were also still just learning how to live.

After living at Diamond Heights for a while, Phil and I migrated to a two-story Victorian on Belvedere Street, a hop, skip, and a couple jumps away from 710 Ashbury. I now had Susila with me. Phil was still with Florence. The guy who hosted that San Jose Acid Test lived down the block from us and we smoked a lot of hash at his place. Pigpen and his girlfriend moved onto that block too, at some point. For some reason, I remember that we had extremely strong coffee every morning. Little details.

But before that happened, in May 1967, the Grateful Dead took another extended band trip that brought back the spirit of Olompali and Camp Lagunitas. My friend from boarding school, John Warnecke, invited us up to his family's encampment on the Russian River. We ended up setting up camp there for a little bit—a couple weeks or so. It was a really far-out place for us. Warnecke's dad was a famous architect—John Warnecke Sr. He's probably most known for designing John F. Kennedy's tomb at Arlington National Cemetery but he also designed Hawaii's state capital building. He built a beautiful vacation house for his family, with all these cabins around it—wood platforms with canvas tents on them and beds inside—on the Russian River, a couple miles shy of Healdsburg. We stayed in the cabins and it was a perfect situation for us. One of the wood platforms, originally intended for a campsite, was right next to the river. We set up all the equipment on that platform and played out there. Naturally, we took a lot of acid and had some really outrageous times. I don't remember drinking that much there, but I do remember taking a lot of acid.

The Russian River area of Sonoma County is a popular vacation spot and road trip destination for city dwellers from the Bay Area. They drive up on Highway 101 and camp out for weekend getaways and stuff like that. It's also the home of the infamous Bohemian Grove. But we had our own little bohemian groove going on. We set up our speakers facing the river and we'd wait until people kayaking downstream would get right in front of them and then really let them have it with all kinds of birdcalls and frog sounds, really weird vocal jams and stuff, all turned up to 110 db and amplified through speakers. I don't know if any kayaker actually fell over from the shock of what sounded like a giant eighty-foot bullfrog or anything, but we sure tried.

Perhaps the most significant thing to happen during our Russian River trip was that Jerry remembered some words his friend Robert Hunter had sent him. He used them for a lyric in a new song that we worked up called "Alligator"—and that was the start of Garcia and Hunter's incredible song-writing partnership.

I think Jerry came up with an initial sketch for "Dark Star" while we were on that river trip, and Weir and I also came up with an idea that would eventually form the basis of "The Other One."

The Russian River was also just a really great place to practice and experiment, because it was outdoors, during that graceful transitional time when spring turns into summer. It's in the middle of wine country so there are beautiful vineyards everywhere. And that time of year, it never gets too hot during daytime, nor too cold at nighttime.

We played a lot of music there and became a better band. Pigpen was still our leader and he wrote a bunch of tunes during the stay. The band always liked being in the country and, in those days, we also liked living together. The closer the better. We only had one car, really—mine—so that mandated being close. That was a good thing. Those were good days and Russian River was a good trip.

Not long after that, we got to do what every rock band in the world dreams about—we played New York City. The holy grail of venues, Madison Square Garden, was still a dozen years away, for us. Eventually, we played the Garden a total of fifty-two times, and, for the longest time, we even held the records for the most shows and sell-outs until Billy Joel beat us . . . decades later.

But our first gigs in New York were far different experiences from headlining the big top. We had to outrun a gang one night, on our way back to the hotel, and Weir almost got mugged another night. It was a tough city back then. Still is, but not in the same way that it used to be. The reason I'm bringing this up is because it's so different from anything we had been exposed to, growing up in Palo Alto or even living in San Francisco.

New York was like a pickpocketing dragon, capable of burning you and swallowing you whole—but it also was a really exciting place to come and play music. We were so excited that it was hard to sleep at night. The rock scene was just getting started and the clubs were just starting to put on rock shows. The Rolling Stones had been around, the Beatles had been around, and when Jimi Hendrix hit that scene, that was it—it was all Hendrix then. The Grateful Dead were unheard of.

We played free shows in Tompkins Square Park and in Central Park, to a very different audience from the kind we were used to in San Francisco. We established a residency in an area called Greenwich Village. That neighborhood served as the birthplace for the Beat Generation, which was interesting to us because the beats' other geographical focal point became a neighborhood called North Beach—in San Francisco.

Back home, we had been hanging out with our champion—and Beat Generation hero—Neal Cassady. But, a decade earlier, he was in the Village, hanging out with Jack Kerouac and Allen Ginsberg and all the famous beats. Most of which also made their way to San Francisco. The two cities had some kind of underground connection, even though—on the surface— they were worlds apart.

By the time we got there, Greenwich Village was also home to the East Coast folk scene, with Bob Dylan leading the charge. It was pretty neat to be in the epicenter of this movement that was distinctly different, yet directly and spiritually related to the one we were a part of, nearly 3,000 miles away.

We set up shop at the Café Au Go Go, a small club on Bleecker Street, reminiscent of the Matrix in San Francisco. Lenny Bruce, the comedian, made that place notorious a few years earlier when he was arrested on obscenity charges for a pair of shows there. Back then, the First Amendment didn't always apply—you couldn't swear onstage. There were certain things you just couldn't say. But you could jam, so that's what we did. (Before we were in a band together, Garcia actualy took a job transcribing recordings of Lenny Bruce's routines at the Café Au Go Go for use in Lenny's obscenity trials.)

There was a theater right above the café and Frank Zappa happened to be playing there. I went and watched him throw tomatoes at the audience. I picked up that he was brilliant, but it didn't get me off to see food being used as a gimmick during a rock concert. It was like Gallagher smashing a watermelon and calling it comedy. A backstage food fight is sometimes a necessity, but Zappa's food theatrics just distracted me from his music. And that's why I was there—for music. I wasn't yet hip to the idea of having fire dancers onstage or anything like that, but I would warm up to it in time. I loved being in New York City and I still do, to this day.

A few weeks later we were back west, headed to the Monterey Pop Festival on California's Central Coast, just above Big Sur. The festival took place at the town's fairgrounds from June 16 to 18, 1967 and the lineup featured Simon & Garfunkle, Otis Redding, Eric Burden and the Animals, the Mamas and the Papas, and a bunch of Bay Area bands—including three we were rather accustomed to playing with: Quicksilver Messenger Service, Jefferson Airplane, and Big Brother and the Holding Company. As Big Brother's front woman, Janis Joplin's performance at Monterey was a career-maker. Especially since, unlike the Dead, they allowed their set to be filmed. You've probably seen the footage.

Monterey wasn't a career-maker for us, though, but—we were kind of fucked from the start on that one. Here we were, this young band—"the Grateful what?"—and we were sandwiched right in between The Who and Jimi Hendrix. I was intimidated. We didn't really have our own thing yet and we had to follow The Who. They were a great English rock band that was already established back in their homeland, and they really knew how to put on a spectacle; they wore all these beautiful show costumes and delivered power-chord anthems with visual flair. Then, after us, came the Jimi Hendrix Experience. Hendrix was at the top of his game and to top it all off, at the end of the set, he even set his guitar on fire. And we had to play in between these two giants?

It was a very scary gig for me, because of that. I remember throwing up before we went on. I was so frightened, so nervous, that my left hand locked up while we were playing. I was terrified of being onstage at such an overwhelming event. In time, I would get used to playing shows like that, but it took awhile to really get comfortable. By any standards, it's pretty unusual to be squashed between The Who and Jimi Hendrix. I went back and listened to our set sometime later and it was actually quite reasonable—it wasn't all that bad.

Monterey was the first big gig we played with real stars walking around backstage. David Crosby was there with the Byrds, and he sat in with Buffalo Springfield, a new sensation that featured his future band-mates Neil Young and Stephen Stills. (For Buffalo Springfield's set at Monterey, David Crosby was a substitute for Neil Young, who had taken a temporary leave.) We had seen a Buffalo Springfield gig on the Sunset Strip in L.A., back when we were living at the Pink House—but at the Monterey fairgrounds, we were on the same playing field.

We became friends with all of those guys that weekend. Crosby was wearing the classic, hippie, high-roller leather coat with fringes and the whole nine yards. But he was such a kind person and he taught our guys some tricks to help them sing harmony parts. A few years later, he gave us hands-on instruction when we were recording *American Beauty*. Thanks, David.

The Who were another band at Monterey that were social and engag-ing that weekend, and they all came by my hotel room the night we both played. They stopped in for a little while just to say hello. It was Keith Moon's time—the wildest drummer they ever had. He passed away in 1978, darn it, and The Who were never quite the same without him. He could've been a great actor, too, because he was Mr. Personality. I remem-ber watching him tear up his drum set and throw it all over the place, and seeing Pete Townshend smash his guitar all to hell at the end of some song. It was as over the top as Hendrix setting his guitar on fire. It really sur-prised me when, back at the hotel, there was a knock on my door and the Who were all just standing there, like, "What are you doing? Want to hang out?"

The Who teamed up with the Grateful Dead for a pair of stadium shows a decade later, and Townshend sat in with us in Germany once, but I didn't become friends with him until 1993, when he did a theatrical version of *The Who's Tommy* on Broadway. I got to see the dress rehearsal for that, because the Dead were in town for a multiple-night run at Nassau

Coliseum on Long Island. Townshend and his son became friends with my son, Justin, and they've worked together on some video projects. They keep in touch and all of that.

Although I never had the opportunity to become close with Keith Moon, it was an honor to have met him and an even bigger honor to have shared concert stages with him, over the years. He was one hell of a drummer. As it turns out, a few months after Monterey, I ended up meeting another drummer that wasn't too bad, either. Meeting him would forever change the identity of the Grateful Dead and, in turn, my life.

The first time I met Mickey Hart was at the Fillmore Auditorium in August of 1967. The original Fillmore, which is still going strong at the corner of Fillmore Street and Geary Boulevard, is in an old jazz district of San Francisco that was once nicknamed "Harlem of the West," back when jazz and blues nightclubs lined the strip.

The Grateful Dead had performed at that historically significant venue many times before I had been introduced to Mickey, enough that it was almost like our second home. In fact, we were the house band. We played that room no less than thirty times in 1966 alone. Our first Fillmore show was on December 10, 1965, about a week after we had changed our name from the Warlocks. We returned to the Fillmore on January, 8, 1966, for an Acid Test.

When we came back there a week or so after that, for a Mime Troupe Benefit, the promoter, Bill Graham, thought our name change was bad for business. He was thinking only about that night; we were thinking about the rest of our career. Finally, we came to a compromise—the first of many with that guy—and he listed us on the bill as "The Grateful Dead: Formerly the Warlocks." Which was—and is—true.

Graham is perhaps the most famous live music promoter of all time and, even though we lost him in 1991, his legend lives on. Deservedly. He was a true trailblazer. Many of his innovations have become, and remain, standard practice.

But one thing that was uniquely Graham's, and which has largely disappeared following his death, was the creative way in which he'd string a lineup together for a show. He wanted to educate his audience and he saw it as a service to music fans—he'd take the hip new thing and put them on a ticket with overlooked royalty, introducing young crowds to the masters. He'd bill upstarts next to immortals. Sometimes (like, say, March 17, 1967) the kids came for the upstarts (like, say, my band), but then had their skulls cracked open by the legends (like, say, Chuck Berry). And other times, Graham would give a brand-new band their first big break by putting them on as an opener for a local favorite, essentially handing them hundreds of new fans in a single night. Regardless of genre or age or anything like that, if you were an incredible artist, Graham would book you at the Fillmore. And he wouldn't book you there otherwise. So, as fans, we'd just go and listen and discover. It was our music school.

The headliner the night I met Mickey Hart was Count Basie. *The* Count Basie. His drummer was Sonny Payne and watching him play was fascinating and inspiring. You could barely hear Count Basie count the band in, but then all of the sudden, out of the clear blue, Sonny would stomp on his bass drum. The volume alone would startle you. And that was without a bass drum microphone. I was blown away.

I was staring at Sonny in total awe when I felt someone tap me on my shoulder. It was Mickey Hart. I had never seen him before, but he introduced himself as a fellow drummer and friend of Sonny's. We started talking all about rhythms, anything and everything to do with drumming, and he told me about stuff he could do that I wanted to learn. That was convenient, because he was a drum teacher. Matter of fact, the year before we first met, Mickey beat his dad in a drum championship. His dad was defending his title from the year before and lost to Mickey. They were in some kind of lifelong competition with each other and the ramifications of that would end up having significant consequences for the Dead down the line. Both of Mickey's parents were award-winning drummers. But that night, we weren't thinking or talking about family matters. We were thinking and talking only about drums.

And everything Mickey told me that night turned out to be true: he was a great rudimentary drummer. He had one of his drum students with him at the Fillmore, a guy named Michael Hinton, who went on to become the premiere drummer for the Broadway production of *Les Miserables*. I got to see him perform it with the original cast and it was amazing. Hinton also drummed for Jefferson Airplane at one point, among many other accomplishments, some of which have certainly overlapped with the Dead's universe over the years. (On the other end of the spectrum, I heard he spent years touring with Liza Minnelli. Solid work. Steady work. Hey, whatever works.)

After Count Basie's set, Mickey and Hinton cajoled me to come out to their car and they both took out their sticks and started doing tricks that I didn't know how to do. I mean, I knew how to play drums and all, but I sure didn't know how to do this stuff. I knew immediately that it would be beneficial for me to learn these things. Later that night, I took them to the Matrix to check out Big Brother, with Janis Joplin in fine form. The whole scene was a new discovery for Mickey, a Brooklyn street kid that had just recently wrapped up a stint in the air force. My new discovery that night was Mickey himself, and the idea that this guy could actually make me a better drummer. And that was my mission.

I had developed an off-the-wall style that worked for me, and it seemed to work for the band, but I didn't want to just be something that worked. I was reaching for mountaintops that were a hell of lot higher than that, and in order to reach that altitude, I needed to pack a few more tools in my rucksack. I realized this that night.

I needed to uncover what rudiments meant to drumming and I wanted to attain the freedom that they had to offer. The way rudiments are set up, you can play two beats with one hand, which gives you time to move your other hand to a different place. That way, you can alternate naturally by going side to side without missing a beat. Mickey was all about teaching this and he taught it to me. He also had me play marches and I got pretty good at them—well, actually, I wasn't great at them. But I got so that I could play them. I didn't like them any more than I did when I was a kid, though.

Under Mickey's guidance, I practiced the fundamentals until they became embedded in my foundation and then I used the rudiments as if they were bricks that I then cemented together, forming a bridge between the drummer that I had been and the drummer that I wanted to be. And then I crossed it.

I'm going to get technical for a moment, so bear with me: a single paradiddle is four beats; a double paradiddle has two more beats than a single paradiddle (six beats). A triple paradiddle has two more beats than a double (eight beats). It may sound simple but it's tricky.

Mickey made up this great rudiment called a false-sticking double paradiddle. It has the same number of beats as a regular double paradiddle (six), but you accent the first beat on the same hand every time, instead of alternating. The divisions are split up differently, but with the same number of beats, so it sounds the same. His false-sticking trick works out particularly well when you're playing in 3/4 or when you want to accent three against four. Learning these techniques from Mickey proved instructional; watching him play around with them was inspirational. The end result is that I became a better player.

Somehow the idea of having Mickey sit in with the band came up, so I invited him to come practice with us over at the Heliport in Sausalito. The story goes that he tried to make it out there, but he got lost and couldn't find the place. Maybe that's true or maybe it was just an excuse for not showing up. The statute of limitations has worn off by now, Mickey. We wouldn't be mad at you . . .

Regardless, I still wanted him to sit in with us, so I invited him to come down to the Straight Theater, where we had scheduled an interesting run of shows on September 29 and 30, 1967. The theater was on Haight Street, at the intersection of Cole, just a few blocks away from 710 Ashbury, and our friends were running things. But this was during that challenging time in history where dancing at a rock concert was like ordering booze at a bar during Prohibition. It felt right, but it was banned by law, unless you had a dance permit. San Francisco was certainly not going to issue the Straight Theater a dance permit for a pair of shows by the Grateful Dead. However, we found a delightful little loophole and the defiant act of exploiting it made the shows especially satisfying for us—you needed permits for a dance concert, but not for a dance *school*. Class was about to be in session. We charged a "registration fee" instead of selling tickets and everyone got membership cards on the way in. The cops were there but couldn't do a damn thing. The media loved it. And we taught some people how to dance, all right.

Mickey came down on the second night and, during set break, we rounded up a second drum kit. Even though Mickey didn't know any of our songs, or the other guys in the band . . . or anything about us, really . . . I thought it would be a fun experiment to have him sit in with us. Nobody could've predicted that from that moment on, Mickey Hart would be a member of the Grateful Dead.

⌒ Class was in session at the Straight Theater on Haight Street, September 29, 1967. The next night, Mickey Hart played with us for the first time. (*Jim Marshall*)

But sure enough, that's what happened. After the show, Jerry allegedly said something along the lines of, "*This* is the Grateful Dead!" and, just like that, Mickey was in the band. He even moved in with me, in a closet underneath the stairs at the Belvedere house—the same kind of "bedroom" that Harry Potter's guardians gave him on Privet Drive. Like Potter, Mickey Hart seemed capable of magic. He later proved this to be true. (He used to drum at the very edge of it.)

As a side note of sorts, Weir also moved into Belvedere at some point. So, I suppose, with Phil and me (and our ladies) in the two respective bedrooms, Mickey under the stairs, and Weir sleeping God knows where—hence, four of the six active band members—it silently transformed into the "real" Grateful Dead house. 710 Ashbury was more for show; something to give the tourists.

But first, before Weir moved out of 710, there was the famous pot bust that happened that fall and which made headlines (including a piece in the very first issue of *Rolling Stone* on November 9, 1967, and a photo in the local paper showing an irreverent-looking Weir handcuffed to Florence on the front steps). I wasn't a part of it and, luckily, I wasn't even there that day. I probably had contraband in my possession at the time—but over at Belvedere. I was never even a suspect. They were busting the house more than the occupants. The cops just wanted an easy target to make some cheap headlines, just as public opinion was beginning to sour on the whole Haight-Ashbury scene. The one and only "Summer of Love" was officially over and the police department wanted everyone to know it. So they raided the house and they arrested whoever happened to be at the house that day, including the one guy in the band that didn't use drugs—Pigpen.

Also: their search failed to turn up an entire kilo of high-grade pot, Acapulco Gold, sitting on the top shelf in the pantry, not even hidden, just waiting to be discovered . . . or smoked. Bobby and Pigpen ended up paying small fines, as did some of our management and crew. In the end, the publicity was probably good for us. After all, it got us into the pages of *Rolling Stone.* So we should probably thank both the snitch and the police department for the extra help.

Anyway, as I was saying, when I invited Mickey to sit in that night at the Straight, I didn't think it would result in an invitation to join the band. I didn't think we needed two drummers, but it was kind of nice having another drummer there to buddy up with and play off of—both literally and figuratively. We became a special unit within Team Dead. Partners, brothers . . . "Rhythm Devils."

Instead of hazing Mickey, we had our own initiation rite—we fed him acid. That's the day he became our brother and, after that, things immediately got even more interesting. We rented a new rehearsal space inside the SF city limits where we really gave birth to a new subgenre of rock 'n' roll—one that, to this day, only the Grateful Dead could ever really play.

The rehearsal space was in an old synagogue, right next to the Fillmore, on the Geary side, where a post office now stands. Sometime after we left there, it was converted into some kind of a concert hall, known as Theater 1839 (for its street address on Geary). The Jerry Garcia Band played a few legendary shows there in 1977. After that, I think the name changed to Temple Beautiful and it began hosting punk rock shows for a while. When we used it, in the fall of '67, Bill Graham may have actually owned the building. If so, that would explain why we rented it. Never mind the fact that it was right next door to the Fillmore. ◦

In 1989, the building, as we knew it, burned down. Come to think of it, a lot of buildings that were connected to us through the years have burned down—the induction center in San Jose, the original estate at Olompali, a house in New Jersey that we stayed at for a bit, and so on. Weird. Also weird: right next door to the synagogue was a Masonic temple—the Alfred Pike Memorial Scottish Rites Temple—which became the headquarters for the Jim Jones's Peoples Temple during the '70s. Right before they departed for Guyana, never to return. That whole thing remains a genuine American tragedy and while the Grateful Dead had stopped practicing there a couple years before Jones and his people moved onto the block, it's just one more crazy connection, for whatever it's worth. You know, "There goes the neighborhood."

Anyway, Neal Cassady would sometimes stop in at the synagogue when we were rehearsing and Mickey would get nervous about it, for some reason. Cassady would shake my hand in this way that really shook my entire arm, and he'd say, jokingly, "Are you loose, Bill? Are you loose?"

There was also a wonderful synchronicity to Cassady's appearances there, because it was in that exact time and space where "The Other One" really came into focus, and the song is partially about him. With the eight limbs of two drummers behind it, we got into that groove, that 6/8 thing, and it became its own animal. Appropriately enough, given the subject matter, the song is really just an open invitation to bust loose and it's one of those all-terrain vehicles that is designed to take you down different roads every time, seeing around corners as you go. That's definitely all Cassady, and that song is definitely one of my favorites.

It wasn't until Mickey joined the band that we started experimenting with time signatures. Before then, we mostly played in fours—4/4. Then, with two drum kits set up at the rehearsal space (and two drummers), we started doing these more advanced things. All this also coincided with Phil turning me on to John Coltrane and Elvin Jones. I remember when I listened to Elvin for the first time, I thought, "This is legal? You can do that?" That kind of thing inspired us to enjoy and honor freedom in a musical sense; we began to push the boundaries in any direction, at any given time, in any given time signature.

It was there, at the old synagogue, where we first started playing rhythmically without worrying about the "one." The "one" is the first beat of any measure. Put simply: It's the downbeat. The thing that goes "boom." We experimented with it. "Don't play it anywhere!" Then we tried floating it—putting it in different places or throwing it out until the jam either suggested or demanded that we land on it. We'd create a new "one." I'd throw it down and the whole band would drop into it so fast, you'd think we planned it that way. But we didn't. We weren't reading sheet music; we were reading minds. "Floating the one" would allow jams to shape-shift at will.

Sometimes we had to alter the "one" rapidly because we'd jam and Jerry would take solos and we'd stretch everything out and play some weird stuff in there, and then, suddenly, Pigpen would come back in—but he'd be on the off-beat. To make it right again, you have to take half a beat off, immediately, and make it the on-beat instead. If you're on the off-beat and you take off a half beat, it becomes the on-beat. If you take off another half beat, you're back on the off-beat. And it just continues like that, forever. It's a mathematical thing at the quarter note level. Anyway, we'd be doing some rave, like "Love Light" for instance—Pigpen used to do some of his funkiest raving on "Love Light"—but he'd come back in sometimes completely off beat. We'd have to just switch it around; nobody in the audience even suspected it. That was kind of good practice, doing that shit.

Mickey was a great lobbyist for the drums. He was just so passionate about anything to do with them. We built a couple of drum sets together, over the years. We were both playing sets that had double rack toms, and we decided to push it further by putting a third rack tom up there. Nobody ever did that. As soon as we tried it, though, we began to see them everywhere. Maybe it was just a sign of the times.

Mickey always chased perfection in whatever it was that he was after at that particular moment. He taught me that the act of drumming was as much about motion as it was about contact—a great drummer will use their whole body, not just their wrists. You can hear such a difference.

Working with Mickey continued to help me throughout the Grateful Dead's career. With him in the band, I was always game to accompany him on just about any experimental journey. I even allowed him to hypnotize me once, and I think it worked. As far as I'm concerned, he still has me hypnotized today.

I always felt like we became this four-armed, four-legged beast, instead of two human drummers. Mickey had a zany kind of energy that was persistently infectious to me; it reminds me of the wide-eyed enthusiasm of a little kid, with all this energy just pouring out purely and without restriction and without agenda, and it's really a beautiful thing. You add that to his perfectionist side and he ended up with some wonderful stuff.

I've recently listened back to some shows we played in the 1990s, particularly the "Drums" and "Space" from the Spring '90 tour, and there are really a lot of remarkable moments. It sometimes makes me wonder how I can even think about playing in other bands now, after that. Listen to some of that shit. Everything changed when Jerry left, and we'll get to that in due time, of course. But fuck, man—with Mickey there, we became really good.

He and I also became prankster partners, like the Blues Brothers of the drums. We were playing somewhere in L.A. once, I can't even remember the gig, but afterward we had a really lame limo driver and he went missing for a moment too long, so we stole the limousine. Mickey put on the driver's hat and just started driving. I was in the backseat, laughing my ass off. We drove all around and and started to get hungry, so we high-tailed it to Canter's Deli. We were just digging into our food, when the driver came up huffing and puffing. We handed him his keys back. "There you go, buddy. We're all good, right?" The limo was parked and there was no damage or anything like that. So it was all good, after all. It was all just kicks.

Long before that limo incident though, the band temporarily moved back to L.A.—in November 1967—so we could work on our second album. We scheduled a couple of shows at the famed Shrine Auditorium (where we debuted "Dark Star" on December 13) and blocked out some time at American Studios in North Hollywood.

Once again, we all moved in together, this time at a house that belonged to our friend Peggy Hitchcock's family. Her family also owned an expansive compound in Millbrook, New York, that became headquarters for Timothy Leary's intellectual gang of acid dropouts—we visited them briefly, earlier that year, when we had a few days to kill at the end of a brief Canadian tour. But that stay turned into a string of mishaps that ended up in something less than a story. (And it left us feeling less than thrilled about Leary and his whole head trip.)

Hitchcock's compound in L.A. was a stone's throw from the famous Ennis House, which was designed by Frank Lloyd Wright. A lot of flicks, including *Blade Runner*, were filmed on location there. It was a giant fortress with creepy, long slitted windows, perfect for horror films. We mistakenly thought that Bela Lugosi lived inside its veiled walls, but I think that was just an urban legend.

We moved in down the street and found ourselves right at the smog line, so there was often a red cloud, right at eye level from the house, which made it kind of weird. We played really hard in that house, though. I'd practice by myself, then I'd spend hours with Mickey going over drum stuff, and then we'd play full rehearsals with the band. Every day.

In the studio, we recorded "The Other One," "New Potato Caboose," "Alligator," "Turn On Your Love Light," "Born Cross-Eyed," and some others. They didn't sound quite right just yet but we were basically just demoing them. We planned to react to the frenzied and frenetic pace of our debut album by really taking our time with this one until we got it right.

So we traveled to New York City in mid-December and set up camp there for a couple weeks, moving into a friend's house in Englewood, New Jersey. We'd record all night, every night, at two separate studios in Manhattan. At first, David Hassinger was behind the knobs again but he quickly lost patience with us. Maybe he thought he could cut our follow-up album in a few days' time, like he did with the first one. He was wrong. Again.

When Weir asked Hassinger to reproduce the sound of "thick air," Hassinger bolted. He quit. He couldn't handle us. He wasn't alone in that. We went through a number of engineers and even studios, in both L.A. and New York. Phil could get rather abrasive and the rest of us backed him up because we were chasing after the idea of a perfect album, having just released a debut that none of us were really all that wild about. Phil became a liability in the eyes of our record label because he had a temper, but he also had a point: You should love your albums. We didn't love our first one and this was our chance to fix that.

Going into the studio, any studio, was always really hard for me, because it felt contrived. I'm guessing my bandmates all have similar feelings about that because we were never able to make our best music in a studio.

So, yes, you should love your albums, and although we were struggling

with that, we could all agree that we loved our live shows. We were playing them fast and furious at this point—in 1967 we conquered all the Bay
Area ballrooms. We built off our success from the year before and started
to reach out to the great beyond. Wherever we went, we gigged, and we
gigged wherever we went. So, naturally, we set up some shows during our
time in New York, including a two-night stand at a tumbledown room on
Second Avenue called the Village Theater. Snow leaked in through the
roof one of those nights and I needed to wear gloves just to get through the
gig. When we returned there half a year later, Bill Graham had taken over
the place and transformed it into the Fillmore East. To this day, the Fillmore East remains one of New York's most storied venues, even though
it was only open from 1968 to 1971.

Warner Brothers wasn't very happy with us, but what did we care? Our
record contract permitted us an unlimited amount of time in the studio,
and we had fought for that unusual clause for a reason. My, how things
have changed—there are stories these days of some bands taking a decade
or more between releases. With the album that became *Anthem of the
Sun,* we're talking about a matter of a few extra months. Granted, we
burned through a lot of studio time, and that came with a hefty price tag,
but we were footing the bill for that. As is standard practice, the label fronted
our expenses but we had to recoup them before turning a profit. So they
could piss off. We retreated back to San Francisco at the start of 1968, and
although we weren't empty-handed, we had less than half an album and
a handful of fragments. Clearly, we were still in an experimental phase.

Back home, we were happy to get back to what we loved and knew
best—playing music. Live. In front of people. At some point, it must've
dawned on us, "Hey, we can't get the sound we're looking for in the studio, but we sound great live, so why not overlap the two?" Without a professional producer willing to stick it out with us, we brought in our new
soundman, Dan Healy—Bear's replacement—and went for it. When I say
we went for it, I mean we *really* went for it. Instead of turning the album
into a live release, we layered different versions of the same song on top of
each other until the notion of infinite possibility revealed itself. One key

reason why Deadheads kept coming to show after show after show was that no two performances of a song were ever the same. We couldn't have done that anyway, even if we tried—but of course, we weren't trying. Improvisation was both our aesthetic and our ideal, and it was something that we could explore only through experimentation. There just was no blueprint for this stuff.

Many bands, including jam bands, talk about their studio releases as picture-perfect postcards, where they capture the band at a moment in time, and where they capture the songs in their most realized form. But we were always a different band from one second to the next, and a song like "The Other One" was only realized when it was shape-shifting into something else entirely. A postcard wouldn't work—we were a moving picture. But how do you capture that?

Phil and Jerry were the ones who figured out that we could exploit studio technology to demonstrate how these songs were mirrors of infinity, even when they adhered to their established arrangements. It's the old paradox of "improvisational compositions." Jazz artists knew all about the balance between freedom and structure, but a few rock bands were now catching on. Most rock bands, however, tended to head in an opposite direction, afraid of the uncertainty of improvisation. We decided that *Anthem of the Sun* was going to be our statement on the matter.

So, in the Spring of 1968, we started recording all of our shows. We played the album sequence live, twisting and turning it different ways every time, and at every stop along the way. We did a short package tour of the Pacific Northwest with Quicksilver Messenger Service called "The Quick and the Dead," and we focused our set heavily on the proposed album material. We also couldn't resist playing our new exploratory showpiece—"Dark Star"—often, taking it to different cosmic places every time, although that tune would be even more problematic to capture on a studio release. We realized this.

We played Jerry's song, "Cryptical Envelopment" sandwiched around "The Other One," without a break in the music, and we played the hell out of "Alligator" and "Caution" and even "New Potato Caboose" and

"Born Cross-Eyed." Then, Jerry and Phil went into the studio with Healy and, like mad scientists, they started splicing all the versions together, creating hybrids that contained the studio tracks and various live parts, stitched together from different shows, all in the same song—one rendition would dissolve into another and sometimes they were even stacked on top of each other. The result was *Anthem of the Sun*, which was finally released on July 18, 1968. It was easily our most experimental record, it was groundbreaking in its time, and it remains a psychedelic listening experience to this day.

Warner Brothers wasn't so sure about it at first, but I think they got over it. Initially, label president Joe Smith was rather displeased that the album wasn't ready by February; he wasn't impressed with our attitude or our methods, and he was fed up with reports of Phil's temperament. We gave him no choice but to deal.

Just as Jerry proclaimed, "*This* is the Grateful Dead!" the night Mickey Hart first played with us, the same could've been said after the first time anyone listened to *Anthem of the Sun*. It was the Spring of 1968 and we had arrived.

Remember when the Grateful Dead ran a music venue? Because I sure don't. I mean, I remember the basics—kind of—but it doesn't surprise me that I don't remember the details because I was a musician, not a nightclub owner. To this day, I just want to play music, not operate a venue. But it is true that the Dead partnered with Jefferson Airplane and Quicksilver Messenger Service to take control of a space in San Francisco called the Carousel Ballroom. Yeah, well—that lasted just a number of months. But it's surprising that it ever happened at all.

The Carousel Ballroom was at the intersection of Van Ness Avenue and Market Street, on a corner that wasn't really in any particular neighborhood so much as being the axis between a number of them—the Mission, the Lower Haight, Hayes Valley, Civic Center, SoMa, and downtown were all right there, depending on which way your compass pointed. For many years now, the building has been a Honda dealership. The only music that remains is the radio station that gets played in the background. If that. Twitter's headquarters is now just down the street and there's been a basic redecorating of that entire stretch.

During the Carousel Ballroom days, there's no doubt that the whole area was a bit on the shady side. Also, it wasn't all that far from the Fillmore or the Avalon and it was in direct competition with both of those rooms. Regardless, I loved the location because it was close enough to the Belvedere house that getting home after a show was never a problem. You could take all the drugs you wanted and still end up in your own bed. Or someone else's.

A hustler named Ron Rakow, who conned his way into our little circle and who would continue to lead us astray throughout many ventures, somehow convinced all three bands to form a theoretical partnership called Triad, under his stewardship. This was Rakow's first real leadership role with us. That's probably why I don't remember most of it. I mostly remember the music. There was a lot of great music at the Carousel. All three owner-bands obviously played there a lot, along with the usual Bay Area suspects: Santana, Steve Miller, the Charlatans, that whole scene. Our whole scene.

I didn't really take an active role in the whole Triad enterprise. I just sort of went along with it and was usually told details after the fact. I was hands-off and didn't sweat the small stuff. At all. But I do remember playing a few really fun gigs at the Carousel, and I also remember seeing some other bands there that really got me off. The business side of it wasn't that memorable—but watching Janis Joplin take that stage is something I'll never forget. This one night, I took some PCP and leaned against the back wall, just listening to her—this was with Big Brother—and it was nothing less than incredible. Maybe, on paper, I was some kind of part owner of the Carousel, but during that show, there was no mistaking that Janis Joplin was boss. She owned every one of us in the room that night.

In the very beginning . . . of our little band, I mean . . . I suppose you could say that I took on the role of manager for a brief spell, but I don't even know if we used that word. If so, it was just a name. I didn't keep a book. I never wrote a thing down. I didn't really do any business for the band. I just made sure we got paid and then counted and handed out money at the end of the night, when nobody else would do it—or, at least, nobody else that I trusted. Not that I always trusted the people we later hired to do that for us. Turns out, I had good reason to be cautiously suspicious of our managers: we ended up getting burned in a massive way, and we'll get to that, soon enough.

I never wanted to deal with the business side of things, but I had to deal with the people who did. This one time, in Paris, I fired our tour manager on the spot. I trusted him as a person, but I didn't trust him to get all of our money from some of the thieves who call themselves promoters. He was a nice guy, bless him, but you don't always want your manager to be the nice guy. You hire them so that you can be the nice guy instead.

The manager I fired was named Jon McIntire, a real sweet man who we lost not that long ago, darn it. Before he started working for the band, he was a part of the Carousel staff. As with most people who worked there, he got the job because he was one of our friends, and he learned the job on the fly.

As our tour manager, McIntire was supposed to settle with the promoter at the end of the night and get whatever money was called for in the particular contract. After a gig in Paris one year, McIntire wasn't able to do that. Promoters aren't always the most honorable guys, especially back then when rock concerts were still like the Wild West and crazy shit could go down at any given moment. Tour managers need to be able to get the band paid, even in situations like when the fucking gig is completely packed, and there are thousands of people there, and the promoter says, "I don't have any money for you guys." That was the situation in Paris, and the promoter in question was wearing a sport coat with pockets that were just bulging with money, even as he was telling McIntire that he couldn't honor the contract, that he had no cash to pay the band.

The way it went that particular time, I had to grab one of our equipment guys—a really big, strong dude—and he and I took the promoter in the back room and locked the door. The equipment guy, Sonny Heard, brandished his brand-new switchblade and then literally grabbed the promoter by the ankles, turned him upside down, and shook all this money out of his pockets. He was completely full of francs. Full of francs and bullshit. He'd made a ton of money off us. We knew how much we had agreed upon, and so we looked in his briefcase—he didn't dare move— and it was filled with money. So we got paid. That's why I fired McIntire. Because it was his job to do that and he just didn't have it in him. I loved him, and everybody else did too, so they all gave me a ration of shit for firing him. I don't even know if anyone took it seriously because other people remember that McIntire quit after a different night, right around then. I may have been out of line by trying to fire him on the spot, but all I wanted to do was to get the money to the band. We were basically living hand to mouth. You play a gig, you get paid for the gig, you pay your bills. That's how it worked.

Somebody once told me that Jerry Garcia always felt a special bond with me because of those early days when I looked after the money and made sure everyone got their due. Jerry knew that it was a very important task, but he couldn't bring himself to do it. It just wasn't who he was. It wasn't who I was either, but it needed to be done, so I just did it. Well, for a minute or two, anyway, very early on, and that was enough for me. After we hired Rock Scully and Danny Rifkin, I never had to deal with that side of things ever again.

But, perhaps because of something to do with those early dealings, Jerry and I had some unspoken trust where if he went a certain way with a de-cision, I usually did too. He had some great fucking ideas. The generation we came from wasn't one that communicated very easily on any deep level—at least not verbally. It probably would've helped the band if we did, but that's hindsight.

Instead, Jerry and I learned how to read each other's faces. When it came to business proposals—and the people putting them forth—we knew what the other one was thinking. In fact, one time, Jerry even joked with me, "Bill, I wish you weren't so intuitive."

There was something that Jerry saw in Rakow that he really liked, like maybe his outlaw spirit, but I don't know why we hired him to handle any-thing that had to do with our money. I don't think we ever formally did, actually—I think we just went along with him. He was always scheming, always trying to sell us a used car, metaphorically speaking. Funny enough, he once struck a deal for us that actually involved each of us getting a real car. Fords. Ford Cortinas, to be exact. Not surprisingly, most of those vehicles ended up getting repossessed and the whole thing ended in disaster. Just like most of his deals.

In 1973, Rakow was the man responsible for the Grateful Dead launching its own record label—two of them, in fact. Grateful Dead Records for albums by the band, and Round Records for solo releases and side projects. Just like the Carousel, Rakow had somehow convinced us all to jump on a sinking ship and try to set sail. Turns out, it was a ship of fools. Also, just like the Carousel, running our own record label is a venture that I remember less about than you might think. Again, I was hands-off with that stuff. But I know it almost did us in. To this day, similarly minded bands have looked to it as a lesson in what *not* to do. Eventually, we got rid of the label and walked away from Rakow. He was a charming snake oil salesman, but you never hand the keys to your business over to a hustler. I think he believed in all of his get-rich-quick schemes, he just didn't have the know-how to see them through.

Because we were part owners (at least in theory), the Carousel was kind of like our clubhouse during the Spring of 1968. All fun and games. Rakow oversaw a remodelling of the interior, complete with velvet couches that lined the perimeter of the dance floor. It made seeing live music there a whole lot of fun. We had a grand reopening on March 15, on a bill we shared with Jefferson Airplane. By summertime, it became obvious that our little adventure just wasn't sustainable. Apparently, the terms of the lease alone made it financially impossible to keep the place afloat. It would've been tragic to see such a great venue shuttered, but only a masterful businessman would've been able to turn it around. Enter Bill Graham, who took over the lease that July and transformed it into the Fillmore West. Out of respect for rock history, he kept the Carousel marquee out front, right where there's a giant "H" for "Honda" these days. Then he made his own rock history with the place.

The day before Graham officially opened the Fillmore West, he closed the original Fillmore. (The original Fillmore—on the corner of Fillmore and Geary—has since be reopened.) The Fillmore West lasted from July 1968 to July 1971 and it carried on the spirit of the Carousel while turning it into a respectable business. A big difference between Graham and when we ran that room with Rakow was that Graham had the wherewithal and the know-how to get the best acts and promote the shows properly. He also knew across all lines—he knew different musicians from all different worlds and had a knack for bringing them all together. We already talked about this because of the night when I first met Mickey Hart at the Count Basie show.

Graham continued this tradition at the Fillmore West. For the Grateful Dead, that meant—among other things—that we got to play on a bill with Miles Davis. A four-night stand beginning on April 9, 1970. And Graham scheduled Miles *as the opener*. Naturally, we thought that was totally ludicrous and ass-backwards. "What's he opening for us for?" This was during his *Bitches Brew* era, when he had that bitchin' band that included Chick Corea on keys, Dave Holland on bass, Airto Moreira on percussion and Jack DeJohnette on drums. They blew the house away. It was intimidating because after he finished, as we were picking our jaws off the floor, Graham was like, "Your turn, guys. Get up there! Time's a-wasting!" We did what we could, and we didn't play half bad, but we felt sufficiently humbled. (For his part, Miles must've been satisfied with these shows because, two years later, he released his set from the second night as a live album called *Black Beauty*.)

In addition to having a venue that we could essentially run wild in, we also had a new practice space, which we took to with all the fervor and hunger typical of any up-and-coming band our age. At least, any serious one. The new space was called the New Potrero Theater. As the name implies, the theater was in Potrero Hill, an old working-class neighborhood that has since become way more gentrified, probably because it sits on a hill that breaks away from the city's notorious fog, so you have a lot of sunny days there, year-round. The district has always been family-oriented, with picture-perfect views of the bay and the downtown skyline. At the bottom of the hill, there are a lot of cheap warehouses and industrial spaces that artist types started snatching up, beginning in the 1960s and continuing to this day. Also: O. J. Simpson used to live in the neighborhood, but we never ran into him. At least, as far as I know.

In the Spring of '68, we rented the theater and went and practiced there every day. Diligently. It was once a classic movie theater, but they ripped out all the seats. It went down a slope to where the screen used to be, and it was kind of run-down, but it was perfect for us. Down on the corner was a hamburger stand, so we became real friendly with those people and ate there quite often.

Mickey was still being worked in and we were coming up with stuff that no other rock band was doing at the time. Really far-out things. We learned a lot of music—and a lot *about* music—there. That's when and where I first started believing in our abilities to truly explore different time signatures and play music that was free and far from ordinary. Rhythmically, we started playing around with sevens—we'd never done that before. We got away from being a blues band and started being more of an outsider jam band. That's really what we did best.

The New Potrero Theater is also where we worked up "The Eleven," which is significant because that tune, in particular, represents this new kind of thinking beyond boundaries that I'm talking about. Phil wrote the music for "The Eleven," and Robert Hunter came up with the words. Traditionally, rock music is written in 4/4 time. Four beats per measure, right? You probably know this. It's the standard. Sometimes you'll find a 2/4, especially in country music. But for "The Eleven," we took 12/8 and subtracted an eighth note to make it 11/8—hence the name of the song.

Right after we came out with that, the Allman Brothers did the same thing on the intro to a tune that would become one of their biggest songs— "Whipping Post." The key is different, the changes are different, and when the vocals kick in, they slide it into a 12/8 blues. But the intro cheats that one beat, too. It's 11/8. I wonder where that came from? Of course, I can't say for sure. That's for their story. Not mine.

In addition to all the shows at the Carousel, the tour with Quicksilver, and the free show on Haight Street that we talked about in chapter 4, another concert from that spring that probably deserves mention is one that took place at the Memorial Auditorium in Sacramento on March 11, 1968. We had a pretty good band on the bill with us that night. A power trio from England called Cream—Eric Clapton. Jack Bruce. Ginger Baker.

Watching Ginger Baker was always a trip for me, just because of the kind of drummer that he is. And I've always loved Eric Clapton's guitar playing. It was really soulful. The three of those guys were just incredible together and they played some great music.

We were on the same bus back to San Francisco and we stopped at a restaurant, somewhere on the road there, and Clapton sat down at my table. He was a good cat and everything, but I was pretty well awestruck by the guy because I just loved his playing so much. I can't recall what we talked about, really—it was a casual dinner conversation that took place more than four decades ago—but I can tell you that he was a sharp dresser. Those red shoes really worked for him.

There was also an incident in New York City that I don't remember all that much about, but, instead, I have these images in my mind that are like postcards from my past. It was a free show that we staged at Columbia University on May 3, 1968. There had been a student strike, politically motivated of course, and the campus was effectively shut down. Police guarded the perimeter, which, naturally, stirred the prankster pot in all of us.

We weren't political hippies. We were the much more dangerous kind— fun-loving, peace-seeking, do-as-you-wish hippies that just wanted everybody to get on with their getting on, whatever that may be. For us, that meant loading into the back of a bread truck, sneaking onto campus, and staging a bit of a caper—just for kicks. Nothing to it. We set up on the stone steps in front of some university building, as fast as we could so we wouldn't be shut down, and then we played some music and that was that. It was completely unannounced, guerrilla-style. Nobody was hurt and nobody was arrested, as far as we knew. I do think that we confused some of the students, and I'm not sure how many new fans we picked up that day, exactly—we probably fared better a couple days later when we threw a freebie in Central Park—but at least we all had fun. And we got to pull a fast one on the authorities, which we were always fond of doing.

As for that gig in Central Park, I just remember that Mickey's lady at the time had a bottle of Methedrine on her. Liquid speed. She administered a shot of it to both Mickey and me—right in the butt—so that we'd get through the gig, because we had been up really late the night before. It worked. We were in the heart of New York, the Big Apple, the city that never sleeps, so all of that seemed completely appropriate.

We returned to New York just a month later, on June 14, 1968, for our first run of shows at the newly renamed Fillmore East. On opening night, we were paired with the Jeff Beck Group, a young band from England. It was their American debut and the audience seemed to really love their lead singer. A guy by the name of Rod Stewart.

We played the Fillmore West a bunch that summer, too—both before and after it changed over from the Carousel. We had a few pickup gigs in places like Lake Tahoe and San Diego, as well as a festival in San Jose where we appeared alongside the Doors, the Animals, Ravi Shankar, Taj Mahal, the Youngbloods, and some others. We also played some festival of some sort in Orange County where we assaulted our friends in Jefferson Airplane with cream pies. Each man had a mark and mine was their bassist, Jack Cassidy. I got him good, man, but he didn't like it one bit. He was so pissed off at me that I still don't know if he's ever forgiven me for it. I'm sure you have, Jack.

I bet you the cream pies were Mickey's idea, because he loved that tactic. He even got me once, on a birthday, but I didn't mind—I like pie.

Our second album, *Anthem of the Sun,* was finally released in midsummer—July 18, 1968—and then, about a month later, the band went through a rather uncomfortable period that included two distinct attempted lineup changes. "Attempted" being the key word in both of those instances.

First, there was a meeting in which some members of the band tried to fire Bobby and Pigpen. I had nothing to do with it. I didn't give it credence and I didn't play into it. But Phil had really been on Bobby's case for whatever reason; he didn't think Bobby could keep up with the band's growth, or he didn't fit into his idea of where it was going, or whatever. Phil may have also thought that Bobby was partying too much, or drinking too much, or having too much fun. I just remember him really being on Bobby's case all the time. It seemed personal.

I was getting as high and having as much fun as anybody, so I wasn't about to point any fingers. In any case, Phil must've been really bothered by something and he brought Jerry into it. Now, Jerry was the most non-confrontational person in the band, so that didn't quite work. Management was briefed on the situation and they called a meeting and we all sat around and kind of skirted the issue. Nobody could actually come right out and fire them, outright. Things were said . . . but, in the end, nothing was decided and it didn't last, that's for sure.

Bobby and Pigpen didn't stop showing up and nobody turned them away. Their persistence paid off and, if anything, their determination to succeed led to greater contributions to the band. In Bobby's case, especially, he made himself irreplaceable. It was the best possible resolution to that whole conflict.

Some people will find this interesting so I'll mention it: There was chatter in our ranks about approaching another guitarist in our scene—David Nelson—to possibly take over Bobby's spot, should it open up. It was brief and just talk and I didn't feel any of that because I didn't play into it. I didn't think that either Bobby or Pigpen should leave and I was glad when they didn't.

The other nonbinding, attempted lineup change that happened that year was also instigated by Phil. It may have been related to his reasons for wanting to get rid of Pigpen. Since that wasn't going to happen, Phil came up with a different solution. Remember, this was during the Grateful Dead's most experimental phase where we really got *Out There* every night. Pigpen was a straight blues guy. He formed the group because he wanted a blues band. His rave-ups were a hallmark of the early Grateful Dead and, as a frontman, his command of an audience was second to none.

But with Mickey now in the band, and with our forward motion into all these new, complex song forms, we were getting into territory that Pigpen just wasn't suited for, as a bluesman. He was in over his head. We all were.

But Phil had some history with an old friend of his, a keyboard player named Tom Constanten (aka "T.C."), who, in theory, had the chops to accompany us on these weird musical journeys through other dimensions. Phil had already invited him into the studio with us to record some trippy keyboard bits for *Anthem of the Sun,* and that worked out just fine.

There may have been a band discussion about it or it may have just been a few people in the band, or it may have just been at Phil's directive—nobody seems to recall—but beginning on November 23, 1968, at the Memorial Auditorium in Athens, Ohio, T.C. started playing with us, live. He and Pigpen shared organ duties and it also freed Pigpen up to just sing and rave and wail away on harp and percussion.

There are conflicting views about T.C.'s official role but, in my mind, he was never a card-carrying member of the Grateful Dead. He just didn't fit the template. He was a transitional player for us, someone who was able to provide the keyboard parts that Pigpen couldn't and someone who showed us that that role did, in fact, need to be filled. But it wasn't going to be T.C. All in all, he would play with the Grateful Dead for just over a year—his tenure ended on January 30, 1970. There was no big blowup or anything; no showdown. He just left. We felt no animosity toward him and I hope he didn't feel any toward us—it just wasn't the right fit.

I got along really well with T.C., as I did with most people, and I thought he was a cool enough guy. However, he had this thing where, for whatever reason, he would perform at rehearsals pretty darn well, but then, when we'd be in front of an audience, it was like he froze or something. He just couldn't let go. When things got strange and strayed from form, he couldn't trust the music to lead, with the faith that it would all go somewhere wonderful and then somehow we'd be able to bring it all back home. That's what jamming is all about. That's what the Grateful Dead was all about. If you can't do that, you can't be in the band.

That said, I used to like getting drunk with T.C. on airplane flights. We'd drink cocktails and he'd loosen up. There's no mistaking that he was a strange dude. I don't remember ever taking acid with him but he was the straightest far-out character I'd ever met, to the point of being awkward, and he often seemed uncomfortable in his own skin. But he was smart as hell. He understood music theory and, in theory, he had a solid foundation for all the avant-garde stuff that we were getting into. But comprehending the concepts and being able to play the parts isn't enough to make you a good musician. You also have to have that feeling—you have to get in contact with who you are inside, somehow, and let it connect to the music and then the music will connect to the audience. That's how I see it, anyhow. I sometimes wanted to tell T.C., "Forget everything you know; forget what you learned in school. Forget yourself."

I also found it interesting that T.C. was a Scientologist. He often seemed unresolved to me, and I wondered if his religion was partially to blame for that. Scientology can browbeat you, giving you the feeling that you're not good enough so you need to be audited and you need to clean up, or whatever their trip is. If God really is an outer space man, then so be it. But auditing just sounded like punishment to me.

It's not Scientology that I have a problem with, though. It's all religions. All *organized* religions, anyway. Some have said that the Grateful Dead was a religion but what they mean by that is simply that it was a spiritual experience for them and certain things about it became rituals in which they would get some kind of fulfillment in their lives—be it the act of filling out mail-order ticket forms, or of traveling thousands of miles to ring in the New Year with us, or of dancing all freaky in an arena concourse while we played to the tide. But, despite the analogy, the Grateful Dead were never an organized religion. We offered an alternative to all that noise.

I want to make it clear that we were not a cult. Jerry Garcia was not the messiah. We weren't gods. We were there every night for the same reason the Deadheads were. We wanted the music to take us to a place of transcendence and elegance. We wanted to reach that group consciousness

ᵕ Feeling IT: I love the Deadheads just as much as they love us. *(Jay Blakesberg)*

so that we could realize that there was something that was bigger than us—and whatever *it* was, we all were an equal part of it, from the guys sweating it out onstage to the girls in line for the bathroom. We are all the same and we are all just a bunch of atoms. As I've said many times before, I was actually the first Deadhead, going all the way back to that night in 1965 when I saw Jerry play banjo at the Tangent.

Back to the plot, shall we? After all, this is an action tale, and a lot of big moments were just around the corner for us, from Woodstock to Altamont. But first, another thing that happened during 1968 that had a significant impact on the band, both in the immediate and in the long term, is that we all began migrating to Marin County. One by one we left the city and one by one we left each other to find spaces of our own. Most of the effects of the move out of the city and away from each other were subtle but they were also myriad and insidious. Our days of being a San Francisco band ended in the Spring of 1968. After that, we were a Marin County band. Again.

We loved Marin during our stays in Olompali and Lagunitas and so when everybody started moving up there, I found a place in San Rafael on Lucas Valley Road. It was right across the street, basically, from where George Lucas eventually built Skywalker Ranch. This was way before he was there—the name of the street is just one more weird coincidence. I moved into that house with Susila and the way the Grateful Dead had our finances set up back then, the band covered rent. So it was great.

Bobby remembers living at that house with us for a little while but I don't. He's probably right. He probably did. I was so happy all the time and in love with the band and in love with Susila, that I wouldn't have noticed a detail like that. Phil was in Fairfax and Jerry was someplace with Mountain Girl. Mickey found a ranch in Novato.

Even though we were scattered around a rural county, we were still friends and would still hang out. My place on Lucas Valley Road was tucked away from other houses, so some of the guys would come over and we'd do stupid things, usually involving guns or firecrackers, and drugs or alcohol. Take your pick. Mix and match.

In the summer one time, when the wild oat grass was tall, Jerry and Bobby came by. We taped cherry bombs to old LPs that weren't any good, threading the fuse through the hole. You know where this is going. We lit them and threw them like Frisbees over the field, down the hill. When the inevitable flames broke out, we ran like all hell to get the hose and we managed to put out the fire by the skin of our teeth. There were other days like that, too. Plenty of them.

I enjoyed living there but then the damnedest thing happened. We were making our third record, *Aoxomoxoa,* and we were down in a studio in San Mateo, which is a town in the South Bay—about an hour from my place in San Rafael, on the opposite side of San Francisco. We were recording studio tracks that I'm not even sure if we ended up using, but we may have. (We ended up recording that album twice, as you'll read about in the next chapter). Anyway, I got this message that I had just gotten busted for marijuana and I said, "Shit! That's now the second time I've gotten busted when I wasn't even there." Except when 710 got raided, I wasn't actually busted. This time, I was. I just wasn't around when the police swarmed the house and raided it. Unfortunately, Susila was home and she was arrested and taken down to the station and thrown in jail. She was pregnant with Justin.

This time we weren't busted just for possession. I had pot plants on the property. I was trying to grow my own, so I had a small outdoor grow down behind the house, about 100 yards down the hill, facing north and everything. What happened was, the landlord who rented to us was this really uptight motherfucker—I don't even think he wanted to rent to us in the first place, but he did. He came over one day and it happened to be the same day that, like an idiot, I'd left the garden hose running down there to water the plants. The landlord was the kind of guy who, once he saw the hose, decided he needed to check it out. He followed it to the end, discovered the plants, then ratted me out to the police. Goes to show, you don't ever know. Right?

Well, that was the end of that. The pot wasn't even any good anyway. It was never going to yield anything too kind or dank. I didn't know a thing about growing weed. I don't think I even knew the difference between male plants and female plants. I probably would've raised a male, thinking, "Oh, this is cool," not knowing any better.

But anyway, that happened there and I got a spanking for it. They put me in jail for ten days in Marin County for that one. They made Susila serve time, too, separately, right after she gave birth to Justin. We had to take him over to his grandmother's so he wouldn't be taken to family services or something. To her immense credit, Susila is able to laugh it off now, remarking that at least the jail was in the new Hall of Justice building, designed by Frank Lloyd Wright. Almost two decades later, the Grateful Dead would record our bestselling album in that same complex. (*In the Dark* was recorded at the Marin Veteran's Auditorium, which is part of the Marin County Civic Center complex that Frank Lloyd Wright designed.)

There's another twist to this. Right before I went to serve, I had been busted again—oops—this time in New Orleans, with the whole band. The New Orleans incident happened in January 1970. I did my time for the Lucas Valley grow just a couple weeks after that, because I remember the fucking prosecution said, "You know, Mr. Kreutzmann was just arrested for marijuana possession in New Orleans."

So what if I was? I hadn't been tried on that charge yet and, in this country, you're supposed to be innocent until proven guilty. Granted, I was guilty. Of course I had marijuana on me, and with me, and certainly in me during our stay in New Orleans. Still, what happened that time was such a setup, such a scam, such complete nonsense.

We were playing our first shows in New Orleans and, usually, no matter how late it is, you can't sleep for hours after playing a gig. So you go out and you look for more trouble—you look for a reward. You just played this great concert, you're feeling great, you want to go out and celebrate. I'm always one to celebrate. So after one of those gigs in New Orleans, Mickey and I went out together after the show. We went nightclubbing on Bourbon Street, checking things out and having fun. When we walked back into the hotel, I remember looking around and I knew something was amiss. I said, "Hart, how come all these guys are standing around this lobby, in suits? It's four in the morning. They're not tourists. What the fuck is going on?" He said, "Oh, don't worry about it, Bill."

We went into one of our rooms—I forget whose, exactly—and naturally we started smoking some pot. It wasn't seeded or stemmed, so we used the drawer to clean it—it was probably a couple ounces. Pretty soon there was a knock at the front door. Since this was in the French Quarter, there was also a back door, which, naturally, I started going for. But the cops were there already, too. We were surrounded. Oddly enough, they were rather nice to us, despite the circumstance. They didn't beat us up or do anything weird to us and they were actually quite polite throughout the whole ordeal. They booked Owsley that night and it turned out that's who they really wanted—they knew he was the big gun and they were after him. It actually ended his career with the Grateful Dead, a second (but not final) time.

Eventually, they dropped the charges for everyone but Owsley, even though I don't think they caught him with anything big. He never traveled heavy, as far as I know. We didn't go back to New Orleans for a long time after that, although I never took that bust personally—they knew the Grateful Dead were coming to town, they knew the Grateful Dead meant drugs, and they were right. It's simple. To this very day in New Orleans, marijuana is a big no-no. You can't smoke a joint on Bourbon Street and expect to get away with it.

My thing, and it's important that I talk about this, is that I think you *should* be able to smoke a joint on Bourbon Street. Or anywhere else, for that matter. I think pot should be legalized in this country. It's time for the prohibition to end. I follow this stuff closely and I applaud all the states that support medical marijuana. I live in Hawaii and I have my card.

Listen, the medical benefits of cannabis are no joke. For instance, I know firsthand that smoking cannabis is extremely effective for treating a staggering variety of ailments, from nausea to insomnia. It's also a proven pain reliever. Furthermore, cannabis can now be made into a medical preparation using strains that are very high in CBDs and low in THC, which means there's no psychoactive effect; it's medicine. It can be given to kids instead of prescribing them harsher and more dangerous pharmaceutical drugs such as Ritalin. And it's significantly more effective.

Medical marijuana laws are not just a loophole to get high. Of course, I also like to get high just to get high, and I feel strongly that recreational use should be legal. If anything, it's a crime that it's not. As for the recent wins in Colorado and Washington, well, you can bet those states are going to see my dollars. Good-hearted Americans have used the democratic process in two states to say, hey, stop wasting my tax dollars prosecuting something that is more harmless than alcohol. Instead, tax it and regulate it and generate millions of dollars in state revenue at a time when we need that most. More states will soon follow. Hopefully by the time you read this.

Whether you smoke it, vaporize it, eat it, or even use it as a salve, there's nothing wrong with cannabis—if anything, there are a number of things *right* with it. I'm not afraid to say that. So, for the record, the drummer from the Grateful Dead smokes weed and thinks it should be legal—is that any surprise?

7

The year 1969 was a huge one for the Grateful Dead and it started off with a couple of bangs—literally. First, there was the Led Zeppelin photo shoot that we photo bombed in our own way, you could say. We didn't mean to scare off Led Zeppelin but we scheduled a photo session at Herb Greene's studio on the same day that they did—it was their first time in San Francisco and maybe even in America. They weren't really well known over here quite yet and they had a gig at the Fillmore West that ended up being some kind of breakout show for them.

Their photo shoot was first, before ours, and we were getting tired of sitting around. Every successful band has dealt with the "hurry up and wait" methodology that afflicts the music industry; there's just no way around it. This has led to a lot of truly destructive (and/or self-destructive) behavior by a lot of bands over the years, including us. At that photo shoot, I remember that Pigpen brought a .22 Colt-style six-shooter with him. He used to flaunt that thing around and scare people with it. Anybody who knew him would've found this amusing because Pigpen was the sweetest guy in town. He never would've hurt a single living thing and he never once did. But he did love to have fun with this gun—when he got restless, he'd sometimes shoot it off for amusement. He'd brandish it in conversation and then fire one off in some direction just to make his point. And for humor. At the Led Zeppelin photo shoot, when we all got tired of sitting around, he fired a round into the ceiling, I believe. It was all horseplay. But that was enough for Led Zeppelin. They ran. It's comical and ironic to think of now, given some of the truly unruly and outright evil behavior they later exhibited, once they became big enough to get away with it. We were harmless in comparison. But don't tell them that.

We had another comical encounter right after that, but instead of guns, this one involved Playboy Bunnies and LSD. We were invited to be the musical guest on a TV show called *Playboy After Dark,* hosted by Hugh Hefner. The show was totally weird and awkward. It was supposed to be a variety show that kind of brought the magazine to life and it tried to sell a fake version of what life was like at the actual Playboy mansion.

We arrived on the set and, again, were subjected to the "hurry up and wait" phenomenon. The show was conceived to look like a house party but it was actually filmed at CBS Studios in Los Angeles, on a giant soundstage that was kind of intimidating just by its size alone. One of the things I noticed about this place was that it had a giant coffee dispenser—one of those three-foot-tall things, for the union and for all the people working the show. And everybody was drinking coffee.

We went through the long and tedious process of getting ready: we had them put makeup on us, Mickey and I got our stuff together, we all agreed what songs we were going to play, and all of that. Bear—you know, Owlsey—was back with us at this point. He had a brief revival as our sound guy, until that bust in New Orleans. With Bear came his long delays with getting the sound "perfect," so we had to put up with that, in addition to all the normal sitting around and doing nothing that is standard fare for television shoots.

Pretty soon, though, I noticed that some of the stagehands and cameramen were having a bit of trouble doing their jobs. They were saying things like, "Joe, you're out of focus." "No, number 13, you're out of focus."

"Is this thing on?" "Hi! Who is this?" "Cameras are weird, man." There was all this broken communication. I finally figured out that Bear, or at least someone in our ranks, had gone to that coffeepot and electrified it. Everyone was dosed. Including Hugh Hefner who, at the end of the night, tried to thank Phil and me. You could see he was really trying, and he really was being sincere, but he was also really high on acid and it was hard for him to talk. It didn't quite come out right. All we could do was laugh, cackling the whole way to the end of CBS Studios, because we were really high on acid, too. Everybody was really high on acid—the entire film crew, the band, the actors and actresses, all the Playmates. They all got a surprise taste of Owsley's finest that day. So it ended up being a fun time after all. Like a guerilla Acid Test. With bunnies!

Our performance from that broadcast found its way over to YouTube, if you care to watch it. We played "St. Stephen" and "Mountains of the Moon." You can't really tell that everyone was tripping their brains out . . . but they were.

I don't condone dosing people without their prior consent, but consider the context. If you recall, the Grateful Dead started out as the house band at the Acid Tests, which were thrown by the Merry Pranksters. You could argue, then, that as a band, we were literally born out of a psychedelic prank. Therefore, certain things were just woven into our DNA. And when various members of the band stopped eating acid as part of their diets, well, the pranks, at least, continued.

Bobby was a natural prankster and going through hotel lobbies or airport terminals could be especially hazardous with him. Especially in the days before TSA, before 9/11 and all these heavy-duty regulations. One time, I think we were in Portland—I don't know what year—Bobby thought it would be funny to pull out a toy cap gun. It looked just like a snub-nosed .38 and he whipped it out in front of the ticket counter and just started firing it off in the airport. He got arrested for that one. The rest of us went on to wherever and left him to pay for his sins.

I think Bobby was kind of afraid to prank me too much because he knew that my retaliation might up the ante beyond his comfort zone.

Payback is a bitch. But he would tell front-desk clerks or airline ticketing agents that so-and-so, usually a tour manager, was stoned out of their mind and carrying a lot of drugs on them and things like that. Little things for amusement. His amusement.

One particular prank that I remember, very clearly, inadvertently involved former U.S. senator George McGovern. In 1972, McGovern was running for president on the Democratic ticket against Richard Nixon. It's a presidential race that will always be remembered for Nixon's scandal at the Watergate hotel. The Grateful Dead somehow managed to pull off our own little hotel scandal involving McGovern that year. Unlike Nixon, we didn't get in trouble for it. Or, at least, not enough that we needed to resign.

McGovern's campaign had reached out to us, seeking the Grateful Dead's endorsement. We weren't ready to do that, even though none of us could stomach the thought of a second Nixon term. McGovern was the much better choice and we probably should've supported him, but we were an adamantly apolitical band back then. We ended up meeting McGovern in person, on an airplane—by coincidence, we were on the same flight. He invited us to play the White House if he won. We declined. He lost, anyway.

In late October 1972, with both campaigns in overdrive, the band happened to be booked at the same hotel as McGovern. Two different types of parties—the Democratic and the Dead. This was somewhere in Wisconsin, around Milwaukee. I don't recall the name of the hotel . . . but it wasn't Watergate.

We were destined for trouble at that hotel. Perhaps as some kind of prelude, I got into a fight with Bobby on the way back from the gig after the first night. The argument was over the very important distinction of which freezes first—asphalt or metal. I swore up and down that it was metal. Bobby swore up and down that it was asphalt. To settle it, we jumped out of the van and I wrestled Bobby to the actual asphalt. I had him pinned to the ground and I was trying to smash his head against the curb when one of our roadies, Ram Rod, very carefully put his boot under Bobby's head so he wouldn't get hurt. We were into it pretty heavy. Ram Rod's boot snapped us out of it, and we dusted each other off and continued being rowdy.

That kind of energy followed us back to the hotel the next night, too. We didn't know McGovern was there at first, so that had nothing to do with it.

We were in the middle of a tour and we must've gone through states where fireworks were legal, because we were stocked up on them. Band and crew alike. We had pounds upon pounds of firecrackers, and just as many pounds of bottle rockets. The hotel was horseshoe shaped, with an atrium in the middle, so the rooms all faced each other on the inside, going however many stories up. There was that great wide-open space that over-looked the indoor courtyard or whatever. We kind of got wise to where we all were and we took stock of each other's room numbers. Then, we opened our inside-facing windows and started shooting bottle rockets at each other. It was amazing. They were powerful enough that they'd go across the hotel atrium and into a room; not always the right room that you were hoping for. They weren't exactly ballistic missiles and aiming them was a loose concept. So there would be some poor guy with his windows open who suddenly had a bunch of bottle rockets explode in his room. We proceeded to battle, launching bottle rockets back and forth. We'd light strings of firecrackers—hundreds of them—and chuck them down on the courtyard or mezzanine below and they resonated so beautifully, it was like firing cannons in the Grand Canyon. There was this incredible echo. And because we just played a show, we had all this energy that we were letting out.

While I haven't told you about Keith Godchaux joining the band yet, and we'll get to all that, he was our keyboardist at the time. This tangent should've come with a spoiler alert. Sorry. Anyway, Keith was with me in my room and we were just firing our ammunition away like crazy. We also had cases of Heineken with us and, as we're drinking, we're filling up the entire bathtub with broken beer bottles. That's a lot of Heineken, I guess.

We're drinking and we're firing off bottle rockets and we're lighting off firecrackers and nobody's really getting the upper hand or anything. It's just chaos. Apparently, downstairs and throughout the rest of the hotel, McGovern's Secret Service men had heard the explosions and hit the deck. They thought they were under attack. If that Nixon don't get you, then the Dead sure will.

Ram Rod's room was right next to mine. Directly above him, one story up, was our lighting designer for that tour, Ben Haller. Now, as with many of those old hotels, air would get sucked into the room through the outside window and blow out under the door. So, being the smart guy that he was, Ben cut open a down pillow and emptied the whole pillowcase while leaning outside, right above Ram Rod's room. Every one of those feathers got sucked into Ram Rod's window and when he came out of there, it looked like he had been tarred and feathered. He had been sweating from the firecracker war, so the feathers stuck all over him—he was completely covered in them. Head to toe. It was the ultimate pillow fight. And that was the end of it: Ram Rod lost the war. Ben won. That's how you win when you're playing with us.

We would've all been able to celebrate the victory and take part in the spoils, but just at that moment, there was a loud knock on my door. I opened it and saw two rows of gentlemen facing me. The first row was the local heat and the next row was the Secret Service. McGovern's men had really been freaked out and dove for cover and had reached for their guns and all of that, so now they were trying to get to the bottom of it. "Are you guys lighting firecrackers?" "No." I was leaning with my left hand up against the wall and when I went to move, I had so much gunpowder on my hand that it left a perfect imprint on the wall. The cops laughed—they had never seen anything so incriminating.

I reminded the McGovern party that they had asked us to endorse them or support them or maybe even play for them in Washington, and I played that card: "You're not going to be mean to us now, are you?" That must've worked, because they just made Keith and me go to a different hotel. There was one right across the street, so it was fine. But they only moved the two

of us. It was like they thought we were the most contagious, or the insti-
gators or something. A bunch of troublemakers. Two of them.

Also: I may have gotten into some kind of thing at the front desk, which
contributed to being kicked out of the first hotel. But that's just going by
eyewitness reports; I must've blacked that part out.

When we checked into the new hotel, I was still wired and going nuts
and probably still something of a liability. But then I turned on the radio
and it happened to be tuned to the most incredible jazz station and I started
blasting it. Even though the music was really outrageous, it had a calming
effect on me. It put me into this blissed-out state of being; after all that
excitement, I had found inner peace and I was really thankful for that.
Nobody was hurt that night, and nothing got too damaged, except maybe
the manhood of some of the Secret Service agents who ran for cover.

So, yeah, pranks: we loved them and we managed to pull a couple of
them off, in our time. We also loved guns and explosions and all of those
things—I remember Pigpen and I had pellet guns at one point and we'd
"borrow" the hotel's phone books and set them up across the room and
take target practice. We'd completely decimate the books, and that was
how Pigpen and I would keep each other entertained during downtime.
They were just pellet guns and we didn't shoot them at each other and
we didn't rob banks or anything. Good clean fun.

But where were we in this tale? Back to the beginning of 1969, following the "Playboy Acid Test." We got our hands on the latest in recording
technology—a sixteen-track recorder (which, of course, is antiquated these
days)—and we hauled it up the steps of the Avalon, and later the Fillmore
West, and we became the first band ever to make a live sixteen-track
recording. We weren't trying to make history; we were just trying to record
a live album. We released it toward the end of the year, on November 10,
1969, as *Live/Dead*. It was our first live release and it remains one of our
best-loved albums. Its appeal was that it took great "you-had-to-be-there"
live versions of songs like "Dark Star" and "The Eleven" and put them right
in people's living rooms. Studio versions could never do those songs justice,

but advances in live recording (some of which were at our own hands) meant that we could bring the live Dead experience to vinyl.

That said, I didn't even remember what the cover of *Live/Dead* looked like until I started digging through everything for this book. I didn't have much to do with the whole process behind it, since it was live—I just played my heart out at those shows and that was that.

But we were also recording a lot in the studio during that same time period, working on our third studio release, entitled *Aoxomoxoa*, which doesn't mean anything—it's just a cool palindrome. People have surmised over the years that you could read the "Grateful Dead" lettering on the front cover as "We Ate the Acid" which, I suppose, is true enough, if you look at it just right. Was that intentional? I'm not telling. But I will say that, despite rumors, that's not a five-year-old Courtney Love on the back cover in the group photo. That's my daughter, Stacy.

The recording of *Aoxomoxoa* was notable for several reasons. First, the sixteen-track technology came along only after we did our initial recording using an eight-track at the end of 1968. But when the studio procured one of the first sixteen-track recorders in the world (the same one we used for *Live/Dead)*, the decision was made to toss everything we had already done and record it all again. From scratch. This time we could go deeper and experiment with things no other band had done yet. Being able to utilize twice as many tracks essentially doubled the possibilities of what we could do with each song. The end result was dense and cumbersome in places, and all that studio time cost us a fortune, but we were experimenting on the sonic frontier, exploiting cutting-edge technology.

Mostly, what I remember about those sessions, is this: We took pinhead doses of STP to use as speed during the recording, and then we brought nitrous oxide tanks into the control room during the mixing process. We called those sessions the Barbed Wire Whipping Party. (We recorded a song of the same name, with words by Robert Hunter, but it never made the final album.)

The real-life Barbed Wire Whipping Party was at Pacific High Studios in San Francisco. When you're mixing down tracks while sucking nitrous oxide, it's like anything else: You think you're driving great until you wake up, wrapped around a tree. But at least we all had a lot of fun with that one, which wasn't exactly typical of our studio experiences. We spent an excessive amount of money on *Aoxomoxoa,* because we basically recorded the same album twice and then spent countless hours in production. Once again, Warner Brothers wasn't happy with us, or with the enormous debt that we accrued with them, but whatever. It was worth it in the end. *Aoxomoxoa* came out on June 20, 1969, and it eventually went gold. It only took about twenty-nine years.

My son Justin was born ten days before *Aoxomoxoa* hit the shelves, on June 10, 1969. "Just in" time to go to Woodstock. There's actually a shot of him, in Susila's arms, getting off the helicopter, backstage, in the *Woodstock* movie. The Grateful Dead didn't make it into the documentary, but Justin did. Which was prescient, considering that he now directs music documentaries and concert videos. We'll get to Woodstock, but my son comes first.

In advance of Justin's arrival, Susila and I decided to get married. I took her to Reno, but unlike my previous marriage there, this one was legit. We were living on Benton Lane in Novato, at a tumbledown shack of a place, on a hill, just across town from Mickey's ranch. We moved there because we got kicked out of the Lucas Valley house following the pot bust. Like Mickey's ranch, our place was technically outside the town limits, which means it was unincorporated, which means the local police didn't have jurisdiction over it, which means we could shoot rifles there and go crazy. A highway patrolman owned the property next door and would shoot solid steel bullets clear through oak trees, despite the Geneva Convention (which had banned solid steel bullets). Needless to say, we left him alone and he afforded us the same luxury. Susila has said that this was during my cowboy phase, when it was all dynamite, horses, dogs—and baby.

About that baby: When Susila started going into labor, I went into a high state of panic. We went to a hospital in Novato but they wouldn't let me into the delivery room with Susila. They said, "Husbands aren't allowed in." I said "Bullshit!" and Susila said "Bullshit!" and we got into an ambulance and we hightailed it to San Francisco and went straight into French Hospital.

I'd been hitting a little bit of the Jack Daniels to help my nerves. I got in there and they washed me up and put the gown on, and they put Susila in the stirrups and the whole thing, and you see a little head sticking out, just a teeny bit, and you watch a little more of the head come out, see some blond hair, and these eyes, the cheeks, the chin, the neck. Like most men, I really wanted a son. So, when his dick popped out I went, "Yeah! A boy!" The doctor looked at me like, "Would you be quiet please?" but I wouldn't—I was a little drunk and I was just yelling up a storm. I was so excited at the birth that the doctor wiped him up but before he even cut the umbilical cord, he handed him to me, and it shut me up, because I was holding this child that was still connected to his mother, and I was just blown away. And that's Justin.

We left home in such a rush that we didn't take anything with us, and Susila got into the ambulance after the first hospital wearing only a sheet. I must've forgotten to grab her clothes, because she didn't have anything to change into when we left French Hospital. She had to borrow clothes from someone. She was mad at me about that one, and it was really embarrassing for her, I'm afraid. But it was also just really exciting for both of us, to have a son, and it still is to this day.

About two months after Justin's birth, we took our first family trip—to Woodstock. August 15 to 17, 1969. It wasn't really a vacation because Daddy had to work. Just like at Monterey Pop and all the other big shows, the Grateful Dead blew it. We didn't play that well. Because of rain and problems with grounding, we were getting electrocuted on stage—Bobby especially—and Bear had his usual delays with getting the sound just right. Meanwhile, the sound on stage was damn near impossible to work with. We couldn't hear each other. In the end, I don't even remember what songs we played. It wasn't a memorable performance.

I took a tiny speck of STP before the gig, for energy, and I think most of us took acid before our set—no surprises, there. If you weren't at

Woodstock, then you've at least read about it, so you have some idea of what it was all about. Three days of peace, love, and music. Some of the other artists included Jimi Hendrix, the Who, Jefferson Airplane, The Band, Santana, Sly & the Family Stone, Creedence Clearwater Revival, Janis Joplin, and Crosby, Stills, Nash & Young. You can watch some of those bands give the performance of their lives in the theatrical documentary, but—once again—we declined to sign the release forms and passed on being included in the film. For the Grateful Dead, our performance was anticlimactic, although it was still thrilling to be a part of it.

The one memory that really sticks out, oddly, is when we tried to get out of there. We helicoptered in from our nearby hotel. But when we went to leave, it was after dark, so they had us load up into a vehicle. Then they drove us out—through the middle of the fucking crowd. It was like trying to part a sea of people half a million strong. Quite literally. I'd never seen that many people in one place in my life and I got freaked out. Afterward, I realized it was all fine. The Deadhead community didn't fully exist just yet, but these people acted just like the Deadheads did later. It was part of the same continuum. They were just incredibly gentle and kind to each other and that's really what made Woodstock so beautiful and historically significant. It was the best of everything that the Haight-Ashbury scene had once promised, but this was on a national scale. With the world watching. And the scene really shone through. Strangers were stopping strangers just to shake their hands.

And then came Altamont. Four months later. The two historic events are often juxtaposed against each other because, as people are quick to point out, they were somehow related (Altamont was even nicknamed "Woodstock West," though it didn't stick). But if the two were siblings, then Altamont had to be Woodstock's evil twin—there was light and then dark, good versus evil, and it all played out in extremes at these two festivals. Woodstock was the culmination of the entire hippie movement. Altamont was its death. As if to punctuate this, the festival took place on December 6, 1969. There went the '60s. Wave good-bye.

Earlier that fall, the Rolling Stones came to the United States for what may have been America's first real rock 'n' roll arena tour. People have called it that, anyway. Ticket prices were outrageous—$7 or $8 at the high end. The shows were reportedly electrifying. And the Rolling Stones were every bit the first real rock stars. They weren't outlaw cowboys like the Grateful Dead, or pop-culture gods like the Beatles. They were rock stars.

The Stones reached out to us because they wanted to stage a free concert in San Francisco as the tour closer, and they knew that was our domain. We agreed to play it with them, and help them organize it, but things got fuzzy from there. They sent ahead their road manager, Sam Cutler, and we had a meeting at Mickey's ranch.

I'm going to say a few words about Cutler here because, in the wake of Altamont, the Rolling Stones kind of disowned him—and the Grateful Dead adopted him. He was a smooth talker, a natural salesman, and he could wriggle his way in and out of stuff with a certain elegance. Being a road manager demanded all of those things—the street hustle and the handshake charm—so he was good at his job. He was also good at shaking people down, when necessary, and he wasn't the type to back down. If you can hang with the Rolling Stones, then you've got your chops in that department, and you can hang with the Grateful Dead for sure. We trusted him, we liked him, and we still do. But, being from England, he didn't always understand American pronunciation, and that was sometimes amusing. "Hey, want to go play in Ar . . . Kansas?" "No, Sam, you mean Arkansas."

Anyway, we had meetings about the free concert with the Rolling Stones in the weeks leading up to it, and in some ways, part of the problem was that nobody was particularly in charge. Cutler—and, by extension, the Rolling Stones—called some of the shots. Rock Scully—and, by extension, the Grateful Dead—called some of the shots. Ram Rod and some other people who worked for the Dead were working that Stones tour, so there seemed to be this natural feeling of collaboration, even though the two bands represented two very different camps. The Rolling Stones thought, "Hey, we'll let the Dead put this together, because that's what they do, and we'll come and headline." Alternately, we looked at it as a way to share a bill with the Rolling Stones—and we saw it as their thing. They were headlining. It was their deal; we were more like guests than hosts.

During one of the meetings at Mickey's ranch, we were eating dinner in his barn—Jerry, Phil, most of the band—and these three skunks snuck in under the table. I had my Great Dane with me, lying down in the corner, and I saw him raise his eyes, lift his head, and start to growl, like he was about to pounce. I jumped on him as fast as I could to shut him up because if those skunks—they were civet cats, more specifically—fired off, then the whole barn would've stunk too much to discuss Altamont. Meeting adjourned. But I sat with the dog, and the skunks looked around, sniffed our feet, and left. Everybody has a "bad omen" story about Altamont and that was mine. The astrology was all off. All signs were bad news.

When Mick Jagger announced at a high-profile press conference that the Stones were going to close their tour by throwing a free concert in Golden Gate Park, that's when things really started to come undone. He knew that he wasn't supposed to announce it in advance like that. The stealth element was one of the ways we were able to pull these free gigs off. The publicity meant that now we wouldn't be able to secure the proper permits to hold it in the park after all. We had to move it outside the San Francisco city limits. We found a place in Marin called Sears Point. A racetrack. It was a rather good location but the Rolling Stones and the company that operated Sears Point played politics and, ultimately, that site had to be scratched. Two days before the show. After an insane scramble, Scully was able to make arrangements with Altamont Speedway, which was located on a desolate stretch in Alameda County—the East Bay, past Oakland, about an hour outside San Francisco. Despite its proximity, the scene in the East Bay was significantly different from what was happening in San Francisco. It was a lot edgier, a lot tougher.

On the speedway, the stage was set up only three feet off the ground. With 300,000 people streaming in for a show—on a site that was built for significantly smaller crowds—we needed some kind of security to guard the stage. Nobody hired security. After all, it was a free show. But some members of the Hells Angels had a good relationship with the Dead and at our free shows before this, they would help out by making sure nobody fucked with the generators. Stuff like that. Nobody hired the Hells Angels to work security at Altamont. But somehow a loose kind of deal was struck with them where they would do things like make sure nobody rushed the stage in exchange for free beer for the day. Easy. Who made that call? Fingers point in all directions but at the end of the day, it doesn't even matter. It doesn't work like that. Everyone approved it, or allowed it, one way or the other. Either we're all to blame or else nobody's to blame.

Yes, concerns were raised about that decision and bigger concerns were raised about the facilities and the staging, but in the end, the desire to make this show happen, even in the face of all this adversity, clouded people's judgments. Objections became nothing more than duly noted asterisks in the fine print.

The whole gig was just bad juju, man. They were flying bands in via helicopter, so we went to the heliport in Sausalito—the same one we used to practice at—and at one point, as Jerry and I were waiting around, Mick Jagger showed up and he was trying to figure out the score and we were just trying to get to the site and something was off, even then. You can YouTube the footage of all of us there making small talk. Jagger was gracious but there was some kind of charged energy that was just awkward. It was all disorganized and chaotic.

On the ground at the racetrack, it was a grim and grizzly mess. The crowd up front was crazed and they were encroaching upon the stage, or being pushed up on it by the sheer volume of people behind them, hundreds of thousands strong. The bikers were beating them back. But, like, really beating them. Overzealously. They had their bikes out with them and they were protecting those too, of course, but people were stumbling on them or trying to climb over them to get a better viewing position. The bikers started using pool cues as weapons, and some had their knives out. I don't know—it was just a bad scene.

When our helicopter landed, the drummer for Santana, Michael Shrieve, came up to us—I think he and some of his bandmates were trying to hop on the next copter out of Dodge. He looked a bit roughed up.

"What's happening? You okay?" "No, man, things aren't right. The bikers are knocking people out." So, right then, we were like what the fuck did we just fly into? It felt like we landed in the middle of some kind of turf war. And, in a way, we did.

Shrieve told us that when the Jefferson Airplane took the stage, their frontman, Marty Balin, jumped into the audience to stop some of the bikers from beating a fan with pool cues. In return, Marty got punched out. They punched him out a second time, after he came to, for good measure.

Even backstage, the bikers had free rein to bully at will. There was nothing stopping them. No police. No security. The bikers *were* the security but, of course, they weren't on the payroll and they answered to nobody. It showed us all that even freedom had an ugly side. It's true that some of the Hells Angels were our friends and they remained our allies back there. But others, whom we had never seen before, were roughing people up just because they could. One of these unruly newcomers even threatened Phil at one point, seemingly for no real reason. The threat was serious. Phil was forced to retreat to the back of the pickup truck where we were all waiting for our turn to play. We felt like captives. And definitely not safe. When Crosby, Stills & Nash had the stage, we watched as Stephen Stills finished his set while bleeding, because he had been attacked.

The day's lineup was supposed to be: Santana, the Flying Burrito Brothers, Jefferson Airplane, Crosby, Stills & Nash, the Grateful Dead, and the Rolling Stones. But we scratched ourselves off that list. I don't remember any real discussion about it. There was no way we were playing. No way we were going out there on that stage. Not a chance in hell we were playing under these hostile conditions. It was a simple survival instinct.

The Rolling Stones should've gone on at that point, but they waited several more hours until it got dark. Their true motivations came to light: they were filming the concert to use as the climax of their tour documentary. So it wasn't free after all—they planned to profit from it. Maybe that had something to do with the dark shadow over the event: In our own experience, free concerts only worked when they had no other agenda. We could play or not play at will—there was nothing at stake either way.

We watched the Rolling Stones perform that night and, to their credit, they gave it their all. I couldn't give it my full attention because I was also watching out for my hide and trying to monitor the chaos. Right in front of the stage, during "Under My Thumb," another scuffle broke out. This one ended in murder. Someone in the audience, Meredith Hunter, pulled out a gun and he was stabbed to death by a Hells Angel. The courts later ruled that the biker was acting in self-defense. Meanwhile, the Stones kept playing, later claiming that they weren't fully aware of what just happened. But they did play as if their own lives depended on it. Jagger always held himself as the devil and the band's newest album was entitled *Let It Bleed*— all of that stuff kind of factored into the vibe, I'm afraid. It got ugly.

We took a helicopter back to San Francisco, where we were scheduled to play at the Fillmore West for the third consecutive night. I called it off. After seeing all that shit, after a guy got murdered during a concert we were connected with, after all the day's horror, I didn't feel like going out and playing music. It just didn't seem right to me. At dinner, I said, "I'm not doing the gig." The band backed me up on it. Bill Graham was furious about that, but that's just how he was. I think everybody understood.

We may not have been a political band but that doesn't mean that we didn't have certain principles that we held sacred. We backed out of Altamont mostly out of concern for our own safety, sure. But the decision was also a statement about our views on violence—and our reaction to it. The era of peace and love had come to a close. And our refusal to play even later that night, miles away from the speedway, was our moment of silence.

In the wake of Altamont, something else happened to the band that perpetuated this sudden darkness. Eventually the storm would pass, of course, but not before we got soaked. In short, we got ripped off by one of our managers. But that manager happened to be the father of a band member.

Sometime in 1969, when we realized the colossal debt we got ourselves into with the decidedly indulgent making of *Aoxomoxoa*, we realized that we needed to get a handle on our finances. We were a group of altruistic troubadours, a traveling psychedelic circus. We had gotten used to living hand to mouth and, now that we had reached a certain level, we were able to cover our costs of living. Great. We didn't need anything else. But that kind of thinking had led us into a massive debt with our record label and no real money in our individual bank accounts. We were at a point where we at least wanted to be able to afford houses. Cars. The occasional vacation. The stuff people with real jobs all get to enjoy. Our affairs were a picture of chaos, and we needed someone who could help us do a little spring cleaning. Someone who could lock down the front office while we played ball out back, so to speak.

Mickey suggested that we hire his father, Lenny Hart, to help us get on track. Jerry and I were skeptical from the start and I don't think I was ever fully convinced that it was a good idea. I kept my hands in my pockets and shuffled my feet as Mickey tried to sell us on it. Mickey's pitch was that Lenny was a businessman and now he was also an evangelist—a self-ordained fundamentalist minister. He was a man of God . . . at least, in theory. Plus, he was connected to us by blood. Meaning, if nothing else, we could trust him. It's amazing some of the lessons you learn in life.

Lenny had this whole Southern Gospel rap that he'd throw on us. He didn't try to convert us, but he did try to convince us that he was doing the Lord's work by managing us and that he brought a sort of divine providence to our organization. Consequently, none of us—particularly Jerry or me—liked the guy very much. We couldn't confide in him. He wasn't one of us. I think his intention all along was to rip us off, and that's exactly what he ended up doing.

There had been a number of signs that we ignored because we were naïve and because we weren't paying close enough attention and because we didn't believe that one of our fathers would have the heart to steal from us. There was this one show that we played in San Jose that was kind of reminiscent of the show in Paris, years later, where I fired Jon McIntire because the promoter told him we didn't turn a profit. This time, it was our manager with that sad refrain. The venue was completely packed and, afterward, Lenny told us that we didn't make any money. That was hot air. We made money. He just kept it, that's all.

At one point, Pigpen had an organ repossessed—they came and took it right from the stage—because the payment wasn't made on it. There were other omens like that, as well. Too many of them. And Ram Rod knew— he was the whistle-blower. When we couldn't ignore our suspicions anymore, we decided to simply let Lenny go. But first we asked to see the books. And that was the end of Lenny Hart. He fled to Mexico. And our money went with him.

Naturally, the band discussed what we should do about that, but there wasn't a whole lot that we could do. After Altamont, we weren't exactly going to hire bikers to go take justice in their own hands or anything. The idea was brought up, but we would never actually follow through with that. That just wasn't our style. The other option meant having to go to the authorities and get the police involved and that wasn't our style, either.

We were a band of hippies, so we decided on taking the hippie high road to justice: let karma get him. And it worked. Eventually, Lenny Hart got caught by a detective—somewhere in San Diego, I think—and he ended up doing some time behind bars. Also, we recovered a fraction of the money he stole from us. But this was all still a few years down the line.

In the meantime, Mickey took all of this the hardest. We were careful not to put any of the blame on him and we made it clear that he was still our brother—but this was his father that we're talking about. The rest of us had just been ripped off by our manager, but Mickey had just been ripped off by his own dad. How do you think that made him feel?

By 1970, we were a successful band—we could headline theaters, ballrooms, and college gymnasiums all across the country. We were on a major label and had just played Woodstock. And yet, Lenny left us hobbled. Broke. Funny things happen from hard situations: you learn to survive. I had a family to feed at home and I wasn't about to go back to selling wigs or giving drum lessons . . . so I started poaching deer for the dinner table.

When the band wasn't touring or rehearsing or recording, I would sometimes go out and do a little bit of pickup work for a cowboy named Tony Veranda who had a private cattle ranch out in Point Reyes—still in Marin County, but on the Pacific Coast. His 1,000-acre slice was called Hand Mountain and there were a ton of deer on the property. Tony was a true cowboy from Arizona and knew that I was hard up at the moment, so he said, "If you want, I'll show you how to hunt deer." He taught me how to shoot them and how to clean them, which can be pretty tricky— you have to be careful not to cut the scent glands and all this stuff. It was poaching but it was on my friend's land so I didn't get in trouble for it.

The only reason I did it was because I was flat broke. I wasn't hunting for sport. I was poaching for food.

There was this one time when I shot a deer and the bullet went right through her neck and killed the baby deer that must've been standing right next to her, on the other side. They both dropped. Yes, that's sad, but that also meant the Kreutzmanns wouldn't need to worry about food for a while—I suddenly had a good stash of meat. I did all the nitty-gritty stuff that you have to do when you're doing it yourself: I cut off the head, skinned the deer, wrapped it in sheets so flies couldn't get in there and lay eggs, then hung it to dry for three or four days. When it was time, I took it all down and cut it up, but I'm not much of a butcher. I cut it up in approximate steaks, with a big accent on "approximate." I took the back strap, which is one of the best parts of deer meat, and cut it into really long strips that could be rolled into a roast. Bear would've been proud.

Susila put garlic inside the layers of the roast and tied it all up with string and we started cooking when Lesh drove up to the house unannounced. "Hey Phil, want to join us for dinner?" "Yeah, sure." So we sat down with full plates of vegetables, potatoes and—for the entrée—the venison roast. As we're eating, Phil goes, "This is the best beef I've ever eaten." When we told him it was venison, he just about choked. He wasn't down with that, even though he loved the way it tasted. If we hadn't just been ripped off by our manager, then maybe we would've served filets mignons. We were making do.

We lived the cowboy lifestyle out at Mickey's ranch as well. Not by tending cattle or doing any sort of wrangling, per se—but we did ride horses. I think Mickey and I were probably more into horseback riding than the other guys, but the whole band learned to ride. We got into a situation where we had to. The previous year, somebody, Lenny, probably—thought it'd be a good idea for us to be a part of this western movie they were making down in Hollywood called *Zacharia*.

I owned my own horses and riding them was a big part of my downtime during that whole period. But, in preparation for this movie, everyone in the band sharpened their horseback riding skills at Mickey's. Including

Jerry, who we'll just say wasn't a natural. He didn't want anything to do with it, but we got him up there and riding. It was a fun group activity, even though the movie didn't work for us. We backed out of it. In the end, they got John Coltrane's drummer, Elvin Jones, instead. Joe Walsh appeared with his band James Gang; I think Country Joe & the Fish were also in it; and the actor Don Johnson had a starring role. I watched it once, years ago. So it goes.

Anyway, since Mickey's ranch was remote enough, we'd have shoot-outs there all the time. Not against each other. We'd bring all of our guns to this creek bed that ran through the ranch and we'd set up old television sets and stuff to shoot at. I remember we had a poster of a certain actor named Ronald Reagan, who at that point was our governor in California, and we'd unload all of our guns just shooting at it. It was a picture of him dressed up in his cowboy costume and we shot the shit out of it. There were at least 200 holes in it. I remember we all got paranoid about it afterward and were like, "We've got to get rid of that. If anybody else sees it, they'll think we're terrorists." This was way before terrorism was really much of a threat, as such. This was also more than a decade before Reagan became president and launched the "War on Drugs."

We used to blow the shit out of everything down there and just go completely crazy, without anyone around to tell us otherwise. It's really amazing that nobody got shot or hurt and that there were no accidents or anything. We dodged the bullet on that one. Literally.

Two things happened, during one particular afternoon, that still stand out. First, I walked out there after target practice and there was brass all over the ground. Empty shells. I looked at where we had been shooting and this tree, probably less than a foot in diameter, suddenly fell to the ground. It had been hit with so many bullets that the wind was able to finish it off. It toppled over. My friend and GD crew member, Sonny Heard, came along and, when I told him what just happened, he said, "That's nothing. Check this out."

He'd gotten his hands on something called a four-sticker, an explosive package that construction workers use. It's the equivalent of four sticks of dynamite and he assembled the detonator cap and wrapped it up with a three-minute fuse and then stuck it in a hole that he dug near the creek bed. He buried it with rocks, thereby essentially making the world's biggest grenade. He lit the fucker and walked away with his back to it. I suddenly remembered some of those gunpowder lessons in my backyard with my dad and so I had a bad feeling about this. I found a big fat oak tree and hid behind it and it turned out to be a good thing, too, because sure enough, the rocks flew as far as 200 yards, with some of them landing on the metal roof of Mickey's main house where our friend and den mother, Eileen Law, was cooking all of us dinner. She came out screaming, "What the fuck have you guys done?" The rocks completely pounded the whole area. They came thundering down on the roofs in a way that made hailstorms seem like whispers by comparison. Sonny just stood there with his back to the explosion. He assessed the damage and said, "Okay. Cool." He was a lucky son of a gun that time, although he's no longer with us, darn it. Anyway, that was a great ranch and we had a lot of adventures there.

The greatest adventure of all started at that ranch and it took me east to Nevada and it transformed me from a cowboy into an Indian. At least, in spirit. It was under the charge of an actual Native American—a great one, at that—named Rolling Thunder.

Mickey's thirty-two-acre ranch continued the communal vibe that we had at most of the Grateful Dead houses over the years—it was a safe-house for transients, with an open-door policy, where friends could come and go. Various Hells Angels lived at Mickey's ranch at various points, as did Rock Scully, members of the so-called "Pleasure Crew," (friends of ours who had all-access, but not officially employed—at least, not by us), and, for a little while one summer, me and Susila. (Justin was at his grandparents.)

We moved into an old hay barn on the property and, even though it was summertime, summer nights in Northern California can still get quite cold. The barn was made out of redwood and the walls had more holes in them than your average conspiracy theory. This was all in a tree-lined area where there were scrub oak trees, and we went out and got wood and anything else that we could to patch it up and make it more habitable. It had a dirt floor and we literally put blankets right up against the walls for insulation and we were just happy as hell. We were out there in this country setting and it was quite beautiful. There were no creature comforts whatsoever. I don't think we had a bathroom. We had to go into the main house for that, or to shower. We didn't stay there for very long.

But I remember that while we were there, Phil would come over with an incredibly powerful rifle that he would test-fire. It was so damn loud, he had to put on ear protectors. He started calling it the Ray Gun because we could shoot it over the road, 500, 600 yards, and as soon as you pulled the trigger, you'd see the dust blow where the bullet hit. It was that fast. Phil would sometimes put up targets not far from our little barn, and that scared the hell out of us so we'd flee to the other side of the property. Survival instincts kicked in.

But it was on this ranch, Mickey's, where I met Rolling Thunder. He was a Shoshone Indian medicine man who lived in Carlin, Nevada. For a reference point, Elko is the bigger city, just past it—we're talking about four hours east of Reno, on Highway 80. Rolling Thunder was the real deal. He was an authentic medicine man; very spiritual and very rooted in his people's traditions and rituals. If you were going to have a cigarette, you had to offer him one first. He didn't drink—he hated alcohol. He didn't smoke marijuana. He thought we were a little too loose with the LSD and that we should be a little more reverent with it. Of course, we didn't listen to that talk too much, except to nod our heads, respectfully. But when he needed a ride from Mickey's ranch back to his home in Carlin, Susila, and I thought, "Shit! Let's go live with a Native American for a while and see what that's about."

We bought a tepee and cut down poles for it at Mickey's ranch. We loaded them up on the top rack of my old Toyota Land Cruiser. And off we went to Nevada with Rolling Thunder and one of his braves, who was another young person around our age. It was a long drive but we did it in one day. Rolling Thunder's property had a run-down, wooden house where he would welcome company, and then a separate cabin across the street— his private quarters. He thought of the rattlesnakes under his floor as his friends, which he could communicate with. A part of the rite of passage for him to become a medicine man was that he had to let a rattlesnake bite him on the calf and not take the poison out. That's part of the ceremony: If it doesn't kill you, you're a shaman. You could tell something got him on the leg and probably infected it and all that horrible stuff. But he survived.

He had another unbelievable thing happen to him: He got caught between two railroad cars by his midsection and somehow he lived through that. He had massive scars on his chest from where the couplers got him. It must've been a horrendous accident. There were a lot of accidents like that involving the Native Americans and railroad work. The railroad companies really didn't treat them well, sad to say. The Central Pacific Railroad ran through Carlin and the town was a classic western railroad town until the 1960s, when mining companies moved in and became the major employer. The Native Americans were used for their labor but hardly treated better than slaves. It's important to me to mention this because it was just so unforgivable, the string of injustices that Native Americans faced ever since our ancestors came and took their land.

Rolling Thunder was a Native American traditionalist, practicing the traditional ways. As such, he was a righteous spiritual leader and he helped so many people in the community. People would offer trades for his medicine, or they would give him whatever money they could, but they didn't have much. Therefore, neither did he. He had to continue working for the railroads. He was the protector of the Native Americans in that area; he was their healer, their medicine man. He wasn't afraid of the cowboys, even though the cowboys were ruthless. It went beyond racism. It was even nastier. They would shoot at the Native Americans and really do horrible things, just for kicks. But Rolling Thunder would strike back. He told us stories: things that happened to him, things that he had to do to survive; things that he had to do to defend his community and his people. As he talked, you'd realize that the stories all took place right where we were walking. "This happened right here!" There was no guarantee something wasn't going to happen at any moment.

There were hot springs that were a fair distance from the highway but which you could still see from the road—it's pretty flat in Carlin and you can see for a long way. As we were walking there, RT told us about one time when he was with his braves—that's what he called his friends and family. They were all soaking in the hot springs when a bunch of rednecks crouched down behind the metal barriers along the road and started shooting guns over their heads. Just to rile them up. The next time Rolling Thunder took a group there, he led a little side expedition where some of his braves stayed behind and hid and caught these guys red-handed. They ambushed them and confiscated their guns. Then they took them out to the desert, miles away from anything, took their boots and left them there. They had to hike back. That is, if they made it. We don't even know. Nobody asked them to call when they got home to say they made it back safe. That's the kind of heaviness that was there.

Now, I'm immersed in this. I'm living in this thing. Susila and I go to our first prayer session with Rolling Thunder—to clarify, it wasn't really a "prayer session" in the Christian sense. Rolling Thunder never called it that. I never prayed in my life before then and it made me very nervous to think that I was going to ask for anything from the universe, or to even believe that you could ask for anything. I was in my early twenties and I had definitely never gone to church with any belief that praying did anything real. This was more about aligning with the Great Spirit. This was something different.

We took my Toyota and went down a dirt road for miles and miles into the desert. We crossed a creek bed and ended up in an oasis. There were all these beautiful giant green trees that lined the banks of the creek, away from the desolate brush. They were poplar trees or whatever they're called—with white bark perfect for making canoes out of. We were suddenly in the midst of them, alongside a creek bed. We parked and Rolling Thunder got out first and went ahead of us, then immediately stormed right back and I don't think I've ever seen a man in my entire life as mad as he was just then. His face was bright red and you could see the pained shadow that forms when anger clashes with sorrow. It had taken over his entire aura. He was foaming, ferociously mad, and yet there was also a sadness there that was tender around the corners. You could feel his bitter disappointment. A family of eagles lived in those trees, and it takes a few months before young eagles can fly. Well, these redneck sons of bitches came with shotguns and stood beneath the trees and killed all the birds. It was as if somebody came into Rolling Thunder's church and blew his altar away.

Eagles are sacred to the Shoshone Indians and when Rolling Thunder got back to the car, he couldn't even talk. He made us stay in this one area, away from the carnage, and for the next two or three hours he picked up every feather and prayed over every last one. They were scattered everywhere, these white eagle feathers, and he attended to all of them in turn. When he was finally finished making his medicine over these dead animals, he looked a little more resolved. He explained what happened and pointed out the shotgun shells that were littered all around the trees. Then he cleaned up the whole area. He buried all the birds and kept only the feathers that he was supposed to keep.

We were there for a couple of weeks and had made our camp in an area where three trees formed a natural triangle. Our tepee was set up right in the middle. Before we put it up, Rolling Thunder got down on the ground and prayed and created a protected bubble for us. He told us that if anybody came into that triangle and intended to do us harm, they would leave crazy and confused and might even face death. That was one of his protection prayers that he would use to shield himself from people who tried to hurt him. He'd say, "They can't mess with you—they'll go mad out in the desert."

Susila reminded me recently that we used to test our protected area— we'd go outside of it and the coyotes would suddenly start to take notice of us. We'd jump back inside the lines and it was like we became invisible. It's tough to say if something like that is just in your head, put there by the power of suggestion. It sure seemed real. It was real.

It was actually kind of a funny scene when we first went to put up the tepee, because Rolling Thunder insisted that his braves set it up for us, but it became obvious that they didn't know how to set it up any more than we did. This embarrassed RT, I think, and he started getting on their case, telling them how to do it and issuing orders. In the end, it was a perfect setup: the tepee was tight as hell, the top flap was adjusted just right, the cover around the bottom was perfectly snug, and this saved our hide one night.

I knew it was going to be a long haul from Mickey's ranch, so I took a little bit of street speed—meth—with me, just in case I needed an extra boost of energy. My reasoning was that truckers use speed all the time. But I didn't end up touching it, and when we set up camp, it was still wrapped in tinfoil.

So, anyway, one morning, Sue and I were awoken because we heard a pounding that sounded just like double bass drums. Something was hitting the tepee from the outside. Thump, thump, thump. They were blackbirds. Ravens, actually. Crazy as it sounded, I began to theorize that the birds had gotten into the little tinfoil pouch of speed, which I had placed in the crux of a tree the night before. The ravens were having a party—they were high on speed. They were crashing headfirst into the tepee, again and again, as if it were a mosh pit. But luckily the tepee was tight and they couldn't get in or knock it down. It was tense in there for a few minutes. I was sitting inside, clutching my .22, knowing that it probably wouldn't have done me any good. The ravens were straight-up attacking the tepee. It was just like a scene out of the movie *The Birds*. After things quieted down, I peeked outside. When it was safe, I went up to the tree and, sure enough, they pecked all that speed to pieces. So that just goes to show: Don't ever give meth to a raven. Not a good idea.

On a different day, we were just having fun, shooting that .22 rifle that I had brought with me—a .22 becomes little more than a peashooter in a space as vast as the Nevada desert. There's no power to it. You shoot it at a rock cliff and it would seem like twenty minutes went by before you'd hear the bullet go "ding." But it was still fun to play around with. So we're out there, doing that, and suddenly, for whatever reason I got the feeling I should turn around. It's that intuition you get when someone is right behind you. I turned around and saw two guys walking right toward us, not making a sound. Sue and I got on our feet pretty quickly and I held the rifle at rest. But, without me intentionally doing it, the thing fired off. I swear I didn't pull the trigger . . . even though, technically, I must have. The shot landed right between the guys' feet and it stopped them in their tracks. We were downwind and thought we could smell alcohol on them. When they got closer, we were sure. They were slammed drunk and in a really bad way. That accidental shot had stopped their approach though and, to this day, I honestly believe it was Rolling Thunder's prayer that protected us and that caused the semiautomatic rifle to go off without actually hurting anyone. If I had tried to do that intentionally, I probably would've hit one of them and it would've been a whole different end to this story.

As it stands, those guys backed up and told us not to shoot. "We just wanted to see who you were." They were just some jive-talking rednecks and they were so completely trashed that you couldn't really be that nervous; they wouldn't have been capable of much. It turned out that they had a cabin about a quarter mile from our encampment and were curious about their new neighbors. We walked back to their place and it was a pretty random scene. There was another couple that was staying in a van or something nearby and they started hanging out, too. They were about our age and closer to us in spirit than the drunk fucktards. We struck up a game of horseshoes but the drunks were in such a way that they couldn't throw well. We kept winning and that pissed them off, all over again.

Sue saw rhubarb growing in the garden and, out of nowhere, offered to make a rhubarb pie. She cooked it in their kitchen as a peace offering. And it worked—it made everybody happy. Also: It was just an outrageously delicious pie. That worked out pretty well. The lesson we learned there is that wars can sometimes be won with pie.

During our stay, Rolling Thunder had taught us about eagle feathers and the magic they possess. He made me a wand out of five or six feathers and I used it in healing ceremonies, brushing energy, moving energy, all that good stuff. When we finally left to head back to California, there was no air-conditioning in the Toyota and we had all the windows open. We were discussing everything we had just experienced, questioning what was real and what was imagined. So much of it seemed like fantasy. And yet, all of it actually happened.

We had all the sacred feathers that Rolling Thunder gave us, folded up safely in a piece of newspaper, underneath the passenger seat. They were secure. All of the sudden, with the windows open and the wind blowing through the car, a feather swirled around our heads. Susila dug into the back, reached under the seat, and got the package with all of the feathers. She made sure it was wrapped tight and placed it under our camping gear. There was no way any more of them were getting out. Rolling Thunder had given them to us as a gift. They held meaning; they were special. But then another feather went flying by. Then another. They started dancing in the wind. I tried to grab them and Sue tried to grab them but we couldn't hold on to them. Some of them just flew away, back to where they came from, I think. When we went to tell Rolling Thunder about it, later on, he already knew what we were going to say. How does that happen?

It had really been an amazing couple of weeks. The reason I had to come home, though, was because, the day before we left, I got a telegram from the band. They had sent me a message through Western Union that said, "We need you here. We're going to start work on our new album." That album became *Workingman's Dead*. Right before I got that telegram, Rolling Thunder and I had made plans to go on a vision quest, up in the mountains outside of Carlin. Seven days with barely enough water and only a little bit of food. We were making preparations when suddenly I had to leave; I had to record *Workingman's Dead*. It's always remained a question in my mind, though—I have to ask myself, "What if I had gone on that vision quest instead? What would've happened?" We'll never know. But I do know this: I did go on a vision quest after all. A vision quest of the Grateful Dead kind. I made it home and went straight into the studio with the band.

We recorded *Workingman's Dead* at Pacific High Studios in San Francisco, the same place where we had those nitrous oxide mixing sessions for *Aoxomoxoa*. But *Aoxomoxoa* had cost us a fortune and Lenny Hart had

run off with whatever money we had left, so we made a conscious decision to be more economical on *Workingman's Dead* and work briskly. The
album represented a multitude of changes for the Grateful Dead. It pushed
us in a different direction and that, in turn, led us to different places and
the whole thing definitely ushered in a whole new era for us. The 1960s
were over. Most of the people in the band had stopped taking acid regularly. We were now onto cocaine and other stuff. Welcome to American
life in the 1970s.

I n conversation, I often get *Workingman's Dead* and *American Beauty* mixed up with each other, but there's an acceptable reason for that. I mean, besides the fact that we recorded them pretty much back to back, more than forty years ago. Combined, these two albums represent the Grateful Dead's "Bakersfield era," where we were playing music that reflected our lifestyles during a very specific period. We were good ole American boys living in the Wild West. A little bit country. A little bit rock 'n' roll.

In 1970—the year both albums were recorded and released—we were beginning to see signs of wear and tear, both inside our circle and out. We had witnessed births and deaths of entire scenes and their accompanying ideologies. We lost Jimi Hendrix and Janis Joplin in the fall of that year, which was tough. There were other losses going on around us then too, involving various band members' parents—that's in addition to the father that ripped us off.

So we had songs like "Dire Wolf" and "Black Peter" on *Workingman's Dead*, and then "Brokedown Palace" and "Box of Rain" on *American*

Beauty. Songs that reflected our headspace after we watched the 1960s crash into the wall on a raceway in Altamont. Those two albums also carried some of the biggest hits of our entire career: "Uncle John's Band," "Truckin'," "Friend of the Devil," "Casey Jones," "Sugar Magnolia," and others. These are songs that have gone beyond our own little community and into the American musical vocabulary. They're on the radio and on pizza parlor jukeboxes. You don't have to be a Deadhead to know them by heart. And pretty much every Dead tribute band (including most of the "official spinoff" groups) keeps them in heavy rotation in their live repertoires. They're the standards.

The Grateful Dead definitely went through a number of transformations and makeovers over the years and it felt like the individual songwriters all went through those changes with the band. The songs were unique to their respective songwriters—and I'm about to say my piece on that—but just as we had a "group mind" with improvisation, we generally shared the same "group mind-set" in regards to what mood we were in, musically, during different periods. During the "Bakersfield era," we tried to be like a Bakersfield country band—but one that still sounded like we were from 300 miles north of that town, in the northern part of the state. Which, of course, we were. We held to our psychedelic roots but, in the studio, we wanted to try our hand at a more steady approach. That's what that music called for. Also: it just felt like the right thing for us to do at the time. Forward motion.

Whenever any of the band members came up with a song and wanted to do it, we did it. Once, anyway. Despite our own preferences, solidarity was important to us, as was the unwavering belief that everyone who wanted to be heard, deserved to be heard. It was the way we conducted business on the stage, in the studio, and even in the office. Every opinion mattered. So, I'll finally give mine. I liked the Jerry Garcia songs the best. That should come as no surprise. Jerry Garcia's music with Robert Hunter's lyrics was the best of what we had to offer and getting to play those songs was the reward for being a good sport about the rest. When I got up onstage every night, all the way to the end, I couldn't wait to play the Gar-cia/Hunter stuff. That's what really got me off. I think most people feel the same about that much.

Phil's songs were always the hardest to play. He wasn't the strongest vo-calist and he liked to put a lot of changes in the arrangements. I think he took an academic approach to songwriting, using it as a chance to exper-iment and play around with theoretical concepts. It was like the band was his guinea pig. Some of the songs came from the head more than the heart. They just didn't swing. He had this one thing called "Wave to the Wind" which could have been used maybe for the theme to *The Love Boat*.

I recognize that most of our fans really love "Box of Rain," but even that could feel too contrived to me when we played it. It wasn't an easy song to play, even though that's the illusion that it gave off. There were often issues with the tempo. Jerry's songs never felt that way because the groove was always there. I'm not saying this to be mean; I'm just being honest. And keep in mind, I'm generalizing here: Phil wrote some keep-ers, too.

The Bob Weir songs were more fun to play, but even some of those could feel a bit too contrived to me. Or clunky. Don't forget that I played these songs for decades, and I would play them again in an instant. In fact, I still play "The Other One" often, no matter who I'm touring with. And I really connected with "Throwing Stones"—I locked into the message behind that one and I think it's as relevant today as it was back then. "Lost Sailor," on the other hand, used to drive me nuts. The words don't get me at all. I guess they were written by Bobby's lyricist, John Perry Barlow. It's just not one of my favorites. However, it used to be fun to play anyway, because Mickey would mock the lyrics, off mic, and make all sorts of funny faces that would entertain the rest of us. There's always a silver lining, you know?

Some of Bobby's other songs felt like they were drudging along to their finish lines. I hope you don't hate me for saying this, Bobby, and I think when you play those songs by yourself, they're strong. But when the Dead played them next to Garcia's songs, they just didn't sound as good. I'm sure a lot of people would disagree with me about that. Although . . . not everyone.

Also, jumping ahead of our narrative for a moment, later on in the band's career when a keyboardist named Brent Mydland joined the group, his songs were a real change for all of us. They could be fun, but mostly because they were so abstract compared to the Grateful Dead songbook. They were more like pop songs. It was challenging for me to try to play them that way, but I thought we did a pretty good job of incorporating those songs. I went back and I listened to some of them recently and I was pleased with how they sounded. The lyrics—some of which came from Barlow—were more direct than our other songs; Brent was singing straight-up about his love life and about his joys and sorrows. I could easily relate to a lot of that. But I don't think a song like "Blow Away" was ever really a Grateful Dead song. It was its own thing. Weir's songs were Grateful Dead songs. Lesh's songs were Grateful Dead songs. And Jerry's songs were the very best Grateful Dead songs.

When Jerry would come to us with a new song, it was almost a fully realized entity. He'd show up to rehearsal, sit down with his guitar, and play it for a little bit by himself. The whole essence was already there. He didn't have to tell you how to play your part. He didn't have to suggest anything. He already knew what key he wanted, what the changes were, and where they were going to go. He knew the decoration as well as the architecture. He was open to different ideas, out of some kind of grace or duty, perhaps—but he wasn't easily swayed, because the song was already complete. He worked it out way before he came to rehearsal. Those were my favorites.

You never had to guess anything. You already knew what to play. You could hear all the parts already there, embedded or implied. It was like the music conducted you.

Both Phil's and Bobby's felt forced by comparison. It doesn't mean I'm right—this isn't about right or wrong. I'm just talking about my own taste in the music that I played for all these years, and the other members of the band have their own preferences and the fans all have theirs, as well. It's a wonderful thing. Anyway, in my own opinion, all the songwriters had their moments . . . but nobody could compete with the songwriting partnership of Jerry Garcia and Robert Hunter. That's all I'm saying.

And jumping back into our story line here, 1970 is really around the time when Robert Hunter established himself as a member of the band in his own right. He didn't play with us or sing with us, but he became a full-time employee who ranked about as high as any of us on stage. His words became the words of the Grateful Dead, and when people quote us, they're usually quoting him.

The two 1970 companion albums—*Workingman's Dead* and *American Beauty*—are what really put Hunter in that position. His lyrics worked on a much more elevated level than your typical love ballad or rock anthem—they belonged to literature. I'm not surprised that Bob Dylan, an artist whom many consider to be the greatest songwriter of all time, has used some of his lyrics. That's our Bob. Hunter, I mean.

Workingman's Dead was all about discovering the song. Half a year later, *American Beauty* became all about having the harmonies to do that. The singers in our band really learned a lot about harmonizing by listening to Crosby, Stills, Nash & Young, who had just released their seminal album, *Déjà vu*. Jerry played pedal steel on one of the songs ("Teach Your Children") on that record. Stephen Stills lived at Mickey's ranch for a few months, right around that time, I think, and David Crosby enjoyed partying as much as we did. So our circles overlapped.

When we were recording *American Beauty*, those guys were in the same studio as us, working on various projects and solo albums. There was a lot happening in that studio—Wally Heider's in San Francisco—all at once. Every room had a band making something historic in it, and we all bounced around each other. In particular, though, I remember Crosby really giving our singers a lot of advice and help.

From the rhythm standpoint, everything had to be suitably simplified that year. For *Workingman's Dead,* I had just gotten back from Rolling Thunder's and I was in a real healthy frame of mind, given all the stuff that had just happened. I brought that strength into the studio with me for those sessions. I made it clear to Mickey, "We can't use two drum kits on this stuff—it just doesn't fit." So Mickey came in with shakers and percussive stuff and I played minimal drum parts. It was more like just laying down basic rhythm tracks. Once we took the songs live, of course, Mickey and I would do our thing with them—but in the studio, the drums needed to be as bare and essential as the music itself. We were there to serve the songs.

Now that we had some more accessible tunes alongside our wilder jam vehicles, we broke apart the live show into different sections. In the Spring of 1970—after we recorded *Workingman's Dead* but right before it was released—we started performing shows that we called *An Evening with the Grateful Dead*. The only other band on those bills was a group called the New Riders of the Purple Sage and, at that time, they were really more of a Grateful Dead side project than their own entity—Jerry, Phil, and Mickey were part of the lineup. Jerry was on pedal steel. They opened for us. Then we played an acoustic set. Then we played an electric set. And then we played *another* electric set. Do the math: the Grateful Dead played three sets a night (with half the band onstage for four).

Eventually, that morphed into the format we kept for the rest of our career: long, two-set shows, often without even an opening act. It was a lot more music than most bands played in a night.

Many Deadheads considered the first set to be some kind of warm-up, but I never looked at it like that. I took the first set as seriously as I did the second. It was just a different approach. The second set was more open and free, with a lot more jamming and improvisation. It was deep in the heart of that set where wild things could happen at any given moment. It became the portion of the night where you'd be more likely to find one-time-only adventures.

I know that Mickey felt the same way the fans did. He felt the first set was kind of jive and he was always just waiting for the second set to come around. That wasn't my style, though. I like to be in it, right now.

The first sets were always a lot of fun for me and I always really enjoyed playing them. I take song arrangements seriously. The drummer has the responsibility of setting up various parts of the song by playing breaks that lead into changes that keep the song moving forward. You have to do lead-ins and fills and if you don't do that in the song, then you're not playing the song. You're not expressing its personality.

Take, for example, the traditional ballad "Jack A Roe." That song has a trick intro. Jerry would play this one particular lick that would drop the song right into the groove. You had no warning for that lick, you'd just have to listen closely to what he was doing and come right down on the groove with him. I'd play threes on the bass drum and I'd play 2/4 with my hands, giving the song this nice kind of New Orleans rotation underneath it. That's something we'd play in the first set, but that wasn't just warm-up material. It was something really unique and interesting and a lot of fun to play live. I really took a lot of pride in playing the first sets. There may not have been as much stretching out, but it was still just as cool.

To this day, Deadheads love to discuss our setlists, because—once we built the repertoire—no two sets were ever identical. You could run analytics on them and find all kinds of patterns and translate them into statistics . . . and from those statistics, make tie-dyed tapestries or fractal maps of the stars or create whole new cosmologies and zodiac calendars or weave them into clothing for unicorns or whatever. And while that's pulling a lot more out of it than we ever put into it, some Deadheads have found this kind of analysis to be pleasing in the same way that sports fans might enjoy running numbers with baseball. I can see why that might be engaging, but the truth is that our setlists unfolded out of happenstance and chaos. There was no grand master plan. We would often only write down the first and last song of the second set, maybe some other song as well, and just go from there. It wasn't done with much of a method and most of it was just on the fly. As the spirit moved. I rarely had anything to do with that, directly. I preferred to let the singers figure it out.

After we did that first "Evening with . . ." tour, we went on another great adventure that has since become a part of American history. Or, rather, *North* American history—it took place in Canada. I'm talking about a traveling package tour called the Transcontinental Pop Festival—but you know it as Festival Express, because that's the name of the documentary. The movie hit theaters in 2004. The actual tour took place in the summer of 1970. It was a traveling single-day festival-style event that started in Toronto and went across Canada—but the thing was, the promoters chartered a train to get all the artists and crew from show to show and that became the main attraction for us, more than the gigs themselves. The gigs were cool, too. But you load more than 100 musicians on a train and it's going to be full steam ahead, all right. The other bands on board included The Band, Traffic, Delaney and Bonnie, Buddy Guy, Mountain, New Riders of the Purple Sage and, in one of her last great hurrahs, darn it— Janis Joplin.

One thing I want to comment on is that this was the best I ever saw Janis. She was a friend of ours and had come up onstage with us and we played so many gigs with her band and got to watch her perform a lot— but she was at her absolute best on the Festival Express. She was performing at a super-high level, both on stage and on the train. I think she felt really loose and comfortable during that trek, maybe because so much of it was just for her friends instead of for an audience . . . but she was in her finest element. She and "Marmaduke"—John Dawson from New Riders of the Purple Sage—had a great romance going during the trip. At one point, when the train stopped somewhere for something, a bunch of us disembarked and looked back at the train and we could see Janis and Mamaduke going at it in one of their cabins. They'd forgotten to pull the curtain down, so you could see these two naked bodies making love in there. We started throwing rocks at the window just to fuck with them a little bit, and Janis casually flipped us off and rolled the curtain down and that was the end of that. She didn't miss a beat.

There were more than a dozen cars on the train, including a dining car, but I hardly remember eating at all. There wasn't time for it, between all the drinking and whatever else we were doing. The big theme for the journey was alcohol. We had other things too, but we were running on alcohol, even those of us who weren't usually heavy drinkers. Janis bragged that she got Jerry drunk—which was something worth bragging about.

There were two lounge cars that doubled as music cars. Initially, one was for blues and the other for country, although all lines like that became as blurry as our vision, and just as fast. There were instruments all set up and being handed off or passed around and it was one jam session after another. Janis and Pigpen would drink whiskey together and then sit and sing and it was mind-blowing. I was in awe. I played percussion a little bit here and there, but there were plenty of other drummers there too, and so I didn't have to play. Just being there was my trip. There were all these different, rotating combinations of blues musicians and other types of musicians that were jamming at all times as we hauled ass across the Canadian landscape through all different kinds of country. All these different scenes.

One of the scenes was of a black and desolate landscape; a horrible, dead area. It looked worse than a wasteland and it was black as death. We couldn't figure that one out. Looking back on it now, I'm thinking it must've been the tar sands that are found in Alberta. I wish that weren't the case. These days, we know that if we use oil from tar sands, it will put us past the tipping point of climate change. We're probably past that point already. But tar sands would remove all doubt.

Back on the train, each band member had their own little suite, which leant itself to all kinds of merry craziness. Wasn't that the whole point of putting us on the rails? Or was that just a by-product? The minute we left Toronto, everything shot up to maximum. Everything was turned up to eleven. Everything was going by real fast, both inside the train and outside the windows. It was the ride of our lives.

We made an emergency stop along the way in a desolate area right after we realized that we had run the train dry—we were all out of booze. We thought, "God, there can't be anything here." It might have been Saskatoon. It might have been Chapleau. Maybe it was a Sunday. Regardless, the whole area looked closed. But Canadians must have a really good sense of judgment and value because they put a liquor store near the train tracks and it was the only store still open. With a train full of musicians, everyone threw in some money and had the managers lead an expedition to go into the store and clean it out. We bought every last bottle in the store. Everybody thought that was cool as hell and off we went, down the tracks, full steam ahead. And as if it wasn't wild before, it was now the best party ever.

We had a couple giant bottles of whiskey that were so big, they came with spigots attached. They had to be at least a couple gallons, each. I remember watching Ram Rod get underneath one and pour a steady stream of whiskey straight into his mouth. It had gotten to that point. So things were pretty rich on that trip. We'd stop, get out, play music, and then load on up. All aboard.

There were some troublemakers at the kickoff show in Toronto who wanted the event to become free, like what happened at Woodstock. To keep the peace and spread goodwill we ended up playing a free set the next day in a public park. Then there was another show where only something like 5,000 people were inside a giant stadium. I think that one was in Winnipeg. It must not have been advertised very well. There were also cancellations at one of two of the scheduled cities, because of last-minute permit issues or the like. So we ended up playing at only a few "real" stops during the week and a half journey. The promoters had to have lost their shirts on the whole enterprise, but they can be at peace knowing they created an extremely cool moment in rock history.

I remember one night we all leaned out of our windows because the northern lights had come out for us, even though we weren't way far north. They were all white and beautiful and everyone looked up at them in awe, saying things like, "Look at that one!" "Hey, it's the Marshmallow Man!" "I'm just glad you guys are seeing this too!" And then suddenly Ram Rod got hit with an ember from the old steam engine. Funny, some of the things you remember most. That very night, Ram Rod needed help getting back into his room. Not because an ember had flown into his eye, but because he was so stoned and blackout drunk that he couldn't even walk. He was on all fours, holding up his room key like it was some kind of memento, but there was no way he going to make use of it without assistance. He wasn't the only one in that way.

We celebrated Janis Joplin's birthday at the last stop the traditional way: with birthday cake. In keeping with our own kind of tradition, somebody—within our ranks, I would imagine—had secretly infused the cake with a decent amount of LSD. So it quickly became an *electric* birthday celebration. Allegedly, some generous pieces of that birthday cake made it to the hands and mouths of the local police who were working the show. "Let them eat cake!" (To be fair, I didn't have anything to do with that . . . I was just another cake-eating birthday reveler, that night.)

And that was it for the Festival Express. It was a wonderful time and I think what really made it great was the level of interaction and camaraderie among the musicians, day and night, as we were all trapped on this train careening across the great north. It probably helped that we were all trashed the entire time. Whiskey was in the conductor's seat on that ride.

I hear they tried some kind of Festival Express–inspired revival tour recently, taking a few modern bands like Mumford & Sons across the United States by rail, and I'm sure that was cool in its own right. But there will never be another Festival Express quite like the one from the Summer of 1970.

Shortly after we got back to San Francisco and got accustomed to the ground being solid beneath our feet once again, we went into Wally Heider Studios to record *American Beauty*. I already talked about that album, earlier in this chapter, but it might be interesting to note that we munched on psychedelic mushrooms during those sessions. It was always something with us. And it was usually fun.

I know I also already mentioned that there were a lot of other artists all recording at Wally Heider's during this period, so there was a lot of cross-pollination and a lot of us became session guys for other bands when we weren't actually in a session ourselves. Just like on the Festival Express, there was a lot of camaraderie and a strong sense of community.

The most memorable session that I took part of was with Little Richard. I don't think I've ever really talked about this before. But, yeah, I played with Little Richard in that very same studio and we were playing some kind of rock 'n' roll thing and getting totally wasted along the way. Little Richard enjoyed his distractions and, in those days, we all agreed with cocaine, so there was a pile of white powder on the grand piano. It sort of looked like Halley's Comet had crashed right on the piano. I don't know how much actually got accomplished during that whole thing because, unfortunately, that drug makes you feel like you're doing great, but when it's all gone, you can sometimes scratch your head and think, "Gee, I must've lost my drumsticks," or "Man, we must've forgotten to press RECORD," because there can be little to show for the time spent.

I did some sessions with Jack Casady as well, but when I reach back to recall specifics on that, it mostly just reminds me that our respective bands—the Grateful Dead and Jefferson Airplane—had a softball game over in Fairfax, a small town in Marin where Phil lived. Those games were really something, man. Our pitcher was Sonny Heard, and he wasn't that good a pitcher, but he was a great intimidator. He could scare the shit out of you if you were up to bat. It was hard to hit his pitches because they came with so much verbal abuse, just ridiculous redneck quips that would constantly stream from his mouth.

I'm not sure that we were always matched against the Jefferson Airplane for all of those games, but they kept beating us, which really pissed me off. I don't know how they did it—they must not have been as high as us. Mickey could hit home runs. I think Bobby played first base; he's athletic. Jerry might've played some, here and there, but he was also definitely on the sidelines, yelling.

I slid into third one time and cut my leg somehow and I ended up with a really horrible infection, because my immune system was teetering. It wasn't at its optimum during those years.

I don't remember who played what on Jefferson Airplane's side, I just remember Jack Casady on the field. And I also remember being really pissed off when they would win because I always thought we were a better band than they were, even though they were the more successful one at that point. That all came out during the softball games. But it was all fun and games. It's not like there was a crowd there watching us or anything, and none of us were worth a shit as athletes. The most entertaining parts were the comments from the peanut gallery or the stream of shit talk coming out of the mouths of people like Sonny, who was constantly raving about something or someone. The weather was great and everybody—on both teams—had a good time. But they beat us every time, darn it.

And now for something completely different: death! I'm not making light of loss, it's just never an easy transition. But sure as there were drunken train rides and carefree softball games, there were also heavy prices to pay for our way of life. First soldier down was Jimi Hendrix. He died on September 18 of that year, 1970, of asphyxiation that was attributed to barbiturate use. The details and cause of death remain mired in controversy with an array of choose-your-own conspiracy theories. But the cold hard fact is that Jimi Hendrix died at the age of twenty-seven, at what should've only been the start of an unmatched career.

I can remember one time, we were on a bill with the Jimi Hendrix Experience—maybe at the Fillmore East—and after we played, Hendrix walked right up to me and said, "Hey Billy, nice set." I know that may seem like nothing, but I remember it because of the way he said it and the sincerity in which he approached me. I was really taken aback by how gentle and open he was. He didn't have any of that big-star nonsense, none of that bullshit, and he was really present and genuine.

His drummer, Mitch Mitchell, was also great. A really wonderful drummer. He's left us now, too, unfortunately. Those two cats were the band, really. No offense to Noel Redding, the bassist, but that's the truth. There are famous stories about that. But I can remember that gentle exchange with Hendrix and then watching him blow the house down afterward. That band was so fucking loud. They played with a wall of Marshall stacks behind them, and it's funny that I should call them on that because of where we went with our own sound system a few years later. They got there first.

I don't remember where I was or any of that classic stuff when I first heard that Hendrix was gone. Jumping ahead by a decade, for a moment, I do remember where I was when I first heard about Bob Marley's death. It was May 11, 1981. We were playing a gig at the coliseum in New Haven, Connecticut, and I didn't know anything unusual had happened, but then Weir went up to the microphone and told the audience. I heard his announcement through the monitors and that's how I found out. I don't remember the gig; I just remember Weir doing that and suddenly the world was without the great spirit that was Bob Marley. For whatever reason, finding out about Hendrix wasn't as memorable, even though it had just as much of an impact. It might've mattered even more, because we hadn't experienced death among our peers just yet. But all that would change fast.

As for Janis Joplin's a few weeks later, on October 4, that was really difficult. It hit a lot closer to home because she was a part of our San Francisco family. Also, it was a heroin overdose, and I wasn't aware that she was using heroin. We played a gig that night at Winterland Arena in San Francisco, on a bill that also included Jefferson Airplane and Quicksilver Messenger Service. So, you know—Janis's friends. But nothing was said onstage or anything. It was too heavy.

When people die, you sometimes recall the smallest little detail or some insignificant exchange with them and somehow that becomes an important part of your memory of who they were and how they mattered to you. With Janis, I remember one time we were all staying in the same hotel in L.A.—although I don't think we were playing the same gig—and Janis had this wardrobe case that was a few feet long. She couldn't possibly hang it up in the closet by herself, so she came storming into my room and said,

"Bill, come and help me." I could barely lift that thing up myself, she had so many dresses and all that other far-out stuff that she wore, all packed in there. I guess the point is just that all of us in that scene related to each other on real levels with everyday stuff, and I remember that side of Janis as much as her towering stage presence.

We had another loss shortly after all of this, in the beginning of 1971, but it was of a different nature entirely. As a band, we were still feeling some of the repercussions of being ripped off by our manager. But as that manager's son, Mickey was doomed to suffer the worst of it. He wore it heavy on his shoulders and the weight was beginning to really drag him down. I'm sure it affected his relationship with all of the band members (and beyond), but he and I were kind of a unit within the unit. We were connected. After all, we were the Rhythm Devils.

Thus, it was no easy task when I had to tell him that he needed to take a break and step down from his role as a member of the Grateful Dead. That responsibility fell on me, although I did it at a band meeting with everyone there, at our new office on Fifth and Lincoln in San Rafael. We had to ask him to leave; I had to be the one to do it. This was in February 1971, after we played one of our legendary runs at the Capitol Theater in Port Chester, New York.

Those particular Capitol Theater shows are significant because one of Mickey's academic friends, Dr. Stanley Krippner, performed an ESP experiment using the audience and a remote participant at a hospital in Brooklyn, more than an hour away from the venue. The audience influenced the remote participant's dreams, as they tried to telepathically send him a string of images that were projected onto a screen during the show. The results were published in a reputable psychology journal and the experiment was considered somewhat of a success.

Dr. Krippner was a strange guy. When I met him, he was wearing a sports coat but no tie. I couldn't help but notice that there was a family of ants crawling around his breast pocket. I said, "Doctor, do you know that there are ants in your pocket?" He said, "Yeah, I know." "Cool. All right. Okay. You have ants living in your pocket." I'm not really sure how Mickey knew him, but I think he and Jerry ended up having several lively conversations about science, the universe and the nature of reality. That sounds about right.

But Mickey himself was in bad shape during that run and ended up sitting out for most of it. He had been getting into dark drugs from what I recall, and I think all the pressure on him because of what happened with his father probably led him down that path. This was before either Jerry or I had really gotten into heroin. I had tried it by this point, but it was hardly a regular part of my diet. And it had just killed Janis Joplin. Thank God it didn't kill Mickey Hart. But it did get him bumped from the band he loved the most, for a little while.

It wasn't simply one thing, though: Mickey wasn't able to play at the level he was capable of and it was beginning to affect our performances. He was getting really spacey and just getting so far out there that he wasn't able to deliver the music. It became impossible for me to play with him. It wasn't out of anger or meanness, but we had to address it and deal with it. So our brother Mickey left the band and retreated back to his ranch in Novato and it really strained our relationship for a while, sad to say.

But he didn't fight it. He agreed to step down without any big hassle. I think he was relieved in some ways. Underneath, I know it hurt him like crazy. I know he was deeply hurt by that. But the rest of us couldn't deny that the band didn't sound as good with him in it, during that time, and it would've been hard to argue otherwise. He had stuff he needed to work out and he needed to do that outside of the Grateful Dead.

The first show without Mickey was pretty tough for me. I was used to being a part of an eight-limbed multi-beast and suddenly half of it wasn't there. I had lost some limbs. So the first couple of shows sounded thin to me. I got into playing more demonstratively and playing more stuff. It really led into a developmental period where I learned how to take four limbs and make them sound like eight. I said to myself, "Fuck, man—it's just you. You're open. You can play anything you want." And that was a cool thing. It freed up the music and it added a bounce that was unique to this period. It ended up being a really great period.

"Little Drummer Boy": Palo Alto, around Christmastime. *(Photo courtesy of the Kreutzmann family archives)*

This must be the gun for the ace I had drawn. *(Jim Marshall)*

I have no memory
of this. It could've
been . . . *(Jim Marshall)*

Mickey and me, doing
our best drug-
smugglers imperson-
ation. Circa 1968.
(Rosie McGee)

"Bill Kreutzmann, P.I." *(Jim Marshall)*

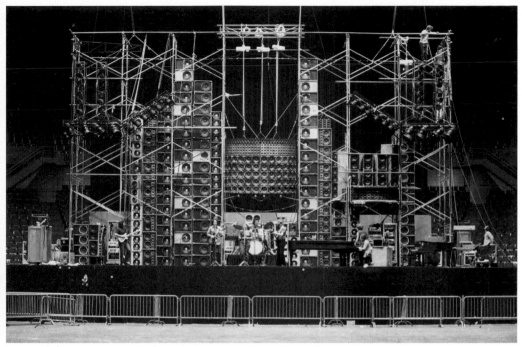

The Wall of Sound, May 7, 1974. Ahead of its time, but I was glad to leave it behind (Vancouver, BC, Canada). *(© Richard Pechner)*

When you're in it, you're in IT. Grateful Dead live, 1977. *(Ed Perlstein)*

That's Jerry's roadie Steve Parish
lighting a joint for Ken Kesey.
Meanwhile, Bill Graham watches
the Rhythm Devils blow past reality.
1977. *(Ed Perlstein)*

"Hey there!" *(Jim Marshall)*

Captured by the sound: Jerry and me, 1977. *(Ed Perlstein)*

On the good nights, our movements were dictated by the music and the music was dictated by magic. December 26, 1979, Oakland, California. *(Jay Blakesberg)*

In the drums' space. With my rototoms and flying bass drums. Live, 1979.
(Ed Perlstein)

Under the spell: Jerry and me on a good night. May 4, 1979, Hampton, Virginia.
(Jay Blakesberg)

Puddled in the moment, with blood, sweat, and tears. Or, at least, sweat. Circa 1979.
(Ed Perlstein)

The Greek Theatre in Berkeley, California, was just across the bridge from our San Rafael headquarters. It was frequently foggy and often chilly—there's no place like home. May 23, 1982. *(Jay Blakesberg)*

Many people said that Jerry Garcia was their hero, but Bob Dylan was ours. Having him join the band never got old. July 19, 1987, Autzen Stadium, Eugene, Oregon. *(Jay Blakesberg)*

Grateful Dead shows were always a celebration—especially if the show fell on Mardi Gras. February 16, 1988, in Oakland, California. *(Jay Blakesberg)*

This is what bliss looks like: October 24, 2006, at the Chicago Theatre, Chicago, Illinois. *(John "Nunu" Zomot)*

During a 7 Walkers show in 2009, with Papa Mali, special guest Karl Denson . . . and a larger than life George Porter Jr. *(Jack Gardner)*

Sometimes the light's all shining on me. *(Photo © Susanna Millman)*

This just says, "I love you." Me and Aimee having fun at an Earth Day festival in Topanga Canyon, California, circa 2011. Our friend Teresa Gardner is in the background. She approves. *(Jack Gardner)*

Seeking the source and finding new horizons with my friends Emmeth Young and Jabar, at the Lebeha Drumming Center in Hopkins, Belize, January 16, 2011. *(Lee Nyhus)*

Performing with George Porter Jr. was always a thrill. And it showed on our faces. This was during a 7 Walkers set at a music festival in 2011. *(Jack Gardner)*

Playing music at the Le Petit Theatre in New Orleans in 2011. There's a lot of voodoo in that city and . . . what's that flying cymbal behind me? *(Jack Gardner)*

An interstellar moment with BK3. Oteil Burbridge on stage left, Scott Murawski on stage right. And alien energy all around. *(Michael Thut)*

My shirt says "Escapist" and if you look at my face in this photo, it is clear that drums are my escape. Or are they just my reality? Either way, it's the best place to be. *(Jack Gardner)*

Not bad for a first show: Billy and the Kids' debut at Warren Haynes' Christmas Jam. December 12, 2014; Asheville, North Carolina. *(Michael Weintrob)*

Catch of the day. With my local fishing buddies, Ryan Cameron and Esteban.
(Eleni Cameron)

Hard at work with my cowriter Benjy Eisen. Well . . . not that hard at work. Moloa'a
Beach, Kauai, March 20, 2014. *(Aimee Kreutzmann)*

One thing about being the only drummer—and this is true today, not just in the '70s—is that it affords you the ability to make really quick changes. You can make an oblique really fast, turning in the opposite direction inside the music and everybody can be right there with you. You don't have to worry about whether or not the other drummer is following you or if you're connected. That kind of thinking doesn't apply.

Meanwhile, as I've alluded to already, the rest of us had been turned on to a drug that didn't serve the music either, and that was cocaine. And it would stay with some of us for the rest of the band's career, in waves and varying levels of intensity. But by the early '70s, cocaine had become the common wash for everything. Somebody always had it. Some people had way too much of it. It became an issue with me later on in our career because I felt like I couldn't perform music onstage unless I had it. Phil got on my case once and said, "Bill, you have a snort before every single song." I went, "Oh, really?" But it was true. I would have my drum tech bring me the cap from a soda bottle or some such low-profile thing, with a bump already laid out for me in it, and he would pretend to make an adjustment on my kit while I would do the bump. This was in between songs, in front of stadiums of people, without anyone noticing. Except Phil, perhaps.

It was like the magic fairy dust for everything, except that it wasn't magic—it was cocaine. The very first time I ever did cocaine was at 710 Ashbury, back when I was still living in the neighborhood. This must've been toward the very end of the Haight-Ashbury days and it's pretty indicative of why that scene collapsed on itself, forming a fireball that crashed into the front gate of the 1970s. The good drugs turned into bad drugs.

I snorted my first line of coke with a guy named "Curly Headed Jim," who suggested that we take a walk down to Haight Street and plug into the street vibe, digging everything we crossed paths with along the way. Before we even made it to the sidewalk, I felt like I was walking on the king's stilts—elevated, though not necessarily high; powerful, though not necessarily in control. I never experienced anything quite like it. I suddenly had another drug that I liked. I also realized, right then, that this new one might not be for the best. Fortunately, we didn't have any money in those days for luxuries like coke, and I wouldn't have known where to score it, anyway. But it came around. That was the problem.

10

As 1971 gave way to 1972, we began to plot our first major tour of Europe; it was a tour that would become one of our most notorious adventures. But first we had some big changes to make on the home front. Including a whole new lineup—with Mickey on leave and Pigpen chronically sick and unable to really pound the keys, an opportunity arose for new blood. And it came serendipitously. Chalk it up to that ole Grateful Dead synchronicity thing.

Around this time, we moved our office to a spot in downtown San Rafael, on the corner of Fifth and Lincoln. We started calling it by the uber-creative and "How the hell did you ever come up with that?" nickname of . . . Fifth and Lincoln. I already mentioned it by name in the last chapter because this is where Mickey's leave of absence became official. Anyway, that office really worked well for us, and we kept it for the rest of our career. Some people might find it interesting that another one of the world's biggest bands, Metallica, have their operations just down the road from there. So while San Rafael might not be seen as a rock 'n' roll destination, don't tell me that town ain't got no heart.

Our office at Fifth and Lincoln was actually an old Victorian house, with bay windows, and all the classic Victorian architecture stuff. It had a large kitchen and we turned all the bedrooms and everything into offices. On just about any particular day, you could come in and find Jerry there, as early as nine in the morning, sitting at the kitchen table, doing whatever—maybe reading, maybe playing guitar, maybe giving an interview, maybe talking to somebody. He was there all the time. It became a hub for all of us. We'd come in and get our mail there—we each had our own mailboxes, as if it was a student union on a college campus or something. It was a meeting place and a place to catch people on the coming or going.

A few years after we got Fifth and Lincoln up and running, we also took over a warehouse just a couple miles away at 20 Front Street that we turned into our permanent rehearsal space. We sometimes called it Club Front because it became the boy's club. It was a place for music, partying, recording, working on cars, whatever. It often felt like we spent more time just hanging out, than rehearsing. Especially in later years; it kept moving in that direction, unfortunately. Toward the end, it became a lot of waiting around; waiting for everyone to show up, waiting for drugs to be delivered, and then waiting for the last person to come out of the bathroom. If it wasn't too late by the time all that criteria was met, sometimes we'd pick up our instruments.

Fifth and Lincoln was our actual business headquarters—all kinds of people came in and out of there, from the visual artists that were working on cover art to music industry types for this, that and the other. Everybody would sort of gather around the kitchen table and hold great discussions. It was the place to do that.

Five, six years into our career it seemed as though, despite all the uncertainty and shape-shifting, we had become established. We would each, individually, still move around some—both literally and figuratively—in the years that followed, but San Rafael was now our permanent home base. In 1971, we weren't quite the business entity that we eventually became . . . but we were on our way.

And yet, Jerry and Mountain Girl didn't have the funds to buy a house that they really wanted out in Stinson Beach, a secluded Marin enclave on the rugged Pacific Coast where he could find inspiration and she'd be able to tend to a few pot plants without anyone noticing. So Jerry decided to manifest the down payment by recording a solo album. That record kicks off with "Deal" for a reason. He was wheeling and dealing, all right.

Because it was a solo venture, Jerry decided that he wanted to play almost all of the instruments himself, except for drums—he enlisted me for that role. He also brought Ram Rod in for those sessions, doing roadie work essentially, running errands and moving around the equipment and stuff. We're both listed as "production assistants" in the credits. He paid Ram Rod the same amount that he paid me and that still bothers me to this day. But that was Jerry's sense of fairness, which speaks volumes for his character, I think.

Musically, for that album, Jerry led the charge but he also conferred with me on certain arrangements. And, of course, he collaborated with Robert Hunter, who provided lyrics. I was awarded songwriting credits on nearly half the album, which was generous of Jerry. Basically, he would come out with this loose idea for a song—oftentimes, he'd be on piano and I'd be in an isolated drum booth—and I'd just start playing whatever felt right for the song on drums. We'd continue jamming in a certain direction until it crystalized into something a little more solid. Then, as if on cue, Hunter would come running out of the control room going, "Okay, I've got it!" and show Jerry some lyrics. When Jerry tried to place them, sometimes it would require a bit of adjusting and we'd tinker with the parts until they all fell into place. It was cool for me to be involved with that side of the process since, when Jerry brought stuff to the Dead, it was usually after that kind of incubation period.

The album, *Garcia,* was cut at Wally Heider Studios in July 1971 and released by Warner Brothers the following January. There are a lot of songs on there that became Grateful Dead mainstays, in addition to "Deal"— we're talking about straight-up classics like "Sugaree," "Loser," and "The Wheel." Also, "Bird Song" is on there, which, to this day, is one of my all-time favorite Dead songs and one of my absolute favorite songs to play live (along with "Dark Star" and "The Other One").

When I want musicians I'm playing with to learn any of those songs, I give them the *Garcia* versions. They're just so good. I had a really great time making that album. Dealing exclusively with Jerry was the most effortless thing in the world. I didn't have to do anything other than be myself. And play.

Cocaine was our special guest throughout those recording sessions, but you'd never be able to tell because everything was very laid back. I have no idea how we were able to do that, because cocaine isn't exactly known for its relaxing properties. Maybe it was just the dynamic between us that made it all so . . . easy.

I'm pretty sure Jerry wasn't into heroin during the making of *Garcia*; as far I know, he hadn't even discovered it yet. But when he did, during subsequent Grateful Dead albums, it could become difficult just to get him to show up, unfortunately. That got to be really old, really fast, for all of us. We wanted to play music with him so badly that we'd put up with it, which—in hindsight—was crazy. Nobody else in the band would've been able to get away with it; at least, not to the extent that he did. But Jerry Garcia was the exception.

It also opens up a moral question that we can talk about now, but we can never truly answer, since he's not with us. There was a certain feeling, toward the end, that Jerry was using the Grateful Dead to finance his drug habit. That's a sad thought. I don't think he ever intended it to be that way or for it to get to that point or to hurt anyone. He was as pure of a musician as they come. But heroin addiction will change a person in ways that are tragic and discouraging.

If the rest of us had just been able to get outside of ourselves for a second, maybe we would've been able to say, "Hey, enough's enough. We can't support this anymore." But not one of us could do that. We had our own addictions, too. For one thing, none of us wanted to stop touring as the Grateful Dead. By that point, we were addicted to the money as much as the music. I think we knew that he would just find other people to play with, and the problem wouldn't have been solved except that, then, there would be no more Grateful Dead. Which is what ended up happening, anyway.

The best we could do—and we did try this, valiantly—was to try to get him into a rehab program. Those things just never worked because Jerry was as stubborn as he was brilliant and he could talk circles around the doctors. They couldn't get through to him. He didn't appreciate anyone who would try to change his ways—just as he would never impose his own views on anybody else, ever. He believed that everyone should be free to do whatever they wanted, no matter what. There was nothing that could be taken away from him, nothing that meant enough to him, nothing that could be used for leverage . . . to keep him away from heroin. That path wasn't the way it was going to work. And, in the end, that proved true—nothing worked.

But during the *Garcia* sessions, everything was still on the up-and-up. I think that record really made a lot of people in the scene or industry take Jerry more seriously as an artist, by himself. It was proof of his genius. It drew attention to his music, without all the extraneous stuff that came along with the Grateful Dead.

A month after that album was released—so, in February 1972—Bobby walked down the solo path, as well. The Grateful Dead had some downtime at that point, leading Bobby to book a block of recording sessions at Wally Heider's. Ironically, Jerry and Phil were also there during those weeks, in the studio next door, working on sessions for David Crosby. I played on some sessions for Crosby, too, at some point. Up in Studio C. That work can be heard on Crosby's solo debut, *If Only I Could Remember My Name*.

As I did with Crosby and Garcia, I played drums for Bobby on his first solo album. But it was a totally different experience. From what I recall, Bobby had most of the songs together already by the time I got there, and he had clear ideas as to what he wanted to do. It was an enjoyable project to work on. He ended up using the rest of the Grateful Dead as his backing band. It was a chance for him to be boss. We just came in and played his songs. They were pretty straightforward and they felt good to play, actually. Some of those songs made it into the Grateful Dead repertoire and we ended up keeping them. By "some," I mean . . . all of them except one.

"Cassidy" was on there and it became a favorite of mine in the Grateful Dead world. It could be a really fun song to play. I always like the songs that weren't engraved in stone, that you could open up and be a little more freewheeling with, in between sections. You didn't have to follow anything that you'd played in that particular spot before—you could do it differently every time and come at it with new ideas and if they worked, they worked. Those kinds of songs are my kinds of songs and some of the Weir songs from that album became like that. "Playing in the Band" is another obvious one.

"Looks Like Rain" evolved into a Grateful Dead staple, and there were a couple instances at some outdoor shows where it started pouring down rain right after we played it. So then, a few of our fans said, "The Grateful Dead can control the weather." That became the rumor for a while. I'm not going to say if that was true or not, but you know . . . science.

In some ways, Bobby's solo album—which he called *Ace* and which was released in May 1972—did the same thing for him that *Garcia* did for Jerry. It made me take Bobby more seriously as a songwriter, and it somehow upped his standing in the band.

Since Mickey was newly estranged from the Grateful Dead, but still in our extended family, he also recorded a solo album in 1972. He called it *Rolling Thunder* in honor of our Shoshone friend and shaman. Perhaps of note, perhaps not: I didn't have anything to do with that one. Jerry did. Bobby did. Phil did. But I didn't. Maybe it was Mickey's turn to be the only drummer.

As for the Grateful Dead proper, a year before all these solo albums were released—back in the Spring of 1971—we started recording live shows with the intent of releasing another live album. That source material became an album that may properly be called *Grateful Dead,* and is more popularly known by the nickname *Skull and Roses.* But the original name was going to be *Skull Fuck.* This was a time long before rap artists like

Eminem numbed concerned citizens to the idea of offensive language in music. Warner Brothers freaked out on us. They said stores would boycott, it and we wouldn't be able to get it on shelves. So we didn't end up calling it *Skull Fuck*. But we did try.

Whatever you want to call it, it ended up being a double-live album that is still a favorite among many fans and it was our first release to be certified gold. It dropped in the fall of 1971. We were in a new state of transition at that time, as we had slimmed down to a five-piece again. But with Pigpen's ailing health (and, perhaps, abilities) preventing him from really taking charge on organ, we had sonic holes that, we felt, longed for keyboard parts. So Jerry brought in a guy named Merl Saunders, whom he worked with on some solo projects, to do a handful of overdubs for the album.

But that still didn't solve the problem of the missing Grateful Dead keyboardist. Merl worked out great for the overdubs and, to be honest, I don't know why we didn't invite him to join the band. I have no idea. Maybe I don't remember; maybe I never knew. We didn't usually talk about those kinds of things. But, again, that still did not solve the problem of the missing Grateful Dead keyboardist.

When Pigpen took center stage during his selected rave-ups, he was a great blues frontman. But the rest of the time, he was more of a background player. Then, in September 1971, he was hospitalized with a bleeding ulcer and some other stuff. None of it good. I didn't know it was that serious, and even though I didn't ask them, I don't think the other guys did, either. We thought it was just a thing that would heal. Three months later, in December 1971, he was able to return to playing shows with us. But there was no denying that he was in a weakened condition and he was never able to fully recover to his old self after that, darn it.

So, we knew we wanted a full-time keyboardist and I knew that Tom Constanten wasn't it. But we didn't have anybody else on our radar, just yet. Some of the guys in the band—namely, Jerry and Phil—became friendly with a whiz kid who was, at the time, enrolled at MIT, named Ned Lagin. Before anyone had met Ned, he had written the band a letter after catching one of our Boston shows in 1969. Jerry and Phil liked what he had to say. I wasn't all that interested in it and didn't really pay attention until Ned came into Wally Heider's to record a piano part for us, for the song "Candyman," which appears on *American Beauty*.

Despite the starkness of that particular record, Lagin's true specialty was his far-out ideas about the integration of electronics and music creation and of using computers—in real time—as an instrument. He was onto something, of course, because that's where music has gone today. He predicted the electronica movement and EDM and I think his vision had a science-fiction element that captured Phil's and Jerry's imagination. But, like T.C., Ned just wasn't the right fit for the Grateful Dead. He played with us a bunch of times between 1970 and 1974 and he did a collaboration with Phil (and, sometimes, Jerry), called *Seastones*, that they would sometimes play live, in between Dead sets. They may have even toured it together. But Ned was never an actual member of the band. He was his own thing.

Meanwhile, the band auditioned a keyboardist named Howard Wales, who laid down some parts for us in 1970 that we ended up using on *American Beauty*. As was the case with Merl Saunders, Wales came to us through Jerry, who played with him in side projects and whom Jerry would continue to work with for many years. I don't know how or where Jerry found him, but Wales had done some session work with James Brown and the Four Tops before we brought him in for *American Beauty*.

His Grateful Dead audition, however, didn't quite work out. He was a madman on the organ but he was just too wild for us. It was too much "Howard" and not enough "Grateful Dead." I still remember the audition, though, because he was such an insanely brilliant player.

Then, around the same time that Pigpen entered the hospital, Jerry gave me a call telling me to get my ass down to the rehearsal space. He said there was a guy down there with him that I simply had to hear. Nobody else from the band was around, but almost immediately after I arrived, I knew that Jerry was right—this guy could *really* play piano. He was one of the best, if not the best, keyboardist that I've had the honor of playing with. The Grateful Dead have played with some really good ones over the years, like Bruce Hornsby and Brent Mydland, but this guy was just outrageous. He was really competent too, in that he could pick up whatever Jerry and I started playing that day, and just run with it. He didn't need to know the material first. He could learn songs before he was even done hearing them for the first time. And he could play just about anything.

His name was Keith Godchaux and he instantly became a member of the Grateful Dead. Legend has it that the whole reason Jerry even gave him a chance was because Keith's wife, Donna Jean Godchaux, approached Jerry at one of his solo gigs at a small club in San Francisco called the Keystone. She went right up to him and declared that her husband was going to be the Dead's new keyboardist. Fate would have it that we needed a new keyboardist, so Donna had Jerry's attention. At her persistent insistence, he decided to give Keith a shot.

Keith liked to play on grand pianos and, once he got comfortable with us, he brought a Steinway on tour and it sounded great. Our technology had finally gotten to a point where we could bring a grand piano out with us, and mic it in a way that would do it justice. We had to isolate it from the other sounds on stage. That was a big deal at the time, and our sound guy, Dan Healy, basically invented the technique for that. Keith's Steinway ended up having a really nice, clean sound. And, man, he was just absolutely brilliant on that piano. We were all really thrilled to have him in the Grateful Dead. His first show with us was on October 19, 1971, in Minneapolis, at the start of a grueling tour that didn't really end until New Year's Eve. He slid right into it like a champ.

Keith grew up in Concord, California—a town in the East Bay, about thirty miles east of San Francisco. As a personality, he was kind of quiet and understated. Much like a lot of people, though, you got some drinks in him and he could become boisterous and act all tough. Unfortunately, he and Donna used to get into some very ugly husband-and-wife arguments. On one occasion, they had a demolition derby in the parking lot of Club Front. They took turns smashing into each other's identical BMWs, screaming all the while. Of course, that was a little disconcerting to us. We didn't think nice cars should be treated like that.

It was a small parking lot, so they couldn't get a lot of top speed. That limitation might've been the only thing that prevented them from killing each other, but they still managed to destroy the cars. I saw the aftermath of it firsthand. Their uncertainty as a couple could be hard on us as a band. I think the bottom line in this conversation is that the music business is damn hard on couples and families. It truly is. Ask any of my ex-wives.

Donna came from Alabama and had worked in the music industry probably before Keith. She had been a professional singer at the influential FAME Studios in Muscle Shoals and sang backup on the original studio recordings of Elvis Presley's "Suspicious Minds" and Percy Sledge's "When a Man Loves a Woman." She also did work for Cher, Boz Scaggs, and others. On New Year's Eve 1971 at the Winterland—just three months after her husband joined the band—Donna came onstage to sing on Bobby's "One More Saturday Night." It was her first time onstage with the Grateful Dead. After that, she was a member, too.

Donna was kind of shy and insecure about singing with the Dead but we all encouraged her to give it her best shot and we supported her in everything, all the way. She did some country tunes . . . but it was Donna, you know? It was cool—sort of.

Donna is a good person and I don't want to hurt her by saying this, but I never felt she fit in with the sound that we were going for. She wasn't integral. The boys had all worked with Crosby, learning how to fill the spectrum with parts and harmonies. There just wasn't enough space for Donna's voice. Sometimes it felt like Donna and Bobby had to compete for vocal attention and that was an issue for me, because it took away from the music.

She sang in tune, but it wasn't that. It was the timbre. Some voices just don't sound great together. Like art—some colors clash. Even though they're all good colors.

Offstage, of course, we all enjoyed having her around. She brought a feminine energy to the band and sometimes even a feminine kind of love. That is to say, we all loved her and some of us got to express that love with her. It was the 1970s, and a special time in American history. And on that note, we split for Europe.

11

Europe. The Next Frontier. When Deadheads talk about the Grateful Dead in Europe, they're almost certainly referring to our infamous Europe '72 tour, and with good reason—there's a lot to talk about. But that historic adventure was preceded by two prior visits abroad—a festival gig in England and a colorful caper in France that had a surprise ending.

The England gig—our first time on a different continent—was a simple one-off. It was on May 24, 1970, in Newcastle-under-Lyme, for an event called the Hollywood Festival.

The only thing that I can honestly say I remember about that one is that I was dating a doctor at the time and she used to give me these giant, incredible shots of vitamins in the morning. They worked—I had tremendous energy throughout the day. She shot me up with so many vitamins, I could taste them. I don't even recall her name now, but I sure do recall those shots. I've also read somewhere in the years since that the Hollywood Festival was supposed to be filmed for broadcast by the BBC, but the film crew became unexpectedly incapacitated. It was rumored that someone—or perhaps some *band*—dosed them with LSD. I wouldn't know any details about that, of course. Also, I'm pretty sure it's the only time the Grateful Dead shared a bill with Black Sabbath. But don't quote me on that.

The festival in Paris—during the Summer of 1971—was rained out. We flew all the way to France from California and decided that we weren't going to let anything rain on our parade—not even rain. One of the promoters, a respected and renowned composer named Michel Magne, offered to put us up at his crib, an old-world castle some 38 kilometers from Paris, in the rural village of Herouville. The famous Chateau d'Herouville. It offered all the amenities that a young, restless rock band from America would want—a swimming pool, a dining hall, a wine cellar . . . and a state-of-the-art recording studio. We ended up staying there for at least a week. It was an incredible property, with ancient buildings that stood watch over an idyllic landscape. Chopin lived at the chateau at one point and Vincent Van Gogh painted it. He's buried nearby.

The rest of the band arrived before I did and when I walked into the chateau for the first time, everyone was already in the middle of a fantastic brunch with Magne and his girlfriend.. She made eyes at me the moment I entered the room. She shot me a look and made damn sure I knew what it meant. I shot her back the same look. It was the start of a short-lived romance, as fleeting as a fling should be, and every bit as passionate. She was the girlfriend of a host who had graciously offered to feed and shelter us and let us record in his studio . . . but I just couldn't help myself.

The affair was wonderful and all, but we had come to the country to play music. We weren't the only band at the Chateau, either. There were some incredible musicians on the grounds who presumably arrived via the same cancelled-festival boat that we sailed in on.

A tremendous jazz drummer by the name of Jerry Granelli was there with a multimedia art group called Light Sound Dimension. Under the direction of artist and light designer Bill Ham, they developed the first true liquid light show, adding another psychedelic dimension to the scene that we were a part of back in San Francisco. We had shared some bills

with them at the Fillmore, so we already knew that Granelli and his bassist, Fred Marshall, were into wild, free jazz. But before joining Light Sound
Dimension, the pair had already made a name for themselves by playing
with Vince Guaraldi.

An outrageous French group named Magma was also around that week,
and I remember being floored by their creativity and chops. Their lyrics
were all written in their own made-up language and they took inspiration
from John Coltrane, classical, and even choral music, superimposing all
three elements into an early version of prog-rock. Really avant-garde stuff.
We all jammed out in the studio and also just hung out and talked music,
life, joys, and sorrows.

What started off as just another afternoon at the Chateau d'Herouville transformed into our first French Acid Test. Magne invited the
village people, while we set up near the swimming pool. We watched with
wide eyes while we played, as colors and shapes melted into the countryside.
That's another "You had to be there" moment that you can now watch
on YouTube. It may have been the best festival cancellation ever, and it
was a lot more satisfying than being on a lineup with Black Sabbath.
(Pink Floyd, Elton John, and Fleetwood Mac also recorded albums there
after our unplanned visit.)

And then there was "Europe '72." A tour that saw us play twenty-two shows
during a fifty-some-day journey. A tour in which we brought along all of our
significant others, our entire crew and *their* significant others, and even some
extraneous hanger-on types from our "Pleasure Crew." The Grateful Dead
paid for room and board for everyone. Everyone. It was high time in spring-
time, full of wild exploits in strange lands. The band played great and it was
nothing but kicks from the very beginning to the very end. One big holiday.

We went to a number of different countries on that trip, including
little-known Luxembourg. We paid return visits to England and France,
but also hit Denmark, the Netherlands, and what was then known as West
Germany for the first time. West Germany, in particular, became a

problem for me. When it came to German policy, and the genocide that led to World War II, I didn't like my German heritage very much. But most of the really exciting, notorious events of this tour happened in that country, and maybe that's because we didn't know what to do with the energy that we felt there, so we let it out in all these weird ways.

The tour kicked off in London, with a couple nights in Wembley. Not at the famous stadium—at the Empire Pool. But the pool was right next to the stadium and it wasn't actually a pool. At least, not since the 1948 Summer Olympics. After those games, it was converted into a small arena. But even a "small arena," for us, in 1972, during just our second visit to England, was a big deal. History and venue buffs take note: The building is now known as Wembley Arena. We played to about 8,000 people, each night.

We had two tour buses and we quickly formed psuedo-alliances based on which bus we were on. You were either one of the Bozos or one of the Bolos. I was on the bus where most of the seats faced backward. That meant I was a Bozo. Most of the band were Bozos. Just a bunch of clowns, really. Our crew clowned around too, but most of them were Bolos. Who knows what their deal was? Or I should say, who knows what their deal *really* was? Never ask a Bozo about a Bolo. General rule of thumb.

The entire tour became a continual running joke as we would try to put each other down for either being a Bozo or a Bolo and, like everything, we took it as far as we could. At one of the gigs, we went onstage wearing wigs and clown masks, perhaps to publicly declare ourselves a band of (mostly) Bozos. Or to spread the Bozo message to the world. It was outreach. It was also all just one big gag. For our own amusement, really.

Part of the whole Zen head trip was that it mattered tremendously which bus you were on but it also didn't matter one bit because both buses were both things at all times. You were either on one or you were on the other. The Bozo bus and the Bolo bus had one thing in common— European bus drivers with really hard edges to them. They could cut right through traffic as if they were on mopeds, and they were skillfully gnarly on the road, zipping us from country to country. They made for great tour guides, too—they knew all the places to make piss calls and whatever else we needed to stop for. We knew nothing about Europe before this trip and I'm not sure that we really learned much of anything at all during it, either. We were too firmly entrenched in our own Bozo and Bolo culture to take in much of the culture surrounding us.

Most of the crew guys had switchblades that they picked up somewhere early on during the tour. That was a huge deal to us because switchblades were legal in these countries and you could buy them in most of the tourist shops. Want to witness a crew of tough guys transform into adolescent boys in an instant? Give them switchblades. It's that easy. They were happy as kids on Christmas morning. But we took it to the next level, of course: As we rode along on the Bozo bus, they took to snorting cocaine off of these razor-sharp switchblades, while the bus careened around hairpin turns at breakneck speed. I'm amazed that nobody accidentally pierced their nose during those proceedings.

I was so into the music on that journey—and making sure that I could be in the moment within that music—that something came over me. I declared something that I can guarantee nobody expected to ever hear from me on that trip: "I don't want any cocaine this tour." And so I didn't do any cocaine during that entire tour. If you listen to the drums from any of those shows, you'll hear that I was rock steady, so I think that was a solid decision on my part. Because regardless of what that drug makes you think while you're on it, the truth is, cocaine is just not a good drug to play music on. It doesn't serve the music. It may be good for other things and I've had my fun with it. But musically, it usually hurts more than it helps.

I made that decision early on during Europe '72, so to kind of balance it out, or as some kind of trade-off, I drank as much beer as I could. My partner-in-crime in that department was Sonny Heard—the loudest, most boisterous equipment guy in our midst. I've already told you a little about Heard, but he was really just a big redneck from Pendleton, Oregon. We would get piss drunk just about every night, after the show, and that was fun. Acid made the rounds, too, but there's nothing wrong with that.

A lot of fun things happened on those buses. And off them. The crew wasn't getting laid, but they all wanted to, of course. One of our roadies, Steve Parish, somehow knew the owner of a whorehouse at one of our stops in Germany, so off we went on an expedition. It was me, Parish, Heard, Ram Rod, and a friend of ours named Slade—a prominent force on the Pleasure Crew. I was the only band member on board; the crew sometimes had wilder adventures than the band and I didn't want to miss out. I wasn't disappointed.

We checked into our rooms at the whorehouse, but the chicks wanted us to wear rubbers, just to get head. We didn't like that. We all went, "What the fuck?" We were from California; we didn't wear rubbers. Especially not for blow jobs. That was crazy talk. Kids, take note that this was way before HIV or AIDS became a concern; sure, there were other STDs to be had, but it was a different time. Well, not in this whorehouse. Some of the other guys were experiencing other difficulties with their girls, like being misled into paying up-front for false promises. Even though we were in different rooms with different chicks, we almost all started yelling in unison. We could hear each other through the walls. We started yelling the proprietor's name, Hans. Like, "We're going to kill you, Hans, you motherfucker!"

We were wound-up rock 'n' roll animals on the loose. We stormed out of the place and threatened to demolish the building as we left. We went into the bathrooms, turned over garbage cans, and lit the contents on fire. We punched holes in the walls. We yelled a lot of things. We were hauling ass down the stairs when Ram Rod saw this big fucking picture, a two-by-three-foot frame of this drop-dead gorgeous naked chick, and he instantly fell in love with her. So he grabbed the fucker off the wall and took it with us, right in the middle of our getaway attempt. He held it tight, under his arm, as we ran full speed down the street, doing our best not to cause any attention. We began to hear those European sirens going off. The proprietor called the authorities immediately, of course. Later we learned that he accused us of threatening the girls with our switchblades. That was rubbish, of course, but it would be their word against ours and we didn't want to have it out like that.

As we were leaving, a group of Japanese business men, in suits, with cameras around their necks, were all on their way in. We shoved past them, knocking one or two to the floor, on our way out the door.

We hauled ass down the street and suddenly we saw a taxicab about a block away. The cabdriver saw us, jumped out of the car, opened his trunk just in time to take the picture from Ram Rod and slam it in there. "Get in the car right now!" he yelled. He was American. We lucked out. Our American cabdriver drove us away just as the cops came screaming by us with those blue lights on. We got away by a matter of moments. Naturally, Parish heard back from Hans later on that night. He wasn't too happy. What really upset him, I think, was that the other johns freaked out after we flipped out. They dipped out in the middle of the chaos. The other thing was that as soon as the police showed up, they started arresting the Japanese business guys . . . for inciting a riot.

I was already in trouble with Susila, as far as mingling with other girls went, because of something that happened after the second night of the tour. At the Empire Pool. A woman named Christine Keeler was in the audience. I didn't know it at the time, but later I learned that she was responsible for taking down England's Conservative government back in 1963, because of a scandal known as the Profumo Affair. She had been fucking the British Secretary of State for War, John Profumo; she was also fucking both a Russian spy and some hotshot drug dealer during the same time period. It was that last one, the drug dealer, who fucked it up for Profumo, when he got busted for shooting a gun aimed at Keeler's front door. I'm not sure what instigated that, but after that incident, Keeler's personal life became public knowledge. Her affair with Profumo came to light. He was forced to resign.

When Keeler strolled backstage at our Empire Pool gig, nine years after the scandal, she was dressed in a short red dress that was tight as hell. Obviously looking for another scandal. It would've been impossible not to notice her. There was an instant attraction between us and even though Susila was there, I did something that was very rare for me—I got her phone number. I used it to call her and we made plans to meet up at her place, later that night. I left Sue back at the hotel and headed over. There were a couple cars parked outside; authority types, in suits, that looked like they were on some kind of a stakeout. "Get in here, quick," she said. So I did.

I went over there with Kidd Candelario, an indispensable member of the crew and my wingman for the night. He hooked up with her hot friend and I went off with Christine. Well, I can tell you that I made a mistake. I was dismally disappointed. When she took off that hot red dress, she insisted on hiding under the sheets. I became suspicious. I was a hippie musician from San Francisco, used to natural women with soft, lovely breasts that they weren't ashamed of. Christine had giant, fake boobs that were as hard as coconuts. They just weren't very pleasant. Or sexy. I didn't even get off that night. I couldn't—her body looked a lot different adorned in that red dress. I should've left the rest to my imagination because my imagination, at least, had it right.

Meanwhile, Kidd got the better end of the deal with Christine's friend, or assistant, or whoever that other girl was. It was a disaster for me, on all fronts: I got back to the hotel and, naturally, Susila was more than a little pissed off at me. And that was just the beginning of the tour.

Most of the other incidents didn't involve girls, necessarily, but were still about boys behaving badly. The landscape in Bremen, Germany, looked like a scene from a postapocalyptic horror film. Under Nazi rule, Bremen was the site of a concentration camp. During World War II, both U.S. and British air forces bombed a number of targets there and British troops eventually captured the city. That happened more than a quarter century before we arrived, but the memory was still there—on both sides. As was the destruction; the aftermath of war.

We were there to play just a song or two for a television show called the *Beat Club*, but we decided to play a full set for the cameras, and we also decided to take acid for it. We took something else too; I don't recall the specifics, all I know is that it got us unbelievably high. Our hotel that night was in an old classic building and I'm guessing that maybe they had to rebuild or repair some of it after the bombings. After the show, we were in one of those collective moods where we were all just fucking around, jacked with the same kind of energy we had the night of the McGovern hotel scandal.

For some reason, for me, that translated into punching a mirror in the elevator on the way to my room. Well, that wasn't a very good thing to do. The mirror was an old antique. It survived the bombings . . . but not Bill Kreutzmann bombed on acid. The hotel was really pissed at us for that one. To get even with us, they managed to steal one of our acoustic guitars. It was some kind of trade for the broken mirror. They didn't break it or anything—they just took it. This was before eBay, otherwise it may have shown up in some rich hobbyist's garage studio.

At another point, back in my room, I was thinking about crawling through my window because it opened out onto a roof. I looked outside at just the right moment to catch sight of a telephone falling through the air and crashing right outside my window. That was our doing, as well. Our sound guy, Dan Healy, was a couple flights up and couldn't get the hotel phone to work, so he ripped it out of the wall and threw it out his window. We never really did the cliché-rock-star thing of tossing TV sets out of windows; we mostly just stuck to tossing out bad ideas, drugs, and the occasional telephone instead. Oh, sure, we kicked a few hotel televisions around in our day, but I don't think any of them learned how to fly. For one thing, a telephone is much lighter and easier to chuck than a TV set. So is ice cream, as we were about to find out.

When we were in Paris, a French revolutionary type harassed us because he wanted free tickets. He must've heard accounts of Woodstock or Festival Express and surmised that demanding free tickets was a very hip, very revolutionary, very rebellious thing to do. And attainable too. Except, not for him. He was on the sidewalk in front of our hotel, and instead of granting him his wish, someone in our crew dumped ice cream out of their hotel window, right onto the kid. It ruined his day . . . and his fancy jacket.

The next morning, however, when we left for our gig in Lille—about 140 miles up the road—we discovered, through empirical evidence, that the little fucker had filled the gas tank of our equipment truck with something that was . . . not fuel. We looked into every available solution but, all told, we weren't able to get our gear up to Lille on time, so we weren't able to play the gig. I stayed back at the hotel with Jerry, Pigpen, Keith, and Donna. Meanwhile, Phil and Bobby were our ambassadors. Florence, Phil's girl, was fluid in French and went with them as our translator. They headed over to the venue to inform the promoter and break it to the crowd (with the sworn promise that we'd be back and make it up to them).

If only it were that simple. The crowd didn't like that announcement one bit and they turned on Bobby, Phil, and Florence, who retreated backstage and then were forced to make a dramatic escape through the window of the second-story dressing room, climbing down a drainage pipe and jumping onto an escape vehicle in the nick of time. Meanwhile, I'm sure I was relaxed and enjoying the casual downtime back at the hotel.

We did make up that Lille date and it turned out to be a free show, so that little rebel fuck-face got his wish after all. Although I doubt he got a chance to enjoy it. Like most of our free shows, it was all done in stealth mode. Nobody knew about it until it was already happening. This was before social media, so . . . it was "catch us if you can." It was a cold and overcast day and the stage wasn't sheltered. There was a little bit of rain but it was certainly psychedelic.

That make-up gig in Lille is something I call an "endurance gig" because, fun as it was, I had something else on my mind the entire time. As a hobby, Phil and I had been casually getting into car races. Since we were already in France, we decided to spend some free time catching the big Formula One race in Monaco—the famed Monaco Grand Prix.

Our friend Sam Cutler, who, if you remember, we snatched from the Rolling Stones after Altamont, was our tour manager for Europe '72. Cutler had a rental car, which Phil and I commandeered as soon as we finished the afternoon show at Lille. Phil, Florence, Susila, and I all jumped in the car. My seat came with a steering wheel. So I drove like hell through Paris, at breakneck speeds, so that we could make our flight. It was getting down to the wire but we were zigging and zagging our way to the airport, and we weren't talking much, because we were all really high on acid. So we communicated without having to say a lot out loud. Phil was a backseat navigator; a human GPS. He'd just say, "Next street, left" and BAM—we'd career off to the left. "Next street, right." He'd give me just enough lead time to figure it out. But I also had to beat all the Parisian drivers, who are famous for keeping tourists locked in an eternal round-about around the Arc de Triomphe. There was none of that for us. We beat every car around every turn with needlepoint precision, a testament to time spent with Neal Cassady, perhaps, and also a testament to LSD super-powers. We didn't jump out of university buildings thinking we could fly. But we did get to Orly Airport just in time to hop on a plane that could. We didn't have time to return the car to the rental agency or any of that tedious crap, so we left it right there in the parking lot. I called that audible as we pulled into a space. "Okay, everybody, we have to make one little error— we have to abandon the car here and get the fuck out of Dodge," I said. "Maybe we'll own a Ford Cortina after this."

For some reason, though, I reached under the driver's seat and, holy shit—I found a package under there. And, holy shit—it had a big bag of cocaine and another big bag of hash in it. This was during a more inno-cent time of air travel where going through security wasn't quite as intim-idating as it is these days, but still—I didn't plan on getting busted for drug smuggling, especially when they weren't even my drugs. But if we left them in the car, we would've almost certainly gotten busted that way. Someone would've found it. So I thought, "Well, fuck. We have to take this with us. And it's not even mine, damn it." Also, I wasn't too happy about the idea that I had just sped recklessly through all of Paris—on acid—with a large stash of illegal drugs beneath my seat. That could've been serious.

When Cutler was running the game for us, it wasn't unusual for him to be in control of the band's master stash, doling it out to us as needed. I'm sure he'll deny that charge, but it doesn't matter. The proof, with this one, is in the pudding—it was his rental car. He gave it to us. And there it was.

Susila put it in her purse and dumped it in the first garbage can we could find, inside the airport. I was all nerves until then. We weren't even halfway through our first big tour of Europe; getting popped for smuggling that much weight wouldn't have ended well. It would've been heavy.

Remember, I stayed away from cocaine that tour. I had rewired myself to be against it for the season. So to be stuck with the devil in a package as we were about to go through airport security in a foreign country, while still tripping—really freaked me the fuck out. I recognized the irony of the situation, given all the coke that I shoveled up my nose before this, but no bandit wants to be busted by the bank that they didn't hit.

Disasters averted, we made it to Southern France with seconds to spare. We sprinted into the F1 race in Monaco as if we were in the race ourselves. That's when the day's biggest challenge presented itself: fighting with Spaniards and getting into elbow wars with the general admission masses, as we struggled to maintain a decent position along the fence, just so we could glimpse those fucking cars for two seconds at a time as they flew by. And every time they did, we instinctively shouted, "Yeah!"

The Bozos and the Bolos continued on down the road. We didn't take any other field trips like that—at least, I didn't—during Europe '72, but most of the cities we stopped in were brand new to us. It was automatic sightseeing, just by virtue of us being there. The Bozos and the Bolos. The biggest deal was just trying to find food—most of the restaurants along the way kept weird hours compared to American eateries. And by weird, I mean . . . horribly inconvenient.

After the tour, we released a live album called *Europe '72*—a compilation of some of our hottest moments during that tour. It was slimmed down to fit on three vinyls (and, eventually, two CDs). But the entire tour was hot. So, in 2011, Rhino Records released a box set containing all twenty-two shows on CD—it takes up seventy-three discs. I went back and listened to them and it's really one of our best tours, ever. The recordings don't lie. My own playing was solid throughout the entire tour and I'd like to thank the wise man on my left shoulder for that one. His persistent voice wouldn't shut up, as he insisted that I keep my nose clean for the journey.

I did that, and I was able to have as much fun as any other Bozo. And ten times as much as any Bolo, that's for sure.

I loved being the only drummer in the band. And with Keith now on keyboards, I was getting high off the music. Keith really complemented Jerry and that worked out incredibly well—the music was able to get really, really out there. Just the way I like it.

A year before, in 1971, we explored Americana through *Workingman's Dead* and *American Beauty*. But playing American folk songs in Europe was less exciting to us than the idea of test driving our old Acid Test vehicles in front of European audiences. Europe had a lot of moments that we were able to stretch to infinity. That tour was really sponsored by "The Other One" and "Dark Star."

As for the cowboy songs, like "Me and My Uncle," "El Paso" and the others, well, they were a laugh for me. I played them, but I didn't take them seriously. They were in cut time. Real easy to play on autopilot. Whereas with the other ones, like "The Other One," you could get out of yourself and even forget what song you were playing because you were that free. When that happened, I knew it was right. We were able to tap back into our group mind for excursions where we could do anything that we could think of, on the spot, the moment we thought of it. Our imagination was our only limitation. Any experimental idea that we could think to play, we played. And we made it work. I love the songs that let us do that. They're the best. The cowboy songs were almost tongue-in-cheek by comparison. At least for me.

We continued to tour Europe from time to time, for the rest of our career, but none of those tours matched Europe '72. That was the big one. As it was happening, we knew we'd be talking about it for years to come and, sure enough, here we are.

Well . . . okay . . . so, there is one story from our Europe '74 tour that stands out. I remember the night, but not the tour. Isn't that crazy? As I look at the tour dates—September 9 through 21, 1974—not much rings a bell. We played three nights in London; a one-off in Munich, Germany; and then three nights in France. That's a short tour and it was scaled down considerably from the extravagance of 1972. That must have been a business decision—it costs a lot of money to bring everyone you know on a six-week European vacation. For the Europe '74 tour, we weren't in buses. We rented cars. I drove a Mercedes but I'm not even sure who rode shotgun. We're talking about twelve days, once upon a time, in a land far, far away.

There were no Bozos or Bolos that tour, but I insisted on being a bozo anyway, I guess. The tour wrapped up with a two-night stand in Paris and, after one of those nights, I decided to go out partying with some people that I didn't know very well. Locals, I think. They were at the gig but they weren't from our scene and I didn't speak much French. They weren't really friends.

Regardless, they took me to this club, a speakeasy with no name on it. It was one of those things where they knocked on the door and it slid open, and they must've known the password or something because we were let in. All the tables were low and there was a dance floor over to the side. We were seated but instead of bringing us drinks, they brought us fifths of booze. Bottle service, I guess, is what that's called now. There was already a big bottle of rum on the table that I quickly got into. Oh, and I was really high on acid. Are you surprised?

The thing about acid is that you can drink and drink on it and not realize how drunk you are until hours later, because your brain is more concerned with the fact that you're on acid. Those two intoxicants fight for attention from your head, and the acid wins, every time. So, I must've been really drunk and I certainly was really spun, and I decided that it would be a good idea for me to get up and dance. But I couldn't dance. I started falling down. It was embarrassing—I wasn't trying to make a scene, but it was pretty obvious that the Ugly American was getting a little too ugly.

The people who brought me there disowned me, or at least distanced themselves: "We don't *really* know him." Someone showed me the door.

"Fine." I went outside for some fresh air. The door shut behind me and I started walking down the street. But, when I tried to come back, I couldn't find the club. It didn't have a sign and I hadn't thought to log any landmarks. Maybe it was the acid, maybe it was the booze, but the fuck if I knew where I was.

They wouldn't have let me back inside, anyway. So instead I was on the street, by myself, and probably more of a mess than I'd care to admit. That wasn't the problem. The problem was that I didn't know the name of the hotel where I was staying. I didn't know where I was and I didn't know where I was going. And I was high on acid and drunk on rum. Speech was becoming difficult. Not that it mattered—I couldn't speak the language anyway.

What do you do in that kind of situation? Well . . . I knew if I could hot-wire something that I could find my way back to the hotel eventually. Retrace my steps. I saw a moped leaning against a storefront, so I decided to test my little plan. I couldn't get it to start, though. I was so stoned that there was just no way I was going to be able to hot-wire anything, much less drive it. I started to get really frustrated. "Okay," I thought, "I need to get some attention. I don't care if it's from the cops. Hell, I'll get a policeman to come. I don't give a shit."

I lifted the moped up and crashed it into the store's front window. It made a horrible noise. But then, silence. Not a dog barking, not a rat scurrying, nothing. Something was weird. I mean, something, not just me, not just the acid. I had just smashed a window with a fucking moped for chrissakes and it went totally unnoticed by the universe. That didn't seem right to me.

I started walking. Finally, a car came down the street. Yes! Something! A big, black Mercedes. As it passed me, I slapped the trunk with an open hand, as hard as I could. The car stopped. Then it backed up a few feet. Then the driver got out. Oh fuck. The guy was twice my size and he was not amused. I didn't know if he spoke any English and I didn't really care to find out. He must've been a good twenty, thirty yards from me. I was just standing there on the sidewalk. He started walking toward me. I didn't know what to do next, but I remembered some book I read about New York gangs where they would rip the antennas off cars and use them for street fighting. A makeshift weapon. So I did the most obvious thing I could think of: I ripped the antenna off a parked car on the street—it broke off easy—and I started advancing toward the guy with this antenna in my hand. I must have looked a lot scarier than I felt inside, or else maybe I looked just about as crazed as I felt. Miraculously, the guy turned around and ran back to his car. I couldn't believe it. What luck. In truth, he could've ripped my head off and beat me all to hell. Easily. And I knew that.

I didn't really have a plan in mind, so I just turned around and started walking in the other direction. A new start. I probably walked right past the speakeasy, which I never could find. I ended up at an intersection where I managed to flag down a taxi. Finally. I told the driver that I had no idea where my hotel was, or what it was even called, but I held up my key. He recognized it. Everything was about to turn out fine.

"What have you been doing tonight?" he asked me. I decided to be honest. "I'm the drummer from the Grateful Dead and I'm totally lost right now." I'll never forget his response: "Well, I don't like the Grateful Dead very much. But I'll take you to your hotel." Classic.

The next day, student riots erupted in that neighborhood. It was on the Left Bank of Paris. The hip section of town. The theory is that all the cops and all the students were busy preparing for a big showdown, so nobody was out on the streets the night before. It probably wasn't very safe. There could've been people like me out there. Or the guy in the big, black Mercedes. That's one of those things, though, where—without even realizing how much luck was involved—I probably escaped with my life. Thank you, student rioters. Thank you, streets of Paris.

The only other thing I took from that tour is the sweet memory of a girl I met in a hotel bar at one of our stops. I don't remember the hotel. I don't even remember the country. But I remember going to the lobby bar and seeing this stunning lady there, sitting all by herself. There wasn't a guy within ten feet. Everybody at the bar was wrapped up in something else. I made a beeline for her and it may have been the smartest thing I did that entire tour. It was certainly a lot smarter than smashing a moped through a window. After chatting it up at the bar for a while, we went upstairs to my room where she immediately made her intentions clear. They weren't what I had in mind at first, but I went with it: "I want to take a bath with you," she said. Then she got out her lipstick and asked me to paint her body while we were in the tub. I had never painted a naked body before, but it didn't take me long to get the hang of it. I started painting her boobs and stuff and it was great. I felt like Monet in a sea of water lilies. We made love in the bathtub, then in the bed, and then in the morning she just got up and left. I missed her for days after that. But at least we had that one night because, otherwise, it would've been just another tour.

12

When we came back from that first Europe tour—in 1972—we were riding the crest of a wave that, like all waves, we knew would break and tumble before rolling back out to sea. But for the moment, we were poised for flight, wings spread bright, that whole thing. We were full force and tits deep, hitting grand slams wherever we went, even though we had to keep making slight adjustments to the roster. Pigpen had been on and off sick leave for a while by this point. He was on active duty in Europe—some nights more-so than others—but when we returned home, he needed rest and recovery. He did come down to Los Angeles with us for a one-off at the Hollywood Bowl on June 17, but that night would be the last time Pigpen performed live with the Grateful Dead.

We toured heavily for the rest of the year. We were down to one drummer and one keyboardist. The audiences embraced Keith as the new piano player. Nobody forgot about Pigpen, but we had changed so much as a band since our beginnings, seven years earlier, that long-term fans were used to a certain amount of fluidity. It was a physical manifestation of the very ideals expressed in our music, which embraced an improvisational nature. So Pigpen's absence left us with a hole in our hearts, but not in our sound.

Pigpen had been living all alone in the small community town of Corte Madera, a Marin County nook that's nestled between Mill Valley (where I was living) and San Rafael (where we had band headquarters). So he was close by. Susila and I would go visit him sometimes. It was obvious how sick he was. He was really sick.

On March 8, 1973, I was at home with Susila when I got the call. It was one of our managers, Jon McIntire. Pigpen was dead. Something about a gastrointestinal hemorrhage. Bleeding. Complications. And so on. Unfortunately, it didn't come as the biggest surprise.

Let me restate that: Death is always a surprise. Your mind never gets accustomed to those phone calls and your body never adapts to handling that kind of news. It's always a shock, even when you know it's coming. I think I knew it was coming. "But still. . . ." I can't recall the actual funeral or the large, informal gathering that Bobby had at his house afterward. I was in mourning. We all were.

Pigpen's death was juxtaposed against the backdrop of the Grateful Dead's rising success. There weren't exactly any windfalls or anything coming down in big, giant amounts, but money started coming in steady, at least. Susila and I bought a house in Mill Valley right before the Europe '72 tour, and we decorated it with nice things. And I didn't have to drive the band around in a station wagon anymore—we could all afford cars.

In fact, I went out and bought an Alfa Romeo 1750 GTV, a fancy Italian sports car that had a lot of class to it. I loved that car. One day, probably in 1973, I was washing it and got a minor injury on my hand that required stitches. The band put me on the injured reserve list for a few weeks, so I split for the Southwest with Susila, just for kicks. Arizona and thereabouts. We picked up a bunch of decorations for our new house and smuggled a cactus or two back with us, but overall, there was nothing to it. The point is that we never made big plans for bigger getaways. The only vacations we took were impromptu and usually happened by default. I played music for a living, which meant that I had fun for a living. I never even thought about going on vacation because I loved my job too much. All that any of us in the band wanted to do was to play music, so why not play music all the time? And that's exactly what we did.

Business was booming but the bigger it got, the less I paid attention to it. I paid attention to the beat, to the rhythm, to the music. Meanwhile, our managers had managers. As always, we had people around us who tried to hatch crackpot schemes, and because we were the Grateful Dead, we listened to all of them and even agreed to give some of them a shot. One such endeavor that gets brought up a lot in books and stuff was launching our own record label, Grateful Dead Records, and its subsidiary, Round Records. That was a Ron Rakow production, I'm afraid, and he did the same thing with it that he did with the Carousel Ballroom—he took an airship the size of the *Hindenburg* and brought it to a similar, fiery fate. It ended in smoke and ashes.

Really, the only thing worth remembering in regard to our record label was the crackpot proposal for distribution: we briefly kicked around the idea of selling our albums exclusively from ice cream trucks. We must've been really high when we entertained that one—like, Cheech & Chong high. The plan went "up in smoke." So you can see why maybe giving us control over our own record label wasn't the most prudent idea . . . even if it did lead to some "nice dreams" and laughs along the way.

The truth is that the record companies, in those days, were so powerful and so locked into the machine of industry, that launching an independent, band-operated label would've been damn near impossible for anybody to do with any kind of real success. Nowadays, the rules of the game have been so radically changed by digital distribution that running your own label is a hell of a lot easier. But, back then, we would've been better off selling actual ice cream from those trucks.

Talking of bad business decisions, our lawyer, Hal Kant, convinced us at some point to sign a contract that activated a Last Man Standing policy. I don't know if anybody's ever talked about this before, but the idea behind the Last Man Standing was that the last living member of the Grateful Dead would get everything. Under that policy, when a musician died, his rightful royalties wouldn't go to his estate; instead it would be put back in the pot until, eventually, there was only one man left standing. And that person would get it all. Now, how do I say this? Let's start with: "What the fuck kind of idea is that?" We've since changed it and made it fair for the families, but over the years there's been some black humor about that policy. (The Grateful Dead's licensing arm, Ice Nine Publishing, still has an active version of the Last Man Standing clause.)

We made some questionable business decisions and we couldn't sell records, but we sure could sell tickets. We sold around 150,000 tickets for a single show at a racetrack in Watkins Glen, New York, on July, 28, 1973. Yes, and more than 600,000 people ended up coming out for it. The lineup was just us, the Allman Brothers, and the Band. That show, called the Summer Jam at Watkins Glen, made it into the Guinness Book of World Records for what, at the time, was the largest audience ever assembled at a rock concert. In fact, that record may still hold today, at least in the U.S., and some have even proposed that it was the largest gathering in American history. Originally, the bill was supposed to just be the Dead and the Allmans, but our respective camps fought with the promoter over which band would get headliner status. The solution was that both bands would co-headline and they'd add a third, "support" act.

The friendly ("-ish") competition between us and the Allman Brothers carried through to the event itself. And yet, the memory that I'm most fond of and hold most dear from that whole weekend was jamming backstage with Jaimoe, one of the Allman's drummers. We were just sitting in the dressing room, banging out rhythms, and that was a lot of fun for me. Jaimoe backed Otis Redding and Sam & Dave before becoming a founding member of the Allman Brothers, where he remains to this day. He's a soulful drummer and just an incredible guy who is impossible not to like.

As for the show itself, it is a well-known fact that the Grateful Dead always blew the big ones. Watkins Glen was no exception. However, we still got a great night of music out of it—the night before. The show took place on a Saturday, but by Friday afternoon there were already about 90,000 people in front of the stage. I've heard others place that number closer to 200,000. Either way, the audience was already many times the size of any of our regular shows, and the show was still a full day away. The only duty we had on Friday was to do a soundcheck, and even that was somewhat optional. The Band soundchecked a couple of songs. The Allman Brothers soundchecked for a bit. Then, perhaps spurred on by our friendly rivalry, we decided to one-up both bands by turning our sound-check into a full-on, two-set show. Naturally, without any of the pressure of the "official show" the next day, we really let loose and played a good one. There was an eighteen-minute free-form jam that eventually made it onto *So Many Roads,* one of our archival box sets. It's good music, all right, and it still holds its own.

On the day of the actual show, we had to fly into the venue via helicopter because the roads were all backed up, like what happened at Woodstock. People left their cars on the side of the road and walked for miles to the gig. I remember looking down from the helicopter and seeing the most incredible impressionist painting, a Monet of heads, shoulders, tie-dyes, baseball caps, and backpacks, packed front to back. You couldn't see the ground for the crowd. To this day, I've never seen anything else like that.

Nowadays at large music events and festivals, they have golf carts for artists and crews to get around, but back then they used little motor scooters. Early, during the day of our supposed "soundcheck," I commandeered one of these scooters and, because the venue was an actual racetrack, I decided to do a lap. This was before the gates were opened. The scooter went maybe fifteen or eighteen miles an hour, something stupid like that, and it took forever just to do one lap. But I did it. And that's when I first started to get a feel for the scale of the event and just how large it was.

During the Summer Jam itself, I watched the other bands play and I honestly thought the Allman Brothers played better on the big day than we did. As for the Band, well, they always sounded great.

I was friends with their drummer—the late, great Levon Helm. At some point, he invited me to his barn. I stayed there about a week and listened to the Band run through a lot of music. They were all so into it. They were never more than an arm's length from their respective instruments and the music never stopped. Watching them work was as entertaining as watching them play live. They were hip behind the scenes.

In 1983, the Grateful Dead invited a newly-reformed—and Robbie Robertson–less—version of the Band to open for us at our New Year's Eve show. I made a lot of phone calls to Levon throughout the fall, convincing him to sign on for that one. He finally said yes. That made me happy. The Band played some other really big nights with us as well. But Watkins Glen is the iconic show that everyone remembers. It's historic.

Meanwhile, back in the Bay, we had a team of crack scientists and sound engineers who, under Owsley's vision and Healy's leadership, were trying to create the next advancement in live sound presentation, for the benefit of our audiences. They were working on the frontier of live sound. It can be said, accurately, that throughout our entire career, the Grateful Dead organization was responsible for some genuine innovations in concert sound (lighting, too). We had people on salary working on research and development for all of that stuff. Some of the ideas and practices that we came up with are now industry standards. For example: calibrating each individual venue. Our sound guys even sold various venues our sketches and diagnostics of their room's acoustics.

All throughout 1973, we had our team working on a new beast of a sound system. After a beta test at a hometown show (Cow Palace, San Francisco, March 23, 1974) the Wall of Sound made its official debut in Reno, Nevada, on May 12. Fully assembled, the Wall measured something like forty feet high and almost eighty feet wide. That was the indoor version. Outdoors was bigger. We had more than 600 speakers. The Wall of Sound was Owsley's brain, in material form. It was his dream, but it spawned a monster that rose from the dark lagoon of his unconscious mind. Owsley let it out of the cage so that it could sprawl out on the stage with us, night after night—a creature that was supercool to look at, but impossible to tame.

Because the sound reinforcement was coming from a wall behind us—instead of a traditional PA off to the sides and in the front—the system had to use deferential microphones in order to avoid feedback. Each singer had two microphones that were out of phase from one another. They would only sing into one of them. Any sound picked up by both microphones would be cancelled out by the other, thereby eliminating feedback and bleed. In theory, it works. Technically, it works. But in actual use, it just sounds terrible.

That afternoon in Reno, as I made the walk to the stage and saw this thing fully assembled, I had some concern about a safety issue. I was looking at this monumental edifice of speakers, this statue to hooliganism in the sound universe, and it was utter madness. Just madness. There weren't any floor monitors. Everything that you heard, from vocals to the instruments, you heard from right there on stage, coming out of the Wall. It made a row of Marshall stacks look like cotton candy by comparison. Each instrument got its own stack of speakers, on each side of the stage. Phil even had a quadrophonic pickup system on his bass, which enabled him to direct each of his four bass strings, individually, into different speaker towers. The Wall's center cluster was designated for vocals. We're talking about two tons of speakers, suspended above the drums. As I walked to the stage that blustery day in Reno, the whole center section swayed significantly in the wind. Four thousand pounds of speakers, directly above my head. They were hung from one single winch and if something went wrong or if the speakers ever broke free, I would be as flat as a penny on a railroad track. Dust to dust. I insisted that they redesign the rigging with two additional winches, for extra insurance. Then, at my request, they rigged it from the corners instead of just the middle, to achieve greater stability and prevent it from swinging every time there was a gust of wind. It was a lot better that way, but still, it never stopped being disconcerting to look up and see all that weight above you, knowing that it was all assembled and disassembled on a daily basis, leaving much room for fault.

But even beyond that, there were just too many problems with such a cumbersome system. It was really hard to get with the sound. There was so much sound everywhere that the system wasn't very accurate, and it frequently made things difficult for me. Our performances, however—throughout 1974—had many great moments. A lot of those Wall of Sound shows remain fan favorites.

As much as we played out during '73 and '74, we also played in—I mean, we recorded in the studio since, after all, we did own a record company now and record companies need product to survive. In August 1973, fresh from a two-night stand with the Band at Roosevelt Stadium in New Jersey—and with soil from Watkins Glen still on our sneakers—we booked about a month of studio time at the Record Plant in Sausalito, just a stone's throw away from the heliport where we used to rehearse.

The Record Plant was decked out in a classic seventies style, with an array of different-sized pieces of wood covering the walls, just for effect. The studio itself was pretty nice and it was also convenient, being right down in Sausalito, near the boat harbor. None of us had that long a commute. Also—and this is pretty cool—the studio was right across the street from the U.S. Army Corps of Engineers Bay Model, which is an actual, miniature, hydraulic model of the entire San Francisco Bay and the Sacramento–San Joaquin River Delta. It accurately simulates the tides and was created to study environmental impacts. It turns out, that's the perfect thing to be looking at when you're getting high, while taking a smoke break with your friends. We'd walk around its cavernous insides, which mimic the foothills around the Bay—again, the perfect playground for stoned musicians looking to get lost in another world. I have more memories about that than of the time spent inside the studio itself. We were there to record *Wake of the Flood*. Our first release on Grateful Dead Records and our first studio album since *American Beauty*.

In the three years between, we released a pair of live albums. First *Europe '72*, and then, to fulfill our contract with Warner Brothers, we let Bear put together a live anthology—hence the nickname *Bear's Choice*. The official title, *History of the Grateful Dead, Volume One*, reflects its unofficial intent as a tribute and send-off to Pigpen. A lot of later-generation fans got their first exposure to that chapter of our career through that album, as Pigpen soars through several rave-ups, back when he was still on top of his game. Owsley pulled the material exclusively from live tracks that he recorded during our February 1970 run at the Fillmore East.

Wake of the Flood was Keith's coming out party and it had some great Jerry tunes on there, too—"Mississippi Half-Step Uptown Toodeloo," "Eyes of the World," "Stella Blue," "Here Comes Sunshine," and a personal favorite, "Row Jimmy."

Let's talk about "Row Jimmy" for a moment. In the Spring of 1973, we were rehearsing out by Point Reyes, which is on the Pacific coastline near Stinson Beach. "Far west." (This was before we set up our then-permanent space at Club Front). Jerry brought "Row Jimmy" into us one day, and it was really difficult to get a grip on it at first. It has a slow tempo, which makes it seem like it would be easy, but it calls for a slight reggae groove layered over a ballad. Rhythmically, the lengths aren't traditional. They're not just twos and fours. It's deceiving. Basically, you have to play the song in half-time with a double-time bounce on top. It's trickier than it sounds. But once I locked into it, "Row Jimmy" became one of the best songs in our repertoire. Looking back on it now, I have some regret that I didn't take that song with me, into my offshoot bands after the Dead, because it's such a good one. It deserves to be played. That's the best track on that album.

Bobby's "Weather Report Suite" is also on there, which was always more fun to play live than the studio version may indicate. *Wake of the Flood* was released on October 15, 1973.

Not too long after that, in April 1974—between the Wall of Sound's test show at the Cow Palace and its debut in Reno a few weeks later—we went into CBS Studios in San Francisco to record what would become *From the Mars Hotel*. I remember recording that one because of a freaky circumstance surrounding it. The City of San Francisco had been placed on high alert, due to a string of ongoing, racially charged murders after dark.

Nicknamed the "Zebra killers," an organized group of men, at large, were thought to be responsible for more than a dozen, execution-style murders during a six-month crime spree. The killers were targeting whites. Randomly. Residents panicked, tourists went elsewhere, and nightlife suffered. People were terrified to walk the streets at night. The SFPD launched an unprecedented dragnet, as they racially profiled more than 500 "suspects." I remember hearing sirens constantly wailing in the distance, as I'd cross the Golden Gate Bridge, heading downtown to work . . . where the sirens became significantly louder.

From the Mars Hotel turned out all right. It's a mixed bag. Again, the studio felt contrived. It couldn't offer the freedom of playing something live, nor the satisfaction. You get it already, I know. But a big part of the process behind making a studio record involves post production. After you lay down your parts, you go in and doll the whole thing up. You beautify it with smoke and mirrors. It can sound cool in the end, but it's not about being in the moment.

I don't go back and listen to any of our studio albums. I listen to the jams—the "Dark Stars"—from the *Europe '72* box set. I listen to the *Spring '90* box set. My wife, Aimee, will play the archival releases whenever we get them in the mail from Rhino. The *Dave's Picks* and whatnot. It's fun to be able to relive those nights, once in a while.

But I don't even own a copy of *From the Mars Hotel.* Not that it doesn't have its merits. It has "Scarlet Begonias," which is a great song. And it has "Loose Lucy," "China Doll," and "Unbroken Chain." On the flip side, however, it has "Money, Money"—an easy contender for lamest song ever. At least, from our catalog.

One thing worth mentioning is that *Mars Hotel* was named after an actual flophouse in San Francisco. An image of the real Mars Hotel appears on the cover. The building was about a block away from the studio, so we saw it all the time on the coming or going, while we were recording the album. It's since been demolished to make room for the Moscone Center—in a sign of the times, tech companies like Apple, Google, and Facebook now hold conferences on the same corner where the Mars Hotel once housed winos and junkies.

The hotel remains historically significant because Jack Kerouac wrote about some of the depraved nights he spent there, in his book *Big Sur*. Consequently, it was on the Beat Generation map before it was on Deadhead radar. That's another one of those cool, synchronistic connections. The Mars Hotel was a genuinely seedy establishment and, thus, held a particular appeal. Jack liked it. So did Jerry. (The original Mars Hotel can be seen for a few seconds in a David Bowie video.)

And it is true that if you hold the album cover upside down in front of a mirror, the otherwise illegible subtitle reads, "Ugly Rumors." It was originally supposed to be "Ugly Roomers," a self-deprecating dig at ourselves, but we changed it to "rumors" out of respect to the boarders at the hotel. Rumor has it that former U.K. Prime Minister Tony Blair named his college band Ugly Rumours as a direct reference.

Despite our record label follies, our business arm was becoming so profitable that an entire cottage industry began sprouting up around us. Nowadays, that cottage industry has expanded to include everything from radio shows to annual festivals. All of it unaffiliated. But in the early '70s, it started with our own friends and families. Sam Cutler branched off into his own booking agency (Out of Town Tours) and since we were always touring, it made sense that we'd spawn our own travel agency (Fly by Night Travel)—both of these businesses expanded to include a number of other client bands.

Susila opened up a shop called Kumquat Mae. They sold official merchandise including our records, the band shirts that Susila designed, and various other crafts. When she moved the store from San Anselmo to Mill Valley, the name changed to Rainbow Arbor. It was a heady shop and I was happy to see Susila thrive like that. I didn't spend too much time in the store itself, but there was a bar down the street called Sweetwater—the original one—where Weir and I used to hang out all the time, when we weren't on the road.

But we were usually on the road. And in some ways it began to feel like we peaked. The whole thing had gotten so big that the sheer size was beginning to take away from the overall experience, rather than add to it—for us, onstage, as well as for the audience, I think. I remember reading an interview with Jerry once where he said that he wanted to find an escape from the Grateful Dead because, for him, playing music in small clubs with small audiences was where it was at. There was no pressure, everything felt more personal and authentic, and the music was usually better. More alive and breathing than just regurgitated and rehearsed. You could explore the element of risk and danger so much easier in small rooms than in large stadiums, where nuances don't always come across and whims are hard to justify. The stadium shows felt a little too safe by comparison. And safe equals boring.

We played a *lot* of shows in 1973 and 1974 and once we had the Wall of Sound with us, we weren't just a traveling rock 'n' roll circus; we were a traveling institution. Every show was as massive as our sound system insinuated. We had an arsenal of trucks, unimaginable electricity, and production demands at every venue, and we needed two individual stages, which leapfrogged each other on the road, to accommodate the Wall of Sound. While we played on stage in one venue, a second stage was already being set up at the next. For this, we had to have two different road crews. It was a whole thing. It was too much.

I'm not entirely sure where or when the idea of us taking a break—not a vacation but an actual hiatus—came up, or who first verbalized it and brought it to the table. It may have been one of the dyed-in-the-wool crew guys throwing in the towel or something like that that made us first think of it, then consider it . . . then agree to it.

I do know that, once the idea was put out there, Jerry became the biggest proponent of the hiatus. Maybe he's the one who first hatched it. That would make a lot of sense to me. I think we all were probably going on automatic pilot at that time, and perhaps Jerry was able to get out of himself for a minute and see that. In my mind, everything was just fine; the band was really successful, we were playing at a certain level—people still listen to a lot of our music from that era. I didn't think the Wall of Sound sounded great, but our interplay at some of those shows was phenomenal.

At some point, though, that's not enough. The creative drive gets stale and you need to refill those tanks or else find new vehicles to creativity altogether. In a band, as with most things, stagnation is just a step away from death.

The Grateful Dead didn't hit our actual pinnacle until sometime in the late 1980s. Size-wise, early 1990s. But in the mid-1970s, we hit a certain plateau. Success took a heftier toll on Jerry than it did on me, personally, because I could always retreat or go hang out with the crew or something. But everyone wanted a piece of Jerry, all the time, until he had nothing left for himself. He used to take time to talk to that random fan who had taken too much acid and who needed to discuss the universe with him, or thank him, or just have some kind of personal exchange. If they were too high, Jerry would talk them down. If they were too low, Jerry would help them up. When they demanded his full attention, he'd try to give it to them. That was really admirable. Heroic. But when your audience swells to a certain size, you can't do that sort of thing anymore. There's just not enough time and there was always someone else in line, raising their hand, demanding attention. By the end of 1974, Jerry was done being that kind of hero. He was ready for a change of scene. He needed a break from it. I honored his decision and the rest of us did, too.

I could tell that Jerry's spirit had turned restless. He was no longer satisfied with the music, and if the music isn't working, then the rest of it isn't working, either. Overall, Jerry didn't seem as happy as he once was. Looking back, neither was I. We needed to get our hunger back, so it was time to go on a fast.

The risks were certain: If we kept going, we ran the possibility of coming to a standstill. Of course, by stopping, we risked the same thing. There was always the chance that we'd never start back up again.

Before the hiatus began, we played five hometown shows at the Winterland Arena. They were our good-bye shows and we even advertised them as such. It wasn't a marketing ploy—nobody knew when or if the Grateful Dead would ever return. We sure didn't. We each had our own ideas about it and I'd venture to say that even those thoughts varied wildly from day to day. Whatever we told others about regrouping, we didn't always believe ourselves. Sometimes it was just wishful thinking.

The Winterland shows were October 16 through 20, 1974. Our performances from that run, as always, were varied. Highs and lows. I'm sure we rode the emotional roller coaster, as well, those nights. The atmosphere inside the venue was charged, not just because these were our "last shows until . . . ?" but also because Jerry had decided that this might be his only chance to live out his filmmaker fantasies, so he had Rakow hire camera crews to document the entire run. Bill Graham was not happy about that and neither were some members of the audience. The cameras were big and cumbersome and got in some people's way. People weren't used to tripping out or freaking freely with big, professional camera crews around, capturing everything. People weren't used to seeing cameramen onstage instead of just the band. It was a distraction. Graham saw it as a divisive issue and sided with the small group of fans who minded.

But there was a bigger issue at those shows, specifically at the final one. Somebody had convinced Mickey Hart to show up and to bring a drum kit with him, in the back of his car. The thinking was that if this really was the last Grateful Dead concert, Mickey should participate and be a part of it. I was *not* cool with that. At all. I've never really spoken publicly about this, but I'll be clear, here: I objected to having Mickey sit in with us that night and I think I was probably somewhat vocal about that, backstage.

I enjoyed being the only drummer and I didn't want that to change. I got territorial about it. Mickey didn't know the new material and we hadn't rehearsed or played with him in years, so I didn't think that it could possibly be any good—and it wasn't, that night. Personally, I was insulted that everybody else backstage rallied behind Mickey. The whole situation became really uncomfortable for me. And that was the last Grateful Dead show before our hiatus.

13

The hiatus officially began on October 21, 1974. There were points during the hiatus when I honestly didn't think the Grateful Dead, as we knew it, would ever get back together. Maybe it had run its course. Jerry was content and busy and musically satisfied—he had several active bands, including the Jerry Garcia Band and Legion of Mary, and he was touring as much as ever.

I played in a band with Keith and Donna for a little bit, but then they both defected into one of Jerry's bands. Jerry recruited me, too, for some shows that were billed as "Jerry Garcia and Merl Saunders"—just a few at first and then not at all. Pretty soon, I was a drummer without a band.

Before the break, Susila and I bought a second property up in a remote area of Mendocino County, in the small Wild West logging town of Comptche. Today, Comptche has less than 200 residents. Back then, it was probably half that. Booker T. was one of them. Also, Rita Coolidge's sister, Priscilla, lived in the area. Their father, Pastor Dick Coolidge, held Sunday services at the grange. Not that we went. But that meant that Rita and her husband, Kris Kristofferson, were no strangers to the land. It was an odd mix of people and took a certain type. There wasn't much in terms of modern luxuries and it's the type of place where the only gas station is also the general store. Susila describes the town as "kinda Norman Rockwell with an edge."

Comptche is about fifteen miles inland from the Pacific and 140 miles north of San Francisco. Realistically, it takes almost four hours to get to the city limits from up there. That's why we chose it. I wanted to be close to the coast but away from the bay and the band and the whole lifestyle. It was our escape hatch; our getaway. A place to relax and recharge during downtime. A place to run away after a long tour.

The house was physically built by another drummer, John Barbata, who was known for his work in the Turtles and Jefferson Starship—one of those many post-OG incarnations of Jefferson Airplane. He was also Crosby, Stills, Nash & Young's drummer for a while and worked sessions for legends like Eric Clapton. He may have been a better drummer than a home builder, though.

Here's another crazy connection: Barbata allegedly built the house with the help of the real-life Indiana Jones, the real-life Han Solo. Yes, Harrison Ford. Before Ford was a famous actor, he was a starving carpenter.

Susila and I were attracted to the house because of its unusual architecture. It was made of all redwood, with wooden decks, wooden rails, wooden everything. It was like a pirate ship turned upside down. None of the walls were the same size. The windows leaked. It was funky. It was odd. We loved it. We bought it from Barbata and used it as our retreat. All told, I had it for something like twenty-five years and lived there full time for a long time, over different periods.

I built a big barn next to the house, which I used for music when I wasn't on the road. We had more than twenty acres to play around with. Throughout the years, I grew a little bit of marijuana up there and played a lot of music in local places and kept things pretty low key. But, at first, it was just our little adventure place; we'd get cabin fever in Mill Valley and feel the urge to wander around, like hippies do. But instead of getting into a Volkswagen bus, we had alternate lives as ranchers in Mendocino County. It was rustic luxury.

But then Susila and I broke up. This was right before or around the time that the hiatus began, so it was perfect timing. Sometimes you need those kinds of sea changes. The tide comes in and sweeps away your footsteps as you retreat to higher ground. It's not unlike wisdom gleaned from Grateful Dead shows—you can never truly predict where the jam will go next, but you must always know what to do when you get there. Or else it ends and you move on to the next jam.

Susila had been drifting away from me and she wouldn't come home a lot of the time. I drove forty minutes down the road, to the actual town of Mendocino, after I had gotten word that she was there with some other guy. I went to his apartment and found them both in bed together. I had a check for $35,000 with me, because we had just sold the Mill Valley house and I needed her to sign off on it, so I could cash it. Due to the unusual situation that I had just walked in on, she was freaked out and signed the check right there and then, still in bed with this other guy. I left peacefully and alone, and went straight to the bank. And that was the start of my bachelor period. I was around twenty-eight years old. I never really had a bachelor period before. I was ready for it, but it wasn't quite what you'd think.

I didn't get a playboy suite in a big city high-rise and live life inside a rock star cliché. Instead, I rented a little red house in Stinson Beach, about 100 yards from the beach, with sand all around it. I had to put in a fireplace because it was freezing there in the wintertime. Oddly enough, that's yet another place from my past that has since burned down. I went back to Stinson Beach a couple years ago and decided to drive past it, for old times' sake, and it was gone. I was told that it went up in flames. Ashes to ashes.

I really liked living there. It was the first time in my life I had a place to really call my own. I had never lived by myself before. I started dating a beautiful blond chick who would come over and stay with me sometimes. But overall, I was on my own. Jerry and Mountain Girl lived nearby. So did Keith and Donna. I wasn't talking to Susila and Justin was living with his grandparents, so it was a far-out time for me. I didn't have any idea if or when the Grateful Dead would get back together, and I didn't have a steady income. I didn't know what to do.

That was all right because the first part of the hiatus wasn't much of a hiatus after all. After just four months off the road, we went into Bobby's brand-new home studio. I've made it loud and clear that I have problems with studios, and it's true, I do. As you'd assume, recording in a friend's home studio can be laid back and loose—but then that becomes the problem. Since you're not paying by the hour, it can be too relaxed. And too comfortable.

Bobby had a good setup, though, and we had a good working thing going on; we'd start in the afternoon and would play for as long as it was happening. The record that came from that, *Blues for Allah*, had a lot of really strong material on it, but I always felt that my own playing was weak. We should've let the new tunes breathe a bit more before we recorded them, because they really deserved better.

Once we started performing them live—"Help on the Way," "Slip-knot!," "Franklin's Tower," "The Music Never Stopped," "Crazy Fingers"—we turned a corner and it was a whole other ball game. Those songs are among our very best and they lived up to their potential. We had to play them live in front of an audience in order for that to happen. Once we let them outside and started taking them for walks, they each had a growth spurt during which they really discovered themselves. We got to know those songs rather well, over the years.

The album also contained a group of really experimental songs ("Stronger than Dirt," "Unusual Occurrences in the Desert") that bordered on acid-jazz composition. Wild stuff. Deep cuts.

Mickey wasn't technically back in the band yet—actually, technically, neither were we. This was supposed to be our leave of absence. This was our idea of a break. Anyway, depending on who you ask, I'm sure, Mickey was just a "special guest" on *Blues for Allah*. Everyone, me included, remembers his contribution because of the crickets. Mickey and the crickets.

He was starting to get into some of his true sonic pioneering by this point and he definitely was going as far out there as he could with sounds and stuff. He got a whole box of crickets to use as an instrument on *Blues for Allah*. To this day, I'm not sure where you actually can buy such a thing. Maybe a cricket farm. Anyway, he put a microphone inside the box and then manipulated the sound. That was cool and all, and totally Mickey. But I wasn't thrilled about his presence.

We weren't booking tours again, just yet, but we agreed to two one-off gigs, in March and June respectively. Both gigs were already weird and awkward, so we used them to showcase the new experimental numbers—"Blues for Allah" and "Stronger than Dirt." Oddities that disappeared into the ether soon after. So long.

Then, on August 13, 1975, we played at the Great American Music Hall in San Francisco. A private, invite-only show, mostly for the music industry and, of course, our friends. Something about showcasing our new material for radio programmers and the like. You know, stuff I never actually paid any attention to. All I knew was that we were going to play a show. And it ended up being a great show. After cutting an entire album in the studio, we were like schoolchildren waiting for the last bell to ring before summer break. At least I was.

Mickey played the show with us and brought his box of crickets with him, to use as part of the live performance. At some point during the night, the crickets joined the revolution and staged a jailbreak. They liberated themselves and pretty soon there were crickets over the whole goddamn place. They made the Great American Music Hall their home for a little while after that. They were granted asylum.

We played the material from *Blues for Allah* that night and the band sounded great. We were all so into it. The Great American Music Hall is a tiny place with just a 600-person capacity, and we were really squashed on that stage without our usual amount of real estate, but the night was as good as you could ask for.

In my mind, that show was a crucial turning point. I wasn't high on smack that night—I dabbled with opiates throughout the hiatus, which

I'll explain later in this chapter, but I stayed away from all that junk for the gig. It was a very bright, clear, expressive night for the whole band. It was also just a really big moment for me, personally. It was the first time that I thought we could be a band again. And the first time I thought having two drummers again could work.

That one gig spurred a whole lot of energy. Everybody really felt great about the music. *Blues for Allah* is one of the farthest out-there albums that we've ever done. I mean, it's freaking out there. But, to this day, I still really love some of those songs. Maybe the live run-through of the album should've been the album itself. Sixteen years later, we came around to that idea—we released the show in its entirety as *One From the Vault*.

A friend of mine, this guy Slade, came up to me after the show. I drove my Alfa Romeo 1750 GTV to the venue and Slade had his BMW 2002 TII with him. I literally just walked out the front door and got in my car to go home, when Slade pulled up to me. We decided to race—from the Great American in San Francisco all the way to Slade's house in San Rafael, some twenty miles north of there.

Gentlemen, start your engines: We raced the whole way. There was no holding back. We were going top speeds, like, 120 mph across the Golden Gate Bridge. On the Marin side of the Golden Gate, we took all three lanes to make the turns. We were going so fast, we couldn't stick to just one lane. There was no traffic. Neither one of us got pulled over that night and that had more to do with blind luck than with karma.

The moment we left the Great American Music Hall, I could feel it. I knew we were going to push this as far as we could go. It was going to be a real, honest-to-God car race. By the time we hit Lombard Street, we were running all the lights. At first we went fast enough to make all the green lights. Then it didn't even matter anymore. By the end of Lombard, we were running red lights. That's an incredibly irresponsible thing to do and I can't recommend it. No way. Frankly, I'm still amazed that we did that without any consequences. We got away with it and we know that now. But in the heat of the moment, there was no guarantee of any outcome.

There was a reasonable possibility that somebody was going to end up in big trouble that night. Or worse.

By the time we reached the Presidio, at the edge of the city, I had the pedal touching metal. I was in fifth gear. "Show me what you got." We raced through the toll booths—100 miles an hour through those fucking things—and I'm saying to myself, "Okay, I'm going to go to jail tonight. I'm okay. It's okay. I'm going to jail. That's all." My seat belt was on, my balls were out, and I raced like hell. At the end of the bridge, I looked down—you can only take your eye off the road for a split second—and I saw the needle at 120. I kept that up through the tunnel on Highway 101, and could hear both of our cars echoing in there, roaring away like wild things. We were going racetrack speeds on streets that were made for daily commutes, rush hours, and gridlock.

When we got to San Rafael, Slade was just the tiniest bit in front of me. He had me beat by maybe a car length or less. We continued racing all the way through downtown, running everything again. There was no stopping for anything. In the last quarter of a mile of this big race, a decision had to be made. The road split and I had a choice. Left or right. Both sides led to Slade's house. I don't remember if I chose left or right but it was the right call. Slade went the other way. I came in hot around that turn just in time to slide in front of Slade's car, effectively blocking him. He had to slam on his brakes. And that's how I won that race.

It really pissed off Slade, though. Man, was he pissed. There was nothing he could do. I had him blocked. We both drove nonchalantly up his driveway, parked our cars, and got out. I can still remember this: there wasn't a sound to be heard. No wind blowing. No dogs barking. And no police sirens. All I could hear were the exhaust pipes. They make this loud tinkle, tinkle, tinkle when the steel starts to cool down after getting red hot like that. I looked and the pipes were bright red. We looked up and thanked our lucky stars. I'll never understand how we didn't end up getting chased by the police. Maybe there were student riots planned for the next day or something. You watch—I'll get a letter from the CHP once this book comes out. Of course, there's no proof of any of this. It's all hearsay. (Right?)

I'd like to think that a part of us getting away with it has to do with that manifesting spirit thing—if you worry too much, you'll be busted for sure. But if you don't, you won't be. I'm not sure that it really works like that. But, regardless, that was a hairy race, man. It was really hairy.

Slade's co-pilot for that race was a dope dealer who sat in the passenger seat, terrified and wondering what he got himself into. Slade didn't care because when he's competitive, he gets tunnel vision. His passenger could see the bigger picture and it scared him so much, he shit his pants in the car. That's another thing that pissed Slade off that night. Two losses in one race.

Our crew guy, Kidd Candelario, rode shotgun in my car. He didn't shit his pants; in fact, he didn't give a shit at all. We laughed and had a great time. We had that kind of a team, back then. I could hang out with the crew guys and we took care of each other in strange ways, I guess. Kidd had my back and he was cool as a summer breeze on that ride. He was probably happy that we were going to make it to our destination in half the time it usually takes.

I have such a clear memory of that entire night. I really loved it. The racing part was cool and fun and has made for a good bonfire story over the years, but that was just the capper to a very pivotal gig and a great night of my life, overall.

After that, the hiatus began in earnest. Most of the other guys had side projects that they wanted to work on. But me, I didn't have a Plan B and I didn't know what to do for an income. I knew a dope dealer in the nearby town of Bolinas, who was growing a bunch of weed out behind his house. The plants were so big, I just couldn't believe it. This was back way before the medical marijuana movement even started, so it was all the more brazen and radical. And definitely outlaw.

We both had time on our hands, so I used to go over there a lot and play him in backgammon and we got into some serious money with that game. I had a way of destroying him every time, and I was able to make enough winnings and take home enough free drugs to get me through those strange days. I never cheated and I'm not a gambler, but I sure knew how to win that game. I was on a streak. I had to win, because if I didn't, I would've been in trouble. I would've squandered the only money I had to buy groceries and firewood—and I needed plenty of firewood because it got pretty cold out there on the waterfront. I was in the saltwater of it, so to speak. That suited me just fine: I've always been salt of the earth.

It was there in Stinson Beach where I got locked into a serious opium habit. The dealer who I played backgammon with would load me up. Before I knew it, I was smoking a ball of opium a day. Jerry was fully booked with his other bands and was also hard at work on what would become *The Grateful Dead Movie*. Bobby did some extracurricular touring of his own and he now had his own home studio that he could record in whenever he wanted. I'm not sure what the other guys were up to. But, me, I was playing backgammon and getting blissed out on opium.

I can't remember when heroin entered the picture for me, personally. Or for any of the other guys, for that matter. I just remember that I started doing some around the time of the hiatus. It's a damn shame that I ever got into that horrible stuff and I'm lucky in that I never got in too deep with it. I never shot up. I snorted it, but I preferred opium, which some people will say is the same thing, but it's not. "Not quite," anyway. They're both opiates and they're both crap. I don't recommend either.

I never did heroin with Jerry. It's well documented how deep he got with it and how it would continue to plague him and affect the band for the rest of our career. But I never did any with him or saw him do it. We never scored together and I've always felt this instinctual feeling that he was kind of looking out for me, on that level. He didn't want me to do what he was doing, because he knew what it was doing to him and he knew how bad it was. That was the feeling that I got, anyway. It was always a strong feeling. But I also know that heroin is a solitary drug. It's a dark drug. It's not a social thing. It's not like acid or ecstasy or any of those true consciousness expansion drugs. It's not even like coke, which carries its own share of demons. Heroin is much darker, I'm afraid.

I didn't have enough money during the hiatus to go out and do anything lavish. I was just barely getting by as an amateur backgammon player. There were few gigs and the ones I played didn't pay. At least, not much. I was pretty isolated. I think I was in both shock and denial about the band. I was just kind of . . . waiting.

Susila and I started hanging out again. She started coming down to the beach and then, all of the sudden, she was with me again. I don't understand how these things work, of course. Nobody really does. But before I knew it, we were serious again. I knew that I liked that, and I knew that it made me happy, so we decided to go with it. Then we took it further: We wanted Justin to live with us again and to be a real family. Susila's parents, Justin's grandparents, helped us buy a new house in Mill Valley and the three of us moved back there for round two. A new start.

Somehow, a decision was made to get the band back together. In typical Grateful Dead fashion, I don't remember having a conference about it or anything. I think somebody just gave me the word: "Hey, come on down to Front Street for rehearsal."

Then I realized that Mickey was going to be a part of that. Somehow, it seemed like Mickey had just weaseled himself back into the band, full time. I wasn't too pleased about it. I didn't think it was a good idea. Shortly before all of this, he started coming around to my house in Mill Valley, here and there, and I started getting the feeling that he wanted to hit me up for something, or get me to form some kind of alliance. Maybe he was trying to warm me up to the idea of having him rejoin. Parts of me came around a little at a time and then, of course, I did come around. I don't remember exactly when it happened. Years into it, we started getting far-out together and the "Drums->Space" part of our shows became this phenomenal thing that I looked forward to every night. It was the most reliably psychedelic, improvisational, and experimental part of our show. Consistently. So Mickey earned his keep. But at first, I can tell you that I didn't like it one bit.

One reason I let it go and didn't fight his return, or raise as much of a stink about it as I probably wanted to, is that I was still dabbling with heroin and certainly was locked into my opium habit. It made me very malleable; very easy to convince to do something. Here was Mickey going, "Okay, Bill, I'm going to be back in the band," and instead of objecting like I wanted to, I just gave a very stoned, "Okay, whatever you say."

In the end, of course, everything worked out for the best. Eventually. As I've said, "Drums->Space" became some of the most far-out moments of Grateful Dead music, and that would never have happened had I remained the only drummer in the band. That was Mickey's doing more than anything. He's a full-on shaman of that world.

But at the time, I hated it. I remember Phil once told me off the cuff that we made a mistake by having Mickey come back in the band, and maybe he just said that in the heat of a moment. But there were times when it was really challenging to have two headstrong drummers in the same band. It's really hard to achieve subtlety with an extra man on the job, and quiet moments are difficult to execute. Especially when both drummers have very strong personalities and attitudes and want to play as much as they can—you know, two minds powering eight limbs.

Jerry had his stuff, too, with letting Mickey back in. He made Mickey get rid of some of his crash cymbals because they were right at head height, which made it difficult for the singers, given how hard Mickey could hit those things. There were other problems with having two drummers—we're talking purely on a technical, musical level here—but eventually we worked it out. It got better. I was really thankful when it did, and also thankful to have Mickey in the band. All in time.

That first rehearsal was just awful, though. It wasn't just Mickey. I remember that first get-together clearly. It was at Front Street, before we had a chance to really fix it up and make the necessary adjustments to make it a good practice spot. There were no sound curtains or anything at first; it was just concrete. Once we renovated it and it became our permanent place, we had it dialed in. But when we first regrouped there, the actual sound in the room was impossible to get with. And with two drummers making a racket, I just thought, "God, this is terrible." I mean, it was really, really bad.

Then we played that Great American Music Hall show, and things started looking up—except that that's when the hiatus really began. In late September, a month after the Great American gig, we agreed to a quick one-off in Golden Gate Park with our friends, Jefferson Starship. A free blowout just like the good ole days. This was the one where a woman gave birth in the field while we played. So they say, anyway. But if anyone got pregnant during or right after that show, they could've had the child at our next gig—we took about nine months to return. ("Hey man, when's your next show?" "When that lady over there gives birth.")

The Grateful Dead may have been on hiatus but our floundering record label was not. In an effort to keep hope alive, Rakow spearheaded a live album, culled from those "final four" Winterland performances at the end of 1974. It was to be the sound track for the movie that Jerry was working on. The source recordings were problematic to say the least, but somehow we were able to get enough material for an extended live release. I say "we" very loosely there. That was Rakow's project and I think Phil and Bear mixed it. I'm not conveniently distancing myself from the process just because the resulting album, *Steal Your Face*, may have been our worst. I really had nothing to do with it. It wasn't long before our little record label experiment came to a fiery conclusion. Rakow was fired. He cut himself a big fat check with Grateful Dead Records' remaining funds, thereby crippling the label, and then he split. And that was that.

We needed a new label, so we went with the now-legendary Clive Davis, who signed us to Arista Records. I guess he wanted to see if he could make us a hit band or something. He wasn't too far off, although it would take a long minute—more than a decade. Still, the arrangement worked for us, I think, and Clive kept his word and let us do what we wanted, creatively. He preserved the sanctity of the Grateful Dead while enabling us to be us—and to sell a few records along the way. We met with him on our turf, at Front Street, and all I really recall from that meeting is that Davis spray-painted his hair black, because he didn't want people to know that he was balding. He and Weir got into some kind of humorous discussion about it. As for the record deal, we got Davis to agree to our terms. From then until our breakup, the Grateful Dead belonged to Arista.

In the meantime, Jerry was still working long hours on *The Grateful Dead Movie*. It was his passion project but it became a sticking point within our ranks, as it was financed from the band's pockets. Phil thought that it was an unnecessary expense and had some kind of issue with Jerry about the whole thing. It never bothered me that it went so high above the budget, because what are you going to do in that situation? Say, "Okay, you can only have this much money and if the thing's not complete, who cares, wrap it up?" Or are you going to find more money for it and let it become a really worthy project that your band leader and good friend really believes in?

Nowadays, *The Grateful Dead Movie* is still shown in theaters around the nation once in a while and for decades every college dorm in America had at least one kid on every hall with a VHS copy on his shelf. It paid off. It became a huge thing and, as Jerry had known all along, it captured and defined our identity, since it had the visual element to go along with the music, the animation to go along with the interviews, and the B-roll that really showed viewers with their own eyes the circus that was a Grateful Dead show in San Francisco, circa 1974. We were watching the movie, and then we were in the movie.

As for my opinion on the movie itself, all I can offer is that it was a very good home movie. It's not exactly a typical motion picture. It doesn't have a plot; it's a bunch of scenes that are kind of woven together. And still, today, the part of the movie that ate up the biggest slice of the budget and took the most amount of work—the animated sequence in the beginning—is my favorite part. Back then, animation was all done by hand, frame by frame. I like that whole segment the best, and I think most people who watch it agree. Producing that thing really consumed Jerry's time, on a day-to-day basis, throughout the hiatus.

But then, suddenly, the Grateful Dead revved up again. Nine months without a show and we were fucking ready. I wonder if that lady had her baby. We started in Portland, Oregon, and plotted out a little theater tour, hitting our favorite markets for extended runs in Boston, Philadelphia, New York City, Chicago, and—of course—San Francisco. A couple months later we jumped the rest of the way into the lion's den with a pair of sold-out shows at the Oakland Coliseum Stadium on a double bill with the Who. The Grateful Dead were back.

Those shows with the Who were memorable. Stadiums are always a big deal, and this one was on our home turf. Being on a bill with the Who just put it over the top. This was still during the Keith Moon era, and he was one of those guys that just went crazy on the drums. He was more of an entity than a drummer, but it really worked for that band. Those gigs were far-out, man. Jerry and I talked about them afterward and he felt that we had one "on" day and one "off" day. I thought we played well at both of them. There was just so much personality in those shows. They were afternoon concerts, so I could see all the faces in the crowd. Whenever I play in daylight, I develop a real sense of the connection between me, the band, the audience, and the music, because I can see it in action. Moving people to dance was how this whole journey started for me and I'm still on board that train.

The shows with the Who were in October 1976. Four months after our return and, man, were we ever back full force. It ushered in a whole new era that was, in hindsight, another great period in Grateful Dead history.

In fact, some people believe that one particular tour from that period— Spring 1977—is our best. Ever. Does 5/8/77 Cornell (Ithaca, NY) ring a bell? If you're a fan, then of course it does. That recording is a prerequisite for every incoming class of Deadheads, and the jam between "Scarlet Begonias" and "Fire on the Mountain" is guaranteed to be on all of our final exams. You will be tested on all of this stuff. All we need is some Kool-Aid.

When we began to get our heads around making another record, our new record label had a bigger influence on us than we realized up front.

Clive Davis was used to being a not-so-silent extra band member with most of the acts he signed, but he kept to his word and generally let us make our own bed. However, his one sticking point was that we had to agree to work with outside producers.

For our first album on Arista, we settled on a producer by the name of Keith Olsen. If you're a serious music fan, you know who he is. He has Grammy Awards and God knows how many gold and platinum albums to his name. He's produced big ones for Santana, Ozzy Osbourne, Heart, Joe Walsh, the Scorpions, Whitesnake, Sammy Hagar, Journey, Emerson, Lake & Palmer, and I don't even remember who else. He's the producer behind that Rick Springfield ear-worm, "Jessie's Girl." But, at the time, that early in his career, his main claim was Fleetwood Mac. When Olsen came to our attention, he was riding the number one success of 1975's *Fleetwood Mac* album, which was that band's big breakout, really.

It was because of Olsen that Fleetwood Mac hired Stevie Nicks and Lindsey Buckingham, forever changing that band. And it worked—it made them famous. So, as a producer, Olsen's approach was hands-on. Since we had just made Clive Davis promise us that he would be hands-*off,* maybe the secret objective behind making us use outside producers was so that he could have an inside man and get some say with us, after all. Now, there's a conspiracy theory for you.

Regardless, Olsen insisted that we use a studio in Hollywood that he liked, so we all moved down to L.A., again, and rented apartments within walking distance to the studio. It was pretty hard. I was down there by myself, I think. I'm not sure why Susila wasn't there with me. We may have been on the outs again, by that point.

Those studio sessions were tricky because Olsen was kind of a wired fellow and he liked things to sound a certain way. His way. He was strait-laced and took a straitlaced approach to recording. He'd have us play the same thing over and over again, and we're not really the type of band that can put up with that. We can't play the same thing, the same way, over and over. Our very identity is based on the opposite principle. So there was some friction there.

The album that we were recording became *Terrapin Station.* As for the song of the same name, he had us record the entire track from beginning to end, and it was something like fifteen minutes long. Olsen told me that I'd lost my time as the timekeeper; that my rhythm wasn't steady. When we played it back, under the microscope, he realized it varied by 1/25 of a second from beginning to end. Even he had to admit that was amazing. This was before drum machines were big. I was the drum machine.

Olsen had his problems recording us, but the music came out great. Still, we struggled with that title track, with "Terrapin Station." It's a suite and a pretty epic piece of music; it was supposed to be the centerpiece of the album. But it's a complex composition with different parts and all these different, interlocking sections. One night after we'd been wrestling with it, unsuccessfully, in the studio, I came to the conclusion that part of the problem rested on Mickey and me. We hadn't agreed on a precise arrangement, and a song like "Terrapin Station" needs a precise arrangement.

Later that night, I went to Mickey's apartment—we were all in the same basic apartment complex—and I told him that we were going to stay up and work on the song until we got it right. No more faking it. We sat down and mapped it out. I said, "This is how the song goes." I showed him all the parts that I felt worked really well, he added a couple, and that's what the song is today.

We went back into the studio, the next night, and got it right. With the drum parts worked out, everything else snapped together like puzzle pieces. The right pieces. The song was done.

Well . . . except for one little detail that's not so little. Mickey had a cool timbale part that he recorded, with Garcia adding interplay on guitar. But Olsen had another idea. Without telling anyone in the band, he erased Mickey's part entirely and then hired a string section to fill out that passage instead. I was pissed off about it, but Mickey was deservedly outraged. Outraged. I think that he and Olsen had some unspoken tension throughout those recording sessions and, in some way, perhaps this was Olsen just trying to get back at Mickey. Either way, it was a very stupid thing to do.

Mickey wasn't going to be had that easily, though, and so he and Garcia—who sided with Mickey—redid their part. Olsen wasn't going to give up either, so he made sure the strings remained in the final mix. The recorded version of "Terrapin Station" is probably my least favorite version because of that. It sounds really grandiose, like somebody's ego is playing those strings. Anyway, that was a wrap for the record, *Terrapin Station*.

The album kicks off with "Estimated Prophet," which is a Weir/Barlow creation. I did the same thing with Bobby for that one that I did with Mickey for "Terrapin Station." It's a great song but when he brought it to us, something was off. It needed a groove. It was in quick 7/4 but it didn't swing. Yet. For my homework that night, I combined two fast sevens and played half-time over it. The two sevens brought the time around to an even number—the phrasing is in two bars of seven, so technically the time signature is in 14/8. But that's getting technical. In layman's terms, "Estimated Prophet" suddenly grooved.

Terrapin Station is a pretty good album, all told, and it holds up today, I think. I hope.

Meanwhile, Jerry and Mountain Girl had broken up and Deborah Koons entered the picture. She chased him down. Well, down and around. The whole situation between those two was volatile from the get-go. This one time, in New York City, Jerry called me up in a panic. We were in a fancy hotel on Fifty-Seventh Street. We had a gig the night before. It was now the following afternoon. Jerry got me on the phone and said, "Bill, you have to come to my room. Deborah's here and won't leave me alone. You've got to help me get rid of her, man." So I hauled ass down there. I threw on a pair of beat-up blue jeans and a ragged old white long-sleeve shirt, and left the room, still barefoot. I was lucky enough to remember to stuff my room key in my pocket.

I entered Jerry's room and, sure enough, Deborah was there, holding her ground. Jerry told her to leave and she refused. So I grabbed her, firmly but without hurting her in any way, and I forced her into the elevator. I told her, "Don't move! I'm not going to hurt you, but you have to get out of here." I looked at her and realized that she actually looked pretty good—she was all dolled up to attract Jerry's attention. And I was just the drummer in a rock 'n' roll band, so I looked scruffy as all hell.

We got down to the lobby and I wasn't quite sure what to do. I just knew I had to get her away from Jerry. I took her to the front desk and explained that they had to make her leave. The clerk took one look at me, in all my ragged glory, then took in her graceful debonair appearance. He looked back at me again. "Sir, are you a guest here?"

I flashed, in that second, that she could've easily turned the tables on me. She could've flipped the script. But I reached in my back pocket for the only thing I had on me, my room key. They called security and got her to leave the property. If I hadn't remembered that key, I could've been the one escorted out.

Deborah was capable of that kind of conniving, because when I talked to Jerry about it afterward, I asked him why he invited her over in the first place. "I didn't," he said. "She snuck in underneath the room service cart." She paid off the waiter to sneak her in the room and, once he left, she popped out. "Surprise! Nice to see you, Jerry!" Well, he didn't think so.

I heard stories of her getting violent when they lived together, but I didn't see any of that. I don't know what their deal was or when they got together or when they broke up or when they got back together; that's their story, not mine. But I do recall one time at Bobby's studio when Jerry, Mountain Girl, and Deborah were all in the same room together and it ended with Mountain Girl throwing Deborah into the foot-thick studio door. It broke the hinges off. I don't know how Deborah survived that. But what is it that they say? Hell hath no fury like a woman scorned?

Deborah must've been used to running into thick doors, because when she came out on the road with Jerry, he'd get hotel suites with two separate bedrooms. He made sure his always had an additional lock on it. That pretty much says everything, right there.

I should add, however, that she and Jerry shared an interest in film, and he would probably have been as happy as I was to find out that she recently made a documentary (*Symphony of the Soil*) about the dangers of GMOs.

Issues of love and warfare aside, 1977 was a rather memorable year for the Grateful Dead. One of our high points. Right around the corner, 1978 would bring us our greatest adventure yet, in a faraway land, on a whole different continent. The long strange trip was about to get very strange indeed.

14

On May 18, 1978, we were at the final stop of a spring tour and the end of a three-night stand in Chicago. I made them cancel the gig. Actually, I didn't make anybody do anything. But long before our call-time at the Uptown Theater, I was already home in California. For whatever reason, Keith and I got into a major fight back at the hotel, after the gig the night before. I don't even remember what the fight was about. Isn't that something? It was probably some real nonsense.

I stopped by his hotel room and, out of nowhere, he started saying some really nasty shit to me. "Well then, fuck you, Keith!" I was exhausted. It was the end of tour, which usually means you're crispy up top and frayed around the edges. I overreacted and jumped on the first flight out of there, even though we had just one more show to complete the tour. The grand finale. But I didn't want to be in the same building as Keith and I couldn't imagine walking on stage with him and doing something as interpersonal as playing music. It was that bad.

We didn't throw any punches, although I do remember wrestling with him on the floor. We mostly just got into a lot of verbal garbage. Fueled by alcohol, I'm sure. Other drugs too, probably. It was stupid. Keith blind-sided me—with a series of visciously personal insults that were intended to sting. Mission accomplished. My feelings were hurt—deeply—and be-tween my damaged ego and my wounded pride, I wasn't going to stick around to take stock of the emotional carnage.

I pulled the rip cord. "I'm outta here!"

I was in my seat on the flight and the doors were about to close when suddenly Dan Healy came running down the aisle and plopped down in the seat next to me. Sweat pouring off his forehead. "I made it, Bill!" It was his way of saying, "I've got your back." It was a really big way of saying that.

After the tour, I went and stayed at Mickey's ranch for a while and told him that I wasn't going to play in the band anymore. Not if Keith was in it. After some post-tour decompression, I was able to dust off, but it took a minute before I could let bygones be bygones. That's how deeply Keith was able to cut. I don't remember how we healed that wound other than the universal cure-all: time.

Besides, we had bigger fish to fry that year—the Grateful Dead were going to Egypt. It made Europe '72 seem like a stroll to the corner store. Egypt instantly became the biggest, baddest, and most legendary field trip that we took during our entire thirty years as a band.

As kids, Egypt captured all of our imaginations. Sure, we wanted to play there, just as we'd want to play on the moon or under the ocean or in never-never land—but the moment we realized that Egypt might be some-thing more than just a collective daydream—that it might actually be possible—it took on its own momentum. And urgently. It felt like one of those things where the universe wanted it to happen.

Phil gave me a book to read called *The Great Pyramid Decoded*. It was an absolutely fascinating book that explained the difference in measure-ment between the old inch and the modern inch and why we couldn't find the doors and some other stuff that we knew existed inside the Great Pyr-amid. We were using the wrong size measurement to discover them. Pi plays an incredible part in some of the math.

Bringing our caravan to Egypt wasn't exactly as easy as bringing it to London or Paris. And getting permission to do what we wanted—propping up the Grateful Dead big top right next to the pyramids—was particularly tricky.

After diplomatic meetings, both in Cairo and Washington, D.C., a deal was struck: Ultimately, we were cleared to perform three shows at the Sphinx Theater, which was right at the foot of the Great Pyramid of Giza. But we weren't going to be compensated for them. Half the proceeds would go to a children's charity that was connected with the Egyptian first lady— President Anwar el-Sadat's wife, Jehan. The other half would be donated to the Egyptian Department of Antiquities, which oversees the pyramids. We were all too happy to sign off on that. But it meant that we had to pay for everything ourselves. We went on our own ticket and that cost a lot of money. Especially since, once again, we brought an extended family with us.

Our Egypt '78 extended family was different from our Europe '72 extended family. Different lovers, different loves. Members of the Merry Pranksters, including Kesey, came with us for this one. Bill Graham joined us, just for fun. On my end, I brought my wife—but it wasn't Susila. It was a woman named Shelley Pearce, who was an elementary schoolteacher and a really amazing woman. I fell for her pretty hard and our marriage lasted fifteen years. I'll fill you in on all of that, soon enough.

When we landed in Cairo, Shelley and I took a cab to the hotel with Richard Loren, our manager during this period. He had been to Egypt before and pointed things out to us, eagerly, during the ride. We could tell we were in a strange land. The vibe was different. The air was different. Everything looked different. We dug it.

We could see the silhouettes of the pyramids, off in the distance, and immediately felt their energy. It's so flat out in the desert that you can see their outlines for many miles. The crackpot theory that the pyramids may have been used for marker beacons suddenly didn't seem so crackpot. But marker beacons for what?

The other thing I remember about that drive is that it felt like being on that amusement park ride, the Wild Mouse—but without any safety regulations. Traffic lights were merely suggestions and right-of-way appeared up for debate. It was a little too risky for me. I realize that might sound like a ridiculous statement, just however many pages after telling you about the race from the Great American Music Hall to San Rafael. But this time, I wasn't driving.

Our hotel was less than half a mile from the venue—and by venue, I mean . . . the *Great Pyramid!*—at a renowned place called the Mena House Hotel. The hotel was palatial and surprisingly elegant. The stone walls were unusually thick to protect guests from the elements—the desert heat pierces through thin walls faster than a knife can cut through butter at Thanksgiving dinner. The hotel felt like a solid fortress, surrounded by a fifteen-foot fence. It didn't look like much from the street, but behind the walls was a grand resort.

Of all the amenities in my room, the Great Pyramid was my favorite. It was framed inside my window, ready to be gawked at whenever we opened the curtain. Naturally, we gazed at it often, but we learned rather quickly not to leave that window open at dusk, because of all the mosquitos. They came in, uninvited, and took over every inch of our ceiling, as dense as the crowd at Watkins Glen. But unlike most of those folks on the raceway, mosquitos don't like hash. Well, we did—so we smoked them out.

We had tons of good hash while we were there. All locally grown and produced. We didn't smuggle in any paraphernalia, so we would use aluminum soda cans and whatever else we could come up with to smoke out of. We weren't too proud.

There was a nine-hour time difference from San Francisco. At five in the morning on the first night, our internal clocks hadn't yet time traveled. We were stuck in the previous afternoon. Shelley and I were starving and—despite security issues, common sense, and Shelley's protests—I decided I was going to go out and get us some food. I was a hunter gatherer. I got as far as the stairwell when a waiter walked past me with a giant food tray balanced on his shoulder. I offered to buy the entire tray, on the spot.

"Just call room service and I'll bring it to you." I couldn't believe it. We were in a country where a significant portion of the population still went to work on camelback—and yet, here we had twenty-four-hour room service. The same waiter turned out to be our hash connection . . . so we liked that guy.

A lot of people in our entourage got sick because of the bacteria in the food, but I took a preventative measure: I ate yogurt every day. Probiotics. The only yogurt I could get had a really bad stench and was served in jars without lids on them. Every day, I'd take a big dollop of strawberry jam and mix it in and somehow manage to get it down the hatch. I'm convinced that it kept me from getting sick. Shelley didn't do that and she got sick. She wasn't the only one.

It was so hot there during the daytime that, from about 11:00 A.M. until late afternoon, you really couldn't go outside. If you wanted to venture, you'd have to wear all white clothes, a white hat, and go from shade to shade. You couldn't hang out. Everything becomes a ghost town except for a few hardy locals, walking their horses up and down the streets. Nighttime was where it was at, and that's something that we could really get with. In fact, part of the impetus of us being there in Egypt came from Richard Loren, who had visited Luxor and made a spiritual connection between Egyptians and hippies. They had tapestries instead of tie-dyes but it was all cut from the same cloth. And they liked getting high as much as we did.

The Mena House was on the one road that ran up to the Great Pyramid, in an area called Mena Village, which is a little outpost at the edge of Cairo. The downtown is way off in the distance. Mena Village can be a tourist trap during the day for all the travelers going to and from the pyramids.

Everyone on the hotel staff instructed us not to go out after dark. "There's a reason we have a fence around the perimeter," they said. "It isn't safe." You tell the Grateful Dead or the Merry Pranksters not to do something and you know damn well that's one sure way to get them to do it. So we all—individually and in small groups—snuck out. We all found each other out in the street and started laughing our asses off.

The Egyptians were the nicest, most peaceful people I had ever met in my entire life. And at that time of night, after it cools off, they go outside and sit with their hookahs in front of their shops and homes and drink tea and smoke. They didn't drink any alcohol and that was really an attractive characteristic to me—even though we drank a ton of beer, out of supersized bottles, back at the hotel.

The local custom for smoking hash was a bit different than ours. They'd fill their hookahs with black, gooey tobacco and then they'd clean out a little, finger-sized bowl in the middle where they'd place a tiny, round ball of hash. They showed us their way and then we showed them ours—we filled the entire hookah with hash. No tobacco. We put some coals in the middle, so the hash would burn, and puffed, puffed, passed. The local Egyptians scratched their heads and shot each other glances and then got really, ridiculously stoned with us. Everybody had fun.

Shelley and I met a friendly local who invited us inside his abode to meet his family and see his horses. Their horses are a source of great pride, and they treat them like extended members of the family. In fact, the horses actually live in their basements, where the stalls are kept cleaner than any racetrack's I've ever seen. Manure gets picked up faster than the hottest hooker in all of Las Vegas—they use it for growing vegetables. These Arabian horses were so completely trained, they were simply incredible animals.

The rest of the house had the faint smell of horse wafting through it, but it wasn't so bad. With their smell came their heat—the horses became natural space heaters during the cool desert nights.

All of the furniture in this particular house was covered in plastic, so it wouldn't get dirty. I don't know if that was an Egyptian thing, or a 1970s' thing, but the plastic all had the same color and the same design, and I looked at Shelley like, "This is a little weird." But we weren't scared of a little weird.

Our hosts invited us to stay and drink tea, so we sat on the couches, on top of the plastic, and sipped away. They weren't trying to sell us knives or get us to join their religion or rip us off in any way—they were just being friendly. Strangers stopping strangers. The Heart of Gold Band.

We couldn't really say but a few words to each other, because of the language barrier, but we tried knocking it down with a combination of charades and ingenuity. Shelley somehow explained to them that we had horses at home, too, that we loved. But the love these people had for their horses really left an impression on us. They didn't just care for their animals; they respected them.

Everyone we met in the village was just as peaceful and as sweet as could be. When we compared notes the next day, every single person in our traveling rock 'n' roll carnival had similar experiences. There was nothing but love and good tidings. So all that nonsense that the hotel staff told us about the dangerous world outside their protected gates was just hogwash. It always is, isn't it? They probably just wanted us to spend our money exclusively in their overpriced hotel shops and restaurants.

The Sphinx Theater held a couple thousand people and we couldn't sell it out. Cairo wasn't our biggest market. There were a lot of Americans in the audience but not all of them were Deadheads; at least, not in the traditional sense. I looked out at the crowd and thought, "Pretty straight audience." There were a lot of American diplomats and government workers—and their families—mixed in among some extremely stoked foreign exchange students and random travelers. About a hundred seats went to our friends and family, including the Pranksters. And then Basketball Hall of Famer (and "Celebrity Deadhead Number One"), Bill Walton, led his own entourage on this Egyptian expedition. So the crowd was small but mighty.

A really incredible thing happened, in regards to the audience, at those three shows: Only a waist-high cement wall enclosed the outdoor venue. There were even sections where the theater was basically just roped off from the open desert. It was an arbitrary perimeter. If you didn't feel the need to be front and center, you could easily see and hear everything just fine without having to buy a ticket. You could still take the ride. Well, sure enough, on the first night I saw these shadowy figures sitting on camels watching us play. They formed a row around the outside, all the way around. Talk about general admission on the lawn! Except, of course, the "lawn" here was genuine desert.

By the second night, these shadowy figures numbered two and three deep, and by the third, you could hardly see past them, at eye level. Given the outlaw cowboy image that we had back home in the Wild West, we automatically felt some kind of affinity for these camelback riders. They were the Bedouins. Nomadic tribesmen. The real deal. I didn't know anything about the Bedouins, but they had an impregnable presence to them. You couldn't penetrate these people. There was an understood feeling that you were to keep your distance. They didn't put out anything bad or negative in any way—they didn't brandish swords or act in any way that was threatening. As a matter of fact, they acted peacefully. But there was a sense of both silence and space, forming a line that we didn't even think to cross. (Rolling Thunder commanded a similar sense of silence and space, but he invited us to cross it.)

The Bedouins were shadowy in the literal sense—their faces were all hidden and drawn back inside their hoodies. All you could see was a soft red glow, right around where their mouths would be—they were smoking something. They sat almost completely still, on top of their camels, and watched us play.

Nobody in our midst was able to meet them or have any kind of interaction with them whatsoever. Nobody dared. We didn't research it further but communicating with them would've been very difficult—none of us spoke Ancient Arabic as a second language. They had a quiet strength about them that you just watched and respected. And they must've liked the Grateful Dead well enough, because they came back each night in stronger numbers. So maybe the respect was mutual. That's kind of neat to think about.

The stage was right in front of the Sphinx, and the Great Pyramid was right at the bottom of that. It's all built on the same outcropping of stone. There are a number of tombs off the back side of the Great Pyramid. That whole area is one big giant rock necropolis.

Everything about the Great Pyramid is far-out. It's one of the Seven Wonders of the World and the largest known pyramid on Earth. There are three burial chambers inside—an underground one, carved into the bedrock, then the queen's chamber and, of course, the king's chamber is the centerpiece. The master bedroom. No corpses were ever discovered in any of the chambers, and archeologists and theorists have questioned if all three were ever intended to be burial chambers to begin with—especially the queen's chamber, which one popular theory posits was meant to hold a sacred statue of the king.

In 1978, when we went there, they hadn't even discovered a blocked shaft that leads to the queen's chamber—that particular shaft was so well hidden, that archeologists didn't locate it until 2002. And anyway, they never did find King Khufu in the king's chamber, so as far as we know, it may never have been used for what we thought it was supposed to be used for.

We used it for something else that it wasn't supposed to be used for. We had a group excursion to the Great Pyramid during one of our free days in the week leading up to the shows, a little entourage that included the band, wives, Bill Walton, and so on. The walkway to the king's chamber might be four feet tall so Walton, being 6'11", had to crawl on his butt and shimmy up the pyramid backwards, pushing with his hands. Maybe that was good training for the NBA, because he didn't seem to mind. Kesey and some of the other Pranksters were there, too, but on both feet.

As a matter of fact, in a display of Merry Pranksterdom, George Walker climbed a wooden pole at the top of the Great Pyramid and put a Grateful Dead flag on it, which stayed there, untouched, for at least a few days. Back then, they didn't really stop you from trying to climb the outside. If you got hurt, that was on you. Thus, it was on Walker when he got splinters on his legs, sliding down that pole. He didn't seem to mind.

We were granted a private tour of the Great Pyramid, so there were no other tourists coming or going while we were in there. When we got into the king's chamber, Kesey pulled out a harmonica and started playing, "Oh, Susannah." It was the stupidest thing—but we all started singing. Turned out to not be so stupid—the king's chamber is an impeccable echo chamber. The acoustics were incredible and the echo and reverb properties did an excellent job of skull fucking our minds. It was so good that we wanted to use it—somehow—as part of our live concert sound for the shows.

Our sound team, Dan Healy and John Cutler, tried to make that happen. They placed a microphone and a speaker inside the chamber, so they could use it as an echo room—kind of like the world's biggest and baddest delay pedal. They wired it to a transmitter, running the cables to the chamber by snaking them through air holes. The FM transmitter was going to send the signal to the mixing console, giving Healy an unbelievably cool effect to use in his sandbox for the shows. But they couldn't get it to work. We have no idea to this day why it wouldn't work. Some theories involve the will of the pyramids: perhaps they hold a certain power and influence over the electromagnetic field within a certain radius. Perhaps they were just trying to protect their own air space. Of course, another explanation is simply that the only wires we could get over there to rig the thing up were pretty much useless.

Looking back, I wonder: Was it ballsy, on our end, to crawl into a sacred chamber and sing a campfire song, in an ancient power spot where FM signals didn't work and where science may have spoken an ancient dialect?

We visited some of the other pyramids while we were there, too. The old pyramids. They were in Saqqara City, which is nicknamed "City of the Dead." How appropriate. It's a little more than eight miles from the Great Pyramid and is part of a sacred necropolis; an ancient burial ground for the rich and famous which, in those days, meant royalty. We visited one of the step pyramids that they said, on a clear day, you could see all the way from our hotel in Mena Village, and it was a really fascinating pyramid in its own right. It was really worn down; it's a lot older than the Great Pyramid itself. One thing I remember is that it had a carving that looked like whoever carved it was trying to depict a spaceman looking out of a capsule. Parts of that assessment were undeniable. The carving had a round helmet around the head, and what might've even been a breathing tube. And I thought, "How did the ancient Egyptians know about modern space travel?" It's a question that I'd still like answered. Maybe it just predicted the Grateful Dead landing in Egypt. Because the whole thing felt like some kind of outer space mission. Or something. We were definitely strangers in a strange land.

It also cost a pretty penny. Everything was on our dime. In fact, the tab came to half a million dollars. Back in 1972 we took everyone to Europe and it made for one of the greatest adventures of any of our lives. Six years later, we went to Egypt under slightly different circumstances—but we reasoned that the more people we could bring along with us, the more fun we could have. And we were right. It was priceless and perfect and, at half a million dollars, a bargain in the end. Albeit, a very expensive bargain.

Different people at different times would come visit Shelley's and my room and smoke hash with us. It became some kind of ritual. We hosted a daily hash happy hour. At any hour. So that, too, was great fun.

Here's a story for you: It was after the show on the second night, if I remember it right, when a local fella that had about ten horses got some of us together for a little late-night excursion. It was myself, Mickey, Sunshine Kesey—daughter of Ken Kesey—and Mountain Girl, and some others. We set out for a place called Sahara City, which is a nightclub in the middle of the desert that isn't exactly your typical nightclub, by any means. The Fillmore, it was not. We rode in a straight line, kicking up rocks and stuff, with our backs against the moon. It was a full moon rising. We were running away from it, on the way to a tent city in the desert. Not Black Rock. Before we even got there, we could hear the drums, beating their way across the dunes. It was a crazy, outrageous, belly-dancing kind of drumming. Really fast, hard-hitting, bright drumming. The kind I like.

When we finally pulled up, the only parking they had available was a railing, which was nearly filled up with horses and camels. Nobody drove here in their Mustang. Just on a mustang, perhaps. The kind with hooves. We were out in the wide open, under Egyptian skies. In the dark, the vastness of the desert was palpable as our imaginations ran side by side with the realities.

Sahara City was a crazy little scene. There were drumming and dancing, and the vibrancy shocked us out of the desolation of the desert. This was some kind of an oasis; our kind. Our tour guide signaled us to an area of the tent where we posted up, and I barely noticed any of that because I was so taken by the drums, which were loud and incredible. I had never heard anything that sounded quite like that before, although it wasn't for lack of searching. This may have been the most moving music that I've ever witnessed. It had the center of the earth involved. It had lava. It had eruptions. It had pleasure and pain; joys and sorrows. It was fucking outrageous.

The drummers were playing on doumbeks, which are meant to incite belly dancing. There were women belly dancing all over the place, in indiscriminate places—there was no stage or anything. No spotlights. The drummers were scattered all over the floor, and the women were dancing among the drummers, and it was like, "Are you kidding me?"

This was in a large tent, and—after being at the Great Pyramid, playing our own music, then riding horses by moonlight across the desert—here we were, getting to witness this truly insane drumming. Our minds were just totally blown by the magic of Egypt. We were taken away. Mickey and I couldn't even talk; we were literally speechless. It seemed like we'd only been there for a second, maybe a minute, and then *Bam*!—it all stopped. It stopped on a dime. It stopped. Our guide said, "It's over, you guys. It's midnight. Time to go home." Damn. We were hoping the music would never stop.

We hadn't been there all that long—less than a half an hour for sure—but it made a permanent impression on me and left me with a clear memory of those rhythms. It was that powerful. We went outside and we got back up on our horses. Our guide thought I was the leader of this group for some reason, and he asked if it would be all right for him to take Sunshine around and show her off to his friends before we left. His English wasn't all that developed, but he said, "I want her to meet some people." Sunshine was into it and I was fine with the idea, so away they went. The moon was up higher now, and it was brighter. You could see the moonlight reflecting off the tents and the horses and the camels and there was nothing else there, really. Nothing for miles around. Not even a Starbucks.

After hearing that music, your mind is really clear. You're a part of the desert. You just had communion with it. From up on high on my horse, I had an even greater sense of the nothing that surrounded us. We didn't come in on a road. There was no road.

As I sat there, my mind started to wander. I lost track of time. How long had it been since we last saw Sunshine? The thought started turning around in my head, and I started getting nervous. "Oh shit, what did I just do?" I let Sunshine go riding off with a guy that I only met a few hours ago. I didn't know the local scene. Maybe the hotel was right after all, maybe it was dangerous at night. In the darkness, where the fuck was Sunshine? Did I need to go and rescue her?

I continued to work myself up about it, building in intensity as every minute passed by. I decided that I definitely needed to go find Sunshine. This was unacceptable. I was an experienced horseback rider, of course, so I pulled back the reins and kicked the horse and . . . nothing! I pulled the reins back even harder, kicked harder, finally started really kicking the horse hard—nothing! I couldn't move this creature. I realized right away that these horses were trained to do that.

Egyptian horses listen to their masters. Our guide instructed these horses not to move. At the time, I didn't understand that it was to protect us. This way, we wouldn't be able to ride off into the desert, into uncertainty, hot-headed, all alone and out of water. At the time, I didn't pick up on any of that. I was too busy worrying about Sunshine. "Oh my God, what I have done?" And all the while, I couldn't get the fucking horse to move. It had a built in antitheft device. Better than any car alarm.

I was getting ready to launch a search party and take the desert by foot, when here comes Sunshine, all smiles. Our guide was smiling, too. Sunshine told us all about her fun little adventure: "It was great! I went to different families and saw how they lived." They had never seen a blond girl like Sunshine before. They found her remarkable, and she obviously dug it, too; she was fearless in her joy and they could feel the love she brought with her, everywhere she went. Our guide nodded in appreciation as Sunshine recounted the scene.

We rode back, all of us together again, feeling incredible. We had an experience that took us higher than any drug in the world, we heard drumming that was better than any drumming in the world; we were out in the desert at the edge of the world. It was a wild night. As we rode back home, directly toward the Giza pyramids, the moon hung above our heads. We could see the Great Pyramid, all lit up by the moon. Our guide told the horses to run. Fast. Out there in that part of Egypt, the desert floor has more rocks than sand. At the speed we went, the horses kicked up the rocks, causing sparks to fly off their hooves—brilliant, bright sparks like fireworks for equestrians.

I was behind the group, bringing up the rear, taking in the scene and marveling over how far out it was, when I started getting hit by all the rocks. I had to pull my horse way off to the right to get out of it, but it was such a magical experience. We didn't slow down until we got back and only then did we do a collective, "Whew!' and "Wow!" and "Do you believe what just happened?" It was an incredible night. Hugs and high fives all around.

The Grateful Dead went a lot of places and had a lot of crazy times—and I've continued to feed my appetite for adventure in the years since the Dead disbanded—but I can tell you that nothing I've done has been as far-out as our time in Egypt. I'm glad I got to go when I did, too—1978—because I don't think it would be quite as friendly today, with all the Middle Eastern turmoil. It couldn't be. I was shocked when Sadat was cold-bloodedly murdered. It's a different environment, now. Maybe they need more music.

I was so enthralled with the Egyptian adventure that I continued to wear my Egyptian apparel for weeks afterward, in the same way that kids sometimes wear admission wristbands long after the festival is over. I picked up a fine Egyptian cotton galabeya that was white with green stripes, and I'd wear it while running errands in Mendocino. That got me some really strange looks from my neighbors and the townsfolk, but I didn't give a fuck. In my mind, I was still in Egypt.

Truth be told, the shows that we played there weren't our best. They weren't bad by any means . . . but they weren't our best. I know that, for true Deadheads, despite all of the wonderful aspects surrounding the shows and the lot scene and the culture and the road life, it was most important that the music always came first. It was that way for us, as well. It was the heart of the whole thing. But Egypt was about a lot more than just playing music. And it was a whole lot bigger than just a bunch of hippies from California banging out some weird sounds on electric instruments. Egypt rocked but it wasn't all in the name of rock 'n' roll. We went there to tap into the greater spirit of things and to be just some small spec in a much larger experience.

It wasn't any one of our faults that the shows weren't as inspired as the situation. I think we were all just a bit overwhelmed and felt humbled by the weight of the history of it all.

Also: I was playing with a broken wrist. So there's that. The Great Pyramid gigs were in the middle of September (beginning on 9/14/78). A couple weeks before then, on our way to Egypt, we played a show at Giants Stadium in New Jersey (9/2/78) and a two-night stand at Red Rocks, just outside Denver (beginning on 8/30/78). But we had most of the summer off.

About four days before leaving for this great adventure, my friend from boarding school, John Warnecke, came up to Mendocino to visit me at my Comptche ranch. Warnecke, of course, was the guy whose father had the Russian River property where we practiced back in 1967. We had come a long way since then. A few days before his visit, there was an outrageous party a couple miles inland from Mendocino, at a house in the middle of the woods. It was a really crazy-looking house, too. The host had the kind of cannons that you'd find on a pirate ship. So, naturally, we filled them with black powder—like pirates—and tons of fruit—like hippies—and just blasted the booty off into the forest. It made a horrendous noise and produced clouds of white smoke. I loved it. It brought back memories.

At the end of the party, the host gave me an ounce of cocaine. I don't know why, exactly, but I'm not one to turn things down. So I took it home and proceeded to get into it. It was real high quality—the good stuff. Pink on the inside. Shelley gave up on me after a couple of days and was in bed just trying to pry me away from the bag of coke. But as anyone reading this who's ever had an unfinished bag of coke knows, it just doesn't work that way. Then, along comes Warnecke. Cocaine may be the bathroom drug at a house party, but even behind closed doors, it sure loves company. We got into it right away and kept at it until the day before I was supposed to meet the band down at Front Street in San Rafael and embark upon our trip. I was trying to get things in order at home, pack, and all of that. Cocaine can be good for that sort of thing.

We had a horse in the pasture—a large, quarter horse—that I had to bring into the stable. It was my horse, so I went and put the halter on her, but we were on a hill and it was a real skittish horse to begin with. In my altered state, I jumped on her back and she threw me—she reared back, lifted her front legs, and threw me off into the air, down the hill. I was in full flight. I paddled backward as fast as I could, trying to fly. Actually, I was just trying to get my feet under me before I hit the ground, because it was on a slope and was a longer fall than just off the top of the horse. There was no way to straighten out. No way to get my balance. To avoid landing on the small of my back, I managed to get my left hand down under me, but my full weight and the force of impact was too much for it. I broke my wrist. At first, I was in denial. "Oh, come on, it's just a sprain." But it swelled up and the pain became so bad that I had to go and see a doctor in Fort Bragg immediately.

The doctor confirmed that it was broken—he didn't even need to X-ray it to tell me that much—and he wanted to put a fiberglass cast on it. But I had shows at Red Rocks, Giants Stadium, and *Egypt* all coming up. A cast? No can do. So the doctor just wrapped it up, gave me some painkillers, and off I went.

The next day, Shelley and I drove down to San Rafael to begin our crazy adventure. We went to meet the band at Front Street. I knew that it wasn't going to be pretty when the guys found out about my wrist. I thought that maybe if I just wrapped a T-shirt around it and pretended that it was casual, maybe nobody would notice. Well, I don't think I made it more than ten feet inside Front Street when Jerry called me out: "Hey Billy, why are you hiding your wrist?" "Oh, man. . . ." Everyone standing around, in unison, went, "What have you done, now?" I pulled it out and gave the story. I knew this was going to be the start of a long, hard, strange trip. It was already going to be long and strange. But now it was going to be hard, too.

I couldn't use my left hand to play the drums—if I just touched the drum with a stick, it sent a sharp pain up my entire left arm. So I learned fast how to play one-handed and it became a positive experience in the end because I had to learn how to separate the bass drum and the hits from my right hand. So it became, in a strange way, a forced drum lesson. It was a teaching tool. It taught me how to play the snare beats with my right hand and not come down all the time with my bass drum, which is a habit that drummers get into—hitting the bass drum and the cymbal at the same time. It's really productive to learn how to hit them on opposite beats, break them up and know how to keep them separate when you want to. The technical term for that, among drummers, is independence. The uniqueness of it wore off fast, but at least I was able to get something out of it.

When we flew to Denver to play Red Rocks, a doctor convinced me to put a fiberglass cast on it because every time I moved my wrist, no matter how slightly, it would shoot a lightning bolt of pain all the way up to my shoulder. So I put the cast on and for those Red Rocks shows, I still couldn't use that hand for anything. But by the time we got to Egypt, it had healed enough that it didn't hurt anymore. It was still in the cast, and it was frustrating for me to have to listen to so much music without being able to play more than I could.

When they molded the cast for me, I told them to leave a space so I could hold a drumstick in there. The doctor said, "I'm not sure you're going to be able to play without it hurting, but we can go ahead and try that." It didn't work. It was fool's folly trying to get a cast that would hold a stick.

It started to feel better when we got to New Jersey. We played Giants Stadium, which, as many of you will remember, was a massive football stadium at the Meadowlands Complex, just outside of New York. Home of the New York Giants NFL team for many years. Almost as famous as the Garden. We headlined more than a dozen shows there throughout our career, but this was our Giants Stadium debut. I think we booked it mostly to help finance our trip to Egypt. Help offset some of that massive cost, anyway.

At the Giants Stadium gig, during the drum solo, I stood up and went to play these really big drums behind Mickey and me that we used for that part of the show. I started using the cast as a beater and it worked great. It didn't hurt. I couldn't play superfast or anything, but it didn't matter to me—I could use both hands now and use my cast as part of my instrument. When the audience saw the close-up of that on the video screen, they went nuts. Mickey got very, very excited—not in the good way—when I started doing that, for some reason. He insisted that I stop immediately. He started yelling, right over our solo, "If you don't cut that right now, I'm going to walk off." I probably stopped. He was just worried about me, that's all.

I still had to keep the cast on when we got to Egypt, so I wasn't able to play the full-on drum set. That's honestly not the only reason that parts of those shows were so lackluster . . . but perhaps it had something to do with it. In all fairness, the sluggish dream-state that hash puts you in probably played a part in all that, too, and that was a high that everyone seemed to be riding.

I'd like to back up for a moment and talk about Red Rocks. We played our first pair of shows at that incredible venue earlier that summer, on July 7 and 8. We returned at the end of August for the two shows when my wrist was broken. Of note, all four shows were consecutive. We didn't play anywhere else in the six weeks in between.

Red Rocks is one of the most mystical places that I've ever been, much less played music. The only venue in America that can really compete is a newer place in Oregon called Horning's Hideout. That place is a different kind of far-out, though; you're surrounded by trees and away from the city. The Gorge Amphitheater in Washington is a power spot as well, but it has its challenges with wind issues when you're in the drummer's stool on that stage. And it gets really cold there when the sun goes down.

Red Rocks is mystical, though. It's at 6,450 feet elevation, so when you come from sea level like I always did, you get a little buzzed in the weirdest of ways. When you get up to that altitude, the thickness of the lower register just goes away. It takes more energy, more air, to produce really full sounding bass notes—so when you're up in thin air, you get less bass.

Being able to play music at Red Rocks was a privilege and the fact that an amphitheater even exists there is like some kind of miracle. And I saw more kids looking for miracles there than anywhere else. The kids used to climb the rocks on the sides and it would scare the shit out of us because we were concerned about their safety. It was dangerous enough trying to climb those rocks during the day, but at nighttime, you couldn't really climb down safely because you couldn't see. It's one of the wildest venues I've ever seen. Playing in Golden Gate Park in San Francisco was really far-out, but there's just something about Red Rocks that makes it special. Very. And even with the altitude challenges, it sounds great in there. A natural amphitheater carved out of rock, high above Denver, in the Rocky Mountains? Yes, please.

I also want to back up and talk about Shelley for a second. After Susila and I divorced, I was living as a bachelor at my Comptche ranch for a short period of time. Shelley used to hang out with some of my music friends, at a bar in Mendocino that I used to go to a lot and play music. Someone told her I was coming down one night, and she made it a point to stay. We hit it off the moment we first met. In fact, I had a couple of gigs scheduled with some local guys—just some low-key extracurricular stuff for fun—and I remember driving back to Mendocino, thinking, "I can't wait to see her again." Once you have those thoughts, you know that you're in it.

The thing that really sewed us up as a couple, though, is kind of a funny story, involving LSD. Shelley was a schoolteacher in the town of Mendocino, right on the coast, and I was out at the Comptche ranch, fifteen miles away. I was all excited that she was going to come visit. It was going to be a date and I was going to cook for her. I was all nervous. When she got there, she was tired from teaching all day and decided she needed to shower before we could hang out. Afterward, she came downstairs and we started playing backgammon. I taught her the game at some point before this, and she was generally a fast learner. This time, however, she started making up moves that just don't exist. But they really should. Special feature moves. Fifth dimension moves. The kind of moves you might come up with if you were high on acid.

She looked at me and started blinking her right eye and asked, "Was that Murine in your shaving kit expired or something? I put it in my eye and it really burned." I went, "Oh shit! That wasn't old Murine at all! That was brand-new acid!" I didn't know what to do, so I called Ken Kesey and laid out the situation. "Hey Ken, funniest thing happened . . . Shelley accidentally put LSD in her right eye." He didn't miss a beat: "Right on, Bill. Put it in your left eye and have a good time. Bye."

Shelley got as high as could be and just rolled with it. We ended up having a grand old time. I remember waking up, after we finally slept, and the whole floor was covered with vinyl records from the night before. I had played DJ but I didn't put any of the albums back in their sleeves. It was just next one, next one, next one. We had such a fun time, tripping by ourselves inside the house, that it really launched and solidified our relationship.

What broke our relationship, fifteen years later, was cocaine. It also hurt the Grateful Dead. And a lot of other relationships, both within my circle and without. Cocaine has its place . . . but it's a detrimental drug, make no mistake.

I don't remember when Shelley and I got married, exactly. I'm thinking it was sometime just before Egypt. So, 1978. But maybe 1977. I was doing a lot of drugs back then and some things just run together. I'm not even sure if I had a best man for the ceremony, but the wedding was at the Comptche ranch and I know that it was an extremely hot day because the cake started to melt and fall over, so we had to serve it up to everyone really fast. I was on tour right before then and had to drive all the way back from the airport in San Francisco the night before and go straight to all the rehearsal dinner stuff. Bobby and Mickey had to do pretty much the same thing, because they made it up there for the ceremony. So did Bill Walton, who complained and gave me a ration of shit because there is no short cut to Comptche—it's a long haul no matter where you're coming from and the second half of the journey is all on winding country roads through Mendocino County. It's a trek.

One of the many wonderful gifts to come from my fifteen years with Shelley was that she got me into scuba diving, which changed my life and has been a passion of mine ever since. Shelley got certified while I was on tour, and when I heard her excitement about the underwater world, I decided that it was something I needed to check out. So I did, in Laredo, Mexico, when I recklessly went sixty feet under the water for my first time, without certification or instruction. I took Jerry on his first dive, too, and it changed his life as well. But now we're talking about stuff that happened in the late-'80s. We'll get there. First, I have a couple really good John Belushi stories to tell, stemming from the Grateful Dead's first performance on *Saturday Night Live.*

15

At some point in 1975, during the Grateful Dead's hiatus, something happened that would forever change late-night television: *Saturday Night Live*. Groundbreaking in its unflinching use of satire and the unapologetic way that it made fun of sensitive current events—on live television, for a national audience—NBC's new sketch comedy show became an instant smash, and its cast (which, during that inaugural season, included John Belushi, Dan Aykroyd, Chevy Chase, and Gilda Radner) became instant *SNL* stars. I became an instant fan. I never watched much television, but I used to love to get stoned and turn on *SNL*. They had those fake commercials that would get me every time. I just loved that.

Although I didn't know it at the time, one of *SNL*'s top writers, Tom Davis, was a Deadhead. At some point, after Davis and I became friends, I congratulated him on winning an Emmy Award. It was for Outstanding Writing in a Comedy Variety or Music Special—specifically, for his work on NBC's December 8, 1977, *Paul Simon Special*.

I looked at him and said, "You know, I never had an Emmy." Without missing a beat, he said, "You know, I never had a gold record." The logical conclusion was that we should fix that by trading awards. Tit for tat. We were just being silly, but we went with it. So on the bookshelf in my living room now, I have an Emmy Award for an NBC special. And, somewhere, Davis was able to hang a gold album for *American Beauty*.

I should also mention, as a footnote, that Davis's writing and acting partner was Al Franken, who is now a U.S. senator (D.) for Minnesota—and a Deadhead. "We are everywhere."

It may not be immediately obvious, but there are some undeniable parallels—or, at least, similarities—between the Grateful Dead and *SNL*. We both constantly took great risks, which sometimes led to train wrecks but also led us to unprecedented triumphs. We both were seen as renegade heroes of counterculture, rebellious artists that prided ourselves on challenging the status quo. We both were underdogs from the underground that somehow managed to embed ourselves in at least one home in just about any given neighborhood in America. And, behind the scenes, both the cast of *SNL* and the band members of the Grateful Dead were legendary party animals, ravenous for drugs and danger . . . and dangerous drugs. It seemed like both camps would get along.

Still, it was a bit of a shock—and a total thrill—when I found out that we were invited to be the musical guests for one of the episodes. Not everyone in the band shared my enthusiasm. Jerry wasn't into it. I'm not sure that Phil was, either. They had their reasons, whatever they were, but Mickey sided with me and we managed to convince them to do it. We ended up playing *SNL* twice over the next couple of years, but our debut was on November 11, 1978, with Buck Henry hosting. We performed "Casey Jones," "I Need a Miracle," and "Good Loving" and we actually managed to pull it off, bucking the trend of us messing up the big ones.

For me, the best part was getting to have a cameo in one of the comedy sketches with my favorite cast member: John Belushi. I had the simplest part. I played "Cliff Morton from Bakersfield," and I got to drink Budweiser on live national TV. People ask me and, yes, it was real Budweiser. Still didn't calm my nerves. But the sketch worked and the audience laughed. It didn't launch my career in comedy, per se, but it did lead to a fantastic and treasured friendship with Belushi that would get us into some wild adventures in the days to come. Belushi died in 1982, darn it, but boy did we ever have high times 'til then.

I hung out with Belushi whenever I could, especially when the band had shows in New York. We'd kick it at his place, or his office, or wherever we could find trouble. I have many different memories of John Belushi, but the one I'm about to tell you is my absolute favorite.

The Grateful Dead had a three-night stand at the Capitol Theater—not the restored one in Port Chester, New York, where we played a number of historic shows as well, but the one on the other side of the city, in Passaic, New Jersey—beginning on March 30, 1980. We weren't on tour, and I think we probably booked the gigs as a stand-alone run because we were going to be in New York anyway, for our second appearance on *SNL*, on April 5, 1980.

By that point, Belushi had already left the cast of *SNL* to concentrate on film. But we decided to pull off some real life "sketchy comedy," so I met up with him a few days before the shows and we immediately started getting into trouble. And trouble with Belushi almost always meant cocaine. We went on a bit of a bender, just raving the nights away. The day before our opening night, he really wanted me to hear this demo tape of a radio sketch that he was working on for a National Lampoon show. The setup was that he played a drugged-out hitchhiker who was trying to get to a Grateful Dead concert to see Pigpen play with Janis Joplin. He wasn't aware that the year was 1980. It was a classic Belushi sketch. All in the delivery, perhaps.

He insisted that we go down to the studio so that we could listen to the playback. But when we got there, the producer was busy in the control room and we had to wait. As you know by now, "waiting"—for either of us—meant imminent trouble. Belushi waltzed right into the main recording room and started stuffing all these expensive microphones into all of his pockets until he was just overflowing with them in a really cartoonish way. "See how easy it is, Billy? Want a brand-new microphone?" He put them back, but not until after I had a good laugh. Pure slapstick.

After that, we went back to Belushi's office and continued to party. In between blowing lines of cocaine were fits of laughter. Suddenly, I realized that it was approaching afternoon—on the day of the show! We had been raving until the night had passed back into the day. I started getting paranoid. How would I have enough energy to make it through the show? This was night one and I owed the audience my best. I needed to get some sleep and drag my ass over to soundcheck somehow.

But Belushi had a different idea. He took me to a Russian bathhouse that, in those days, were popular places for men to go and get massages and rejuvenate, kind of like what spas are for women nowadays. Belushi was a regular at a few of them in the city. When we got there, he slipped the door guy a twenty-dollar bill and they chatted about nothing for a few minutes. New York City loved John Belushi because of things like that. That's just who he was.

The doorman led us inside, and I remember it being a real solemn place, with some kind of heaviness in the air that I couldn't put my finger on. It wasn't quite my scene and I wasn't totally comfortable with it. In keeping with the custom, we stashed our clothes in lockers and put on robes, then walked down a long flight of stairs to a huge, subterranean area that must have been the size of four basketball courts. It was dark and dingy down there and we went into a giant steam room that was encased in glass. There were old immigrants who were talking quietly among themselves, in near whispers, like they were conspiring or something. We lay down on massage tables and then guys started rubbing eucalyptus boughs on our backs. It just didn't feel right to me, so I got up to leave: "I'm out of here, John. It's just not my thing." But Belushi wasn't going to let me off that easy: "Relax, Bill. Lay down. Trust me."

I was so exhausted that I didn't have the energy to resist. I turned back and ended up falling asleep during a really fantastic massage. I woke up feeling great. We put our robes back on, went upstairs, and got down on the cots, where they brought us ice-cold shots of vodka. Very Russian.

During all of this, some men came in that looked like heavies. Gangsters of old New York. Their eyes were cold and tough—you immediately knew not to fuck with them—and they all wore really expensive, Italian suits. When they went to hang their jackets, you could hear the audible clunk of a heavy object slam against the side of the lockers. They were packing heat. Belushi just glanced at me and said quietly, "You didn't hear that. Don't look up at them. Don't make eye contact." We were surrounded by mobsters.

I went back to the hotel and took a nap and somehow made it to soundcheck on time. Belushi was already there at the venue. "I feel great!" he said. "Don't you?" I did, actually. It was almost showtime.

Belushi loved music and he loved the Grateful Dead. His comedic partner, Dan Aykroyd, turned him on to the blues and he dove into it and became a scholar of the genre. He had a great singing voice and the same knack for perfect phrasing and delivery that he had with comedy. So he and Aykroyd put together a band, which they jokingly named the Blues Brothers. Originally the group was assembled just for a comedy sketch on *SNL*, but they knew they were onto something bigger. The band became real and they cut an album and then made a movie and went on tour. Belushi and Aykroyd created characters for the band—Jake E. Blues and Elwood J. Blues, respectively—but they took the music seriously. They recruited a fantastic lineup of players for it, too. Members of Booker T. and the M.G.s and backing musicians for Isaac Hayes and Howlin' Wolf were in the band, along with a bunch of monster musicians from the SNL Band. Among other things, the Blues Brothers opened for the Grateful Dead on New Year's Eve at the Winterland in 1978.

Well, two years later, backstage at the Capitol Theater after our bath house escapade, Belushi got it into his head that he wanted to sing backup on "U.S. Blues" with us that night. I thought it would be really cool to get Belushi out there with us, of course, so I went and told the band, but Phil was opposed to the idea. He vetoed it. I had to go back to my friend and tell him, "Sorry, buddy, but Phil said no." There were no hard feelings or anything like that; it was what it was.

Why did Phil say no? I can't say for sure, but I know he didn't like my friendship with Belushi. He didn't approve of it. I have no idea why—the two of us just had a grand old time together. But I didn't want to rock the boat, so I respected my bandmate's decision.

I had a really good show that night, and the entire band played well. We encored with "U.S. Blues" as planned and, right before the chorus, Belushi took everyone by surprise by cartwheeling onto the stage. It was a comedic ambush. He had on a sport coat with small American flags stuffed into both of his breast pockets and he landed his last cartwheel just in time to grab a microphone and join in on the chorus. The audience and everyone in the band—except for Phil—ate it up. It couldn't have been rehearsed better. Belushi had impeccable comedic timing, musicality, balls, the works. And, apparently, he didn't take no for an answer.

I really loved my friendship with Belushi and it was especially cool for me because I was such a fan of his work, long before I ever met him. In fact, right before we began rehearsals for our first *Saturday Night Live* appearance, I got his phone number from the producer, Lorne Michaels, and called him up just to tell him how much of a fan I was. I've never done anything like that before, but I couldn't help myself.

After that first *SNL* performance—November 11, 1978—the band joined the cast for a wrap-up party at the Holland Tunnel Blues Bar. It was really just a party space that Belushi and Aykroyd rented, which may or may not have been officially licensed. They put in a jukebox and filled it with blues classics, and they brought in a primitive PA system and some

∽ The night that John Belushi crashed the stage. March 30, 1980. (*Jay Blakesberg*)

house instruments, to encourage impromptu jams after *SNL* tapings—or any other time that was clever. The bar itself was largely unfinished and certainly unrefined. Belushi kept summoning me down to a shady spot in the basement to snort coke and rave about whatever. We had an audience of rats down there; we didn't care. It was a real fun, loose time.

One of Belushi's famous impersonations was of Joe Cocker. We played with Cocker at Woodstock and also shared a bill with him a month prior to that at Flushing Meadows Park in New York—the site of two World's Fairs. Anybody who has seen the *Woodstock* movie, where Cocker performs "With a Little Help from my Friends," knows that he gets a little crazy with gesticulations and facial expressions when he sings. He really feels it and he used to be able to let go and flail about without any self-consciousness. It was admirable, on a level. But then Belushi imitated him on *SNL* and suddenly Cocker got pretty embarrassed by the whole thing and he took offense and it changed the way he performed—he toned everything down. He became more self-aware.

One night in 1976, Cocker was the musical guest on *SNL*. Belushi came out onstage during his rendition of "Feeling Alright." The two were dressed exactly alike and Belushi duplicated every movement, every expression, even the vocals. He nailed it. He didn't exaggerate because he didn't need to; Cocker's stage presence was ripe for parody. Belushi didn't mean any harm by it, of course, and even though Cocker was mortified at first—if you watch the footage, you can see he's a bit thrown off—he was a good sport about it, in the end. At the time, though, I don't think he was too thrilled.

Well, when Belushi and I were hanging out in my hotel room one night, I asked him to do his Cocker impersonation. He left the room and when he came back in, just seconds later, I swear Joe Cocker himself entered the room. Belushi was even funnier in real life than on the screen. If that's possible.

Weir and I hung out with him a couple weeks before he died. On February 21, 1982, we were playing at UCLA's Pauley Pavilion—the same building where Bill Walton rose to fame as a college basketball player—and

I was struggling just to stay awake because, once again, I hadn't slept the night before. One of our roadies said, "Billy, look behind you," and lo and behold, there was Belushi, making all kinds of funny faces at me. I cracked up and my energy returned and we partied with him after the show.

He died just twelve days later. Of an overdose. A speedball, which is a dangerous combination of coke and heroin, is what did it. I sort of want to say that L.A. killed him, but it could've happened anywhere. He moved to L.A. for film work, but they didn't love him there as much as they did in New York.

Hearing the news of his death almost killed me, too. I'm not making a metaphor here. I was living in Novato with Shelley and I was driving home, listening to a Bay Area radio station, when they interrupted the broadcast: "John Belushi was found dead . . ." My heart nearly stopped and I almost got into a horrible car wreck. He was one of those irreplaceable ones. Time has proven that to be true.

If there's one thing I learned from Belushi, it's that humor saves the fucking day. True humor only knows and adheres to itself. It's not about putting someone down or making fun of race or gender. Watching Belushi perform was like going to a little Burning Man of the mind; it was wild, free, full of abandon, reckless, daring, artistic and it spun reality into all sorts of twisted and contorted dimensions. He didn't tell jokes with punch lines; he was both the joke and the punch line. He was an artist and his canvas was humor. And humor saves the day, every time.

16

A couple days after our first *Saturday Night Live* appearance, we released an album called *Shakedown Street*. It was notable for a few reasons. It was the first album we recorded at Front Street. We didn't want to work with Keith Olsen again, but we had to keep our promise to Clive Davis and have someone in the producer's chair—so we hired Little Feat's Lowell George.

I'm a big fan of Little Feat. So I enjoyed having George produce the record. He had a wonderful way about him; he was always really relaxed, which is a great quality to have in the recording environment, and he was a real soulful guy. If he wanted us to work on a song during the session, he wouldn't just talk the talk—he'd put on his guitar and come out and work on it with us. I loved that. He was a musician first and foremost. Maybe that's why he was my favorite producer to work with. He also was the most fun to be around.

Working with him was the easy part of recording that record. The hard part was that the recording studio wasn't a studio—it was Front Street. On the one hand, it was nice being in our own space. It felt like home because it was our home. But it was never really intended to be a studio and, therefore, was never fully equipped as one. It was a raw practice space. There wasn't much in terms of sound isolation or separate booths or a control room or anything like that, so it ended up being more like a really awkward live recording.

As for the songs, a lot of that material just didn't work out so well for us in the studio. Have you picked up on the pattern, yet? The songs were fucking fantastic when we nailed them live: "Shakedown Street," "Fire on the Mountain," "Stagger Lee," and covers of "Dancing in the Streets" and "Good Loving," among other oddities. Mickey and I had an instrumental on there called "Serengeti." It was just an experiment. I don't even think we tried to bring that one to the stage. Some of the other songs on that album are long forgotten, but the ones I mentioned above turned out to be standards and fan favorites. Deadheads refer to this album, and even this era, as Disco Dead. I can see why. The title track has a real upbeat feeling to it and, actually, would make a dynamite disco tune.

As for our cover of Martha & the Vandallas' "Dancing in the Streets," I've heard young bands do that today and they tend to screw it up. It's like they didn't listen to the bass and they don't get the bass drum right. It's supposed to be syncopated, and some of these kids just don't get that. Not all of them, of course, but I heard a band attempt it recently and all I could think was "Oops . . . "

The album cover art, by Gilbert Shelton, depicted the scene outside 20 Front Street, at just about any given time. The song "Shakedown Street" might be about San Rafael at large, although I think it's more about Front Street in particular. You'd have to ask Robert Hunter about that one. Pretty soon the phrase was co-opted by Deadheads to refer to the busiest part of our thriving parking lot scene, where unlicensed vendors sold everything from veggie burritos to ganja goo balls to handmade tie-dyes and bootleg merchandise. You could get anything you wanted before or after our shows on Shakedown, by fans trying to get themselves from show to show.

I went out there a couple times; I liked to see what people made and what they were up to. The scene in Philadelphia, in particular, was always outrageous. I still like to poke around Shakedown and look at all the glass pipes and take one home with me. It was just a really colorful place. You always want your marketplaces to be like that, whether it's in Deadhead-land or a foreign country.

As for the album, given the material and the producer, *Shakedown Street* just wasn't as good as it should have been. But once it was released, it was business as usual for us—which meant, among other things, preparing for our annual New Year's Eve show. Of all of the ones we did over the years, New Year's Eve in 1978 was particularly special. It was on the corner of Post and Steiner in San Francisco—the Winterland Arena.

Our New Year's Eve shows weren't normal concerts. They were a chance for Bill Graham to really have fun with his background in theater. He loved spectacle. Anybody that ever played a show produced by Bill Graham will tell you that, on those nights, they worked for Graham and not the other way around. But on New Year's Eve, particularly, we were Bill Graham's band. He had all sorts of festive things going on that were totally distract-ing and I loved it. It was a good show. Good theater. Graham was really a showman, even in the way he did business. He'd put on the tough guy act or else pull out the "buddy-buddy" routine.

Since New Year's Eve were three-set affairs, I'd pace myself and try not to drink or party too early. I'd do my best to wait until after the first set, at least. Then, at midnight, we'd do the balloon drop and Bill Graham would always be a physical part of it. He used to get dressed up as Father Time and come onstage to officiate at the start of the New Year. To give it his blessing. One year he came onstage, in his Father Time getup, riding in a giant, lit joint ("the SS Columbian"). It was just a prop, of course. Another time, he came out riding a giant mushroom. It was always something different, always a spectacle, and always a fun time.

Well, for the Winterland '78 New Year's Eve gig, the show was a cele-bration for another reason, in a jazz funeral kind of way—it was our col-lective wave good-bye to the Winterland. The old ice-skating rink was being put to rest. The Band held their *Last Waltz* there and now we were playing the Winterland's last waltz. We gave that building its last rites. It served us well during our time there. We played sixty shows at the Winterland, beginning in 1966. It was our traditional New Year's Eve venue, so the farewell concert was bittersweet. But it was an old building and Graham decided to close it. I think there are condos or some such crap there now.

That New Year's Eve show also featured the Blues Brothers and New Riders of the Purple Sage. At midnight, Dan Aykroyd did the countdown. We played for maybe five or six hours. Then breakfast was served.

I remember the Winterland fondly. Musicians would enter through the back door and it was all rundown and old but then you'd enter the pro-verbial fountain of youth in the backstage area—there were pool tables on one end, lots of couches on the other, and every drug and other unspeak-able thing in between. Romances. Cavorting. Shit-talking. Deals and trea-ties. Laughs and follies.

It was another one of those places where all these amazing souls gath-ered, like the kitchen area at 710 Ashbury. It had bathrooms that barely offered any privacy—there was always some kind of action going on in there.

Another great memory I have of us playing the Winterland was this one time, not sure when but I think maybe during a first set, I somehow got Graham's attention because I was worried that the roof was about to cave in. It was raining dirt and plaster and cement. Shit was falling right onto my drum set. I looked up and saw one of our fans trying to sneak into the sold-out show through the roof. It wasn't safe and it wasn't going to work. Graham got the band to stop, shushed everyone in the audience, and then started screaming through Jerry's vocal mic at the kid. Graham's team eventually got him down using rope. It was a whole thing. I was al-ways amazed at the ingenuity of Deadheads but that was just a little too risky. I think he would've stayed up there and watched from there if I hadn't noticed, but there were silver dollar–sized pieces of cement dropping; it was just too disconcerting.

I usually rooted for the gate crashers, though. Not always. Not when they were stupid or when they destroyed property or put people in harm's way or anything like that. But I always had a thing against authority. So, even if we had become the authority, I liked knowing that they got in. A couple at a time, anyway. A trickle not a cascade.

Our final song at the Winterland was "And We Bid You Goodnight." And with that, Father Time ushered in 1979. The beginning of the end of the '70s.

The beginning of 1979 saw us launching into a heavy touring year— the only month that we didn't tour was March and we had a major internal change to deal with, which we'll get to. Right from the get-go, in January, we played Madison Square Garden in New York City for the first time. That's something. You never forget your first. We ended up playing the Garden a total of fifty-two times over the next fifteen years, including two nine-night runs.

The '70s were coming to a close, but before the decade closed up shop, Grateful Dead shows would get a new addition that would take us into the next decade and, in fact, remain a hallmark right through our very last set, as a band. I had played drum solos from the very beginning and they were fun. But with Mickey around, we could bounce sounds and rhythms and ideas off of each other and really transform into the eight-limbed octo-beast. And since "beast" was a good way to describe us, Mickey—always the adventurer—came up with the idea of encasing both of us with a circular metal bar, about twelve feet in diameter, where we could hang an ever-changing arsenal of drums. He called the contraption "the Beast" and it united the two of us inside one big drum ecosystem. It was like we were in our own command center or drum universe. However you want to describe the Beast, it brought forth the age of "Drums ->Space"—the only thing that appeared night after night, even though it was also the part of the show that was the most reliably different every single time. Total improvisation.

Different drums would get hung up on the Beast, leading us to explore different tones, textures, and ideas. We would stand up and beat them with mallets, walking around in a big circle. Also: I would get different hand drums and switch them up to keep it fresh. I had an octoban, which is a set of eight drums of all different sizes that you can spin while playing, making them change pitch just as fast as you cared to spin them. I had a little piccolo at the top all the way down to a bass drum at the bottom. The octoban really opened up a lot of tonal and melodic possibilities, so I played a lot of solos on it. I also used long tubes, anything I could think of, really. Mickey, too. He's a musicologist, so he would bring all kinds of percussive instruments into the mix, from all around the world. We both experimented, constantly. It was always fun for us and fresh for everyone.

Mickey used to play the big drums that produce thunderous lower frequencies. He could make them sound almost like a bass line. I liked to play something that complemented that, so I would go up the sonic ladder and find myself in the higher registers. Together, we created something that sure felt like magic, on a nightly basis.

While none of it was rehearsed and all of it was improvised, before each show, we used to come up with a theme so we could have a common, if vague and elusive, goal in sight. I can't remember most of the themes now, since they were simply abstract ideas to experiment with, but, for example, one night we might say, "It's the end of the world." The next night, it might be the beginning, starting with a big bang. The night after that, it would be totally different. The themes that worked the best or were at least the most amount of fun usually involved the cosmos—going off into space. Some of the other themes were humorous in nature, just to keep ourselves entertained. Like an inside joke where everyone got to hear the punch line. We would go so hard on the drums and just when we—physically—needed a break, the rest of the band would come back onstage and play a segment called "Space," which was the same idea as "Drums" but with all the melodic instruments instead. Their themes were usually different from ours, but they had theirs too. It often got pretty far out there. If you were in the audience, on psychedelics, it could get pretty heavy and lead you into some intense head spaces. I loved that.

I'm pretty sure the first time we used the Beast was at an outdoor gig in San Jose, California—basically, a hometown gig—on April 22, 1979. That night would be remembered for a different reason and a different first:

it was the first time we had a keyboard player by the name of Brent Myd-land join our ranks. His first show.

I guess I need to back up and explain: Like *Spinal Tap* and drummers, the Grateful Dead had a way of going through keyboardists. If they were full-time members, their residency with the band had a tendency to terminate early due to death. Pigpen was the first to go. Keith was the second. But Keith wasn't playing in the band when he died. He checked out of the band before checking out.

Keith felt a lot of pressure in his role as the band's keyboardist and I'm not quite sure he was ever able to fully get a handle on road life. At least, not the way we did it. Some people are wired for the lifestyle . . . but most people aren't. Oh, sure, it's exciting at first; it's like you're on a giant carousel and everything goes around and around and there's lights and music and the horses are going up and down and the scenery is all a blur and things come in and out of focus, in and out of focus, but all you have to do is hang on. That's all you have to do. Hang on. Smile. Let the carousel take you in endless circles. Well, some people get motion sickness from the ride.

Keith's health, both mental and physical, was deteriorating. He was in a heavy place, had heavy things on his mind, and did heavy things to deal with it all. His drug use was through the roof. It was like that for all of us, I suppose, and that's one thing that's always been an unspoken crux of the Grateful Dead family: we all did drugs—some more than others—but we all did them. And we were spokespeople for an ideology of personal freedom. But when someone in our ranks went overboard, we all would start pointing fingers. Especially when it started affecting the music. Our music was the only thing that was sacred and we all wanted to protect it, even though we weren't always the best at that. We were all guilty of our bad nights and of being responsible for causing them. But when somebody else in the band was doing something to cause them to have one bad night after another, repeatedly, then it became a problem. Spoken or not.

Down the line, Jerry would be the one member who could get the hall pass on this. But Keith did not. In fact, toward the end of Keith's time with us, Jerry would get pissed at him because he'd get lazy and start mimicking Jerry's guitar lines during the jams; his own creative spark had been blacked out by then.

Early in the year, as we were touring arenas, coliseums, and big rooms across the country, Keith and Donna appeared to be unraveling as a couple. They had been volatile for a long time and there's nothing worse than having to be around a married couple when they're fighting. Like the time they turned the parking lot of Front Street into a Demolition Derby. It's a drag for them but if they do it around other people, it's also selfish. And marital fighting, while on the road with a rock 'n' roll band, meant trouble. It also meant a lot of trashed hotel rooms.

Well, things got so bad that Donna quit the January tour a couple of shows early. That's the second time that someone in the band left a tour early because of fighting with Keith. We soldiered on without her, but those remaining two shows had a weird air because of it.

So, in February 1979, the Grateful Dead had to ask Keith and Donna to leave. It was a band decision and, ultimately, Jerry was the one to break it to them. It wasn't like with Mickey when that thankless task fell on me. As a matter of fact, Jerry was a little upset with me because I didn't go with him for support, as I had promised, but I tried to avoid those kinds of scenes as much as possible. So did he, of course. To a fault. As it turned out, however, Keith and Donna had both had it with the band and were relieved to be relieved of their duties. There was little heartbreak there, although there were mixed emotions for all of us, I'm sure. It was bittersweet. These things always are.

But Keith and Donna were out and then, just like that, a newcomer named Brent Mydland was suddenly the new Grateful Dead keyboardist. And the carousel went around and around.

We auditioned Brent, of course . . . but only kinda. Bobby brought him in and he really championed him before all of us even had a chance to meet the guy. He played in one of Bobby's side projects—Bobby and the Midnites—and Jerry saw some of that and took a liking to him, musically. We needed a keyboardist. Bobby had one. Jerry liked him. That's all it took.

When we first played with him—at Front Street—it was more of a test drive than an audition. He passed.

By some counts, Brent was the Dead's fifth keyboardist. That's if you count Tom Constanten and a guy named Ned Lagin as former members. I don't. They were fine players and people, but they didn't make the final cut.

From his very first note with us, Brent was as much a member of the Grateful Dead as any of us. His piece just fit our puzzle. He brought in a number of songs, sang lead vocals, and really brought something to the table musically. Like all of our full-time keyboardists, Brent really affected and influenced the sound of the band overall. You can really divide Grateful Dead eras by who was on keys—Pigpen represented the '60s, Keith represented the '70s, Brent represented the '80s, and the '90s, well . . . we'll get there. All good things in all good time.

Brent's B3 playing was really spectacular. I was always energized by watching him play; he was always in motion. He could really play and he could really sing and he was suddenly in the band. He was one of my favorite Grateful Dead keyboard players. Brent and Keith—those are the two for me.

Personality wise, I liked Brent well enough but we didn't hang out much or do anything wild and crazy like I did with some of the other guys in the band and crew. I mostly just met up with him onstage. He had so much energy and he was one of those players, like Keith in the beginning, that didn't just copy or follow Jerry's leads all the time. He had his own ideas that he ran with and they fit right in; he belonged.

Brent's energy and style was a catalyst for the whole band to discover entire new realms within our material. He really kick-started us as a unit and by bringing in a new element to all of these songs that we had been playing for so long, he really opened up new possibilities for the jams. New sensibilities. Some of his originals sounded like they could be hit songs for commercial bands, like "I Will Take You Home," or "Just a Little Light." Brent made them our songs and we made them Grateful Dead songs.

Ever since I knew Brent, he was with his wife, Lisa, who now lives not too far from me in Kauai. On stage, he was really animated—his long, blond hair would blow all around him and he wailed on the organ and keys. He moved around a lot and brought a great, physical energy to his performance. Offstage, though, he was really shy. We'd have some beers together and he'd loosen up, but on the day-to-day, he was somewhat reserved.

He did have one peculiarity and I think it is important to remember for later on, toward the end of his tenure with us: he would tell me that he didn't think Deadheads liked him very much. I might have bought that at first, just because anytime you have a change, people are resistant to it. When you love something, you love it exactly as it is and you don't want it to change. At first. But once you get over the initial shakeup, you adapt. And you just might find that the remodeling did some good; that your old love is now new and improved. Of course, that's not always the case—as we shall see when Jerry left us. There was no replacing Jerry. But once people got acquainted with Brent, in terms of the Grateful Dead, he was generally embraced. People loved him. He blew the roof off of certain songs and when he and Bobby sang together, the result was often greater than the sum of its parts.

Still, he would take me aside and say things like, "The fans don't like me." I think he just wanted a pat on the back; some reassurance. Like he was fishing for a compliment. I always gave it to him. And I was able to do it honestly. Brent was an integral member of the Grateful Dead, beginning with his first show on April 22, 1979, in San Jose. As I said, that's the same show that we debuted the Beast. So 1979 was a redefining year for the band in many ways.

Nineteen seventy-nine was also the year Francis Ford Coppola's *Apocalypse Now* was released to movie theaters. Mickey and I had a hand in that soundtrack, which is pretty cool to think about nowadays when looking back. At the time, you don't think like that. You don't know how anything is going to turn out or how it will be received or anything, really—you just do it. If you believe in it, you do it. That's a reward in itself and then you get to enjoy your involvement in it, in a whole different way, years after the fact. You gain a different appreciation for it. But it didn't work out as well as we had hoped.

Francis Ford Coppola sat offstage behind the drums at one of the Winterland shows that closed out 1978 and he said something that would have a pretty big impact on Mickey and me—he called us the "Rhythm Devils." And from that moment on, it was our joint nickname. Mickey and I became the Rhythm Devils, both in the Grateful Dead and without.

About a decade after the Dead broke up, Mickey and I did some touring under the Rhythm Devils name. We released a live DVD in 2008 and we were active until 2011. After the last time out, in which we had Keller Williams, Steve Kimock, and Reed Mathis with us, we retired the Rhythm Devils. But we sure had our moments while it lasted. During our revival, we had Mike Gordon of Phish, Tim Bluhm of the Mother Hips, Andy Hess formerly of Gov't Mule and the Black Crowes, Jen Durkin, Davy Knowles, and talking drum legend Sikirou Adepoju all join us, at various times, for tours.

As for Coppola, sitting behind both drummers and watching us slay the dragon really left an impression on him. He was working on *Apocalypse Now,* and needed a sound track and he was willing to indulge Mickey's immersive style in the creative process. So Mickey spearheaded the whole thing and, for a while, he staged an *Apocalypse* takeover at Front Street, assembling all different kinds of drums and percussion stations. He would project scenes from the movie on a large screen while he came up with sounds that mimicked walking through the jungle, napalm explosions, and mood-setting pieces. Mickey and Coppola became so obsessed with their work that they couldn't escape Front Street. There were nights when they didn't bother going home, instead crashing on the couches or wherever they could claim space. Front Street didn't make for the most comfortable hotel, but when you're locked into something like that, you're locked into it.

I was into it at first, but I just couldn't take watching all those gory scenes again and again on a large screen. All that bloodshed really started fucking with my head. It had the same poisonous effect on me as the video game *Mortal Kombat* might have on an adolescent. So I didn't stick with it. In the end, neither did Coppola—he only used a fraction of the stuff Mickey presented him with, and then he went down to Hollywood and had studio guys there reproduce the same sounds. Sounds just like Holly-wood, doesn't it? And right as the 1980s were about to begin. How very apropos.

There was one thing Coppola kept from Mickey's efforts, though. Some-thing that even Hollywood couldn't copy. The sound of napalm in the morning? That's the Beam—one of Mickey's contraptions.

Since this is the chapter where we talk about Keith and Donna leaving the band, I should jump ahead for a minute to the Summer of 1980. About a year and a half after they split from the Grateful Dead. During that period, I played a couple pickup gigs with them—in the Healy Treece Band—but I didn't really see either of them otherwise. Being in the Dead was a full-time thing. I didn't have the chance, or very likely the desire, to go and catch up with the Godchauxs.

On July 23, 1980, I was at home in Marin County when I got the phone call. This time, it was about Keith. Nothing is worse than losing somebody,

∾ Keith Godchaux on guitar and me on beer; fucking around backstage at a Healy Treece Band show. May 1979. *(Bob Minkin)*

no matter where you left things with them. Keith came in as a pinch hitter for Pigpen and hit Europe '72 out of the ballpark during his rookie season. He remained on the Grateful Dead roster for almost an entire decade. He was a lifelong member of the family, even if he was no longer in our lineup. So, yes—Keith Godchaux was a member of the Grateful Dead the moment he played his first notes with us, in October 1971.

But on July 23, 1980, the car that he was riding in collided with a parked construction vehicle. I never learned all the details, but it was out on the west side of Marin County, where all the farms are.

I don't think I went to Keith's funeral. The band must have had stuff going on because otherwise I would've gone. I went to Brent's. But that's way down the line. For now, just know that at the turn of the decade, the 1980s, Brent was our hot new keyboard player and we couldn't have been happier about that.

17

The 1980s came in like a lamb and out like a lion. I already told you one great tale from 1980, involving John Belushi and a three-day cocaine bender. The start of the decade couldn't have been better scripted. Unless it was a comedy sketch for *SNL*.

The first quarter of 1980 saw us release *Go to Heaven,* our eleventh studio album and first with Brent on keys. It got slammed, shredded, swiped, and shit on by the music press. It's all right—I never paid much attention to reviews anyway, and in truth, *Go to Heaven* wasn't a five-star album. That one was yet to come. But I think, if you go back and (re)listen to it, you'll find that time has been very kind to *Go to Heaven*. It plays better now than it did back then. That's still no excuse for the cover, though—all six of us, dressed all in white disco suits against a white background (because we had been "driving that train . . .").

We hired an English gentleman by the name of Gary Lyons to produce the album. Gary had success producing Foreigner's self-titled debut, which was glossy and slick and had obvious hits. It sold millions. I remember talking to him on the phone, before we met in person, and thinking that he was going to be great.

We decided, for the second album in a row, to record right at Front Street. It gave us the home court advantage and we were more comfortable and relaxed recording there than in a professional studio. But since it wasn't a professional studio, it made things difficult. There's a reason most albums are recorded in studios. We hadn't yet learned our lesson from *Shakedown Street*.

Once again, we recorded by playing together rather than tracking separately. We tried to get isolation between the instruments and the drums, so Lyons had Mickey and me sit behind curtains, way off to the back of the room, in our own little area. We could hear the rest of the band, but we couldn't see them. We felt estranged. There wasn't a separate control room, so the engineers had to listen on headphones while we played right in front of them in real time. The recording process is hard enough on my patience; having to do shit like that just drove me crazy.

What else about *Go to Heaven*? Well, "Antwerp's Placebo"—a drum composition that Mickey and I wrote—is on there. I haven't heard that in a long time. I don't think we ever played it live.

We kicked off our 1980 touring season in earnest on April 28—the day *Go to Heaven* hit stores. Once again, we found ourselves selling out civic centers, coliseums, and arenas across America. We were in search of our own manifest destiny, and since Alaska was one of the few states in the country we hadn't played yet, we decided to travel all the way up there for our first and only shows in America's "Last Frontier." We booked a three-night stand in a high school auditorium in Anchorage. But, for us, those shows were all about the adventures, before, after, and during. It was my first time checking out the Alaskan landscape and I'm pretty sure most, if not all, of the other guys could say the same. So, as the state motto goes, "North to the Future," we went.

Leading up to the shows, a group of us went on a river-rafting excursion in the Kenai River on the Kenai Peninsula. One of our managers,

Danny Rifkin, was with us, maybe a couple of the crew guys, and maybe even another band member, although I don't recall who. Shelley was with me and we ended up in our own raft—the smallest one—with one of the guides. The three of us brought up the rear. I didn't know anything about river rafting in those days so I put all my faith in our guide. He seemed like he knew what he was doing.

We started rafting down the river and it was as calm as can be. It was flat water at that point and we needed to paddle to get anywhere. On the back of our inflatable raft was a forty-horsepower motor in case of emergencies, but it was raised up out of the water because we were going over so many rocks. The river was mostly calm and I was starting to get a little bored when suddenly we went over a small little rapid. It should have been no big deal, really, but it formed a pond at the bottom of it where there was a hydraulic. Technically, in rafting terms, it's called a reversal. It's a strong, potentially troublesome reverse current that's caused from the force of the water falling and bouncing back against the rocks below. Ideally, your raft clears it, no problem, but it is possible to get stuck in a reversal and you may find yourself in a dangerous situation. That's what happened to us. Our boat was shorter than the one in front of us, so after we went over the rapid and landed in the pond, the front end dipped below the waterline and it swung the back end around. Boom! Suddenly we were sideways to the reversal. The water was falling onto us from the rapid above and pouring into the boat and, sure as shit, we started to sink. The boat was taking water at a thousand gallons a minute. I started screaming at the guide, "Get in the back, start the fucking motor, and get us out of here!" Shelley was screaming in my ear, blowing out my eardrums, in hysterics.

I took her and held her with my left arm and I started leaning way over the left gunnel, using her as a balance to keep the boat from tipping over. That's the only thing I did. We'd fill with water and start to tilt and I'd climb over the side, holding Shelley, until the weight would balance out and drain the water out, and we kept doing this for a while. Shelley is still screaming, the guide can't get back to start the motor, he broke one of the oars trying to push us off from the rocks, and I start studying the river downstream—"Okay, if we go swimming, where are we getting out? What's the closest departure place? What course should we aim for? What do we need to look out for?" and I was going over the training in my head— always float with your boots downstream. There was no easy way out of the river; rock walls lined the side for a ways down river.

I could see the other boat, at this point hundreds of yards downstream. While our boat was tipping and being washed by falling water, all the loose stuff in the boat—sandwiches, supplies, clothing—all fell out and were now floating down the river. Our friends ahead of us watched our stuff float on by. They were thinking, "Oh no. Where are they? What happened?"

I finally just said fuck it, and started cracking really bad jokes ("Well, now we know what it feels like to be salmon!") and doing my best to just stay calm. It got really quiet all of the sudden and I said something that I used to say whenever I was in a real jam with nature: "Rolling Thunder," I said, "Help me out."

We suddenly broke free of the reversal and backed out horizontally to the flow. Without the motor, without us paddling, nothing. It just happened. The guide looked at me and said, "What the fuck was that?" But that's how water is. It's like that. It has that kind of magic to it.

We were safe—drenched but safe. It was freezing cold that time of year, summer in Alaska, and we pulled out of the river where our friends had stopped, and we started drying off and telling them what happened.

I remember that I had a little vial of cocaine, just about a gram, that someone had given me as a gift. I was just praying it was unharmed. I pretended I had to take a leak and went up the hill and, sure enough, it was fine. I figured I might as well test it out to see if it still worked. It did. That was my reward. I did a few big boy bumps and went back to the group and enjoyed the rest of the day. I was so wired, not just from the cocaine but from the whole ordeal. Adrenaline. When you're in a situation like that, there's no guaranteed outcome, only guaranteed risks.

We had to fly in a float plane to get home, taking off in rather dangerous conditions on the lake that served as our runway—we had to fight waves and weather, making take-off sketchier than you'd care to have it. But we managed to get out of there.

The whole adventure had a pretty significant effect on me once I had time to process it. When we finally got back to the hotel and had dinner, word had already spread about what happened and people kept coming up to me and telling me that they were glad we were safe. Lots of things can scare me, and I'm terrified of more than I might admit. But I wasn't afraid that day. Quite the opposite. I liked the adrenaline rush.

As for saying the prayer to Rolling Thunder, it helped me remember that surrender is sometimes your only way out. You can't fight a current or a riptide or a river rapid. You have to surrender to those things, instead. I took care of Shelley, took care of balancing the boat, made jokes, and then sent Rolling Thunder a message. All of that helped.

Another trip we did up in Alaska was ride a float plane over a glacier. This must've been before the run of shows because we were staying in Fairbanks. Shelley and I got on a float plane and they don't go all that fast or all that high, but they're the safest planes in the world. It was simply incredible. The pilot took us over a glacier—with everything that's happening to the environment, that glacier is probably not quite the same today and might not even be there tomorrow. But when we went over it, it was heart-stopping gorgeous. I can still vividly recall the color turquoise that was buried deep within it. It was the prettiest color of anything.

It's like when you're surfing and you watch the top of a wave and it transforms into something translucent and you can look through it and see all these magnificent greens and breathtaking blues, all in different hues, while the foam forms on top and all the colors cascade down. It looked like that. Our pilot flew us to this lake and we landed on it and it was smoother than any landing I've ever experienced on a runway. We were gliding across the water, barely touching the earth. Floating gracefully.

As for the three-nighter in Anchorage, the only thing I remember about those shows is that they were in a high school gymnasium which, believe it or not, is not the ideal place for a rock concert. For one thing, the room was sonically unsound—it was one big echo chamber. There was nothing to soak up the sound and the back wall was terribly close to the stage. Every time I hit a drum, I'd get a report back. Every beat bounced back. With two drummers going full-throttle, it was an acoustical nightmare. All told, those gigs couldn't have been that great. But the adventure sure was fun.

Our flights to Alaska were part of a triangle fare, which meant that on one ticket we could fly from San Francisco to Alaska and then on to Hawaii before returning home. I had been to Hawaii once, maybe twice, before but it was fun to go there with the band. We weren't there to play music; we were there to play around. Goof off. It was recess and we had about a week before our next run of shows, down in Southern California. So we went to the island of Oahu for the week and we stayed somewhere not too far from Diamond Head, which is a volcanic tuff cone that's part of the Honolulu Volcanic Series.

We were all hyperaware of the volcano because of a crazy experience that we had just a couple weeks earlier in Portland, Oregon. We did a show there on June 12 and, about halfway through "Fire on the Mountain," Mount St. Helens started erupting. The synchronicity was classic Grateful Dead.

The volcano, which was slightly more than fifty miles from the venue, had a devastating eruption just a month earlier. May 18, 1980. That one was the big one, the one you know about—it was the most catastrophic volcanic event in United States history. People died. Animals were killed. Homes, bridges, railroads, and highways were destroyed.

When we played Portland on June 12, it was still in the news, still current. It was the aftermath of a natural disaster. During our second set inside the coliseum, Mount St. Helens had a second set of her own—another eruption. This one was the second of two smaller eruptions, and neither caused nearly as much damage as the main event. We had no idea what was going on until after the gig. While an actual volcano was erupting outside, Jerry was singing, "Almost ablaze still you don't feel the heat / It takes all you got just to stay on the beat. . . . Fire! Fire on the mountain!"

I remember leaving the venue and I was still in that hallucinatory space, that imagination zone, that you find yourself blissfully inside of when you play music for a few hours. Especially improvisational music. Grateful Dead music. It's a trance state and it takes a little while after the show sometimes for reality to come back into focus. So, when we went outside, I looked up at the sky and exclaimed, "My God, it's snowing!" Granted, it was summertime. But my mind was still elsewhere. I was an innocent. One of the snowflakes got into Shelley's eyes and that snapped me out of it—it was ash. People were screwing around in it like schoolchildren. All you could see was this gray ash flying around and landing on everything, blanketing everything—to my credit, it wasn't too unlike snow after all. There must've been an inch on the ground.

In the morning we had an "ash delay" before getting on the road to our next gig, just up the way in Seattle. Before leaving, Shelley wanted to buy a bottle of ash that they were selling in the gift shop, taken from the bigger eruption in May. I gave her a look and said, "Shelley, empty out a glass and just go outside." We both laughed. It was everywhere.

I know there are energies in music and that everything is connected, but sometimes something happens that demonstrates that in an undeniable and also beautiful way. That was one of them.

Between Mount St. Helens erupting, exploring the Alaskan landscape, and frolicking around Hawaii—after crisscrossing the mainland for a couple months, passing through Colorado and Arizona, Maine and upstate New York, Georgia and Virginia, I was more and more in tune to the real sense of the sacred in nature. Wherever we went, there were natural wonders. The rivers, the mountains, the coastlines, the trees, the lakes, the birds, the fish, all of it—natural wonders that I really felt connected to. More and more, the more I saw. The earth is an incredible place, one of a kind, really, and with an appreciation for it comes the understanding that it needs to be protected. The earth is not permanent but here we are, doing so much permanent damage to it. I saw the tar sands in Canada, the logging in the Northwest, the pollution in the big cities, the constant construction taking place all across the continent—across the whole world, in fact—and it was beginning to break my heart. I think that's when I first became aware of my own environmentalism. That's when I became aware that it was an issue and that I needed to take an active stand with it. There wasn't a "eureka" moment—it's just something that happened over time, after seeing all this stuff. I'm sure it dates back to my days with Rolling Thunder, too.

Back in the land of the Dead, we decided to shake things up with our live shows just to keep things interesting and to keep covering new ground. In 1980 we were celebrating our fifteenth anniversary, so we put on fifteen shows (that was a coincidence, actually, but let's roll with it) at the Warfield Theater in San Francisco. The Warfield only holds around 2,300 people, which means that all fifteen shows sold out immediately. The venue is located right on Market Street, not too far down the road from where the Carousel Ballroom (aka the Fillmore West) used to be and right along the path of Phil's old mailman route.

These were our first shows in the building and we would return for five more over the next few years but, overall, the place was too small for us by 1980. However, the Warfield became the home venue for the Jerry Garcia Band for many years and, to this day, his name adorns the door to one of the dressing rooms.

Bill Graham produced those shows and the three-week run was one of his crowning achievements. For us, it was an opportunity to experiment with a three-set format: one acoustic set followed by two electric.

We had a hidden motive behind the move: We were all a bit disenfranchised with recording studio albums after *Go to Heaven,* despite the fact that it did reach something like twenty-three on the pop charts. We were over it. Done. For a while, anyway. "A while" ended up being seven years. In the music biz, seven years is the equivalent of several lifetimes. It's like seven dog years.

But we weren't out of the game entirely—we wanted to release live albums. Starting with two off the bat: one acoustic, one electric. Hence, the fifteen-night run at the Warfield, followed by another eight nights at Radio City Music Hall in New York at the end of October. The Radio City run ended on Halloween with a show that was telecast and which featured sketches by some of our *Saturday Night Live* friends.

The Warfield run had a pretty comedic end as well—when we filed backstage after the second set, Bill Graham placed a table onstage with a bucket of champagne and some glasses. We noticed it when we came back for the encore, of course, but we weren't sure why it was there. Ever curious, Jerry went over and, almost hesitantly, picked up one of the champagne glasses. That's when house lights revealed everyone in the audience raising a champagne glass to toast the band, while a "Thank You" banner hung from the balcony.

It was Bill Graham at his finest. Although, so was this: he came running up to Mickey and me after one of the nights and, in a flurry of excitement, told us that he had been in the bathroom, taking a crap during the drum solo, when a couple pieces of marble fell on him. "You guys beat the drums so hard, that it knocked the marble right off the wall!" We laughed. "That's what you get for going into the bathroom during the show, Bill."

About a month later, he presented special plaques to Mickey and me that he had commissioned, with pieces of the marble on it, commemorating the event. It had the date and the venue engraved in bronze and all of that.

The fact that we could blow marble right off walls was a testament to our sound system as much as anything. But that plaque remains one of the only awards I ever earned that I give a damn about. Gold albums, platinum albums; that's just the industry patting itself on the back and the record label showing off how much money you made them. Jerry had that point of view and, once he pointed it out to me, I did too. But a physical piece of marble that you made fall off the wall of a building because you were playing your drums so hard? Now, that's an award!

As for recording those shows, we got *Reckoning,* a double-live album culled from the acoustic sets, and *Dead Set,* the electric counterpart, out of it. The obvious benefit of doing that was that we were able to release two albums over the following year, 1981, without having to go back into the studio and frustrate ourselves again. Made sense.

Another feather in our cap: Just two months after fifteen sold-out nights at the Warfield, we closed out the year with a five-night run across the bridge at the arena in Oakland. It was the end of 1980, fifteen years into our career, and our popularity was only beginning to explode.

The beginning of the 1980s were good to us, from a career standpoint: we established camping at our shows, in the lawns and parking lots around the venue. Those tent cities made Grateful Dead shows feel like even more of an interactive event—a special happening—more than just a concert. And it helped cultivate our own counterculture that, at this point, had long-since splintered off from the hippie revolution of the 1960s. As a movement, hippies were dead. But Deadheads were very much alive.

We also established our own in-house ticketing system. We figured if other people could make money from selling our tickets, then we could, too. We wanted to do as many things under our own roof as possible, just to keep it one big family. Above all else, it was a service to our fans, really. This separated us even further from "every other band," and really highlighted the fact that we had become our own community. Now Deadheads didn't need to line up at the local mall all night to get tickets from a TicketMaster outlet. Instead, they could send mail-order forms to us directly, through their local post office.

After doing battle with TicketMaster, on behalf of the fans, we were able to get a sizable portion of the tickets to sell ourselves. About half the house. Sounds like only half a victory but it was actually groundbreaking at the time and less than a handful of bands enjoy that kind of deal even today. We made the tickets themselves look fancy, knowing that fans would hold on to them as keepsakes.

We founded the Rex Foundation sometime during 1983. The Rex Foundation was—and still very much is—our own nonprofit organization. This way, rather than saying yes to one benefit gig and no to countless others, we could instead play a certain number of benefit shows every year, give all the profits to the Rex Foundation, and have a committee divvy up the money, funneling funds and granting grants to various causes and projects that were agreed upon by consensus. It was a much more efficient and effective way of donating money to all the things we believed in.

We named the Rex Foundation in memory of Rex Jackson, one of our most beloved roadies and road managers, who died in a car wreck in 1976, darn it.

The way I remember it, the idea for the Rex Foundation came partially out of a board meeting at Fifth and Lincoln where we were talking about our kids' educations. I had Justin on my mind. Jerry had his kids. Some of our employees had children. We wanted to start a Grateful Dead school that would serve their education but also work as a nonprofit. Turns out, that's not so easy to do.

Out of those talks and that line of thinking, Danny Rifkin decided that we should take all the potential money from playing benefits and direct it toward good causes and also good people who were coming to us with solid ideas for start-up nonprofits and other creative endeavors. Having our very own charitable arm was yet another expression of our self-enclosed community.

Meanwhile, the band wasn't always feeling the communal vibe within our ranks. We had begun to build resentments and alliances and we were no longer the band of brothers always striving for a group mind. This translated to the stage often enough, although just as often, the music broke through and united us—all of us, fans included—for a few hours each night. Then, after the show, we would all go our separate ways, sometimes without so much as saying good-bye to each other or, you know, "Good show."

We did one show as Joan Baez's backup band (that was a favor to Mickey, since he was shacking up with her at the time). At our New Year's Eve 1982 show, at the Oakland Auditorium Arena, we backed the great Etta James—with the Tower of Power horn section backing us—for an entire set.

We also became the soundtrack band for a reboot of the television classic *The Twilight Zone*. That whole thing was suitably weird. Our friend Merl Saunders—whom I played with in one of Jerry's solo lineups in 1974—was the musical director for the revived TV series. The original was a classic and we were all big fans; especially Jerry, if I remember right. But its revival in the 1980s wasn't quite the same. The creator, Rod Serling, didn't have anything to do with it anymore.

We recorded sound effects and other odd background noises at Front Street. I would just play whatever Merl told me to play. It was an enjoyable experience; quite the opposite of the *Apocalypse Now* sessions.

Phil may have sat this one out, because he was opposed to the idea. I don't know why he had such opposition to stuff, but to his credit, the new series wasn't nearly as good as the original. If that was Phil's reasoning or concern, it's certainly valid.

It's funny: all these things are part of the Grateful Dead story, sure. But they're not necessarily my story. They were just some of the many things we did, as a band, in the 1980s. From our vantage point, it was a pretty incredible place to be. And looking back on it, we weren't wrong.

By the middle of the decade, we had become an American institution and even though we were a different band every single night, we had learned what it meant to be the Grateful Dead. Both sonically and aesthetically. We were getting bigger and bigger while our history was getting deeper and deeper. First fifteen, then twenty years deep.

We were now tremendously famous and making a lot of money. There was this feeling that there was no end in sight. We didn't think that we looked like the rock stars you saw in all the magazines, but we were in all the magazines. We didn't think that we acted like the kind of celebrities you saw on TV—we thought we were better than that nonsense—but the fact was that we could do anything we wanted, whenever we wanted, and get away with it. And we knew it, too.

Our fame afforded us the stuff that money alone could not: it let us live by a different set of rules. When Jerry seemed to be drifting even outside of those lines, we had an intervention for him. This was in January of 1985. He agreed to enter rehab but decided to have one last binge. He was parked in his BMW in Golden Gate Park, by himself, when he got busted by the police—initially because the car didn't have proper registration. But because he was "Jerry Garcia of the Grateful Dead," his arrest didn't amount to much. He had to go to some counseling, something light and easy that didn't get in the way of his habits. Or his life.

I had a similar thing happen a few years earlier. I played a club gig in

San Francisco with a small side project that our soundman, Dan Healy, had put together. The Healy Treece Band. Afterward, my friend and future Grateful Dead publicist, Dennis McNally, asked me for a ride home, because he didn't have a driver's license. We decided to stop and pick up some beers. We had just enough time to make it to the liquor store . . . maybe. Dennis was riding shotgun and shouting out directions. Suddenly, it was like being in Paris with Phil navigating. "Go left! Okay, now right!" One misguided direction, though, and we ended up going the wrong way down a one-way street. "Oops, that's not going to work." I slammed into reverse and got us out of there. But not before a cop noticed. I noticed him noticing me, so I parked and got out of the car before he even had his lights on.

I drank a couple Heinekens earlier that night, sure, but I wasn't drunk. Though I probably still had beer on my breath. I thought my driving was on point and that I pulled a smooth exit maneuver. It was precise and controlled. I didn't argue with the cop when he took me down to the station. If I had been drunk, I probably would've. He gave me a Breathalyzer. I passed it. He threw me in the slammer anyway, where I spent the night. If they think you're drunk, you get an automatic four hours in the tank. I was just glad they put me in my own cell because I could hear some truly terrifying screams coming from some of the other jail cells.

Shelley was freaking out this whole time because this was before cell phones—she didn't know what happened, only that I never made it home from the gig.

Eventually, I had to go to court over it. I didn't have an attorney or any kind of representation. I don't think I took any of it all that seriously. I was beginning to understand that that might not have been the best approach. I was watching all these attorneys give their clients all this serious advice, even though nobody was in there for anything all that big—nobody was shackled or anything. I began to realize that I had no idea what I was going to say and that I'd probably end up putting my foot in my mouth. I started getting the feeling that I was going about this all wrong.

Just then, a guy came up to me, shot me a look of recognition, and said, "Hey, you're Bill Kreutzmann!" He was an attorney. Suddenly I had representation. We met in his office down by the piers and he told me that I had nothing to worry about. "You're going to like this judge," he said with a knowing smile.

When we went back to court, the judge said, "Mr. Kreutzmann, there is no proof that you were drunk that night. I'm going to give you the benefit of the doubt. By the way—I love the Grateful Dead."

While we were still in court, the judge said she was going to make me go to a driving school. "They're going to send you a card in the mail and it will have further instructions." I could swear that, right after she said that, she winked at me. I never got the card in the mail, never got contacted by any school, and never had anything else to do with it. The judge threw it all away while everyone else just looked in the other direction. Just like they did with Jerry when he was busted in the park.

We weren't flashy rock stars, but everyone knew who we were. I remember seeing our numbers posted in *Pollstar* and reading that we were one of the highest grossing live acts in the world. Eventually, we became the highest. That used to blow my mind. We'd come a long way since playing on flatbeds in Haight-Ashbury. And that, back then, seemed huge. Those early gigs were easily just as rewarding and exciting for us as any of our sold-out stadium tours. The money was astronomically different, but the spiritual paycheck may have been even bigger back then.

Despite the intentions of various people around us—perhaps—for the members of the band, making money was never our number-one objective. For some, like Jerry, it wasn't even an objective at all, beyond making enough to get by. Even in the middle of the "Me Decade," we were never greedy.

Our crew was the most spoiled crew in rock 'n' roll. Our roadies would come home from tours with suitcases full of crap that they bought on the road, and even the suitcases themselves would be charged to the band. It was supposed to be taken off their pay—"on account"—but sometimes it was and sometimes it wasn't.

A lot of times, stuff would be bought in the name of the band but the band never saw it. Jerry once commented, when someone told him that there were forty cases of Heineken backstage, "I didn't even drink one." The point is, we had so much money, it didn't matter. We could just waste it and it was fine. I don't think we were all so fine with it deep down, but by that point it was a snowball that nobody could catch. It just picked up speed and mass as we rolled on down the road.

Nothing was going to stop the train from chugging along until, finally, Jerry got sick. We all saw very quickly how fast the whole thing could derail. Money had become an enabler. Jerry could eat anything he wanted. So he did, and then he became a diabetic. Jerry could get any drugs he wanted. So he did, and it began to take away the one thing he couldn't buy—his health.

And then, in July 1986, Jerry Garcia slipped into a diabetes-induced coma.

18

During the 1960s, we were just a bunch of kids with our own ideas about what you could do with rock 'n' roll music. During the 1970s, we became the Grateful Dead. During the 1980s, we became genuine rock stars. From seed to flower to fruit.

It was a bitter fruit, though, as Jerry's coma came just days after we had completed a summer tour that included five stadium shows where we invited Bob Dylan along for the ride. Dylan hired a backing band that went by the name of Tom Petty and the Heartbreakers, and we alternated head-lining slots, depending on the market. We sold an astounding number of tickets.

It felt like we were halfway to the moon when, suddenly, our rocket ship had to be grounded. Our hot-air balloon, deflated. Jerry was in the hospital, in a coma and near death. He stayed that way for five days. It was a scary five days. A lot of stuff went through my mind, most of which I don't care to remember. At first, only family members were allowed to be in his room, so I was left pacing around the hospital. My only comfort was Justin, who kept me company. We talked about anything we could think of, trying to distract each other from the real reason we were there. We were frightened. Nervous. Helpless but not hopeless. Jerry's coma was induced by diabetes but the excessive use of all those recreational drugs couldn't have helped—we were pretty reckless in 1986, that's for sure.

When Jerry finally came out of the coma, his senses were fuzzy and his motor skills were mush. He basically had to relearn how to play guitar, after first piecing together how music even worked. He told me that he had thoughts like, "Will I ever be able to play as well as I did?" At first, he wasn't even sure that he'd be able to play at all. But then things came back to him, bit by bit. Merl Saunders helped him out in the beginning with that, sitting at the piano and going over chord changes and stuff with him until muscle memory kicked back in. And then Jerry's neural pathways fired up again and he was the same old Jerry.

In fact, when you consider the circumstances, his recovery was miraculously expeditious: Jerry returned to the stage just three months after knocking on death's door. He got his feet wet by playing with his solo band—at a small club in San Francisco—that October. And just two months after that, we were able to resurrect the Grateful Dead. Again.

Our "comeback" show was on our home turf, at the Oakland Coliseum Arena. It was a Monday night. December 15, 1986. We opened with "Touch of Grey" and immediately the song resonated on a totally new level—its refrain of "We will survive!" was appropriate, anthemic, and cathartic. That song, still relatively new at the time, suddenly became one of our anthems. It was destined for greater things, still.

Meanwhile, we debuted "Black Muddy River" in that second set. It was the emotional counterpoint to "Touch of Grey," in that the lyrics seemed to point toward death rather than survival. Or, at least, to some kind of inward reflection instead of outward proclamation. ("When the last rose of summer pricks my finger . . . I will walk alone by the black muddy river.") Both songs seemed especially poignant that night. Both songs carried a message. And both songs ended up being right.

That was a special night. There was a lot of emotion in the air—a lot of love and a lot of energy, especially toward Jerry.

It was easy to take the scene we had created for granted. You start believing in its permanence and my, how quickly we all feel entitled. The Grateful Dead carved an arch out of rock, connecting the idealism of the 1960s, with the technology of the 1980s and the promise that music without politics could just be the most effective politic of all.

People came from all different places—spiritually as well as physically—to the Grateful Dead arch, believing that crossing underneath it would lead to a utopian island where the gardens looked like amphitheaters, the mall looked like Shakedown Street and the houses were made out of tents. And every night was a celebration where we got to dance with Dionysus, wrapped up in a music that wrapped around our souls.

Jerry Garcia was the keystone of this magical arch. You take that out, and not only does the arch come tumbling down, crushing all who are stuck beneath, but also, it crushes the only road that leads to that utopian dream. "Dark Star crashes / pouring its light into ashes."

Everything we loved was precarious. We know that now. But, that first night back, we also knew that it was glorious and that it was ours again.

Jerry's concern that he wouldn't be able to play as well as he once did may have touched upon some deeper demon inside of him. I was his bandmate, not his therapist, so I'm not making any kind of formal assessment. But I do recall one time when we were playing at the Shoreline Amphitheater in Mountain View, California. Jerry had recently been released from treatment, so he was clean and sober. I'm not sure he felt entirely comfortable with himself when he was clean and sober, especially when performing for large, sold-out crowds. Maybe that's why those phases never lasted too long. During soundcheck, he leaned over my tom-toms and said, "Bill, I'm terrified! I can't play anything. What am I going to do?" He was really afraid—you could see it on his face.

We had just worked through a tune and he sounded fucking brilliant. "Jerry, you sound great," I told him. "Hang in there, man." I think some things were really hard for him . . . and on him. He had a pinnacle of excellence to maintain, and so he felt a great weight. A responsibility. Two things he hated, for sure.

At the last gig we played before his collapse—July 7, 1986, at RFK Stadium in Washington, D.C.—Bob Dylan came out onstage with us to
perform a couple of tunes: "It's All Over Now, Baby Blue" and "Desolation Row." Both of which were Dylan originals, so he had them in his
wheelhouse, and we already had them in our repertoire. It was easy. Still,
it was far-out—I got to play drums behind one of my childhood heroes.

That was the second time that Dylan sat in with us. The first was just
a few days earlier, on July 2, at a bowl in Akron, Ohio. It was the only
time we played "Don't Think Twice, It's Alright," and we had the honor
of performing it with the songwriter.

I was a junior in high school when I first got turned on to Bob Dylan.
I would put on *Highway 61 Revisited* and play it for my friends, in my apartment in Palo Alto. Afterward, they'd say things like, "This is garbage,"
and "He can't sing," and I knew right then and there that there was a new
divide between my old friends and my new scene. I didn't give a fuck about
his voice. I loved his words and his songs. They meant so much to me.

In the Grateful Dead camp, to a man, we were all still in awe of
him. He must've fancied the collaboration as well, because the following
January—1987—he visited us at 20 Front Street just to fuck around for a
couple days, run through some tunes, and maybe see where that got us.
There was no grand plan, as far I know. "Let's just jam and play and have
some fun." Sure—get our kicks with Bob Dylan. Why not?

Jerry started working up the Beatles' "Nowhere Man" like it was no
big deal, and we had a good time with that one. I don't remember what
else we played at those sessions, although I'm sure we must've recorded
them. Dylan didn't come with an entourage or anything, just his dog—a
cream-colored Great Dane that stunk to high heaven and that would sit
at Dylan's feet, licking himself, while we talked. It didn't have much spunk
and mostly just laid there in a big dog puddle, but it was Dylan's comfort
companion during that visit.

From my perspective, Jerry and Dylan were really friendly with each
other and had some kind of rapport going on. But the rest of us were pretty

shy around him. The novelty didn't wear off—there was our hero, in our practice space, running through songs with us. Dylan must've liked something about it, because he came back in May. And, this time, with a purpose: both of our organizations signed off on a six-date stadium tour, to be billed as "Bob Dylan and the Grateful Dead," for that coming July.

I don't know who came up with the idea, or which side initiated it, but we couldn't have been more excited for the tour. We worked up more than fifty songs—perhaps even double that—during those May sessions at Front Street. Dylan was there for at least a week. I've read that he practiced with us for five days and I've read that he was with us for the better part of the month. I can't testify about those kinds of specifics because my own sense of time was warped; each day was just so surreal that they all now melt into a dream.

What I can tell you is that Dylan was a mess during this period, I'm afraid. He didn't really remember his own songs all that well, but we did our homework, so Jerry would sometimes stand right next to him and whisper the next verse into his ear as we played. Dylan was really loose with all of his arrangements and tempos and everything. We were diplomats for improvisational music—twisting and turning songs on the fly—so we had the right résumé for the gig. We had a lot of experience with that kind of thing, hearkening back to the Pigpen days when he would go off on one of his rants by coming into it off-time, and we'd just have to adjust, dropping half a beat without ever dropping our game. That's when the group-mind thing really came in handy. Still, Dylan threw even more curveballs at us than Pigpen. We knew better than to duck, so we just kept swinging.

The idea for the tour was that we would perform one or two sets as the Grateful Dead, and then we'd come out again for a final set, in which we backed Dylan. During those sets we still sounded like the Grateful Dead—but we became Bob Dylan's band. Just like Tom Petty and the Heartbreakers had done the year before. Just like, perhaps more famously, The Band had done in the mid-'60s.

The tour kicked off on July 4, 1987, at the now-demolished Foxboro Stadium, outside Boston. From there, we hit the Philadelphia, New York, Eugene, and Bay Area markets before wrapping up down in Los Angeles at Anaheim Stadium—I have particularly fond memories of that last show, for sure. That's the night Dennis Hopper came backstage afterward and hung out.

As has been noted and documented elsewhere, Dylan was drinking a lot that tour and he exhibited the same erratic behavior to us that he's notorious for, publicly. Once or twice, he launched into songs that we never even rehearsed with him—in front of crowds as large as 90,000—and we just had to wing it. It was common for him to forget lyrics, so just like at band practice, Jerry would step up next to him and casually whisper the words into his ear. Right in front of the entire audience. Other times, Dylan would take unannounced left turns on tunes that we had rehearsed an entirely different way.

There was nothing wrong with that, though; if anything, it just kept us honest. We were a jam band—we were made for the job. And we were headlining stadiums with our hero. Nothing beats that. A couple years later, we released a live compilation of the tour's highlights, called *Dylan & the Dead*. That's a better prize than any trophy. (And I'm happy to see that Dylan is going strong these days, and is still just as eccentric.)

Overall, 1987 was a great period for us. We were enthusiastic again and more focused than we had been in years. Things were good in GD-land. Two days after the launch of the Dylan tour, we released a new studio album, entitled *In the Dark*. It would become our bestselling album, redefining us for an entirely new generation that wasn't there for the Pigpen—or even the Godchaux—years. We had a whole incoming class of new recruits. This would spell trouble for us down the line as we were rapidly approaching a level of popularity that would prove to be simply unsustainable. But for the moment, we were riding the wave and enjoying the ride.

The band was in great spirits for the recording of *In the Dark*. If you ever want to resubscribe to the good life, try recovering from a coma. It will put the spring back in your step. Some band members were sober during this period; I was not. But we were all in high spirits.

It had been seven years since our previous studio album and a large part of that was that we were frustrated with the process. Hours upon hours spent re-recording the same bit, over and over again, in a soundproof room, while a producer tells you to take it from the top—"although this time with a little more feeling." It just wasn't our thing. And recording at Front Street wasn't the solution that we were looking for. So we stopped recording albums for a while. Besides, many of our fans didn't even bother to buy them. We were always a live band.

And that's where the "a-ha" moment came from. In January 1987, we rented out a 2,000-seat theater—the Marin Veterans Memorial Auditorium in San Rafael—and set up shop almost as if we were playing a live concert. It worked. It didn't feel like a studio, because when you looked out, you saw seats. It was only about five miles from Front Street but, in terms of recording an album, it was a world apart.

In the spirit of shaking things up from our previous disappointments, we decided to keep this one in-house—we had tried a number of producers but none of them quite got us the way we got ourselves. The only outside producer who ever got a second chance with us was our first guy, David Hassinger, and he ended up quitting the second time around because he didn't like the sound of "thick air."

That's okay. Our best studio albums were largely the ones that we produced ourselves, using our own guys in the control room, before the Arista contract called for otherwise. The production credit for *In the Dark* goes to Mister Jerry Garcia and our longtime sound engineer, John Cutler. We were done with hiring outsiders.

We ran all the electric instruments through amplifiers in the basement, in isolation rooms, and kept the drums bright and loud on stage. Everything was fed to a recording truck parked outside the venue. Everybody played their parts in real time, together. When we took breaks, we'd go into the wings by the stage door and sit there and talk about what we'd just done. Talking about the music, then going right out to play the music, then talking about it some more was something that we really should've done more often—the analysis served the songs and the camaraderie served the band. It really put us in a good spot.

We were able to record the basic tracks in just a couple of weeks. No doubt, just like *Workingman's Dead*, the expeditiousness of *In the Dark* certainly contributed to its farm-fresh quality. Hell, we even had time to spare. So—in that classic Grateful Dead spirit—we experimented and fumbled around in the dark, hoping to stumble into happy accidents. That's not a metaphor; we did that literally. Mickey decided it would be a fun exercise, so we turned off the lights in the middle of a jam and things got . . . incredibly weird. In the end, the experiment didn't work but it did pay off by giving us the idea for the album title.

In the Dark peaked at No. 6 on the charts and "Touch of Grey" became our first Top Ten single (reaching No. 9—which still counts), thanks in no small part to MTV playing the video. Our previous studio album, *Go to Heaven,* was released in 1980. MTV didn't exist yet. But by 1987, sure enough, it had changed the entire game. If you didn't have a video, you didn't have a hit. Now that we had a promising single, it was time for us to dabble.

We hired director Gary Gutierrez, who worked special effects on *The Right Stuff* and *The Running Man*. We knew him because he created the animated sequences for *The Grateful Dead Movie*. Which meant Jerry loved him. And we loved his treatment for the song: playing off of the fact that our graphics and logos frequently revolved around images of skulls and/or skeletons, Gutierrez created skeleton marionettes that resembled the frames of each respective band member. They were built to scale. Mine even had a mustache. The puppeteers attended one of our concerts, in advance of the video shoot, to study our individual, idiosyncratic movements and mannerisms on stage.

We filmed the video down by Monterey, California ("Somewhere near Salinas . . ."), during a two-night stand that we had scheduled at Laguna

Seca, an outdoor venue on the same property as the famed raceway of the same name. Deadheads were camped out, on site, anyway, so we literally had a captive audience. After the first show, all we had to do was tell them they could be extras in our first video, and they came streaming back onto the concert field.

The video is supposed to be a live performance, but performed by our skeletons. Even in the final version, you can still see the strings attached to the skeletons, revealing that they're actually just marionettes. That transparency made it charming. At some point during the song, the skeletons transform into the flesh-and-blood band members. Toward the end, a quick, often overlooked, shot hints that it's the puppeteers who are actually the skeletons, manipulating the band's movements. It was an unexpected heavy hitter on MTV.

My son Justin, who was now seventeen, came down for the shoot. He had taken an interest in filmmaking, so he shot a bunch of behind-the-scenes footage and B-roll and created a thirty-minute documentary. We released it as an official home video—back in the days of VHS—entitled *Dead Ringers: The Making of Touch of Grey.* I was a proud papa.

The success of "Touch of Grey" took everyone by surprise because gray-haired rockers from the 1960s didn't exactly fit in with the generation that MTV catered to. The kids that wanted their MTV in 1987 wanted hair metal and power ballads, or pop stars and dance tracks. It was a different demographic. Suddenly, "Touch of Grey" could be seen in the same block as videos from Bon Jovi, Madonna, and U2. It was strange to find ourselves in such company, but, then again, ours was always a long, strange trip.

Naturally, the fact that "Touch of Grey" became one of MTV's most-played videos of the entire year only encouraged us to make more of them. So, for the rest of our recording career, we filmed music videos to accompany the singles. None of them ever came close to replicating the success of "Touch of Grey," though.

The next video from *In the Dark* was for "Hell in a Bucket," a Weir/Barlow tune. That song to me was always a bit of a joke—it was almost a carny tune, if you know what I mean. But it was a fun video to make and, I hope, a fun video to watch.

For the shoot, we rented out a bar called New George's, which was located at 840 Fourth Street in San Rafael, just around the corner from our offices at Fifth and Lincoln. It's still there, although it's now just called "George's"—no longer "new," I guess. It was a rowdy bar at the time, so we took it over for a night and filled it with fake bikers and staged a few bar fights. All the women in our clan—including Shelley—dressed up in high heels and all this makeup, and some of the crew dressed as riffraff, which wasn't necessarily a stretch. The song has a verse that seems like it could be talking about S&M, so there was a scene with Bobby . . . oh, never mind. Just YouTube it.

The street scenes were filmed right on Fourth Street—the heart of town. Mickey and I were in the front seat of a Cadillac, wearing devil costumes and acting rather animated. I guess we were supposed to be escorting Bobby to hell, as the song would suggest. Mickey rode shotgun, which meant I was behind the wheel. I wasn't actually driving, of course—the car was hooked up to a tow truck and they positioned the camera so it only looked like I was driving the thing through the streets. I kept on forgetting I was in the driver's seat; they had to remind me a few times, "Hey, Billy, hands on the wheel, eyes on the road, and make some turns, will ya?" That was fun.

Bobby was in the backseat, lip-synching the lyrics. There was an actress back there with him—his temptress, as it were—and a duck. I'm not sure who came up with the duck idea, or why, but it was a real, honest-to-God duck all right. There's a lyric in the song that goes: "You imagine me sipping champagne from your boot," which basically means, like, you want me to kiss your feet. Well, to illustrate the lyric, Bobby was holding a glass of champagne and, what do you know, the duck starts drinking it. You can see some of that in the final cut. Bobby felt compelled to keep the champagne flowing and before we knew it, we had a drunk duck on our hands. He got pretty hammered. I think it's safe for me to talk about this, now; I mean, he looked like he was over twenty-one—in duck years, at least. We showed him a good time and let him cruise around town with us. It's not like we were smoking quack with him or anything.

We made a third video, for "Throwing Stones," but I wasn't there when they filmed it and the band had to use a stunt double. It wasn't playing hooky, I wasn't hungover, and I didn't call in sick. I was in court in San Rafael, defending myself in a civil lawsuit. I had gotten into some kind of scuffle with a musician named Matt Kelly, that ended with me trying to kick him in the balls. I certainly wanted to. But he blocked it and, in the end, it should've been no big deal. Dust off, walk away. Like a man. Instead, Kelly faked injury and said that I crushed his nuts and that he'd never be able to use his dick again. As if the world should be so lucky.

Matt Kelly is a friend of Bobby's from childhood, and they played in a few bands over the years: Kingfish, Bobby & the Midnites, and an early edition of Ratdog. Kelly sat in with the Grateful Dead more than a dozen times and even played harmonica on a few studio tracks with us.

Kelly wouldn't pay me for a side gig that he hired me for, even though he had the money. That's where the altercation began. The lawsuit wasn't about being kicked in the balls. This was about more than that. Grudges. Sour grapes. But the attempted swift kick to the groin was enough for Kelly to sue me for $600,000 on the grounds that he would never be able to have children as a direct result. During the trial, we had to say the Pledge of Allegiance every morning while looking at a large drawing of a pair of testicles. The two things were unrelated.

My son Justin saved the day. He was at Bobby's fortieth birthday party in Mill Valley and saw Kelly take home a girl that night. A stripper. The one that came out of the cake. The Defense called her to the stand and, sure enough, she told the court—under oath—that Kelly certainly had no problem with his dick on the night of the party. No complaints. No sign of discomfort. And that was that. Needless to say, he didn't get his full $600,000.

Anyway, after my nonappearance in the "Throwing Stones" video, we went back to using Gutierrez as our director. We made videos for some of the songs from our following album, but nothing came close to the success of "Touch of Grey." That's the one where the lightning struck.

With the commercial success of *In the Dark*, we were the same band that we used to be—only, somehow, even bigger. We were in the middle of a sold-out, five-night run at Madison Square Garden when Clive Davis came backstage to present us with the plaques celebrating *In the Dark*'s platinum status. (A gold album means you sold 500,000 copies, and platinum means you sold a million.) This wasn't our first platinum album, and we already had our share of gold—but it was our first to sell that well right after it dropped.

As I already said in the previous chapter, these plated-record awards stopped impressing me once Jerry pointed out that they really were just indicators for how much money you made the record company. They didn't qualify your talent or speak to the actual quality of the music. Thus, it was hard to look at them as "awards."

When we got maybe our third gold record—I forget now which one it was, specifically—we decided to take apart the plaque to see if the actual record would play. We unscrewed the back, took the glass off the top, and put the gold-plated album on a turntable. It played, all right. Even with the gold plating. But it wasn't our album. It wasn't *Live/Dead* or *Workingman's Dead* or whatever it was supposed to be. It was a Johnny Cash album. Johnny Cash!

The funny thing about that, aside from the obvious, is that Cash wasn't even at the same record company as us. It had our label on it, but it was his record. I think we probably crunched the plaque back together and went on with our business, but we had an honest laugh over that one. We didn't take it to heart and, besides—we were all Johnny Cash fans.

To this day, I'm not sure where most of my gold or platinum albums are. I don't have them hanging anywhere. I'm thinking they're probably in my storage unit in Northern California, but some of them may be in my garage or in a box somewhere around my property in Hawaii. I have my Grammy Award on my living room bookshelf—as a bookend—along with my Rock and Roll Hall of Fame trophy. And, although it's in slight disrepair, I keep that Emmy Award from Tom Davis that I already told you about atop that bookshelf, too. But gold or platinum records don't exactly make good bookends and you can certainly find better art for your walls.

Amidst all this success, the band wasn't changing but we were evolving. Our whole trip was that we never played the same concert twice, and in order to do that we had to constantly seek new ground. One major evolution was the introduction of MIDI to our toolbox, thanks to a guy named Bob Bralove. He programmed keyboard software for Stevie Wonder before we hired him as a sound technician. MIDI stands for Musical Instrument Digital Interface and it was the bridge between physical instruments and computerized sounds. Under Bralove's direction, supervision, and programming, MIDI made a significant impact on our live sound. You could argue that, by 1988, we were the first real jamtronica band. Well . . . if not the first, certainly on the forefront. In our own little corner.

Phil and Ned Lagin had begun experimenting with electronic music way earlier, in the 1970s, but it was still a new concept in rock 'n' roll. Of course, rock 'n' roll itself was sprung from the birth of electric instruments, but, now, instruments were actually becoming computerized. It was the great frontier. We were a long way away from all the "MacBook musicians" of today—back then, electronic music was still a lot more physical. We played the notes with our own hands, but the sounds coming out of the amplifiers were electronically manipulated. With MIDI, we could replicate the sound of a flute, or a wind chime, or birds, just by playing our normal instruments—which were patched in to computerized controllers where we could, ultimately, decide on the sound that would come out of the speakers. Jerry and Brent really dove into it and experimented. Mickey and I started tinkering around with electronic drums and triggers and all of that, and Bralove's influence could be heard loud and clear in the "Drums" and "Space" segments of our shows, where we were encouraged to take such risks and go off the deep end. We didn't really go hog wild with it until years later, in the post-GD era, when we toured as the Rhythm Devils. That's still to come.

On the other end of the spectrum, we started incorporating more New Orleans music into our repertoire, which really pleased me tremendously. Brent started singing a New Orleans classic called "Hey Pocky Way," and it fit right in with songs like "Iko Iko" and "Man Smart (Woman Smarter)" that were already in our rotation.

The Neville Brothers opened up for us on New Year's Eve, 1985, and we invited them back at least half a dozen times over the next couple of years, including the following two New Year's shows. We usually had them sit in with us as well, sometimes for the better part of an entire set. I wish I could think of who first had the idea to invite the Neville Brothers to come join us, but it was brilliant and I'd like to thank them, whoever they are.

I always lamented, at least a little bit, the fact that the Grateful Dead didn't play more New Orleans music, so whenever we had a chance to play those songs—or play with the Neville Brothers—it was just over the top for me. "Pocky Way" is a classic New Orleans Indian march, whereas "Iko Iko" has more of a Bo Diddley feel. Everyone plays those songs a little differently, but they always seem to work.

Take a ride through New Orleans funk and all roads will lead you back to the Meters. More than twenty years after I first started playing "Hey Pocky Way" with the Grateful Dead, I brought it to a rehearsal with my band 7 Walkers. We had George Porter Jr.—an original member of the Meters—on bass. He stopped us and said, "No, man, you're doing it the way the Neville Brothers did it! Here's the real way . . ." There was no arguing with George about that one, since he wrote the bass line.

I used to listen to as much New Orleans music as possible. Whenever a new record came out, I'd grab it immediately. I would go home and study the drum parts, because New Orleans music has a different level of syncopation to it that just makes it furiously attractive to me. I get a certain enjoyment out of playing that style of music that I don't quite get from anything else.

It's in my blood. Literally. I haven't really talked about this too much, ever, but my mom was from New Orleans. My grandparents on her side were all from there, too. So I think that the music from there probably resonated with me on deep, subconscious levels and it gave me an underlying love for those rhythms.

After my parents divorced, my mom went back to that area of the country. She moved to Biloxi, Mississippi, about ninety miles outside of New Orleans. We used to vacation there when I was a kid. It was a beach town before it was a casino town and that's the way I'll always remember it. I bought my mom a house in Biloxi but I didn't get many chances to visit. I was a working musician.

Back in Palo Alto, when I was around eight years old, my mom displayed an unusual piece of artwork in one of the bedrooms. And by "unusual," I mean, disturbing. It was a diorama of a human skull with a hole in it. Next to the skull, sitting peacefully on a doily, was a pistol. An actual skull and an actual pistol. I realize that artwork often speaks in metaphors and that true art is supposed to encourage individual interpretation—art isn't supposed to be incriminating; it's supposed to be liberating. Expressive. But, at age eight, I wasn't much of an art critic. I didn't exactly interview my mom about the dark folds of her artistic expression. In fact, I didn't mention it at all. Years later, the collective artistic output of the Grateful Dead would often include skull and firearm imagery. I didn't question that stuff, either.

Around 1988, my mom started writing me letters asking for money. She'd threaten to kill herself if I didn't help out. I took those threats seriously but, after about two or three years, I stopped hearing them. I continued to send her money anyway. I knew what she needed it for. She used it to buy drugs and alcohol. To keep her habits going. I realized, on some level, that I had become her enabler. But I continued to send her money anyway. I loved her unconditionally and I wanted to be a good son. It was simple. Besides, if she didn't spend the money on drugs and alcohol, I would've spent it on that stuff, myself. We both had our vices. And I had the money.

Things were about to change. For both of us. As I'll explain in more detail later, I cleaned up in 1990 and spent the next three years sober. After a stint in rehab, I started going to appointments with a drug and alcohol counselor in Fort Bragg, a forty-minute drive from the Comptche ranch. She wasn't a psychiatrist. She wasn't even a psychologist. She was just a counselor. Not an M.D. I had already straightened out, but I still needed some support. She helped keep my nose free from foreign objects and made sure that my water did not turn to wine. I was doing this for myself, not for anybody else, so it was important to me.

I confided in this counselor and I trusted her. I had to. One day, she advised me to stop sending the checks to my mom. She said I needed to stop being the enabler. Against my own instincts and inclinations, I took the advice. I didn't know what was wrong or right and I still don't. I just wanted to be a loving son. The counselor insisted on tough love and I listened. I stopped mailing the payments.

About two weeks later, my mom took her life. She shot herself in the head with a .38 pistol.

I was salmon fishing near Albion, not too far from my home, when I got the news. I was by myself, on a little inflatable single-motor boat, and I had just caught my first silver salmon. It was a very proud moment for me. And I was clear-eyed that day, which made it even better. I was heading home with the prize when I got a call on my VHF radio. This was before cell phones, of course. They reached me as soon as they could: "Mr. Kreutzmann, you need to come back right now. Something's happened."

I flew to Biloxi and went straight to my mom's house. The one I bought for her. Nothing was cleaned up. There were a couple dozen codeine pills on the side table, and blood all over her bed. It was a crime scene. And, of course, the cops were being dicks: "You should go into her bedroom and check it out."

I had to identify her body at the morgue. It was my first time seeing her in a few years. I know it's common for people to say how peaceful corpses look, after they've been embalmed, but it's true—they hid the gunshot wound by wrapping a towel around her head and the weight of that was juxtaposed by just how incredibly peaceful my mom looked. There was no pain on her face. No sorrows, no struggles, no strife. None of the strain that was in her voice when she'd call me and start yelling about how I needed to send her more money.

I stopped by the police station because they said I needed to go there and pick up some of her belongings. I got there and they handed me the gun that she had used. They said, "Here, you can have this. You can take it home with you." Assholes.

My mom bought the pistol at a gun shop about a block away from her house. She was looking to buy a .22, but when she told them what she wanted it for, they recommended that she buy a .38 instead. Bigger caliber. They must've thought she was joking. She wrote about the interaction in a crazed, drug-fueled note that she scribbled in the weeks leading up to her suicide.

My sister didn't come down to face the music with me in Biloxi. She's an entire generation younger than me—thirteen years—so she lived with my mom long after I left home. I know she loved her as much as I did, but I think the aftermath of the suicide was just too much for her to bear. It's not an easy thing to have to deal with. I had to tell myself to stay strong and get through it, to deal with whatever needed to be dealt with first, then work through it later. Like, for years. Since neither my sister nor my father could be there, I had to do it alone.

I did bring one person with me—a sponsor, to help keep me clean and sober. I can tell you I really would've loved a stiff drink or two. Or three or four. But I stayed true. Dealing with the cops and the cremation and the other necessary arrangements was the final thing I could do for my mom, as her son, and I wanted to do it right.

You're damn right, I blame the counselor for overstepping her bounds and for giving me professional advice that she wasn't really qualified to give. I don't know, maybe it looked like a good idea on paper. Or in a textbook somewhere. But humans are complex creatures and you can't treat them like programmable robots. Every one is different. I don't know. I should've never taken that advice. It was bad advice.

If I hadn't cut my mom off, would she have drunk herself to death instead? Would she still have shot herself? It hurts too much to dwell on such things and, besides, there's really no point. They're questions that are impossible to answer. But it will always be there, in the back of my mind. My soul knows it's there, my body still carries its weight. And it's heavy.

Darker days were still to come.

19

Our next album was a mistake. I take comfort in knowing that the material was easily as strong as anything on *In the Dark*, but we weren't able to give those songs their proper due. I don't think I need to give a spoiler alert here, because we all know where things were heading . . . but had the Grateful Dead survived through the 1990s and into the 2000s, some of the songs on what would become *Built to Last* would've certainly grown into veritable beasts. Some of them did anyway. On a good night, "Blow Away" could breathe dragon fire, while fiery versions of "Standing on the Moon" could thaw the heart of even the most unruly creature. Two new Garcia/Hunter tunes—"Foolish Heart" and "Built to Last"—had all the makings of future classics. The songs could've and should've been the foundation of a great album.

Instead, we came off the success of *In the Dark* by taking everything that worked for us, recording-wise, and throwing it out the window. We reverted back to using Front Street as a studio, and we regressed back to recording our parts individually, one at a time, piecemeal. Tracking by stacking is pretty much standard procedure for most albums, but it didn't work for us and we knew that and we did it anyway.

Jerry and Cutler agreed to co-produce again, but *Built to Last* was the antithesis of doing things our way. It wasn't much of a band effort. We barely even saw each other at all during the recording process—we went in on different days, recorded our parts, and then split. There was no joy in it. The music on *Built to Last* betrays that. It's not the sound of thick air; it's the sound of plastic. A manufactured product. It took us the better part of a year to complete and it dropped on Halloween night 1989. Fitting for such a Frankenstein of an album.

Our live shows from that era, however, were nothing to fuck with. We were named one of the top-grossing live acts in America, by people who keep track of such things, and we'd reach number one on that list in a few short years. We had some massive nights in the late 1980s, sonically as well as commercially. A couple of those tours, between 1988 and 1991, dealt winning hands night after night—royal flush after royal flush.

During the storied Spring '90 tour, Brent played the best organ I've ever heard anybody play. He had the piss and the vinegar in him and he brought it to the table every night. The band, as a whole, had come alive again. Those shows had energy, with thunderbolts of electricity to spare. We didn't wreck drum sets or smash guitars or dress up in elaborate stage costumes; our shows were always about the music and the music during that period was adventurous. It dared listeners to ride shotgun as we went around hairpin turns, whizzing past ever-changing landscapes. Some nights, I could look out from my perch on the drum riser and see the whole house rocking back and forth in unison, a giant wave of people, and those were the nights you knew it was working.

We also had a lot of special guests join us during this period. Actually, we had always invited guests to the stage, going back to the likes of Janis Joplin, David Crosby, and Elvin Bishop in the late '60s, early '70s—people that were in our close-knit scene back then. It was fun to play with all our friends and hear what they could bring to the land of the Dead. But now, either spawned by our high-profile collaboration with Bob Dylan or perhaps due to our general mainstream acceptance and popularity, we were pulling in people from other musical universes entirely.

Bruce Springsteen's saxophonist, Clarence Clemons—the "Big Man" of the E Street Band—sat in with us half a dozen times in 1989. The year before, we had an all-girl pop band, the Bangles, join us in New Orleans. They sang backup while looking awkward during a lively version of "Iko Iko." They may have known how to "walk like Egyptians," but they danced more like soccer moms.

Neil Young, Huey Lewis, John Popper, Edie Brickell, Hall and Oates, Bonnie Raitt, Steve Miller, and our old friend Carlos Santana all joined us on various occasions. Some of them multiple times. And there were others, too, of course. But the two special guests that really stand out in my mind are Branford Marsalis and Ornette Coleman. We're talking about jazz legends who really knew how to blow their horns. They were professional improvisers. So were we. So we got along.

The first time Branford Marsalis sat in with us was on that hot Spring '90 tour, when everything was firing just right and the wheels were fully greased. It was at the Nassau Coliseum in Long Island on March 29. We brought Branford up for a now-legendary version of "Bird Song" during the first set, and it was so good, that we invited him out for the entire second set. The "Eyes of the World" that followed was of such a caliber that we even included it on our next live compilation (1990's *Without a Net*). Branford played with us four more times over the next four years, usually for the entire show. Those were good nights.

Branford became a friend of ours and he said something about us that I'll never forget: he said we all had big ears. Coming from a monster jazz guy like that, it was a monster compliment. We may have helped introduce improvisation to rock 'n' roll, but the jazz cats had been jamming since before Chuck Berry even picked up his first electric guitar. Having Branford validate us like that really meant something to me. He told us that we showed him what's possible within rock 'n' roll and that playing with us was one of the greatest thrills of his life. That, in turn, was one of the greatest thrills of mine.

One of the nights that Branford played with us, he walked outside the backstage door at set break to shoot some hoops at a basketball court that was right by the loading docks. We were using expensive, state-of-the-art, in-ear monitors at the time, which were like earbuds with your own, personal mix in them. Branford put his down on the curb or something and, while he was distracted on the court, someone stole them. We laughed about it and probably cracked a joke or two at his expense, but we didn't make him pay for them or anything. We just gave him replacements. "Nah, you're cool. Here's another pair. Don't lose 'em."

I was clean and sober in those years—which, of course, we still have to talk about—but because of it, I have a really sharp memory of those nights with him. With someone like that on stage, you always want to do your best. It challenges you to perform at your peak level, and it really lifts your game. And although Jerry wasn't necessarily clean and sober at that point, Branford really brought out the best in him, too. Jerry's face always lit up at the sound of a sax cutting through our little hippie stew.

Ornette Coleman was a slightly different deal. He still brought out the best in Jerry, I think, and the two had obvious mutual admiration for each other. Ornette checked out one of our gigs at Madison Square Garden and, shortly thereafter, asked Jerry to lay down guitar on a few tracks on *Virgin Beauty,* which Ornette recorded with his double-ensemble group, Prime Time, in 1988. Ornette's influence on free jazz is impossible to overstate and by the late-'80s he had become a vanguard of free funk, as well.

After my first time seeing him live, I got my hands on a recording of the show—kind of like what Deadheads did for us—and I couldn't stop listening to it for the longest time. He had this 6/8 rhythm thing going on that I just loved. Still do.

Ornette Coleman is an icon and we all respected him a great deal. That's why I really took it to heart when, during one of our performances, he turned to our manager, Cameron Sears, and said, "Man, those guys don't listen to each other when they play." So much for having the big ears that Branford thought we had.

Of course, both observations were correct, depending on the night. On the night that Ornette said that about us, his story checked out. He wasn't being unfriendly, he was just telling it like it is. We had built a foundation on our ability to achieve a group mind, but by the early 1990s, nobody wanted to listen to anybody else, anymore. Not on our stage. It was tough hearing someone like Ornette Coleman call you out on something like that, and yet, I'm not sure that it changed a damn thing.

Ornette sat in with us twice in 1993, and you can bet that we were all listening to him—and to each other—on those two nights. He got far out there, too.

Let's get back to 1990, where we were sailing on wind from such a great spring tour. For our summer jaunt, we hired acts like Crosby, Stills & Nash and Little Feat to open some stadium dates for us. The arenas and amphitheaters, we could sell out by ourselves. The machine marched on.

It was a refreshing start to a new decade, and life was sweet like a rhapsody. The band was playing great, our albums were selling well, and our concerts were selling out. Also: I was healthier than I had been in years. To get to that spot, first I had to recognize that I had landed in a place where I was drinking way too much and downing way too many painkillers. Those two vices were always one of my favorite combos, unfortunately. Served with a side of blackout. It was time for me to call last call. I was ready to stop drinking. Not for always, but just for then. I made up my mind about it and phoned a recovery facility in St. Helena, California— which, ironically, is in Napa County, right in the heart of wine country— and booked myself a lovely month-long stay.

But I had a big tour to do first, so I brought a sponsor on the road with me. He had been in AA for a while, so he knew the ropes. We went to meetings together almost every day, throughout the tour, in whatever East Coast town we were in that particular day.

The first thing I learned by going to AA meetings was that nicotine and caffeine are okay. Two drugs with documented health hazards. But one of the first things you do at an AA meeting is go to the coffee machine and fill a cup, then you go outside and light up a cigarette. Many of the people in those meetings were there because a judge told them that they had to be. They were just logging their time and punching in so that they'd be free to go about their business. All the same, going to AA meetings in the midst of an arena tour helped me stay off the sauce.

After the tour ended, I went and checked myself into St. Helena. My room came complete with a scenic view—of vineyards and wineries. You might as well line up slot machines around the perimeter of a Gamblers Anonymous meeting. At that point, it had been a few weeks since my last drink, but I had become increasingly addicted to Xanax. I was taking a ridiculous number of milligrams per day. Way higher than any recommended dose. I was glad to throw that monkey off my back and kick him to the curb.

Xanax is really a dangerous drug to take recreationally. You build up a tolerance faster than you can blink, and when the addiction kicks in, you stop counting how many you're taking and you start popping handfuls at a time. Xanax is from the same family of benzos that Valium comes from, although it tends to come on quicker and it wears off before it wears out its welcome. It doesn't feel as harsh as Valium, you start with a much smaller dosage, and you're not as groggy the next day—all attractive properties to doctors who, upon its release in 1981, started prescribing it liberally to anyone that was anxious, or having trouble sleeping, or upset about their girlfriend, or worried about their pet, or a little too uptight about the world at large. "Here, take this and relax, son."

I was really happy to free myself of that particular addiction and I've never really gone back to it. I'll take it here and there, like if I need to fall asleep after an acid trip, but I'll never make a habit of it. Not again. And I didn't drink for about three years, from 1990 to 1993. These recovery places are so good at programming you, it borders on brainwashing. They use scare tactics: "If you ever take another sip, you'll fall down dead."

That kind of intentional and malicious misinformation makes me think that it's high time—pardon the pun—to take a stand and stand up against Big Pharma and the DEA. How many years have they told us that pills are safe? And how long have they told us that cannabis is not?

And how much longer will they tell us that cannabis isn't medicine, while side effects from pills—that they've approved—kill us? They can keep telling us these lies, but as a nation, we're finally beginning to see right through them. We're locking up peaceful citizens for using natural medicine while doctors aid and abet the deaths of our friends and loved ones by prescribing stronger and stronger pills. Medicine should heal, not kill.

I know the tides are turning, and I know you already know where I stand with this, but it's time to make cannabis legal once and for all. Federally. Nationally. And if anything can help people shake their addictions, it should be pot. They should be given a joint for every unopened beer can they turn in.

But enough with the weed rap. It was good for me to get off of Xanax and to stop drinking and to be clearheaded for a change. Reality became sort of like an alternate reality in itself, and I was digging the new, natural high.

Plus, I was able to get out to Hawaii to go scuba diving—sometimes with Jerry—and, when you're submerged ninety feet under the sea, there's no fucking chance for survival if you're at all fucked up. You've got to come to it straight. So I did. So did Jerry. And so it is that, for the most part, as the 1990s rolled in, everyone had found their happy place. Everyone seemed to be in a good spot.

Brent may have been the one exception to that. The fighting between him and his wife, Lisa, was beginning to remind everyone of Keith and Donna's domestic warfare. Also, he took the poor reception of *Built to Last* personally, since he had four songs on there—more than anybody else; the most he ever had on a Grateful Dead album. The album was met with harsh criticism and bad reviews. It went gold fast enough, but not platinum like *In the Dark*. Somehow, Brent suspected that he might be to blame.

In December 1989, two months after the album's release, Brent overdosed on opiates of some sort—either heroin or morphine—and was subsequently arrested for possession. He was released on bail, of course, but the very real threat of significant jail time hovered over him like stormy weather as he entered the New Year. If I recall correctly, he also had at least one DUI to deal with, and he was planning on cleaning up after the summer tour.

Overall, you could say that Brent was a pretty disturbed guy but, man, was he ever on a roll with us during the first half of 1990. You got the feeling that he was pouring himself into the music in search of some kind of catharsis, that he was letting it all out through the songs, that he was using music for therapy. But, in the end, it wasn't enough.

This time, I was at home in Mendocino when I got the call. Brent was dead. He was murdered . . . from a self-administered speedball—an often lethal mix of cocaine and either heroin or morphine. You shoot them together, in the arm, so each one can balance out the effects of the other. A potent upper and a potent downer, both at once. Never a good idea, kids.

The overdose was ruled accidental, although some people did whisper that Brent had developed a death wish. I don't think that's true. I think he was just naïve and was going for one last rush before cleaning up. It's a same-old story that you hear far too often. He was thirty-seven years old. That's four years older than Belushi when he died of the same stupid cocktail.

Brent's funeral sucked. All funerals suck. As a band, we tried to make jokes and avoid eye contact as much as possible. And I'm sure more than one person there had the thought that, "Hey, that could've been Jerry," or "Is Jerry next?" For his part, Jerry became noticeably more withdrawn right after this. You could tell it struck a chord in him. I mean, he had his own demons at the time, and when you see similar demons kill one of your friends, it probably should scare the fuck out of you. I'm not sure Jerry was scared, but Brent's death had a certain effect on him, that's for sure.

Brent's last show with us was on July 23, 1990, at a giant summer shed about a half hour south of Chicago. The World Music Amphitheater in Tinley Park. We encored with a cover of the Band's "The Weight." Which means the last line Brent ever sang onstage with us was, "I gotta go, but my friend can stick around." Talk about a weight, all right.

Whenever one of our keyboard players died, we felt it in a way that's usually reserved only for family members and loved ones, because you were a part of something with them. You depended on them but you weren't just business partners: Your souls became entangled through music, across time and space as the tours rolled past the miles and the miles cut through the years. You felt like you lost a family member because you did lose a family member.

I'm not sure how many people know this, but I was in another band with Brent, besides the Grateful Dead. In the fall of '86, when Jerry was recovering from his coma, Brent and I played in a no-frills rock group called Go Ahead.

We had Alex Ligertwood (vocals) and Dave Margen (bass) from Santana's band. And we had Jerry on guitar. Not Jerry Garcia, though; Jerry Cortez. He was with the Youngbloods at the time; more recently, he became a late-era addition to Tower of Power. They're lucky to have him.

Those three players were all in a local Marin band called City Section, which aspired to be a backline band-for-hire. They hired themselves when they recruited me for an attempted group called the Kreutzmann/Margen Band, which morphed into Kokomo, which morphed into Go Ahead. I hated the name Go Ahead, but it was better than Kokomo.

We got our kicks and put on some really great shows. Bobby must've felt like he was missing out because he sat in with us and even signed on for a short tour. We only played sporadically—from 1986 to 1988—and we never really had a grand plan. It was just for fun. Our one and only video, for a Brent original called "Nobody's," was directed by my son Justin with Francis Ford Coppola's son, Gian-Carlo. It aired on TV, but nothing else came of it. With Brent's death, there went the possibility of anything more.

As for the Grateful Dead, we couldn't stop. Even if we wanted to, we had an empire to protect, a business to run, and a hell of a lot of overhead to finance. Employees had to be paid, headquarters had to be maintained, offices needed a raison d'être, we needed work, and fans needed their band—the beast had to be fed. Our live shows fueled all of this, so we had to get back out there as quickly as possible. Like it or not.

There was only a month and a half gap between shows after Brent's death. We had set out to find a new keyboardist immediately, although personally, I was probably back at home in Mendocino during much of that time, resting, recovering, processing.

For a while, Shelley and I lived in a tract house in Novato, which is at the northern tip of Marin. It was close enough to San Rafael that I could go from my couch at home to my drum stool at Front Street in about fifteen minutes. But we hated living in Novato. It wasn't my scene. I owned the place in Mendocino—the Comptche ranch—so Shelley and I decided to move back up there. It was a great decision. During the Grateful Dead's biggest years, I lived on a remote ranch three hours away from it all.

Granted, because that was—intentionally—too long a daily commute, I ended up getting a place in San Anselmo as well, on the other side of San Rafael's tracks, where I could stay during rehearsal weeks or when we were in recording sessions or whatever. The band was working a lot, but I would come back from these mega-tours very happy and very wealthy and could then retreat into my own little wilderness.

At the end of a tour, I'd fly first class to San Francisco and then hop on my friend's commuter plane, a Twin Cessna Flyer, and he'd take me up to Little River Airport in Mendocino, about thirteen miles from home. Those short flights were just me and my pilot friend.

Little River Airport was used to support naval flight training during World War II, in conjunction with operations at the Naval Auxiliary Landing Field in Santa Rosa. Sometime thereafter it became a public-use airport but there's no control tower to speak of. You had to click your radio five times to turn on the runway lights and then pray that there wasn't any fog. I couldn't wait to land because Shelley would be there waiting for me, and she'd have the medicine with her—the cocaine—and we'd get back to the house and get wired and stay up all night talking and raving. It felt like I was escaping the insanity of the city and like I was escaping the insanity of the Dead tour. In reality, I was escaping nothing. I was just trading in one insanity for another. I was pulling a geographic.

Post-rehab, there was a period in Mendocino when I didn't drink or do any drugs. But from, say, 1985 to 1990, the band was doing really well and

I was doing really well and I always seemed to have a reason to celebrate. Life was grand.

I really loved the community up there, too. That's where I first started dating Shelley, if you remember. Then we moved away, then we came back. I sometimes played low-key gigs in the bars up there, just for fun. And I helped the homeless there once, when I found out that they were being kicked out from one of the beaches. We brought them food and donations and stuff.

During the period when Shelley and I were living in Novato, I loaned the Comptche house to my dad. He needed it for a while. His second wife, Gail, had died of cancer and my dad became despondent. It was the hardest thing he had ever gone through and I had never seen him so sad. I was fearful for him, for a while. He didn't have any money and didn't have a place to go, so I said, "Dad, I have a house for you . . ." He took me up on it.

While living at my ranch, my dad met another lady friend, Pat, and she pulled him out of all that darkness. She was his great escape. She also turned him on to a real open style of living, the kind that I was used to but that wasn't so common among his generation. Pat turned my dad onto psychedelics and they smoked joints and threw incredible parties. So . . . my dad took acid! You can imagine how thrilled I was about that whole development. When I moved back to Comptche with Shelley, my dad moved into Pat's ranch, about two miles down the road. The Kreutzmanns were embedded in Mendocino.

For his sixtieth birthday party, they threw a big bash at the ranch. It was a Victorian croquet party; all the men came in fancy dress coats, slacks, boots, and the ladies all wore long, flowing beautiful Victorian dresses. All dolled up to the nines. My dad invited everyone in town to the party and it felt like half of Mendocino County showed up. Everybody was in the right spirit of things.

We played croquet in the afternoon and it was really a thrill for me to watch my dad play because he would cheat, but he did it humorously and cartoonish, in a way that almost recalled Neal Cassady. He turned it into a slapstick routine. When it was time to eat, we all sat down at the tables while my dad and some of his friends attended the grill.

Next to me at my table was Edith, an elderly, local mainstay who came from the Baptist church and ran the store downtown and knew all the gossip for miles around. It surprised me that she showed up, because she knew that all the hippies smoked weed and did crazy things, but she leaned quite the other way. The way we were sitting at the table, Edith's back was to my dad. I looked over her shoulder and couldn't believe it—there was my dad, wearing nothing but a blond wig and a jock strap. He started loading all the chicken on a serving plate and I was nervous about what would happen next. He came over and offered Edith the first piece. "How do you like your chicken, Edith?" he asked, smiling, politely, the consummate gentleman. That was my dad in those days. He really had changed since I was under his roof. Pat really helped loosen him up.

We got sidetracked again, but I did it on purpose: That was what life was like up in Mendocino. It was a totally different universe from that of the Grateful Dead. I'm not sure which one was the escape from the other. They both offered respite and relief—and they both required that, too.

Back in Grateful Dead land, we needed a new keyboardist and we didn't have much time to find one, much less make sure they were shipshape before shipping out on tour. We had just a few weeks—Brent died on July 26 and we put an East Coast arena tour on the books, slated to kick off on September 7 in Richfield, Ohio. From there, we were headed to the Spectrum in Philadelphia for three nights, followed by a six-night run at Madison Square Garden. Then it was off to Europe for October. No pressure if you're the new guy. Not to mention that we didn't exactly have a new guy.

Enter, into the Grateful Dead fortress, Vince Welnick. It was Pigpen's house from the start. Tom Constanten and Ned Lagin were like visitors, stopping by on their way through. Keith Godchaux came a-knocking and we let him in. Poor Brent didn't have a choice—we grabbed him by the collar in the doorway, rushed him past the foyer, and sat his ass down in the living room. "Take a load off, Mydland."

As for Vince, I'm not sure who invited him to the party. We auditioned him, of course, along with a few other guys. I guess one of us, Jerry probably, said "Kick off your shoes and come on in," but the rest of us were like, "Hey, who's that guy in the kitchen over there?"

We had only considered a handful of folks, most of whom came to us by some form of serendipity. They knew at least one of us or we had seen them play somewhere and liked it. Pete Sears was just such a guy. Sears had an impressive résumé that qualified him for the job, including membership in Jefferson Starship (and, later, just Starship). After we passed on him, he joined Hot Tuna. I've sat in with him on occasion at David Nelson Band gigs. Bobby's played with him. Phil's played with him. He's still an active touring musician and he's a great guy and we're friends. There's certainly room for the "What if . . ." question.

We also auditioned T. Lavitz, a decorated keyboard player from Dixie Dregs who, later, formed a rather notable, all-instrumental Grateful Dead cover band called Jazz is Dead, with Jimmy Herring, Alphonso Johnson, and Billy Cobham. If you know your jazz history, you just raised an eyebrow. It was an original idea for a cover band. (When I hear someone cover us, I want the artist to take ownership over their version of the songs. Keller Williams is great at doing that.)

We looked at just a few other keyboardists—at most—but out of all of them, Vince Welnick was easily my least favorite. No question. There was no denying that he had a respectable history: He played in the Tubes, a theatrical rock band that had its own share of commercial success, including a Top Ten single and hit video on MTV in 1983 ("She's a Beauty"). Much like the Grateful Dead, the Tubes built their career on the strength of their live shows. But unlike the Grateful Dead, their live shows seemed to be more about performance art than about the music itself. They were making some kind of ironic anti-showbiz statement, but it was lost on me.

That's not the reason why I thought Vince was the wrong man for the job, though. I just thought he was lackluster. Perhaps a more diplomatic way to put it is that his playing style was understated. Surprisingly, that's what Jerry seemed to like the most about him. That is, until a few years into it when Vince picked up the habit of mimicking Jerry's lines. Jerry hated that with any player, be it Vince or Keith or Brent or Phil.

At the time of Vince's audition, the band was attracted to his abilities to hit the high harmonies, and he was certainly an adequate keyboard player, so he got the job. It was the path of least resistance. Vince got voted in by default.

In addition to the Tubes, Vince had done some road work with Todd Rundgren, who now lives down the road from me in Hawaii. So he had a name for himself. But by the time he came to audition for us—in August 1990—he was flat broke and desperate for work. Perhaps that played into the decision to hire him, too. He told us that if he didn't get the gig, he was going to have to go down to Mexico and smuggle bricks across the border for dough.

As for Vince's personality, I didn't have any issues with him. We got along. I'm sure we partied some. He was a true gentleman and he was easy-going and he was friendly. Of course, he wouldn't have been a proper Grateful Dead keyboardist if he didn't have problems with his marriage. Before marrying Vince, Lori rode the bareback pony in the circus or the carnival or something. She had a pistol-packing cowgirl image, like a modern day carney Annie Oakley. She was one of those real out-there characters that we seemed to attract. But that's neither here nor there.

Another prop I must give to Vince is that he was dedicated. He put the time in and rubbed it with elbow grease. Like Brent, I'm sure he felt the backlash of so-called "purist" Deadheads—stubborn fans who would've resisted any new keyboardist, no matter what. Fools. But instead of taking it as personally as Brent did, it just drove him to work even harder. And he did work hard. He would practice for an hour or more before every gig, just going over the material. He had to struggle to get it right, and I'm not sure that he ever did. But not for lack of trying.

Remember: Vince had but a couple weeks to learn an entire twenty-five-year canon. And he had just days to learn how to read our minds when we veered from the script. Which was often. We had a quarter century of experience on our side. He had a lot of catching up to do. So we asked our friend Bruce Hornsby to lend some assistance.

Actually, the truth is, Bruce Hornsby was our first choice. Before we held auditions, we asked him to join the band. Bruce didn't need an audition. We wanted him. He turned us down. He was already committed to his own vision, but I think he also realized the benefits of being affiliated with us, so we came up with a compromise: He would play with us part-time, as often as his schedule allowed, until the new guy got settled.

Maybe that says something about Vince—neither Keith nor Brent needed training wheels. They were able to hit the ground running.

Bruce Hornsby was such a big player, with such a big personality, that he was almost too much of his own force for our little ensemble. We all loved him, and I still do to this day. But I think he recognized before we did that his talent demanded his own thing. He never would've been happy just being "another band's keyboardist." Even if that other band was the Grateful Dead. Although, he did like it enough to play more than 100 shows with us.

Even after March 1992, when he handed in his badge and went back to concentrating on his own career, he continued to sit in with us, a few times a year, until the very end. He may have only been there part-time, during an eighteen-month stretch, but Bruce Hornsby will always be an honorary member of the Grateful Dead, as far as I or anyone else is concerned.

Looking back, we already had a good thing going with Bruce for a few years before Brent died. Bruce Hornsby & the Range opened for us nine times, from 1987 to 1990, and he sat in with us on half a dozen different occasions during that time, as well—on both piano and accordion. Naturally, it pleased me to learn that Bruce was a big fan of the Grateful Dead long before he met us. He used to attend shows, on the other side of the barricade, going back to the 1970s.

By the time he made it to the stage with us, Bruce already had a couple of hit songs and multiplatinum albums under his belt. He was established.

When he joined the Grateful Dead, albeit part time, everyone in the stadium already knew songs like "The Way It Is" and "Mandolin Rain." They were all over the radio. For whatever reason, we left those songs alone. We did try to bring several other Bruce originals into our repertoire—"The Valley Road," and "Stander on the Mountain"—but neither of them stuck.

It was hard for me to play those songs and I don't think Phil ever figured out the right feel for them, either. Matter of fact, I don't think anyone in the band ever got them right. I never really felt like we were able to pull those songs off the way Bruce intended them and I think that he probably felt the same way. I'm pretty sure it bothered him. He could nail any of our songs with ease but we couldn't do the same for his. It's not that they're such complicated pop songs, it's just that they have a certain Virginia vibe to them—the same sound that Dave Matthews Band later perfected—and it was hard for a bunch of Bay Area natives to get that groove just right.

One more note about Bruce: Every other Grateful Dead keyboardist left their post only when they died or were dismissed. Bruce Hornsby was the only one who walked away. Respect.

20

There are a lot of deaths in this story, darn it. I guess that makes me something of a survivor. Unfortunately, Bill Graham was not so lucky. On October 25, 1991, he was killed in a horrific accident. He was on his way home from work which, for him, meant taking a helicopter back from a Huey Lewis and the News concert in the East Bay. The crash, attributed to bad weather, killed everyone on board. As fast as lightning.

Shortly after the crash was reported and news spread, I realized that I was aware of the exact moment it happened, because the lights in my house in San Anselmo flickered. That was the result of the impact, as the helicopter slammed into electrical lines. But I also knew that it was Graham, flickering the lights as if to say, "Everyone take your seats. The show must go on . . ."

About a week later, a few hundred thousand people all gathered in Golden Gate Park for a big memorial concert that featured many different acts, including Journey, Jackson Browne, and Santana. The common denominator being that they all worked with—and loved—Bill Graham. He launched more than a few careers and nurtured many more. He transformed the concert industry, time and again.

In the Grateful Dead world alone, he took turns being our manager, our booking agent, our promoter, our coach, our pain-in-the-ass, and our friend. Bill Graham's work with the Grateful Dead was substantial. He was one of the few people who could tell us what to do. We didn't always obey, but we always listened.

As for his memorial concert, I know I was there, because we played it. And I know we played it, because there are recordings. Photographs. Setlists. I must have been lost in the mourning process and caught up in the sadness of it all, because I don't remember one damn thing about that day. According to the data, John Fogerty sat in with us for nearly half the set, on a series of Creedence Clearwater Revival covers. How'd it go? Your guess is as good as mine.

It would be convenient if we could make a poetic statement about how Bill Graham's send-off effectively served as a jazz funeral for the Grateful Dead as well, but we still had worthwhile music in us, and still had a few paragraphs to add to the rock 'n' roll history books. We weren't done. No, not yet. However, we may have been showing signs of wear and tear after more than twenty-five years of nonstop touring, which encouraged and supported unhealthy lives of excess and abuse.

Jerry, in particular, looked torn and frayed. We were supposed to be the spokespeople for personal freedom, but we were getting worried about our brother. After the Summer '91 tour ended in Denver, we reluctantly staged an intervention.

It was difficult. It felt like throwing stones, as Bobby might say. Had we become politicians? Or, worse yet, hypocrites? "You're busted!" said the kids from the Acid Tests. "You're busted!" said the mailman who used to shoot speed. "You're busted!" said the military drum student who was suspended from the band when drugs got the best of him.

I had just come out of rehab and yet I was going to join in on that refrain? "You're busted?" Sure. But weren't we all busted flat, at one time or another?

As you can see, participating in the intervention made me very uncomfortable. Jerry wasn't exactly happy with the proceedings, either. He was defensive and angry. That was okay. I would've felt that way, too. But we weren't there to punish him; we were there to help him. Not for nothing, but after the intervention, Jerry started going to a methadone clinic back at home. Drove himself there, even. We were optimistic.

A year later, the pendulum had swung back the other way. Shortly after the Summer '92 tour—which had its share of great moments—Jerry came close to slipping into another diabetic coma. He was living in a plush pad in San Rafael with his then-girlfriend Manasha and their daughter, Keelan. Manasha was a genuine spirit, but had some pretty far-out beliefs.

When Jerry's life-force started to dim, she insisted that he stay home, out of the hospital and away from modern medicine, while an acupuncturist attended to him instead. It wasn't our place to interfere, so all we could do was cross our fingers and stay close to the phone. Naturally, we were thrilled when we found out his health was improving. He lost some weight and had regained some of his spark, but we still had to cancel the fall tour to give him the time and space needed to really recover.

Earlier in the year, we had talked about taking another hiatus. Jerry wanted us to consider it, and I spoke up in favor of a six-month break. The idea was shot down because our operation was a big one, with a lot of overhead, mouths to feed, mortgages to pay, and so on. This is where it gets good: Jerry's health had a wicked sense of humor because it forced us to sit out for a season anyway. To hell with operating costs.

I'm not going to sugarcoat things. Our tours during this period weren't our best. We still had some transcendent jams in us, and they would occasionally breach the surface, but they were becoming increasingly rare sightings. In fact, before Jerry's new set of health concerns came up, Bruce Hornsby called us out on everything. In the Spring of '92, he relinquished his part-time position with us, in part because he was unhappy with our playing.

Remember: Hornsby was a fan of the Grateful Dead. He was in our audience before he was on our stage. Which meant that his complaints had extra bite to them because they came from someone who loved the. music, who loved the songs, and who loved us. He wasn't afraid to recognize that we weren't delivering to our capabilities. Like Ornette Coleman had said, we stopped listening to each other, on stage and off. And the shows suffered because of it.

And yet, our numbers continued to grow. We had more people vying for tickets, not less. After taking medical leave during the Fall of '92, we resumed touring that December, and then played eighty-one shows in 1993, followed by eighty-four shows in 1994. It was business as usual . . . even though nothing about us was usual.

This was the era where we would take over entire hotel floors and throw post-show parties in the Hospitality Suite (aka "the Hostility Suite"). A lot of famous people found their way to our hotel parties, and that was fun. A lot of girls did, too, and that was even more fun. We could do whatever we wanted to in the hospitality suites—especially in the bathrooms—but we didn't need to take the party home with us. When we were done with it, we could pull a French Exit and escape to sovereign territory: our own private rooms.

When the band first started hosting hospitality suites at the hotels, Jerry would go up there and hold court. And he was brilliant. People were as transfixed by his conversations as they were by his guitar playing. He'd entertain thoughts until he settled on a topic, and he'd start riffing on it, turning a tangent into a verbal guitar solo in which he'd play with your expectations as he wrapped your attention around his words. All eyes were on him. Or most of them, anyway—as I listened intently, I'd also be checking out girls on the sly.

Bobby couldn't compete with Jerry—none of us could—but he came up with his own thing: he assembled a portable, custom sound system to power these parties. It was a giant cabinet on wheels. He'd roll it into the center of the room, open it up, and start DJ'ing. He'd turn the fucker up, and suddenly it was a party. We had more fun in that room than Pee-Wee had on his entire Big Adventure.

I remember this one time, we were raging in the hospitality suite and I was enjoying myself in the company of strangers. There was a big sign on the door that read, "Presidential Suite," which was in clear view when I was introduced to JFK's son, John F. Kennedy Jr. He had spent a summer working at John Perry Barlow's Wyoming ranch—or something to that effect—so he was, strangely, connected to our circles. I blurted out the obvious joke: "Oh, look at this! The future president, in the Presidential Suite!" If I had been just a little more coordinated and a little less inebriated, I would've taken my left foot and shoved it into my mouth. (Kennedy—a president's son, of course—was a good sport about it. He even pretended to laugh.)

The hospitality suite was for after the show. Before the show, it wasn't always the crazy backstage scene that you might imagine. We weren't driving Rolls Royces into swimming pools or getting our private parts plastered for posterity. It had been years since we all took acid together, ritualistically, as if it was a sacrament. Acid had become too risky. We had lost the freedom to fuck up, and to take giant musical chances. It felt like the band began to lack the confidence to take psychedelics and step onstage in front of a large number of people, or to go off the deep end, improvisationally. Were we playing it safe? Maybe.

At a certain level—like, when clubs turn into arenas—you become a cog in a very big, little "engine that could." Every band member becomes a cog. And in order for the wheel to turn, churning out music like the player piano on a merry-go-round, every one of those cogs must be well greased and perfectly calibrated to interlock. There are a lot of other moving parts as well, all powering an engine that is dependent on that wheel going 'round. It's a fragile operation.

If the operation fails and the wheel doesn't turn, then you just disappointed 25,000 fans—or more—in one evening. Some of whom drove across the country to see you, some of whom quit or willingly got fired from their shit jobs just to be able to go to the show, many of whom went through considerable effort just to be there in the back of that lawn. Are you really going to risk letting them all down? Well, as the recordings may reveal, some of my band members thought that was okay. And I'm not saying I always had perfect shows. I didn't. But I sure did try. It was an enormous amount of pressure. I think we all felt that weight, regardless of how we carried it.

I would maybe do a bump or two of coke—oftentimes between songs, right onstage—for energy, and sure, I'd have a couple beers to help me ease on into things while getting ready for the show. Maybe I'd take a couple puffs off a joint, on my way to the stage, just to tap into that creative mind-set. But any serious partying would wait until afterward. Instead, I spent the time right before curtain call (and during set break) in my own little onstage cubicle, just gathering my thoughts, warming up, maybe practicing a few patterns with my sticks, maybe doing some stretches.

Every band member had their own cubicle—with curtains for walls—at the back of the stage, and we could do whatever we wanted in them. They were our own private oases, designed to give us an additional protective layer from the backstage scene, which, at that level, was no more private than the parking lot. The best friend of the promoter's daughter wanted her picture with you; someone you slept with once wanted to introduce you to their new lover; someone you had never met before wanted to share their drugs with you. It was a parade of one after another, and it was never ending.

Since the cubicles were on the actual stage, access was extremely limited. Each band member's cubicle had a different vibe. Phil mostly kept to himself, often on his computer, and stayed in his area. Jerry's cubicle was on the opposite side of the stage, and he was often in there cracking jokes with his roadie or various esteemed guests. I liked having my own area because it was a place where I didn't need to be social, didn't need to grip and grin, and didn't need to be some kind of host. Although, sometimes, different celebrities would stop on by, just to get a private meeting, and that could be pretty cool. Robert Downey Jr. wandered into my cubicle one night. We hung out and talked for a few minutes. Then I played the show.

And even though we had been on the road for more than a quarter century, road life was never completely routine. There was always some kind of adventure—or misadventure—waiting for us at the hotels.

This one time, we were in Las Vegas for a run of shows at the Sam Boyd Silver Bowl. A stadium in the desert. We stayed someplace off the Strip, where we didn't have to contend with the casinos. The point was to stay someplace where we could rest and relax between shows. We were awoken at some ungodly hour one night (err, mid-morning) because our rooms overlooked the swimming pool and all these fat, old ladies were in there doing water aerobics. They had floaters on and were paddling up a storm. A shit storm, if you ask me. Well now, Welnick must've had the same thought, because he bought a Baby Ruth from one of the vending machines, unwrapped it, and tossed it into the pool. When the ladies noticed the candy bar, they started screaming and squealing, making a mad dash for the exit. They thought there was a turd in the water. Good work, Vinny. With a freshly abandoned pool, I was able to go right back to sleep. We call that trick the Candy Bar Evacuation. It only works in swimming pools, although, to be fair, I've never tested it elsewhere.

I've gone through much greater lengths to ensure a full day's sleep between gigs. The fuck if I remember when this was, but it was in the South somewhere. Years earlier. For some reason, we were booked in a Holiday Inn. We had just flown in on some little private jet and we didn't get to check in until four o'clock in the morning. Naturally, I didn't attempt to settle down for sleep until a few hours later. Around nine in the morning, I was woken by an intolerably loud noise outside—wars were being fought, bombs were detonating, and countries were being flattened, all in the immediate space outside my window. It wasn't traffic and it wasn't the neighbors. I opened my curtain, naked as the day I came into this world, and there was a guy with a jackhammer, right outside my window. He was taking down the Holiday Inn sign and changing it to a Ramada, or something like that. I needed more sleep and I had a show to do that night, so I started freaking out on the guy, but he didn't pay me any mind. He couldn't hear me. That made me crazier than a dog in heat, so I called the front desk and started barking at them. I explained my situation. Their response was that they were very sorry but there was nothing they could do and they couldn't even move me into another room because the hotel was fully booked. I hung up. I was pissed. Full red flag anger alert. Houston, we have a problem.

The jackass with the jackhammer woke up some of the other band and crew members, too, but not all of them had been up as late as I was, and I seemed to be the most reactionary in that moment. I decided to retaliate. I unplugged the lamp and cut the end of the cord. Then I unscrewed the telephone box and ripped out the phone cord. I took the butchered end of the lamp cord, which was running 110 volts, and placed it on the 98 volts of direct current from the phone outlet. It was like a miniature battle scene. I just destroyed enemy lines. And by that I mean I blew out the phone line. It physically shocked me and left temporary burn marks on my hands and wrists. But the operation was a success—I took down the hotel's phone system. At just past nine in the morning, before cell phones, when lovers are trying to order champagne and Eggs Benedict from room service, when travelers are trying to call the front desk for a late checkout, when business guys are trying to make important business calls . . . when a rock band is trying to sleep. It was as disruptive as the construction, so I figured we were even.

To take credit for the attack, I took a big bowl of fruit that was in my room and put it in the middle of the hallway. Then I took the telephone that I had ripped out of the wall and balanced it on top. It was a memo to the hotel. Don't fuck with tired musicians.

I went down to the front desk to assess how successful my disruption had been, and Lesh was there, complaining that he was unable to make a call. There were dozens of pissed-off business guys there, too. Mission accomplished. I went back to my room and went right back to sleep.

Of course, hotels weren't only for sleeping. Rock memoirs are supposed to be filled with sex, drugs, and rock 'n' roll, and we've already covered the drugs and the rock 'n' roll. I was already married when the Grateful Dead formed and I went through a few wives during the band's lifetime. But that's not to say there weren't nights on the road when stuff happened that, years later, people might want to read about in the book of rock 'n' roll.

The story I'm thinking about involves our soundman, Dan Healy. We were in Boston, which meant there was no shortage of college girls. During the show, while he was mixing and doing his thing, Healy gave out his room number to every pretty girl he saw, and told them to come on by after the show. "You like to party, don't you?"

I didn't know he did that—he never handed me his room number on a piece of paper—but after the show, I stopped by his room for a drink. We used to hang out a lot during downtime on tours. He was one of my road dogs and we would run around together and get all rowdy and hopefully get into trouble and whatnot. Anyway, there was a knock at the door and, one by one, girls started showing up. Pretty soon there were fifteen, maybe twenty girls in the room. It was a typical suite, with two double beds. Healy was posted up on a chair on the other side, playing guitar and entertaining all of us. Everyone was watching him play and digging it and just enjoying the mellow scene.

Before long, a particular blond chick started making eyes with me. Or did I start making eyes at her? Who's to say. She sat down next to me and we started getting into some of this, and then some of that, together. It didn't take but moments before we took what we started and ran all the way with it. That's called a home run, for those keeping score. Right in the room with everyone else there. Healy was in the middle of playing some song, and more than a dozen girls were all about. Instead of clearing the room like a Baby Ruth in a swimming pool, our moans and groans just kick-started it—before all was said and done, Healy and I made love to just about every one of those girls. I kept count and made it all the way to thirteen. Sometimes the girls were piled a few deep at a time. Sometimes it was like musical chairs. After we were done with them, the girls left just like they came—one at a time—and everything was casual. It was all unspoken and easy. After the last girl left, Healy and I continued to hang out and talk and then eventually I went back to my room to pass out. To this day, thirteen is still my lucky number.

Going to Healy's room that night was a good decision. But I made my share of bad ones, too, of course. One night, when we weren't on tour, I met up with John Perry Barlow in a bar in Lagunitas, just down the road from the Girl Scout camp where we lived, communally, back in 1966. I drove home drunk that night—or, tried to, anyway. Barlow rode shotgun. There's only one way home when you're anywhere in the western part of Marin County, and it's by taking one of the curvy, narrow back roads that crisscross Marin's back forty like a couple fallen strands of spaghetti on a kitchen floor. Mountainous terrain, often under a redwood canopy. I was in my Alfa Romeo, but for the last time. I was driving with mismatched tires, which was my first mistake. We were drunk and snorting cocaine, which was my second and third. I pushed it into fifth gear up a hill and around a corner, but I wasn't going to make the turn, so I cheated and swerved into the other lane. Right on cue, a red Mustang came careening down from the other direction, heading right toward us. We had less than two seconds until impact. I made fast with the wheel and steered us into the other direction to avoid the collision. It worked. Except that gravity lifted the car on its side and we slid across the road a few feet, sideways, until the road curved. We didn't curve with it. At that point, we landed upside down in the woods.

We were suspended upside down, in the car, but there was no blood. We were still in our seats, with our seat belts on. So what did I do? I slowly reached for the cocaine and carefully took it out and let gravity do the rest—I barely even needed to snort. The cocaine sobered me up a little but, when the CHP finally did show up, my real saving grace was the fact that we were on a hill. During the sobriety test, I leaned against the hill to keep my balance and stay straight. Both the protagonist and the antagonist in this particular story are gravity.

I told the cops that I swerved to avoid a deer and they couldn't disprove it—there were no skid marks on the road because the car immediately flipped on its side, and then tumbled down into the woods. Without skid marks, they didn't have a case.

Don't think I'm downplaying the fact that I was drunk. I was and there was no good reason why I should've been behind the wheel. Not that time. For legal reasons, I don't recommend trying any of the stuff in this book at home, but with this one especially. Seriously. Don't do it. Driving drunk is probably the dumbest thing a person could do. It's even worse than shooting heroin. It cost me my Alfa Romeo . . . but I was lucky in that it could've cost me a life. Mine or an innocent.

I destroyed another car once, but that one was on purpose. It was an abandoned vehicle that I found right near the place in Novato, where and when I lived with Susila. Kidd Candelario and I wrapped detonation cord—which, by the way, is not a common thing to have (and certainly not street legal)—around the headliner of the car and rigged it with a three-minute fuse. I remembered my dad's rocketry lessons, but this was a little more advanced than a wood swing and a pipe bomb. I lit the fuse and had three minutes to take cover. Three minutes—but I decided to be cautious and only rely on two. The third minute was spent biting my nails in suspense and anticipation. And then, suddenly—*boom*! The dynamite went off. So did the roof of the car. There were sparks and thunder, all right, but the loudest noise of all came from Susila, who was so pissed that I'm surprised I didn't end up sleeping on the sofa that night. The shock wave rattled everything in the house and knocked dishes onto the floor. Of course, if you've read this book chronologically, you'll recognize that nothing in that particular scene was entirely unfamiliar to me. My life has had its share of dynamite, explosions, and pissed-off women.

Sprinkled throughout my life, these explosive exploits all came from wild and carefree days. But, back in the land of the Dead, the wild and carefree days were about to end.

21

Remember that elementary school music teacher who told me that I "couldn't keep a beat"? Well, maybe she was right . . . but on January 18, 1994, I got dressed up in a tuxedo and stood behind a podium with most of my bandmates, at a very fancy and formal hotel ballroom, to accept the Grateful Dead's induction into the Rock and Roll Hall of Fame. Bruce Hornsby had the honor of inducting us and he gave us a fantastic introduction. Bobby, Phil, Mickey, Vince—even Tom Constanten—all approached the podium. I spoke first.

"In Grateful Dead tradition . . ." I took out a prepared speech, ripped it in half, and tossed it over my shoulder. Then I improvised, speaking from the heart, addressing all the people in formal attire who sat around tables, wedding style, in the stately (in other words, sterile) ballroom.

"I'm really doing this tonight because I like to play music," I started. "That's where I come from." I made a few jokes, then recognized our fallen keyboard players—Pigpen, Keith, and Brent. Some of the others said some words too. Mickey brought out a life-sized cardboard cutout of Jerry, in his absence. With that, the band was inducted into the Hall of Fame. (If you don't believe me, you can YouTube it.)

So . . . I'm now a member of the Rock and Roll Hall of Fame. Okay. But what does that mean? What did I get out of it? Well, I now have a little trophy on my bookshelf that makes a halfway-decent bookend. It's not too bad as a paperweight either. But beyond that, it's just another dust collector. I stood up on that podium with (most of) my bandmates and we accepted the trophies and, suddenly, the Grateful Dead belonged to an institution. We were institutionalized.

Maybe that's why Jerry skipped out on the ceremony. While musicians aren't known for being on time, very few artists have been no-shows at their Rock and Roll Hall of Fame induction ceremony. Of the ones that were, some of them claimed that they had other obligations they needed to honor that night, while others couldn't bring themselves to put aside differences with ex-bandmates long enough to stand beside them on the podium. But the Grateful Dead aren't Guns N' Roses. So what gives?

Jerry didn't mean to make any grand statement by not attending. When he found out about it, he just mumbled something like, "Nah, man. It ain't for me." When he said he didn't care about awards or recognition, he meant that he didn't care about awards or recognition. The more prestigious and exclusive, in his view, the worse.

I wasn't at all disappointed that he didn't attend. It was a part of who he was. It had to do with something central to his personality and his beliefs, and I respected that all the way. Every time. Years earlier, Jerry told me that music was such a joy to play, and that it meant so much to people to hear it, that it should be given away for free. "Let them have music!" He really meant that and I think that it became a bigger and bigger conflict for him, the bigger and bigger that we got. I enjoyed the fame and I enjoyed the money and I didn't see those things as taking anything away from the purity of the art that was our music. But Jerry saw those things—money and fame—as a burden. I think he was confused by the fame and felt that the money came attached to an ever-growing list of obligations that formed some kind of algorithm which transformed music into business. And none of us ever wanted to become businessmen. At least, certainly not Jerry. And certainly not me, either.

I think Jerry may have also had some kind of fear that the minute you make it into the Rock and Roll Hall of Fame, you're done. It doesn't have to be that way, of course. But if you're old enough to be inducted into an institution that takes itself too seriously, then you're too old to be playing a young person's game. Luckily for us, the music we made has proved timeless and as we've aged, so have the Deadheads. We've grown old together. We've also managed to somehow attract younger generations too, and while I could speculate on how something in the music that we made hints at some kind of timeless truth, and perhaps even captures the underlying eternal spirit of the American people, no matter how bad the present situation is . . . the truth is, nobody knows how or why we've had the staying power. Somehow we've remained relevant and if you look at the Rock and Roll Hall of Fame, you'll see that we're really an exception to all these rules. But the fuck if I could tell you why, with any real authority. It's all just words on paper, thoughts and ideas, speculation and philosophy—strictly academic. Hence, Jerry chose to be absent at our Hall of Fame induction ceremony. Fair enough.

Maybe Jerry was also a little bit embarrassed that we weren't exactly in peak form at the time they inducted us. When the Grateful Dead peaked, exactly, is up for debate. It's a complicated calculation because we didn't just have one peak—we had many. But they were all in the rearview mirror by 1993. There were some nights when Jerry would be so doped up that he would start to nod off, on stage. I'd hit my crash cymbals as hard as I could, just to wake him up. "Hey, Jerry, you're on stage!" "Thanks, Bill." That actually happened. More than once, I'm sure. (But the time I'm thinking of took place at Soldier's Field in Chicago, at the end of our Summer 1995 tour . . . the end of the road).

Incredibly, even during those kinds of moments, his guitar playing still had that unreal quality to it that made it the stuff of legend. Notes turned into daggers as Jerry took stabs at every bleeding heart within earshot. They may not have been his best solos, but they still had his magic handiwork, nonetheless. His guitar was a magic wand and he could cast spells with it in his sleep. He wouldn't always remember what song he was in and he would mumble sounds instead of lyrics, but I'll be damned if his fingers didn't find all the right notes . . . effortlessly. Maybe Jerry was lost in the music, after all.

Sometimes, it was almost like watching a pothead double over from laughing at a joke they couldn't retell because they already forgot the punch line. Not that Jerry's ailing health and debilitating habits were any laughing matter. Everyone loved Jerry and none more than me. We didn't know what to do. For the short term, we got teleprompters to help with the lyrical lapses during the concerts.

Off stage, we weren't really talking to each other much. I've been much more open in this book than I ever was between my bandmates, and that might just be a sign of the generation that we come from. It's not like today where kids advertise their inner feelings on social media or text each other deep emotions.

We started off as a band of brothers—by music and by experience if not by blood. But toward the end of it, a lot of the time we didn't want to see each other, much less have to interact on any real level. It was a separation without divorce. A hiatus without a lapse in shows, simply because shows were business and business was good. And, besides, everyone needed jobs. We had our jobs and so many other jobs relied on us just showing up to work. The "group mind" was no longer something we even thought about. I didn't want to be in any of their heads any more than they wanted to be in mine. Everybody was caught up in their own little world, in their own proprietary scene.

Our manager, Cameron Sears, would call each of us individually to tell us where to be and when. I wasn't exactly calling Phil and saying, "Hey, man, did you see we're playing Miami next week? In the mood for stone crabs? I'll get us a table at Joe's." There was none of that. There was no unity. No camaraderie. I know for sure Jerry wasn't happy about the state of our union. None of us were really happy about it, per se.

Perhaps the most regrettable thing, in terms of the band at this time, is that we had a new batch of songs that had the potential to evolve into some of our best material yet: "So Many Roads," "Eternity," "Days Between," "Lazy River Road." One song, "Liberty," had a New Orleans feel to it that I really loved. There were some works in progress in the mix— like Weir's "Corinna"—and some hopeless flops ("Wave to the Wind," "Way to Go Home"). But we had enough material to cut an album and enough potential hits to load it with future favorites. While it may be cheating to say this from the safety of time and distance, I really believe we had our best studio album still in us, and I have to imagine that this one could've been the masterpiece we had been chasing for all those years. If you thought *In the Dark* was good, you would've seriously flipped for . . . ah, well, speculation. It's the lost Grateful Dead album.

In 1994, we booked some studio time at a mythical little place called the Site, conveniently located on Lucas Valley Road in San Rafael. A road with some serious GD history. Nothing really came of those sessions. We spent most of our time there just waiting around for Jerry to arrive. Even when he did show up, he was still absent. We didn't know how to handle it, so we just played through.

Our home lives had become disparate as well. I divorced Shelley and I let her live at the ranch while I got a little house out on the coast near the actual town of Mendocino. I spent as much time as I could surfing and I started dating a girl named Pamela Lloyd. Meanwhile, Phil became increasingly distant with band life as he withdrew into family life. I don't really know what Bobby, Mickey, or Vince was doing at this time; I didn't really pay attention. I saw them on stage and, other than that, I was usually in the water out in Mendocino. Surfing or fishing or something of the sort.

As for Jerry, well, he left Manasha and played the field for a bit before reuniting with the notorious Deborah Koons. They slept in different houses. As I already mentioned, when Deborah went on tour with Jerry, they would stay in lavish two-bedroom hotel suites—and Jerry always made sure that his bedroom had a lock on it. I don't know of any other marriage like that. It was uncomfortable to watch, but we all respected Jerry so much that we didn't offer our opinion on the matter. And, besides, interpersonal communication was never a Grateful Dead strong suit.

When Jerry and Deborah got married, the wedding was as awkward and staid as their relationship. I didn't go to the church to see them exchange vows but I went to the reception afterward. It was held on the harbor in Tiburon, at the San Francisco Yacht Club. Very fancy. Very formal. *Not* very "Jerry-like." There was something tense about the proceedings. A band played, people looked like they were having fun, but it didn't feel like anybody was actually having fun. It was as if it was all for show, as if being there was a commitment rather than a celebration. Of course, some of our most loyal fans could've said that about some of our concerts at that time. Still, I do remember watching Jerry sit there with Deborah and he seemed like he was having a good enough time with her and so that was that. Whatever makes you happy . . .

What makes me happy is being out in the water. It holds the same place for me that I fill with music when I'm on land. The reason I was late for Jerry's wedding and could only make it to the reception was because I was still en route back from the Galapagos. I was down there filming a scientific expedition that was part of a larger documentary I was working on called *Ocean Spirit*. I got some really great footage of sperm whales, up close, personal—I filmed many of those scenes myself and was on such a natural high from being immersed in the water, surrounded by such beautiful and benign creatures. After flying home from something like that, slamming into such a staid wedding was a bit of a crash landing. It was almost embarrassing.

As 1994 crossed into 1995, the Grateful Dead crossed the three-decade mark. We had been a band for thirty years. Thirty years! To give you some perspective, the Beatles were together for thirteen years. Led Zeppelin, less than that. The Band was only a band for nine years. We reached thirty without having ever broken up and, although we tried, we never even took a full year off. We only had one real hiatus. Maybe we should've had more of them.

The Big Three-Zero meant that 1995 should've been a big year for us. A chance to celebrate everything that we had done, while getting stoked on what was still to come. Instead, the year was a nightmare. I'll say right now that 1995 was the worst year of my life. All 365 days that I had to suffer through it. There was more than one tragedy, more than one death, and darkness everywhere. It was the worst year of my life.

The spring tour had a few nights where it felt like we had gotten sucked into a black hole, but it was the Summer of '95 tour that plunged us deep into total blackness. Almost every show was catastrophic.

After playing a memorable show to 60,000 fans in a field in Highgate, Vermont, during our 1994 Summer Tour, we returned on June 15, 1995. It was the first night of the tour. Bob Dylan opened. An estimated 100,000 fans showed up—tens of thousands without tickets—and we had to revert back to crowd control tactics from decades earlier; we were forced to open the gates and make it a free show.

The last great Grateful Dead prank occurred in the middle of the summer at Three Rivers Stadium in Pittsburgh, PA. The rainstorms that plagued our tour—a known risk that haunts many bands when they trek across the East Coast in the summertime—were fully present and accounted for that night. The majority of the stadium was uncovered and fans were getting dumped on. We did our version of a rain dance by stringing together a thematic setlist for the beginning of the second set: A cover of the Beatles' "Rain" led into "Box of Rain," "Samba in the Rain," and "Looks Like Rain." (The Grateful Dead did not control the weather . . . but we would sometimes comment on it.)

Throughout the tour, Jerry's performances were weak. Even with a teleprompter at his feet, he mumbled his way through forgotten lyrics and would even need help identifying what song we were playing—right in the middle of it.

It's been said before that with a scene like the Grateful Dead's, whatever was happening backstage was a direct reflection of what was also happening in the audience (and vice versa, I suppose). I've always felt nothing but love for Deadheads and I feel grateful for them to this day. Consciously.

Consistently. But in the 1990s we began to notice a new subgroup that we nicknamed the "railers"—they would ride the rail in the front row, night after night, and they looked just as dazed and confused as Jerry. They didn't look high. They didn't look stoned. They looked . . . strung out. Vacant. Cadaverous. But then I looked at our antihero nodding off onstage, unaware of what song he was playing even as his fingers picked out all the right notes. Things were bad.

At RFK Stadium in Washington, D.C., one night, several fans got struck by lightning in the parking lot. That was nature's fault, not theirs. But about a week later, at Deer Creek Amphitheater, the storm came from the lawn, not from the sky. The thunderclap came when the back wall of the amphitheater came crashing down as thousands of gate crashers stormed the venue.

Located in the heart of America's corn belt, just north of Indianapolis, Deer Creek Amphitheater—which, these days, has been unceremoniously renamed after a speaker company—had become a legendary stop on our summer tours. A typical summer shed, Deer Creek's bucolic setting allowed for plenty of nearby pop-up campgrounds (with names like "Dead Creek") that local farmers would operate, right on their property. It became a favorite Midwestern play for us. Unfortunately, it's now impossible not to remember it as ground zero for our star-crossed and cosmically cursed Summer 1995 tour. (Deer Creek no longer exists. Neither does Great Woods, Irvine Meadows, the Boston Garden, Knickerbacker, or Lakewood Amphitheater. Their naming rights have all been bought by corporations like phone carriers and speaker companies. But, to me and a nation of Deadheads, the original names will always stick.)

The trouble at Deer Creek started with a death threat. We were scheduled for a two-night run at the shed beginning on July 2, 1995. The afternoon of the first show, we received word from the local police that somebody left a message claiming they would attempt to kill Jerry during the shows. The authorities took it seriously, so we couldn't ignore it. But Jerry never let anybody dictate what he could or could not do, so he wasn't going to let the police persuade him to flee just because some nut-job called the station. In true American tradition, the Grateful Dead wasn't about to cower from a coward—whether it was a pissed-off fan or a pissed-off local, they made for a bad terrorist. Who calls a police station to tell them they're about to assassinate a hippie?

Jerry shrugged it off and even made the whole thing into a punch line when he sang "Dire Wolf" that night ("Don't murder me/I beg of you, don't murder me"). But as he sang it, the house lights remained on. Everyone had to pass through a metal detector to get into the show that night, and there were cops everywhere—especially down in front. It was an environment that was quite counterproductive to the Grateful Dead Experience. Also, it was just hard to concentrate on the music while looking out into a fully lit house, watching police intensely survey the crowd. You'd look at people's faces and wonder if they were going to be the one to try to, somehow, murder Jerry Garcia that night.

Then things took a turn for the even worse. Thousands of ticketless fans outside had managed to break through the back wall of the amphitheater and they came streaming onto the field. The sold-out venue held about 25,000 people. Suddenly there may have been more than 30,000 people inside and the gate crashers didn't exactly pass by security. So in addition to property damage and concerns about crowd safety, thousands of gate crashers just negated all the increased security measures that were put in place to protect Jerry from the death threat. It was disastrous. And a heartbreaking scene to watch.

Again, Jerry seemed to comment on it through a song selection but without the black humor of "Dire Wolf"—this time, he launched into "New Speedway Boogie," a tune that he wrote with Robert Hunter following the Altamont murder. "One way or another this darkness got to give."

When the local authorities informed us the following day that the police would direct traffic but not set foot inside the venue that night, out of concerns for their own safety, we were forced to cancel the second show. So long, Deer Creek. Sorry about our so-called fans?

The true Deadheads that were at the heart of the Grateful Dead

Experience suddenly became overshadowed by the intrusion of an army of wookies. It changed the entire character of the scene. There were bad apples, bad eggs, and—sometimes—just bad people.

The next stop on that tour was at the Riverport Amphitheatre, just outside of St. Louis. It's yet another venue that has since been renamed after a phone carrier. The show itself was fine, although the setlist might reflect some of the emotions we were going through that week ("Going Down the Road Feeling Bad" -> "Throwing Stones" -> "Not Fade Away"). Again, the houselights had to be left on. It began to feel like we were playing the show in spite of the audience, rather than for them. At the same time, finishing those shows felt more like a contractual duty than a privilege.

In a rainstorm after the show, some fans at a campground took shelter by crowding onto a nearby porch. The roof collapsed, injuring more than 100 people. One fan was paralyzed. We dedicated the following night's show to those fans, while we braced ourselves for whatever bad news would come next. It was beginning to feel like, as a touring band, we had overstayed our welcome.

We only had two more shows to get through, both of which were at Soldier Field in Chicago. A football stadium that's been the longtime home of the Chicago Bears, Soldier Field is fortified so that gate crashing isn't really a concern. Instead, the concern shifted back to Jerry, who didn't have his best shows either of those nights.

We ended the second show—the final night of the tour—with a double encore of "Black Muddy River" and "Box of Rain." Two songs that, in hindsight, seemed eerily prescient of what was to come. After our final bows, we had our customary end-of-summer-tour firework show light up the sky above the stadium. It was a good one, too. Explosions. Lights. Smoke. Big bangs. Small crackles. "Oohs," "Ahhs," and that was that.

We didn't know it then, but that was the end of the Grateful Dead.

I don't remember saying anything to any of my fellow bandmates after the show. We may have exchanged pleasantries, but nothing substantial— we were all eager to get home and go our separate ways for a while, process everything that had gone down that summer, and recharge until the fall tour. I couldn't wait to get back to Mendocino and get to a place where I could clear my head. A safety zone. For me, that meant being out on the water.

I had no way of knowing, of course, that that would be the last time I would see Jerry Garcia alive. My friend, my bandmate, my brother. All I knew was that he was in need of some serious help. His roadie, Steve Parish, made it sound like Jerry knew that, was willing to face it, and even had a plan. I looked forward to seeing Jerry in another month or so, hoping that by then he'd be in better shape. Or at least on his way in that direction. Something. Anything.

Indeed, just days after the tour ended, I heard that he checked himself into the Betty Ford Center in Southern California. I didn't talk to him while he was there, and they probably didn't allow a lot of outside conversations anyway. But, as it turned out, I didn't ever talk to Jerry again, period.

When he went to the Betty Ford Center, I remember thinking that, for once, Jerry was really going to have a chance. I was cautiously optimistic, as they say. All I could do was send thoughts of love his way, which I did in my own way. But Jerry only lasted two weeks there before pulling the rip cord. That wouldn't do and I knew it. Remember, I had checked myself into rehab in 1990 and I knew firsthand that two weeks was nothing. It's not enough time to detoxify, let alone change patterns and habits. For some reason, twenty-eight days is the magic number in those places, and even that's just the introductory package; the basic plan. The ground floor. The human body can't really undergo the necessary physiological changes in half that time. So when Jerry came back after a mere two weeks, I thought to myself, "Hmm. That's not going to hold."

Jerry knew this, too. Maybe he just had a problem with the Betty Ford Center in particular or maybe he simply wanted to be closer to home, because when he got back, he checked himself into a place called Serenity Knolls in Lagunitas—just down the road from the old Girl Scout camp where we briefly lived during the Summer of '66. Those were magical days.

I was hoping that, just by being on the same road—almost within sight of the old camp—Jerry would find some inspiration, some motivation, some of the spark that we used to start the fire that became the Grateful Dead and whose flame burned so brightly for three decades. I wasn't thinking of the band. I was thinking of my friend's health. We all were.

There is no easy way for me to say this, so I'll keep it simple: On August 9, 1995, Jerry Garcia died of an apparent heart attack. It happened sometime around four or five in the morning, so he had been sleeping when the angels took him. He was just one week into his fifty-third year. I miss him. Every single day.

22

Every Deadhead remembers where they were and what they were doing when they heard the news that Jerry Garcia died. That's something else that we all, sadly, have in common. I was visiting my dad and his wife Patricia at their condo, in the town of Mendocino. I had recently broken up with Pamela, who was my girlfriend following my divorce from Shelley. I guess you could say she was my rebound. We split amicably, and she called me that morning, at my dad's house. August 9, 1995.

Nobody has ever received a phone call from an ex-girlfriend that started with the words, "Sit down" which they haven't remembered for the rest of their lives. So I sat down. Yet, despite all logic and probability, I wasn't ready to hear what came next. "Jerry's dead," she said.

I mumbled something to my dad and his wife, stumbled out of the house, got in my car, drove back to my place, and sat there. All shock and tears as I looked out at the cold, vast ocean from the relative safety of the Mendocino bluffs.

"Fuck," I thought. "I've got to do something. I can't just sit here, sobbing like this." I put on my wet suit, grabbed my surfboard, and went to battle the unmerciful Pacific Ocean—fierce by nature, unforgiving by force, and totally unfuckwithable in every way. The ocean didn't give a damn that Jerry just died. It's not that the ocean is apathetic, it just doesn't have time for the small stuff—like life and death. I spent a few hours surfing, just to get out of myself, transcend, and connect to something bigger. I caught waves by muscle memory alone. My head was somewhere else; neither here, nor there. I guess that's called trauma or shock. Surfing was my shock treatment. My therapy. I didn't even attempt most waves. I just floated on my surfboard, more than anything, and tried to stare past the horizon, hoping to discover a place beyond the sight line where I could disappear or else make everything perfect again, in a way that it hadn't been for years.

Open water has that magical ability to wash away your problems. To make them go away. Yeah, well . . . not this time. Jerry was gone and nothing could bring him back. Not even the tide.

I was in the water for a few hours. I didn't know where else to go. There was nobody at my house. I didn't want to be alone, but I also didn't want to be with people. I wanted to be on the water. It was the one place besides the middle of a Grateful Dead jam where I could feel the arms of the universe wrap themselves around me and tell me that everything was fine exactly the way it was. Even if I wasn't happy with immediate events. The waves come and crash over you regardless. You can ride, float, or drown. It's that simple.

Meanwhile, Bobby had a gig that night with one of his other bands—Ratdog. He didn't cancel the gig. He told the evening news cameras before the show that Jerry would have wanted him to continue to put music in the air. I wouldn't have been able to keep a beat that night, but everybody deals with death differently. During an emotional "Throwing Stones," Bobby ad-libbed, "Papa's gone, we are on our own." It was a harsh reality. But he was right. "Papa's gone, we are on our own."

His words rang even truer for me, personally, than he intended. About a month after Jerry died, my actual papa passed away. I was on my own. I was single, orphaned, and in a band that had just lost its centerpiece. I felt crippled by loss. It didn't matter that I was in one of the biggest bands in the world or that I was rich and famous. That's surface success. It doesn't do a damn thing to protect you from grief. And in 1995, I had lots of grief. I dealt with it by taking a lot of painkillers and drinking bottomless what-evers until I bottomed out. I hit rock bottom. So to speak.

The only good thing about hitting the floor is that you have nowhere to go but up. It's a choice . . . with the only other option being death. I wasn't going to let the Reaper take me. He already had enough of my friends and family to keep him busy for a while. I felt lost but I wasn't a lost cause. Finally, I called a friend and said, "I need help. Get me to therapy."

And that's when I went to rehab for my second—and final—stint. Set two. But let's back up for a moment so I can tell you about my father's death. It was from complications of old age. His body just gave out on him. I went to be by his side, along with his wife, Patricia, and some of his best friends at the hospital in Fort Bragg, just up the Mendocino coast. We watched over my father as he went into a coma on a Saturday afternoon. By Sunday afternoon, he was gone. It was a sunny day in a part of the coun-try that is perpetually foggy, and a train whistle blew as my dad drew his last breath. It was fitting; he loved train whistles. He had a thing for them in the way that some people have a thing for ice cream or roller coasters or fancy cars. It made him happy, that's all. I think when he heard that train whistle blow from his hospital bed in Fort Bragg, he thought, "That's my cue. All aboard." And there he went. In peace. As sad as it was for the loved ones he left behind, it was a beautiful moment at the end of a beautiful life.

Back when my dad lived with his second wife, Gail, in Carmel, Cali-fornia, he did this thing where he used blow his train whistle as loud as he could, intentionally disrupting the neighborhood. He loved doing that sort of thing. He had a few recordings of train whistles and he'd blast them from his stereo on Sunday mornings with the windows opened wide, all these noises—the train whistle, the steam engine, the chug-a-lug—spilling out onto the street and into the ears of neighbors who were not thrilled.

My dad didn't care. In fact, I think he even enjoyed that part of it. He loved that sound so much.

I must've inherited that love from him—or maybe that sound became a reflection of my love for him—because eventually I incorporated a train whistle into my drum repertoire and I would use it sometimes in "Drums -> Space." I still have that train whistle to this day; it's in my barn.

Consider this: Before my dad died, Jerry died. Before Jerry died, the Grateful Dead had that catastrophic final tour. Before the final tour, my girlfriend—Pamela—got lung cancer and I held her hand through weekends of chemotherapy. And throughout all of this, I was drinking a couple bottles of wine every day—often by myself—and downing fistfuls of painkillers. All in all, 1995 was not my favorite year. In fact, it was my least.

The general public didn't know about my dad's passing, but it seemed like every last person on Earth knew about Jerry. I couldn't avoid it. Wherever I went, somebody was there to remind me. In Mendocino, locals that I recognized but never directly interacted with would approach and say things like, "Sorry about the bad news . . ." ("Yeah, me too . . .") And whenever I ventured elsewhere, strangers from all walks of life would offer their sympathy. Condolences are always awkward and I didn't know how to handle them. I appreciated the thought, but after a while, it just got to be too much. It became part of the burden. I didn't need to be reminded of that which I could not forget. And I didn't need comfort from strangers.

At one point, I was visiting a beach in Hawaii that happens to be just a stone's throw away from where I live now. I was by myself and I parked and started walking to the beach. Two huge Samoan guys just got back from spearfishing and they emerged from the water like creatures from the dark lagoon. They were as massive as sumo wrestlers and they were carrying spearguns with them, for fishing purposes. But, you know, a weapon's a weapon. And to prove it, they had dead fish hanging off their belts. They were nothing to fuck with. I kept my cool when they started walking right toward me, but I'd be bluffing if I said I wasn't a little bit nervous. When they approached, all they said was, "Sorry to hear about da kine." They were speaking in Hawaiian Pidgin—local slang—but they were talking about Jerry Garcia. He would've loved that, like it was some kind of prank that made up for that time the dive instructor in Kona asked him for his autograph, twenty feet below the surface. It made me smile. Jerry was "da kine." And it also showed just how far and wide his reach was and how deeply he was embedded in the American consciousness. You couldn't escape it. I couldn't escape it. And I didn't want to. But I did need a break, to give me time to mourn, for both Jerry and my dad, and to put the pieces of my life back together again.

Jerry's funeral was an open casket. It was held in St. Stephen's church in Belvedere, a real wealthy area near Sausalito. But it was a funeral, which meant, it sucked. It was painful to look at people's faces. I tried not to. Everyone was just a mirror of all of our sadness. For me, the worst fucking part was the open casket. Jerry looked like a toy model of himself, but it wasn't very complimentary. It was like some oddity from a wax museum. Who would want to look at that? It was Jerry . . . but it wasn't Jerry. I would've preferred not to have seen him like that. I would have preferred to keep him in my mind the way he appears in my memories. And I've done that. But the way his body appeared in the casket was some mortician's idea of what he was or what he looked like, when there is just no way that even the world's best mortician could've come within one millionth of one percent of replicating the life energy that Jerry was capable of emanating, effortlessly, every time you caught eyes with him. The way he looked in that casket bothered me.

Still, I went up there with my bandmates and we huddled around him like the unit that we once were, lifetimes earlier. We even made some stupid jokes. "I wish we had a battery, because we'd kick-start you, old pal."

I tapped him on the chest. "How you doing, brother?" I knew that he wasn't there at all. It was all for show. I said some things, both to him and to the others. I said all of these words and I heard them come out of me and I meant them, but I was hardly even paying attention. I remember my final good-bye, though. "I love you, Jerry," I said. And that was it.

On August 13, 1995—about a week after Jerry's death—there was a memorial held for him in Golden Gate Park. It was in the Polo Field where we once played some of our biggest shows, for free. And just like it was back then, thousands of Deadheads from all over the country showed up. The memorial was a big, beautiful celebration of Jerry Garcia's life and of everything that he meant to so many people, and it was almost like some kind of happy event; but I didn't feel happy. And I know you're supposed to get drunk; but I didn't get drunk. I didn't go wild. It was a very beautiful gathering and with wonderful intent—an Irish wake, a hippie send-off—but it didn't have anything going for me. I guess I was more private in my sadness and more isolated in my grief.

Mickey gave me this big drum to play as we marched through the crowd but I didn't want to play a big drum. Everything seemed awful. Except, of course, for the Deadheads. They were there to pay tribute to Jerry and to honor him and to celebrate his life and that part of it was wonderful and moving and made the day special for a lot of people and it gave so many others the closure that they, too, needed. I had to see outside of myself to see that, because I was so blinded by loss. By personal loss.

There was a giant picture of Jerry on some kind of shrine and everybody was really respectful—there was no separation between band and audience and yet nobody asked for autographs or anything like that. Everybody was truly there just to support each other and to come together as a community and to deal with Jerry's departure. But dealing with it was something that for me, personally, I needed to do by myself. And, in a way, I'm still dealing with it. My father's death, too.

The first time I saw the rest of my bandmates after that—at this point, sadly, we can start to say things like, "The surviving members . . ."—it was at our new rehearsal space, which was in an old Coca-Cola plant in Bel Marin Keys, not too far from our longtime headquarters in San Rafael. We had run into some kind of trouble with the landlord back at Front Street, or something like that, and we had just moved into this new space. It wasn't even fixed up yet and the studio wasn't fully built or operational.

It was just a big empty space, which made our meeting there even heavier. You could feel the loss in the air. And the weight of it all.

We got together in one of the front rooms and everybody just kind of gazed down at their shoes. Nobody even bothered making wisecracks, which, of course, was a sure sign that everything had changed and that nothing was the same. Nobody faked a smile. What was the point? We kind of batted around talk of, "So, are we going to keep doing this?" "Should we start to think about auditions?" "What next?" and that sort of thing, but it wasn't even halfhearted—it was completely empty-hearted. The light had gone out in the Grateful Dead's attic and there was nobody home. I think there was talk, probably initiated by Phil, about creating a permanent home, museum, concert venue, store, and mixed-use space called "Terrapin Station." And there was some talk already about merchandising, I think. Everything from that time is a blur to me. If it wasn't the mourning, it was the alcohol, and if it wasn't the alcohol it was the painkillers. Or the holy trinity of all three. Fuck, man. Not a good look. Not a good scene.

Jerry's death, the funeral, and the Golden Gate Park memorial all happened in August. My dad died in September. And then, in December we had another band meeting. Before we called the meeting, I knew one thing already in my heart—the Grateful Dead without Jerry Garcia would be like the Miles Davis Quintet without Miles Davis. Had Jerry still been alive, we would've ended up taking time off anyway, maybe go on another hiatus. We were burned out. I had been burned out since 1993. I did things on the road to make it work for me, like paying more attention to my health and whatnot, but it still wasn't a very healthy lifestyle. I surfed a lot at home but there was never enough time to get enough exercise on the road. I realize that complaints like that are all just rationalizations and justifications. I think the heart of it was just that the band itself was not healthy and the band was my life—so if the band wasn't great, my life wasn't great. It was a ruthless fucking feedback loop.

I think Jerry wanted to take another break from it, too, and maybe even put an indefinite halt to the Grateful Dead. I don't think that would've been permanent, but I do think some kind of a break was imminent. Undeniable. Unavoidable. That's my honest feeling about it.

Before the December '95 band meeting, there were rumors flying around as to who might "replace" Jerry. David Hidalgo, Carlos Santana, and so on. They were (and are) all great players, but nobody could ever replace Jerry Garcia. Let's be honest: Nobody is the next anybody and the only way to replace someone is to imitate them and that's not art. It's a reenactment, nostalgia, mere bathos. Regardless, I'm not interested in being a rodeo clown. Or a puppet. I knew that, without Jerry, it could never be the same. That, in itself, is fine. After all, no two shows were ever the same. But the harsh truth is just that it could never be as good. So I wanted out. Besides, I was in no shape to go back out on tour anytime soon—I was in such a bad way, that I had to call into the meeting. I couldn't even make it there, physically. It was too hard for me to get out of bed.

I think my bandmates knew that I was done with it before that meeting, but that meeting is where I made it clear—I was done. The Grateful Dead were over. Some say I pulled the plug on it but that plug was pulled when Jerry was ripped from this Earth. I was just trying to be respectful.

I became very, very depressed. I can see that for what it was, looking back on it now. When I was in it, however, my head was too convoluted to see the fog for the clouds. I was washing a lot of Vicodin down with red wine and I got to a place where I couldn't even go out to get my own dinner. I was that helpless, that low. I stopped surfing. I turned visitors away. I didn't have a therapist. I didn't have anybody that I felt I could relate to; so, I didn't have anybody. It was bad. I was lost in all directions without a sail, a map, or anyone to carry me home. And no one waiting up for me when I got there.

I had to go into rehab because I couldn't even carry a conversation anymore. So I had a friend check me into Sierra Tucson, a treatment facility in Arizona. I was determined to not meet the same maker as Jerry. And that's when I started to get better.

At one point, my therapist told me to assign each of my problems to a different piece of furniture and place those pieces in the middle of the room. Well, I didn't stop rearranging the furniture until every damn piece was in the pile. I promised myself I would take those things and turn them into a bonfire inside me that would eventually burn off all the pain.

I completed a four-week program and I then insisted that I stay for another week, just for bonus points. Who willingly signs onto rehab for an additional week, after putting in a month already? I did.

Things had turned around in there and I wanted to make sure that they would stick; that I'd be ready to be released without regressing. I waited until I was strong enough. It was such a relief to, physically, feel good again. And besides, I knew that getting healthy was the only way I'd be capable of turning the page and starting a new chapter. The first, since I was nineteen, that didn't involve the Grateful Dead.

I didn't really want to live in Mendocino anymore. My dad had departed. I divorced my wife, Shelley, and later I broke up with my girlfriend, Pam. I didn't have anything keeping me there but ghosts. I moved to Hawaii and I knew right away that I wanted to be somewhere on Kauai. The Garden Island. Kauai is to Hawaii what Mendocino is to California. It's not as densely populated, or as overrun with tourists, as the other islands. It's small and, except for an untamable stretch of the Napali Coast—where there are no roads—you can drive around the perimeter of the island in under two hours. Kauai is rugged. It has picture-postcard beaches and waterfalls and mountains and valleys. The locals are kind . . . mostly. Gentle but strong. As are most of the surf spots. The weather is perfect, the views are scenic, and the rest is history. I moved to the largest town on the island, Kapa'a, with a population of just over 10,000. I knew right away that I'd never leave the island. And whenever I do, I can't wait to come back. I moved up the coast to the island's North Shore and bought a house from a drug auction. The irony was not lost on me.

Later on, I would move back to California for a short period of my life that I'd choose to forget. I made a mistake and married someone I shouldn't have, someone I didn't love. But then I realized that the whole marriage was one giant blunder, a misstep on my behalf, and I filed for divorce and the first thing I did after signing those papers was to move back to Kauai where I belonged. Even when I was living back in California (in Marin), I kept my house in Hawaii. There was no way I was going to part with it. So when I came back, I already had a place to live. I love it here and I'm happy. Locals don't know me as "Bill the Drummer," they simply know me as "Billy." I'm just a local. A lucky man who had a crazy life back on the mainland. But now I fish and I snorkel and I married a girl I'm crazy about, Aimee, and I spend many days helping her out on her organic farm and I jam with friends and I eat well and I just enjoy the hell out of island life. My island life.

I had to divorce myself from music for a while. It didn't feel right. At my first house on Kauai, a friend of mine brought me this old funky black Ludwig drum set. It sounded like dog shit, but it was something for me to bang on and some local guys—aspiring amateurs—would come over and want to jam. After playing in the Grateful Dead, that kind of open-mike jamming just wasn't that much fun. So I didn't do it that much. I didn't start playing music again for a while.

As for listening to music—and specifically the Grateful Dead—it took awhile. I had to get away from it before I could get back to it. I closed the door on everything Grateful Dead for a bit because I had to. After we disbanded, I needed to untangle. And then I went into treatment and I wasn't even allowed to listen to music, or watch TV. I was there to heal. Of course, you could argue that there's no better healer than music, but what I needed most at that time was silence inside my head. And that required counseling and treatment.

When I got back to the island, after my five weeks at Sierra Tucson, I listened to a lot of reggae and what I guess you would call stoner music. Not that the Grateful Dead isn't music for stoners, but I could only listen to stuff that I wasn't so attached to. Back in rehab, my roommate snuck in a Peter Tosh cassette and I used to listen to it every night, religiously. But I didn't listen to any of my own music, even after I got out and had the freedom to hit play on whatever I wanted.

I've since had a Grateful Dead reawakening, thanks to my wife, Aimee, and thanks to some of my good friends who, recently, began playing me some of the great shows and tours. Our current record label, Rhino, has been releasing great box sets and archival packages and I'll play those CDs in my living room after dinner, or around a bonfire when I have friends over, and it really makes me emotional. When I hear that music now, it transforms me and it heals me. And it redeems me. But it also makes me miss Jerry.

23

It's an old adage that time heals all wounds, and, in the end, I suppose that's true. But some wounds take until the end of time to heal. Or so it feels like, when those wounds are yours. By this point, I've built up a lot of scar tissue, and looking back, I can agree that it adds character and all the other things they say about it. Look: everybody has to deal with loss and with death. Many of us also have to deal with things like addiction and depression. All of those demons hang in the same ugly gang, and I had to fight them all at once. I was outnumbered, I'm afraid. I put up a fight, but 1995 kicked my ass and I was still licking my wounds during the year that followed.

Bands are like marriages and, in 1995, I had to end a thirty-year band marriage. I wasn't looking for a rebound band. I wasn't looking for another band at all, really. I was just looking for peace, love, and understanding. At the age of forty-nine, I had to figure out who I was again. Because who I was had just changed, seemingly overnight, from the drummer of the Grateful Dead to . . . ?

In the Summer of 1996, some of my former bandmates—Bobby, Mickey, and Hornsby—decided to combine forces and hit the road with their various, respective new groups as part of the first Furthur Festival. It was a traveling, daylong circus that toured the amphitheaters of America throughout the summer season. The other bands included Los Lobos and Hot Tuna and, sure enough, there were plenty of cross-pollinations and nightly jams. I had no particular problem with any of it; I just didn't particularly feel like participating. So I didn't.

When I decided to start playing music again, it was a situation that was easy and that didn't require the same kind of massive commitment and energy that going on tour with the Furthur Festival would have required. I needed things to be simple. In 1997, two years after my last show with the Grateful Dead, I formed a band called Backbone with some local players on Kauai. I don't think we ever "toured," per se, but we did play some casual shows, mostly around the island.

Backbone was a trio that featured my friends Rick Burnett and Ed Cook. We weren't that great, to be honest, but it was what it was. It got me back in the game; or, at least, got my feet wet again. (Actually, all four limbs, considering that I'm a drummer.) We recorded an album in Burnett's home studio, mixed it in Marin, and released it on BMG/Arista in 1998. Self-titled. About ten originals and the obligatory Dead cover; in this case, "New Speedway Boogie." That was about it for the lifespan of that little trio. Don't hold your breath for a reunion.

Meanwhile, the Furthur Festival went well enough for my former bandmates. It was a profitable enterprise for them and the idea of bundling all their groups together on a package tour made it appealing to Deadheads. They went out again in the Summer of 1997, but this time the headliners were the Black Crowes. The groups led by Bob Weir and Mickey Hart (Ratdog and Planet Drum, respectively) were in afternoon slots, along with Bruce Hornsby and some other bands. I thought that was a bit odd.

A Grateful Dead concert it was not, but I heard reports that the parking lot scene looked just about the same. Except maybe less electric. Less optimistic. There was a new unspoken sadness, like everyone knew that they were there chasing spirits long gone. The ghost of the Grateful Dead.

That's how I imagined it, anyway, which is why when Bobby, Mickey, Hornsby—and, now, Phil—decided to put as many pieces of the band back together, I declined to participate. I knew it wouldn't be anything like the Grateful Dead that our fans remembered. But at least, now, my old bandmates could headline their own festival. They called it the Other Ones. The name said it all. Interpret that as you will.

The first incarnation of the Other Ones featured other players that were familiar to our scene: Steve Kimock and Mark Karan had the unenviable task of filling Jerry's shoes. Those shoes were so large that the two of them, together, could step into them and they still didn't fit just right. It was something different, which isn't to say it wasn't something good. Hornsby's guy, John Molo, was on drums. And they brought in a saxophone player—Dave Ellis—as well, for whatever reason.

When the Furthur Festival came to Shoreline Amphitheater—a venue that Bill Graham built and that, allegedly, resembles a Steal Your Face from space—I made the questionable decision to go check it out. It was the last night of the tour. July 25, 1998. I happened to be in the Bay Area, on some kind of visit, so it made sense at the time. I made it to the venue—albeit, late—and I ended up sitting in for a number of songs. I played a talking drum, but they didn't really put me in the mix. I was turned down and placed off to the side. It was more for show. Their show. That was fine by me, because I was decidedly drunk and it was probably obvious that I didn't really want to be there. It brought back too many memories. Memories that were great when we made them but which became painful after Jerry's death. My heart wasn't ready. I felt like a stranger on that crazy night.

My next project had to be just as casual as Backbone but a little more enjoyable for me as a player—and House of Spirits was born. We were a Hawaiian jam band that just stuck to the islands. Nothing too fancy and certainly not so serious. We partied and played music, simple as that. The guitarist, Steve Inglis, really had a knack for interpreting Garcia/Hunter songs, and the other guys—Calvin Schaeffer and Eric Peterson—were enjoyable to play with too. We formed in 1999, but not everything is built to last, and so we didn't quite survive Y2K. Easy come, easy move on.

At some point, probably in early 2000, I happened to be in the old Coca-Cola Bottling Plant in Marin that the Grateful Dead business arm was still holding on to, God knows why. I eventually did a little bit of re-cording in there and I bet I wasn't the only one, but imagine the album that the Grateful Dead could've recorded in there . . . I tried not to. I don't know why I stopped by there that day, but the Other Ones happened to be rehearsing and it also so happened that they were looking for a new drummer. Not knowing this, and without an agenda of any kind, I deci-ded to jam with them for a song. It was total happenstance. But the mo-ment I sat down behind the drums, it already felt different from the Shoreline disaster. Phil couldn't make that tour and a great bassist named Alphonso Johnson had joined in his place. I wanted in. I was ready. I think it was actually Alphonso who said, "The original drummer? Oh yeah, let's take him!"

And so it is that I had come around and joined the Other Ones for their Summer 2000 tour and those were really enjoyable gigs. Initially fa-mous for his membership in Weather Report, Alphonso had also played in a band called Jazz is Dead, which reinterpreted Grateful Dead songs in a sort of jazz-fusion way. So he knew how to go down that razor-thin line between respecting the song and reinventing it entirely. Every night. After all, it was a practice that we had adopted from jazz in the first place. (Of note for a few paragraphs down the line: a guitarist by the name of Jimmy Herring was also in Jazz is Dead).

Touring with the Other Ones in 2000 was nothing like touring with the Grateful Dead during any of our thirty years. Individually, none of us were all that risky anymore. Onstage or off. We had grown up. We weren't quite rock 'n' roll. At least, not on that tour. Nobody would've wanted to make a reality TV series about being on the road with the Other Ones. There wasn't much in the form of backstage craziness. None of us nodded off onstage or lit any fireworks in the hotel lobby after the gig. It was a professional enterprise run by a bunch of aging adolescents. But it was still a pleasant tour and I'm glad I did it.

Alphonso Johnson had a lot to do with that and, after the tour, I sold him a Jeep that had been sitting in my Mendocino property for far too long. I still feel guilty about this, but I warned him in advance that the truck was unsalvageable. It looked all right on the outside and the engine ran fine, too. But a small nation of mice declared sovereign territory for themselves under the hood and even when I launched a war on them and ran every last one of those fuckers out, they left the Jeep with an intolerable stench. I told this to Alphonso, but he didn't seem too concerned. He liked fixer-uppers and said he'd be able to work on it and restore that new car smell by the time he was done.

I saw him years later and he admitted that he had to junk the car. He couldn't do a damn thing about the smell. I felt so bad, I wanted to offer him his money back—but I didn't.

The Other Ones took a year off and then regrouped for the Summer of 2002, this time with Phil back on bass. The Other Ones had become all of us standing. All of the originals, anyway—we didn't have Vince Welnick or Bruce Hornsby because we opted to have both Rob Barraco and Jeff Chimenti on keys instead. Jimmy Herring on guitar. Susan Tedeschi on backing vocals. While the tour is worth mentioning—and we (both the band and the audience) had a great time that summer—there is nothing in particular that was particularly remarkable.

The year 2001 fell between the two Other Ones tours, and I always thought 2001 was supposed to be some sort of space odyssey . . . from the future. But by the time that future arrived, I had gotten together with some friends of mine from the Bay Area and haphazardly formed another band. It was almost by accident. Neal Schon, the guitarist from Journey, wanted an excuse to fuck around with a bunch of effect pedals and other gear that he had recently acquired and Journey's manager, Herbie Herbert, just wanted to be in a band, period, I think. Herbert called himself Sy Klopps and became our vocalist. The remarkable thing about Herbert is that he had worked his way up from being a security guard at the back door of the Fillmore to being manager of a really successful, platinum-selling band—Journey. But by the time he sang in a band with me, it seemed like all he really wanted to do was roll joints. Which was fine by me. We smoked a lot of weed.

We rehearsed at that Coca-Cola Bottling Plant in Marin; the Grateful Dead owned it and I figured I might as well get some use out of it. Sy Klopps used the space to twist up doobies and we'd smoke them, one right after the other. I suppose he was just trying to live up to our band name: the Trichromes. The core band included Ralph Woodson on guitar and Ira Walker—and, later, Michael DiPirro—on bass. They all came with decent enough résumés and they all could play. We released one EP and one full album. The feather in our cap was our lyricist: Robert Hunter.

Schon was the odd man out in that group; he used to bust our balls for smoking so much weed, but you play in a band called the Trichromes, with the drummer from the Grateful Dead, what do you expect? I think he was too embarrassed to be a full-timer with us, but he helped write some of the songs and he did some recording. Pete Sears participated in that project as well.

When the Other Ones regrouped to tour again in 2003, we decided that we might as well call a spade a spade, which meant, in this case, call the Dead the Dead. Without Jerry Garcia in our midst, we could never again be the Grateful Dead. But with Bobby, Phil, Mickey, and me all in the band, we felt like a part of the Dead had risen. We called up Joan Osbourne instead of Tedeschi but, other than that, we kept the same roster from the previous Other Ones tour. We were a band again. Out of reverence to the dead, we were no longer the Grateful Dead. But we were the Dead. Again.

We kept it going the next year, too, and kept things fresh by adding Warren Haynes on guitar. Warren came from the Allman Brothers Band and was also in the process of building his own band, Gov't Mule. No matter what band Warren plays with, he's always comfortable just being himself. That much understood, you could still say that Warren was brought in to be Duane Allman's replacement in the Allman Brothers and now we hired him to fill in for Jerry Garcia in the Dead. I never talked to him about his feet, but he obviously wears big shoes.

So now we had both Warren Haynes and Jimmy Herring in the band. Two insanely talented guitarists with their own respective styles. They didn't sound alike and, more importantly, neither of them sounds like Jerry.

Interestingly, a few years before this—in 2000—Herring substituted for Haynes in the Allman Brothers. When Haynes returned, Herring transferred to Phil Lesh and Friends. Not long after that, Haynes also joined Phil and Friends. So it seemed natural—if somehow incestuous—to have them both playing in the Dead. The problem, as I saw it from my drum riser, was that both of them were so hyperaware of the other, that neither of them took charge. They were careful not to step on each other's toes; perhaps too careful. It didn't work, in my opinion. The music was fun and it was great to play our songbook again, but there wasn't much risk in it. We didn't jump off of any cliffs—and, as you know, cliff-diving music is my favorite. Instead, everyone played it safe. Because they could.

After the 2004 tour, we put the Dead to rest again, this time for a five-year hiatus. To be honest, I'm not sure why we let five years pass. It took a politician and a presidential election to raise the Dead from our slumber. Maybe we had learned a lesson back in 1972 when we refused to get wrapped up with George McGovern's campaign, but then complained something fierce when Richard Nixon won the office. Or maybe things had just gotten so much worse on Capitol Hill in the years since. But after two terms of George W. Bush in the presidency, all of us had become completely fed up with the government. We all wanted change. And, just as it was for a brief but brilliant moment in the 1960s, we could feel in the unrest of our fellow citizens that change was, indeed, afoot. We decided to do whatever we could to chime in and make that happen. So, for the first time in any of our careers, we endorsed a presidential candidate when we endorsed Barack Obama. And then he brought about change before he was even elected: he brought back the Dead.

It was once again obvious throughout that tour just how much things had changed. I mean, things always change—that's been the nature of our music and that's just the nature of life. But in the Grateful Dead, even when things changed—the drugs from fun to terrifying, the money from rags to riches, the friendships from everything to nothing—we were still a band of hippies. There were certain things about us that were too intrinsic to our identity to change beyond recognition. We were proudly leaderless. We cared about our fans and wanted to give them an experience that was worth a thousand lifelong returns for every fleeting penny they spent on tickets. We gave them music for free, but we charged for the experience. Under the new guard as just The Dead, however . . . it became a business. A corporation. And corporations have never been good at making music. And they're not exactly known for their customer service.

The end of that tour spelled the end of the Dead. There are several reasons and, I'm sure, all of the involved parties have different perspectives on what those reasons are and why they exist. But you can bet that most of it involves money and egos and personality clashes. Very little of it has to do with the music.

The head trips were so monstrous and so big in that scene, with everyone—including non-band members—fighting for another piece of the pie. Or for more power. Or for more control. Eventually I decided that, for me, personally, it wasn't worth it. I don't want to have to fight battles of the head just to play the music from my heart.

I don't want to be in a band where the musicians in front of me don't get along and somehow manage to put up with each other just to do the gig. That's no fun for anybody and the music suffers because of it. At that point, you're doing it just to earn money and that's not good enough. It doesn't honor the music or the legacy.

After the Dead dissolved again, people thought that Furthur was the next incarnation. But it wasn't really. It included just half the surviving members of the Dead (Phil and Bobby). That was fine, but then they got a guitar player who they chose because of his ability to copy Jerry. That approach is automatically going to leave me out in the woods. Playing Grateful Dead music with a fake Jerry just seems disrespectful to me. If you want to hear those songs, with a guitarist that sounds exactly like Jerry, you can go online and stream or download the thousands of shows featuring the real Jerry Garcia. There will never be another.

When I first started writing this book, I imagined that I would go into a little more detail about the reasons why the Dead dissolved after the 2009 tour and why, for years, there were never even talks of reforming. I had dinner with Bobby and Mickey a couple times and we'd text here and there, and we're doing that more and more these days. During the Furthur era, there was very little direct communication between us. Even indirect communication was limited. That's changing, lately.

I felt—and still do feel—that Deadheads deserve to know certain things, like why their band is no longer a band. But I've decided that what I just said is enough. I'm writing this book out of love, and for love, and I'm not here to whine or complain about things I can't control. In the end, it doesn't matter anyway. I'd rather not have it distract from the music, or the memory of a show that you might have gone to, or the sanctity of the holy ship of the Grateful Dead. Even if we were, admittedly . . . joyfully . . . a ship of fools.

The sad fact is that, after Garcia died, some people in my band changed. Others remained the same. And not all the pieces were compatible anymore. I have a lot of love and respect for everything that all of us accomplished together—together—but I decided that all I can do now is to just keep being me, and to keep being the same Bill Kreutzmann that I've always been. I get the honor of being Bill the Drummer. Bill the Organic Farmer. Bill the Fisherman. Bill the Surfer. Bill the Husband. I get to live in paradise with a wife that I am madly in love with and we spend our days with much happiness and laughter and our nights surrounded by great friends, great food, and great music. I've got no complaints. I am a lucky man. And I'm not done yet.

I miss making music with my brothers in the Grateful Dead but I know that if I'm patient and put my intention out there, we'll make music together again. When we're all ready. I'm ready now. But until we all are, I still have a lot of other music in me and I've been enjoying walking down all of those avenues as well.

In 2009, I formed a band called 7 Walkers. We released an album the following year. The 7 Walkers lineup included Reed Mathis—whom I think is perhaps the best bass player in the game today—keyboardist Matt Hubbard, and guitarist/singer Papa Mali. Due to scheduling conflicts, Mathis couldn't go on the road with us. Somehow we managed to land, as his fill-in, legendary bassist George Porter Jr., from the Meters—one of the original architects of New Orleans funk. A hero, for sure.

Just like the blues, just like jazz, just like any genre, really, no one musician or band invented funk. Not if you really know your history. But the Meters brought a particular brand of funk to the table. One that originated in New Orleans and that, arguably, was defined by the way George Porter Jr. plays bass. If you need an example, cue up "Cissy Strut" on Spotify. You've heard it before—it's one of the most sampled songs of all time. When you play with the engineer of a genre like that, and at that level, well . . . it's about as good as it gets. It was so much fun that I sometimes laughed out loud in the middle of songs. The syncopation grooved so hard that it was a drummer's delight.

The Meters opened up for the Rolling Stones but they never played with the Grateful Dead. The first time I met George Porter Jr. was at the first gig we did together with 7 Walkers, in Chico, California.

Following the album release, 7 Walkers hit the road pretty hard but we were just a baby band compared to the gig I had for thirty years before then. We didn't have much of a road crew and we couldn't tour with a big production. There just wasn't enough money for it. When I walked into the venue that afternoon for soundcheck, I was running a little bit late. George was already there and ready to go, so while he waited, he decided to put himself to use by setting up my drums for me. Boy, was I ever humbled. George Porter Jr.! Setting up my drums! (And I was glad he did, too, because I didn't really know how to set them up that well—we were using a local rental.)

Like many of the other post-Dead bands that I either formed or joined, 7 Walkers wore thin after a while and I called for us to disband. I needed time to write this book. Now that the book is almost over—for you and for me—I'm picking up the sticks again.

I really enjoyed sitting in with Phish at Red Rocks back in 2010, although I had to keep telling Fishman to "play harder!" I guess I'm just used to Mickey beating the hell out of things. That set was a whole lot of fun, though.

In the Summer of 2014, I sat in with the Disco Biscuits at a couple of shows, including Gathering of the Vibes. Their music is so different from what I'm used to, but it comes out of something that I was a part of with the Grateful Dead. It's the next stop on the continuum, and the same adventurous spirit drives that train. It wears a different generation's cloak, that's all.

The Disco Biscuits were early pioneers of a style of music known as livetronica (or jamtronica). Whatever you want to call it, it evolved out of the jam band scene. And that brings up a really good point: People often say that the Grateful Dead started the whole jam band movement and that our music remains influential, even today. No other band has managed to sound exactly like us, although plenty have tried . . . to sound *exactly* like us, I mean. There have been a plethora of tribute bands—perhaps too many—and then, too, a lion's den of copycat bands.

That's a huge compliment and I'm respectful of that aspect, but it doesn't make me feel especially proud, because those bands don't really honor the true spirit of the Grateful Dead. The true spirit has more to do with innovation, experimentation, risk—and whole-band improvisation—than it does with a particular guitar sound, or having two drummers and a bassist that doesn't play a repeating pattern. It's bands like Phish and the Disco Biscuits that really make me proud of what the Grateful Dead did, because they keep our spirit alive by taking what we created and doing their own thing with it. If people insist that we were the forefathers, well then the kids have all grown up and moved out and given birth to babies of their own. Music should never be stagnant.

Right before 7 Walkers, I toured with a trio that I called BK3—featuring the Allman Brothers' Oteil Burbridge on bass and Max Creek's Scott Murawski on guitar—from 2008 to 2010. That whole thing started because of a benefit gig that I played with Phish's Mike Gordon and Murawski, and it continued to evolve over the next couple of years. With BK3,

I really liked to get as far out there as I could. I took a little bit of acid before some of those shows; just enough to get out of myself without losing myself. The very fact that I was taking psychedelics for gigs again really spoke volumes.

I still feel that, because of business factors that weren't handled as well as they could've been, some of the musical treasures that BK3 dug up were overlooked by the fans. People just haven't heard those jams, but some of them open pathways to other dimensions. Psychedelic journeys. BK3 really owes its existence, in part, to Mike Gordon. He's the one that introduced me to Scott Murawski and the three of us played a couple gigs together. The prototype for BK3. Then, Gordon suggested Oteil Burbridge as his replacement when he couldn't commit to a tour, following a gig we played in Costa Rica. The Jungle Jam.

There's a funny story about that gig: Mike Gordon's parents owned a place near Jaco, Costa Rica, not far from the festival site. They invited my wife, Aimee, and me to stay with them, and we took them up on the offer. But we only lasted a few days. Mr. and Mrs. Gordon were lovely folks, but it felt like a sleepover at your friends' parents' house when you're in grade school. They were straight as an arrow. Mike's stepmom told us warmly that they had stocked the refrigerator with beer for us. But when we opened it, there was only a six-pack. We were out of there pretty quick. Much love and respect to them, though.

I already mentioned in a previous chapter that Mickey and I resurrected the Rhythm Devils, several times and through several incarnations after the Grateful Dead disbanded. Gordon played in the first Rhythm Devils tour in 2006, alongside Steve Kimock. But the story I have about a Rhythm Devils tour took place in 2010 or 2011 when we had Keller Williams out on the road with us. Mickey can be a bit of a control freak when you give him that power and, for some reason, he thought that Keller was drinking too much vodka on that tour. So he took the bottle of Grey Goose that Keller had on the tour bus and threw it in the trash. On a bus, the trash goes down a shoot to the underbelly but it doesn't immediately get dumped out. The driver saw all of this happen and as soon as Mickey left the bus, he went and fetched the booze and put it back in the fridge. "That stuff's too expensive to throw away like that," he said. We all had a good laugh, and Keller was able to maintain his Irish pride.

There were other tours with other bands, too, and in between all these lines, I played, sat in, or jammed with more musicians than I can even remember.

My latest project is called Billy and the Kids and it's making me feel like a kid again. Although, funny enough, "the kids" themselves are all in their thirties. Reed Mathis back on bass, the Disco Biscuits' Aron Magner on keyboards, and Tom Hamilton from American Babies on guitar. It's a group of all-stars that can really do some damage. I mean that in the best possible way. Billy and the Kids is my reward for finishing this book. I put in a lot of hard work; now it's time to play.

So the Dead stopped touring but the music never stops. Nor will it.

24

It's no secret that you're born alone in this world and, one way or an-other, you die alone. In between, we have each other. Well, okay, we also have music and laughter and adventure and drunken nights and lazy days and hardships and sunshine and tickets to the ball game and a good book or two and maybe some pets and, if you live with someone named Owsley, maybe half a dead cow in your fridge. But family is important. Family and music are the top two things that have gotten me through this life, although sometimes I've had difficulty balancing the two, or honor-ing the two . . . but I couldn't have come this far without either of them.

I've made my mistakes along the way; we all have. "Making mistakes" belongs in that list above, of things we have or do between life and death. Humans make mistakes. But we also, if we're lucky, make up for them.

I already told you, way back yonder in this tale, about my grandfather, the famous football coach. One of the teams he coached was the Chicago Bears and I have such a fond memory of a particular game that they played against the San Francisco 49ers when I was a kid. This was back when the 49ers' home field was at Kezar Stadium in Golden Gate Park, right where it borders Haight-Ashbury. The Grateful Dead played there twice, during the early 1970s, and it was impossible for me not to feel some connection to my grandfather at those shows.

But going back to that football game which, by the way, he lost: He introduced me to all the players that night, but he wouldn't let me go down to the bench with them. He didn't want me to see the nitty-gritty of what went on there. He was trying to protect me, that's all. I watched the game in the stands, with my parents, and afterward we drove back home to Palo Alto in frozen silence because the Bears had been beat.

Years passed, as they have a way of doing, and my grandparents retired in Santa Monica, California. In the late 1960s, the Grateful Dead sometimes played shows at the Shrine, about half an hour from their house. During soundcheck at one of these shows, one of our crew guys told me that there were "two old people" outside who said that they knew me. Immediately I knew—my grandparents found out about the gig and, in the innocent way that grandparents do, they wanted to see what their grandson was up to. I didn't invite them to the gig, though, and that was intentional. I didn't want them to see the nitty-gritty of what went on there. I was trying to protect them, that's all.

I've always stood by my lifestyle and everything that being in a rock 'n' roll band entails and I lived my life in a way that I saw fit. So then, why would I be embarrassed to show that world to my grandparents? I suppose it's because I didn't think they would understand . . . or approve. I was afraid of disappointing them.

But I wasn't going to turn them away at the door. So I grabbed a couple metal chairs for them to watch from the wings and they sat down and took it all in. It was a long soundcheck but they stayed for the whole thing and afterward I went back with them to their place and we sat around and ate Kentucky Fried Chicken for dinner and caught up. I loved them very much and I saw, in that moment, that they loved me too and that I had nothing to be embarrassed about. They loved me not only for the child they knew when I was growing up, but also for the man I had become in the years since. They were proud.

I learned a very serious lesson that day: Never hide who you are from your family. They will love you no matter what. If they don't, they're not good family. And if you find that out, well, love them back, anyway. It's important. Same goes for your friends; in fact, never hide yourself from anybody.

As Jerry used to sing so beautifully, "Without love in the dream, it'll never come true."

Brenda, my first wife, took my daughter with her when we divorced. Stacy. When Stacy grew up, she got married and—as is the custom—assumed her husband's last name. I think she may have remarried since then, but since I don't know who the husband is, I don't know Stacy's last name anymore. I doubt she goes by Kreutzmann. It's one of the great tragedies of my life, not knowing my own daughter's last name. I don't know where she lives. I don't know what she does. I know I have two grandchildren, but I don't know their names, either.

After Brenda and I split up, Brenda moved back down to Palo Alto and then, at some point, married a wealthy gentleman from San Jose. The details are fuzzy because I was too wrapped up in the dog days of the Grateful Dead to really pay that close of attention. I wasn't capable of being a good father back then, I'm afraid. I wasn't the best husband and I certainly wasn't a very good ex-husband. I barely kept in touch with Brenda and I didn't see Stacy as often as I should have. I didn't abandon her . . . but I wasn't always there for her, either.

When she got to be a certain age, maybe sixteen or seventeen, she reached out to me and we started spending quality time together, again. I wanted to be the long-lost dad. I wanted her to be in my life. After all, she's my daughter.

She went away to college and got into some kind of trouble in Boston. She called me asking for help. She was in a sort of situation with a drug dealer over there, and I happened to know the guy because, I mean, I was in the Grateful Dead. During that time period, if you were a dealer in a major American city and I didn't know who you were, then you weren't that big a dealer and you weren't that big a deal. Or else you were doing something wrong.

Well, I knew this guy and he was doing something wrong, anyway. He knew that Stacy needed money, so he tried to hire her. I wasn't going to let Stacy make that kind of mistake, so I flew over there, rented an apartment for her, and got her back on her own two feet. I stayed with her long enough to make sure everything was okay, before I had to get back to the band.

Eventually, Stacy moved back to Northern California—Petaluma—and started working for the Grateful Dead family. A lot of our kids did. Stacy worked on our calendars and stuff like that. I didn't get to spend a whole lot of time with her, sadly, but she worked out of our offices, so at least I got to see her regularly. We were connected.

Then one day she told me—on the phone—that she couldn't come and see me anymore. She was going through a hard time and her therapist said she needed to cut me out of her life because I was the reason she was having difficulties. I know that I was hard to reach, as a father, during her adolescence, and I know that really has an effect on children. But I still think that severing ties was bad advice from the therapist. It wasn't a solution.

I didn't think I was the problem, but I didn't want to become the problem. I wanted her to get better. To live a happy and complete life. So I respected her wish and I haven't talked to her since. It saddens me as much as you think it'd sadden me, and I still hope that it's just a phase, just a process.

It was a much more stable time in my life when my son Justin was born. I mean, it was 1969, and my career was still just getting off the ground in some regards. Being a traveling musician in a full-time rock 'n' roll band is always going to have its challenges on home life, no matter how successful the band is. But Justin's mom, Susila, was still with me throughout his childhood, so we felt more like a family. We were a family.

I had to be out on the road a lot, so Justin spent entire spans living with his grandparents, and I'm sure that wasn't easy on him. I wish that hadn't had to happen, but it did and I can't change that now. His grandparents spoiled him at home, but he had a hard time in school for some reason. Even when he was living with Sue and me and he seemed happy, his teachers gave us a different story. He stayed with me after I divorced Susila and married Shelley, and then he went to a couple of different prep schools. He had difficulty at those, too.

One year, I gave him an eight-millimeter camera for Christmas, just because I thought he might enjoy playing around with it. Sure enough, suddenly we started spending a lot of time out in the garage together, making stop-action videos. We'd set up pieces and move them the tiniest bit and shoot two or three frames at a time that way. It was a lot of fun for me, but Justin really had a knack for it. He dove into film as an art form and that's what he does for a living, today. They didn't teach him that stuff in school; he was just a natural.

He and Jerry used to talk about film a lot, since they both fantasized about being big-time directors. They were film buffs and could discourse endlessly on various movies. I think Jerry really influenced Justin as a filmmaker, and that's neat for me to think about, because it means that Jerry's influence on people knew no boundaries. It wasn't just limited to guitarists and musicians and Grateful Dead fans. Jerry and Justin would talk about filmmaking while we went through airports or had too much time to kill backstage before the show.

Justin was one of the "Grateful Kids" on tour with us. It wasn't a usual upbringing by any means, but I didn't see anything wrong with it. He was sixteen and on the road like a rock star, with his own hotel room each night, sometimes throwing wild parties till dawn with the other kids and stuff.

He's all grown up now, with a lovely wife and two beautiful kids of his own—my grandkids. Justin's been working for my old bandmate, Bob Weir, at TRI Studios in San Rafael, so the fluid notion of Grateful Dead family really does continue to this day. TRI is Bobby's "playpen for musicians." It's a state-of-the-art studio for both audio and video—with a visionary emphasis on webcasting—and Justin directs a lot of the videos that they record there. I'm really proud of him.

I'm giving you what I can on the Kreutzmann clan but the real expert on my family tree is my sister, Marcia. She knows it all from the deepest roots to the weirdest branches. She's thirteen years younger than me, and that discrepancy was prohibitive at first. We didn't really have a chance to bond the way most siblings do. At least, not till years later.

When I was growing up, my parents would have periodic marital difficulties. They went through a challenging period where it seemed like things weren't going to work out, but then they reconciled—and suddenly my mom was pregnant with Marcia. I was thirteen and a new sibling meant just one thing to me: I was no longer an only child, no longer the star attraction. Suddenly there was a baby in the house and babies demand a lot of attention and that meant attention lost for me. I didn't stick around long enough for it to balance back out—a few years after Marcia was born, when I was around sixteen, I moved into my own apartment. So I didn't really get to know my sister when we were growing up.

At some point, maybe in the early 1980s, Marcia came to a Grateful Dead show at the Forum in L.A. She and her friend had been partying, which, of course, was a pretty common thing to do at a Grateful Dead show. It's the reason a lot of Deadheads *didn't* want to bring family members with them to shows. They didn't want to expose them to the nitty-gritty. They were trying to protect them.

Anyway, Marcia and her friend came backstage and it was pretty obvious that they were pretty well tuned up. They were lit. They insisted on singing "Happy Birthday" to me and I was a little embarrassed by it, at that time. Of course, it was even more embarrassing because it wasn't actually my birthday.

I got to know Marcia a bit better later on in life and she's a wonderful, artistic woman and I love having her as my sister. We send each other e-mails and laugh about different things and keep in touch. Marcia runs a dog grooming business in Santa Rosa, California and I love that about her. She can make nice with the nastiest, gnarliest dogs—but she refuses to groom them. She knows the problem isn't with the dog, so much as with the owner. Smart.

In the early 2000s, Marcia and I hung out about once a month. In one of my life's greatest missteps, I left Hawaii and moved back to Marin. Oops. It was a seven-year misstep. Double oops. There was a silver lining, though, and that's that I got to really know my sister during that time. I had two golden retrievers that I would take to her to be groomed, but it was really just an excuse to see her. We'd have a great time over nothing and the appointment would take hours because we wanted it to—we would talk and talk, and I just loved it.

But I didn't love much else that was going on in my personal life during that period. In 2000, I bought a house in Ross, California—just a couple miles west of downtown San Rafael—primarily because my wife at the time was tired of living in Hawaii. I kept my place on Kauai, but from 2000 to 2007, I spent most of my time in California.

It worked out—even if the marriage didn't—because those were the years when the Other Ones, and then the Dead, were touring. We sometimes practiced five days a week, leading into a tour, and I couldn't have done that had I still been living in Hawaii. Okay, so maybe I'm just trying to rationalize it. Airbnb didn't exist back then, but I've stayed in hotel rooms once or twice before. I'm sure a few more nights wouldn't have hurt.

Moving back to California was just a symptom of a much larger problem—I never should've gotten married in the first place. It was a loveless marriage on my part and, as you know, "without love in the dream, it'll never come true."

After that situation, I tried to lay low and mend my heart, which was still bleeding from losing Jerry and my father and my band and the life I had known back on the mainland. I was living in Anahola, fishing with Big Joe, and just kind of fumbling around. I don't remember how I met Linda, but she lived a few miles up the shore in Kilauea. It's a small island; people meet each other.

She wasn't a bad person or anything like that, but our relationship didn't inspire me, either. For whatever reason, she just kept showing up at my house and making herself present. I don't remember ever really inviting her, but I was pretty low at that point in my life. And I was really lonely.

Maybe Linda thought she was doing me a favor because she kept coming around, and to be honest, I didn't mind the company. It was better than being alone. But before I knew it we just, somehow . . . started dating. On my end, it was more out of convenience and passivity than anything else. Well, that and the fact that I was just so lonely. I didn't have the strength to resist.

After a few years, she started pressuring me to get married and, one day, I just said . . . yes.

This is how hard it was for me: The day of the wedding, I prayed that I'd have the strength to call it off. To say, "No." But all the relatives were there, and there was cake, and I just felt like I had to honor my commitment. For better or for worse, I had already said yes. So now I had to say "I do." Although it wasn't fair to either of us.

I try to let everyone just live their own life and make their own decisions and I try not to interfere or to offer unwanted advice or to preach. Even in this book, when I tell most of these stories, I really hope they don't come across as me trying to spread any agenda or send a particular message, other than the basic, "Marijuana is fine, GMOs are not, and God bless the Grateful Dead." But I did make one really big mistake with my life that I really hope other people can learn from: marriage without love will not work. Linda was a lovely woman with lots of redeeming qualities and I liked her, but I wasn't *in love* with her. So, after seven years, I finally pulled the rip cord. The marriage wasn't right for me. I told her that I was going to file for divorce and I finally had the courage to stick with it.

I think those seven years had a purpose, though, and that was to get me ready for the most important thing to ever happen to me. Which was falling in love with the love of my life—Aimee. I wouldn't have been right for her when we first met in 1996. I wouldn't have been ready. I had lived a lot and loved a lot and toured the world for thirty years as a member of the Grateful Dead, but it takes more than that to be a good husband. Especially to a wildflower like Aimee. In 1996, I hadn't lived life enough yet. I still had some learning to do, so that I could be ready for her.

Through marriage—I learned this from my sister—some of my ancestors owned the oldest sugar plantation in Hawaii. I'm not a big proponent of sugar, but I am a big proponent of Hawaii. I was destined to end up on this island. And even though Aimee had followed me around the country on Dead tours, I had to come here, to her island in the Pacific, to meet her.

Before I ran away to California with Linda, Aimee and I went on a blind date. That's how we met. We both were single back then and I hosted a little dinner party at my house in Anahola, and Aimee was my date. I heard that she had creole blood in her and, since my mom was from New Orleans, I thought that I would play that card to connect us. I didn't know yet that she was a Deadhead.

The way that Aimee tells this story, that was the night that I tried to kill her. I figured I'd impress her by cooking something that reminded her of home, something that spoke to her roots in Louisiana. I wasn't much of a cook, I'm afraid, and I think I just figured that if I rubbed everything in habañero peppers, it would end up tasting like Cajun cuisine because of the spice. But it wasn't the same kind of spice.

Aimee took one bite and her mouth exploded in flames. If there was a fire extinguisher within reach, she would've grabbed it. Instead she begged for a beer. Something to cool down the heat. But this was shortly after I had left Sierra Tucson. I was still sober. I didn't have anything stronger than water. She thought that was outrageous, coming from a member of the Grateful Dead, and the date was a total disaster.

But I'm a drummer, so I know a thing or two about timing. It was time to wait it out. Years passed. She got married and started an organic farm; I got married and moved away.

When I came back to the island, my ex-wife's sister was living in my house and I couldn't simply evict her. It was a process. So I couch-surfed at my neighbor's house and, one day, he invited Aimee over. Suddenly, I was sitting across from her again and I couldn't believe it. The timing was finally right.

Before this, Aimee's husband had passed away from cancer and she needed to mourn before she could start to heal. I had just gotten divorced and I needed time to recover from, well, just about everything that I had gone through in the decade leading up to that moment. But that moment finally came. We started dating. I blew it the first time, but the second time around, I was ready.

Aimee has lived a pretty incredible life and one day maybe she'll write a book about her life story. I'd certainly buy it. She owned and operated several businesses on Kauai, including a children's eco-tour company, and she was an organic farmer, but every Saturday night, she turned into a DJ at the local radio station KKCR. She hosted the Grateful Dead Show. I called in once and requested "Black Muddy River." It's still curious that I chose that one in particular, because it's a sad song and I was in a euphoric mood.

"Nobody ever requests 'Black Muddy River,'" she said. "Did you used to go to shows?"

"Yeah."

"How many have you been to?"

"About all of them."

When I told her that, she laughed and said, "Oh, I know who this is!" I was waiting outside the gate at the end of the radio station's driveway for her.

Aimee's farm is thirteen acres and, as fortune would have it, it's less than two miles from my house. It's just one road down and over. Aimee was worried about her land because the plot right next to hers—about eight acres, overlooking the ocean—was up for sale. If it fell into the wrong hands, the wrong neighbor could've seriously fucked up her little corner of paradise.

One day, I called her up with some unexpected news: "Somebody bought the property next to yours," I said. I could hear the concern in her voice, so I tried to reassure her that it would all work out: "You have a new neighbor . . . me."

We've spent the past few years building our dream house there and we're getting ready to move in. So that's how that fairy tale goes.

I proposed to Aimee in 2011, in New Orleans. I had kinda, sorta asked her to marry me several times before then, but she was stubborn and pushed me away: "If you're gonna talk like that, you damn well better have a ring in your hand, dude. This isn't idle chitchat." So I got a ring. Then I waited for the right place / right time.

I had a couple of gigs down in New Orleans for Jazz Fest, and we stayed in a beautiful suite in an old French hotel, complete with a fake fireplace and marble everything. I sat her down on the couch and—like a man—got down on my knee. She said yes . . . but then made me wait a year to go through with it. As impatient as I was, I also knew that I'd be with her for the rest of my life. I had gone through four other wives. The fifth's a charm.

I wanted her hand in marriage so badly, that we had three weddings. The first one was right before I went out on tour with 7 Walkers and it was just a paperwork wedding. I wanted to make it official before I left for the open road. The second time we got married, it was a crazy party with all of our friends and an extravagant island celebration. The third one was the real one—it was a spiritual wedding. We had a Hawaiian enchantress come in and bless the land and the ceremony was stunning and we held it on the winter solstice—December 21—the shortest day of the year. After that day—after the day that she took my hand in marriage—I knew that all my days would start to get longer and longer because the sun seems to shine more and more every day that I'm with her. Still, to this very day.

So yeah, I played drums in the Grateful Dead. And, yeah, I recorded platinum albums and toured the world. I've sold out stadiums and played with Bob Dylan and had a hit video on MTV. I went to rehab twice and I went to hell and back a lot more than that. When I look back on it, so many years collapse onto themselves and the thousands of shows that I've played all melt into one. But I remember the very moment when I saw Aimee again, after moving back to this island. I remember the very moment she walked in the door at my neighbor's house, when I was still crashing on his couch.

Every experience that I ever had in my entire life suddenly made sense—it was all one long suspension bridge, leading me to her. My whole life had been a passageway, and all my experiences were an unconventional mode of transportation, getting me closer and closer to my destination—her. Aimee Kreutzmann.

Deadheads can thank Aimee for getting me out there to play music again. It was because of her that I discovered that there's more music inside of me yet. And it was because of her that I feel motivated to get it out to the world, to sing my song, to sound my beat and to beat my drum.

So, through all the highs and through all the lows, in the end, this book is really just a simple love story. It's the story of how Bill met Aimee. It's the story of how life leads us to some pretty crazy places, but even if you feel like you're at the edge of a cliff and you're stumbling around blindfolded, as long as you let your heart guide you, it will never lead you astray. I did that for thirty years with the Grateful Dead. We got far out there, in every way and in every direction. Far more than just being a long, strange trip, it was an incredible journey, and I've remained grateful every step of the way. Let me assure you that this adventure is far from over, my friends.

And that's how I get to live happily ever after.

To be continued. . . .

ACKNOWLEDGMENTS

When I Had No Wings to Fly

This book would not have been possible without the love and support of Aimee Kreutzmann or the patience of our editor, Marc Resnick. We extend a very heartfelt THANK YOU to both of them.

This storyline would not have been possible without Jerry Garcia, Bob Weir, Mickey Hart, Phil Lesh, Pigpen, Keith and Donna Godchaux, Brent Mydland, Vince Welnick, or any other musical brethren who shared a song or a stage along the way.

For various reasons, including support (emotional or otherwise), wisdom, memories, magical gifts—and airport rides—Bill and Benjy would like to collectively thank, in alphabetical order:

Adam Haft, Albert Hoffman, "Pinch-hitter" Bob Minkin, Col. Bruce Hampton (Ret.), Chelsea Levy ("Photo Editor"), Chris Joseph, Chris Steffen ("Transcriber"), Cloud 9, David Dunton, David Lemieux, Dennis McNally, Emily Schwartz, Estee and Andy Summers, Jack and Teresa Gardner, Jason Elzy, Jeremy Eisen, Jerry Cortez, Jesse Jarnow, Justin Kreutzmann, Kathy Borst (and ABC too), Ken Weinstein, Kevin Runde, Kidd Candelario, Lauren Sparacino, Lee Nyhus, Marcia

Kreutzmann, Matt Busch, Matthew Dodson, Matthew Rosenberg, Nicholas Merriweather, Pamela Faith Eisen, Peter Eacott, Robert Levy, Rosie McGee, Ryan Kingsbury, Ryan and Eleni Cameron, Sam Cutler, Scott Gallaway, Stu Nixon, Steve Fisher, Steve Parish, Susila, Trixie Garcia, and so on and so forth.

INDEX